# ROCK AND ROLL

## A SOCIAL HISTORY

ROCK

# AND ROLL

## A SOCIAL HISTORY

Paul Friedlander

UNIVERSITY OF THE
PACIFIC CONSERVATORY
OF MUSIC

Westview Press
A Member of Perseus Books, L.L.C.

Published in 1996 in the United States of America by Westview Press, Inc., 5500 Central Avenue, Boulder, Colorado 80301-2877, and in the United Kingdom by Westview Press, 12 Hid's Copse Road, Cumnor Hill, Oxford OX2 9JJ

Library of Congress Cataloging-in-Publication Data
Friedlander, Paul.
  Rock and roll : a social history / Paul Friedlander.
    p.   cm.
  Includes bibliographical references (p.   ) and index.
  ISBN 0-8133-2724-5 (hardcover).—ISBN 0-8133-2725-3 (paperback)
  1. Rock music—History and criticism.   I. Title.
ML3534.F74   1996
781.66'09—dc20                                                              95-37864
                                                                              CIP
                                                                              MN

The paper used in this publication meets the requirements of the American National Standard for Permanence of Paper for Printed Library Materials Z39.48-1984.

15

# ♪ Contents

# Illustrations

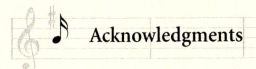

# Acknowledgments

*Good music simply means music that moves the listener into a heightened state of being.*

**Tom Manoff, composer and scholar**

---

Thanks to Gordon Massman, my editor at Westview, for his enthusiasm and support and to Connie Oehring, project editor, Gail Renlund, designer, and the rest of the staff at Westview for their warm professionalism; also to Jon T. Howard for his meticulous copy edit and rock and roll spirit.

My friends and colleagues Herman Frankel, Carl Woideck, Stephen J. Paul, S. Lea Jones, Linda Nettekoven, Bob Pfefferman, Dan Mack-Ward, and Linda Willis-Kilgore provided invaluable assistance in refining the history and ideas contained in this book. I appreciate the vision of the late Robert Trotter, the late Edward Kammerer, and Morrette Rider and their support of my rock music classes at the University of Oregon. The students of my rock history classes at the University of Oregon, Lane Community College, and University of the Pacific constituted much of the inspiration for the development of the Rock Window model and continue to remind me that rock music lives and has meaning.

The International Association for the Study of Popular Music (IASPM) is a scholarly organization devoted to the interdisciplinary study of popular music, providing an active forum for dialogue and inspiration in its wisdom and exploration. Charles Hamm and Portia Maultsby have been especially helpful with their guidance. As chair of the American chapter of IASPM, I have appreciated the support and feedback from our members, especially Steve Jones, Peter Winkler, Les Gay, John Covach, and Venese Berry.

I owe a debt of gratitude to my father Mark and my mother Miriam Friedlander, who helped to shape the intellectual tools with which I now view the world; they offered a perspective that still makes a lot of sense. My wife and partner, Sherry Bloker, has been most generous with her hard work and dedication to create our home, from which I venture forth into "book-writing mode" and its many lengthy periods of absence.

This volume is dedicated to my son, David, who at the age of five has the music in him. To learn about the past is to better understand the present and be ready for the future.

*Paul Friedlander*

# 1· If I Were Reading About Rock Music, I Would Want to Keep in Mind . . .

*(Rock and roll is) the most brutal, ugly, desperate, vicious form of expression it has been my misfortune to hear. [It is written and sung] for the most part by cretinous goons [and] by means of its imbecilic reiterations and sly— lewd—in plain fact dirty—lyrics . . . (it) manages to be the martial music for every sideburned delinquent on the face of the earth.*

**Frank Sinatra at 1958 congressional hearings, as quoted in Steve Chapple and Reebee Garafolo, Rock and Roll Is Here to Pay**

*If it screams for truth rather than help, if it commits itself with a courage that it can't be sure it really has, if it stands up and admits that something is wrong but doesn't insist on blood, then it is rock n' roll.*

**Pete Townshend of the Who**

*Rock n' roll, at its core, is merely a bunch of raving shit.*

**Rock journalist Lester Bangs**

*One crucial way in which the institutions of popular music try to maintain their dominance is through ignoring musics which contain elements of alien discourses (e.g. politics, obscenity, explicit sexuality), for if those elements are brought into popular music, they may have a disruptive effect. When they are brought in . . . there are procedures for incorporating those external elements (be they rhythms, hairstyles or lyric statements) to minimize their disruption of orderly consumption.*

**Music-history scholar Dave Laing**

T HIS BOOK CHRONICLES the first thirty years of rock/pop music history. Picture the various musical styles as locations on a giant unfolding road map. As you open the map, you travel from place to place, stopping at each chapter to sample the artistry. Take in the tales, pictures, sounds, and feelings of each location; remember the people you met there. And don't forget to dress your imagination appropriately for this trip, because each genre is affected by the societal topography and climate that surround it.

If you brought your camera, snap some mental pictures of the visits; they will be wonderful mementos of the journey and can be recalled at any time. For example, when thinking of rural blues of the 1930s, picture a Saturday night party in the Mississippi Delta. A black man in his twenties is playing a beat-up acoustic guitar, singing in a rough and emotional voice about hard times on the road in the South. You can almost hear him. Try visualizing other musical styles (locations) described in this book.

On occasion, step back from the map to see where you've been and ponder how those places are reflected in the story. Take a look at how artists are influenced by and borrow from different sources—the evolutionary flow of rock music, the big picture. Have a wonderful trip.

## One: Terminology

Each book on this subject comes with its own definition of the term "rock music." Some authors use "rock and roll" to signify the music of the fifties and "rock" to represent all subsequent styles. We take a slightly different tack. The music covered in this book is "rock/pop." This reflects a dual nature: musical and lyrical roots that are derived from the classic rock era (rock), and its status as a commodity produced under pressure to conform by the record industry (pop).

The numerous styles created during rock/pop's first thirty years have been given specific names based on their roots, musical characteristics, lyrical content, and relationship to the surrounding cultural and political environments. Thus, the music of Chuck Berry, Elvis, and other early artists is termed "classic rock," whereas their late 1960s Bay Area descendants are dubbed "San Francisco" rock artists.

## Two: You Can Listen on Two Different Levels

*There is always some kind of combination of feeling and thinking in our responses to music, some combination of emotional and intellectual elements.*

**Music educator Joseph Kerman**

*You can intellectualize about a lot of rock and roll music but it's primarily not an intellectual thing. It's music that's all.*

**Rolling Stone** *magazine founder-editor Jann Wenner*

Most people first experience rock/pop music on an emotional, or visceral, level. They listen and it makes them feel . . . you can fill in the blank yourself. The music is received at an intuitive level, one that contains a rich variety of knowing and feeling without the process of logical thinking that accompanies what we usually think of as understanding. For example, were we listening to Aretha Franklin's 1967 version of "Respect," our intuitive reaction might include Right on! and Tell it, sister! or simply Wow!—based on feelings evoked by the song.

Another way to engage this music is to follow an approach that is best described as "analytical." It involves listening to a piece of music with the goal of collecting a wide range of specific information about it. The listener, then, is in the position to make judgments for herself about the nature of the music, its quality relative to other music, and its societal context. Using the previous example, our listener might wonder why this version of "Respect" is so powerful, listening to see what instruments are being played and what beats emphasized. She might also reflect on Aretha's gospel background in order to explain the potency of her voice. And she might examine the artist's personal history or current lifestyle to find a situation—such as an abusive husband—that gives the artist's demand for respect additional urgency.

Discovering, organizing, and making judgments about the meaning of a broad range of relevant information enriches our understanding of the piece of music. Thus, the two levels of engaging a piece of rock/pop music, the intuitive and the analytical, are valuable and complimentary. They enhance our ability to "know," feel, and understand, and they make listening to the music we love a richer experience.

## Three: The Rock Window—One Way to Understand Music

Although a random search for pertinent information about a song and its artist might turn up valuable facts, I would like to suggest a more organized method, which I call the "Rock Window." I developed this device during my ten years of teaching rock-music history at the University of Oregon School of Music. It is a way to systematically collect and organize information received from listening to, and reading about, the history of rock/pop music. By organizing her search, the listener ends up with a wide range of relevant information and finds herself comparing apples to apples rather than apples to bicycles.

The following outline provides a brief description of the Rock Window categories and is intended to point out some major components of rock/pop music, lyrics, artist histories, and societal contexts. Try to broaden your understanding by collecting some of this information the next time you listen to your favorite music.

I. MUSIC

    *a) Ensemble*: What instruments are present?

*b) Rhythmic Emphasis:* What is the dominant beat? What instrument or instruments carry this beat?

*c) Vocal Style:* What words would you use to describe the vocal delivery? What musical styles does this vocal style come from?

*d) Instrumental Solo:* Is there an instrumental solo (generally defined as an improvised melody in the absence of lyrics of one verse or more in duration)? What is its stylistic derivation?

*e) Harmonic Structure:* What chords are present?

## II. LYRICS

*a)* What are the song's major themes? Does it tell a story? Suggested topical classifications: romantic love, sex, alienation, justice/injustice, introspection, rock/pop music, and others.

*b)* Is there an explicit or underlying political or cultural message?

## III. ARTIST HISTORY

What are the important elements of the artist's personal history and career that enhance your understanding of the music? This information can be divided into three areas:

*a)* psychological, social, and economic conditions during youth;

*b)* musical history; and

*c)* important career landmarks.

## IV. SOCIETAL CONTEXT

How did the surrounding political and cultural climates influence the artists and their work? This information can be divided into three areas:

*a)* youth culture and its relationship to society;

*b)* cultural and political movements, including the struggle for civil and human rights for minorities, peace and antiwar movements, and establishment of counterculture alternatives; and

*c)* the music industry and its current point of development.

## V. STANCE

Which elements of the artist's live performances and public actions or behavior provide us with a clearer understanding of the music itself?

Some rock/pop music fans believe that the collection and analysis of information detracts from the intuitive experiencing of the music. I have found that the more I know, the richer my experience. See Appendix B for an example of how the Rock Window can be applied using Chuck Berry's "Johnny B. Goode."[1]

## Four: The Meaning of Rock/Pop Music—to Whom?

*There is a tug-of-war between what he calls rock's "two differing forms of existence": on the one hand an aesthetic-cultural function as the cultural praxis of young people, on the other an economic form as a mass-produced and mass-distributed commodity.*

**Ian Watson, on Peter Wicke's book Rockmusik**

It all seemed so simple at first—a song meant what the artist said. Then sociologists and historians decided that it wasn't enough to interpret the song by analyzing the music and lyrics alone; the work had to be viewed in the context of the artist's personal history and the song's relationship to surrounding society (or the societal context). These two factors, artist history and societal context, were now added to the analysis. Mass communications theorists then suggested that every listener interprets the song differently, depending on her own life experience. Thus, the song's meaning was different depending upon who was listening to it.

So we examined the listener's life: youth, family background, musical tastes, peer groups, and socioeconomic status. This, we hoped, would tell us about the lens through which the listener interpreted the song. It became apparent that a forty-year-old mother found different meaning in a song than her fifteen-year-old daughter. Now, our interpretation included a judgment about the artist's intended meaning, an analysis of the work, and an awareness of how the listener colored the meaning of the song with her own subjective life experiences.

Mass communications scholars have also suggested that we take into account what aspects of the artist's work individual listeners deem crucial. For some, fashion choices, music, and onstage style are more important than lyrics. In fact studies have shown that many youthful rock listeners don't actually understand the lyrics of the songs they listen to, even those of the songs they classify as their favorites. For other listeners, songs appear shallow and uninteresting unless they contain lyrics that comment on some aspect of society.

There is also a range of uses to which the listener can put rock/pop music. Some people barely engage it at all, placing it pleasantly in the background while performing other tasks. Others become more active consumers, listening to and purchasing rock/pop product. This listener might find it relaxing, stimulating, or enlightening. Toward the other end of a use/involvement spectrum, we find subcultural groups, such as the sixties San Francisco counterculture, the seventies punks, or the eighties metalheads, who are immersed in a particular musical genre and to whom the music offers significant knowledge and identity.

It might be interesting, while reading this book, to think about the many ways in which a song acquires meaning. Some meaning comes from the *artist*. The song then changes during the *production process*, being altered by the recording personnel, the record industry, and the era's technology. The work is frozen in time on record and released as the text (or product). This text is presented to the audience within the context of certain societal conditions that shape perceptions of the text (*societal filter*). The work reaches the listener (*receptor*) who endows it with further meaning based on her life circumstances.

|  | industry | | conditions | |
|---|---|---|---|---|
|  | technology | | SOCIETAL | |
| ARTIST——PRODUCTION——TEXT——FILTER——RECEPTOR |
| life | PROCESS | work | | life |
| experience | | | | experience |

I hope that this brief discussion provides some informative new ways to think about the meaning of rock/pop music and that this will allow the reader to experience it more fully.

## Five: The Anatomically Correct Rock and Roll Doll

One interesting way to learn about an artist or group, and to judge the impact of a song or album, is to ask yourself, What part of the body is most affected by the music? We created the Anatomically Correct Rock and Roll Doll for just such an exercise.

MIND (intellectual)

HEART (emotional)

GENITALIA (sexual)

FEET (dancing/movement)

Consider the three major British invasion groups: the Beatles, the Rolling Stones, and the Who. My students would say the Beatles and the Who appeal to both the head and heart—even though they don't sound very much alike. The Stones appeal to the genitalia and feet. What do you believe? Try it with other artists.

## Six: Dividing the Years into Eras

There exist natural divisions during rock/pop music's first quarter-century, the boundaries of which can be best delineated by the occurrence of major creative explosions. During these explosions, dynamic new genres arose from the existing musical landscape. These new genres didn't spring forth from thin air, but were crafted by creatively fusing elements from existing styles. The new styles tended to emerge and exist at the regional level, hidden from the greater public, before exploding into mass awareness. This developmental dynamic was true for all four major rock explosions (classic rock, the British invasion, hard rock, and punk). Aside from these major creative explosions, there are also important minor ones, such as the folk-rock synthesis, soul and Motown, and rap—the difference being the level of impact on the course of rock/pop music history.

Major identifiable rock-history landmarks are: first, 1954–1955—the classic rock and roll explosion; second, 1963–1964—the British invasion; third, 1967–1972—the golden era (the synchronous maturation of artists from several genres, including the first British invasion, soul, the San Francisco sound, and the ascendance of the guitar kings); fourth, 1968–1969—the hard rock explosion; and fifth, 1975–1977—the punk explosion.

## Seven: Lifecycle

Musical styles usually go through lifecycles. These cycles can be observed in single, small genres as well as in rock/pop music as a whole. In the beginning, emerging styles seek form and shape, in a process that can be called formulation. Like the proverbial growing alien species from a sci-fi B movie, they borrow available elements from nearby sources on their way to becoming a survivable form. The next stage is a process of maturation, when artists experiment with ways to improve and enhance the basic form and work to become better crafters. The final stage is where artists achieve a period of normalization, often unwilling or unable to evolve further in any significant manner. At this point the form may stagnate and become a caricature of itself, losing touch with its initial values and exchanging them for symbols and images. The final two stages generally coincide with greatest commercial success.

## Eight: Themes That Transcend the Eras

Two themes, romance and rebellion, transcend temporal and stylistic boundaries and are major components of most rock/pop genres. As to each era, however, these themes are manifest in different ways, depending on the musical style and its relationship to contemporary values and standards.

Romance was the dominant theme for popular music, long before the birth of rock and roll, and continued to dominate rock/pop as the music celebrated its silver anniversary (around 1979). In the fifties and again in the seventies, teens were rock's primary target. It is not surprising, therefore, that romance—and its Siamese twin sex—were the music's major preoccupations. Studies of songs show that 67 percent of fifties classic rock hits (Friedlander, 1987), 65 percent of a sample of 1966 hits (Carey, 1966), and 69 percent of early-1970s #1 hits (Anderson et al.) were love songs.

Rock/pop music wasn't as saturated with rebellious lyrics as critics and defenders would have one believe. This doesn't mean, however, that artists and their audiences weren't participating in conscious as well as unconscious acts of rebellion. The lyrics themselves provide only part of the picture. When Jerry Lee Lewis commanded, "Shake it, baby, shake it" ("Whole Lot of Shakin' Going On," 1957), critics viewed that as a lewd, immoral suggestion. Lewis was engaging in startlingly rebellious behavior, what James T. Carey would call "newer-value" lyrics (which Carey defines as critical of conventional roles and/or society, in contrast to older-value lyrics, which depict acceptance of conventional values, morality, and relationships). Yet these sentiments from Lewis would hardly have raised an eyebrow, and probably would not have even been interpreted as rebellious, during the 1970s.

It is important, therefore, when evaluating whether behavior, music, lyrics, and dress contain rebellious elements, to understand how that behavior relates to what is considered normal for the period—the societal context. The Rolling Stones classic "Let's Spend the Night Together" was controversial in 1967, but it would have been blasphemous in 1957 and yet gone unnoticed in 1977. Bluejeans, t-shirts, and black-leather jackets—de rigueur attire for any true-blue rocker— were rebellious symbols in the fifties, merely fashion statements in the eighties. It is important to be able to look and listen with the eyes and ears of the era you are reading about.

## Nine: It Is Not Always Either/Or

The answer to a question doesn't always have to be *yes* or *no*. When you are thinking about whether a certain song is rebellious or not, try to reframe the question to ask, What parts of this song are rebellious? You thus frame the question in *and/and* terms (rather than *yes/no* terms) and allow for a more insightful answer.

Another way to frame these kinds of questions is to view them on a continuum, that is, placed somewhere between the two ends of a straight line. For example, in discussing why musicians took psychoactive substances (such as marijuana) in 1967 San Francisco, some people might conclude that it was for escape purposes (*E*). Others might conclude that it was to achieve an enlightened, artistically creative state of being (*N*). Using an *either/or* perspective, one would have to choose between the two. If, however, we believed that the answer was a combination of both, we could feel comfortable using the *and/and* model of analysis. This could be visually represented by placing an *X* somewhere between *E* and *N* along the continuum, thus representing quantities of both in the answer.

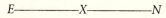

*E* = escape

*N* = enlightenment

*X* = something that blends elements of both *E* and *N*

## Ten: Commercial Success and Roseburg Status

Throughout this book you will read a lot about hit records and mass commercial success. There is a definitive difference between artistic success (as judged by listeners and critics) and commercial success (mass popular acceptance based on radio airplay and nationwide product sales).[2] Those artists with a sufficient level of mass penetration are said to have achieved Roseburg status. Roseburg, a city in western Oregon, had approximately 20,000 people and one top-40 radio station during the sixties. We hypothesize that if a song received airplay in Roseburg, it had sufficiently penetrated the commercial marketplace to be available to the listeners and purchasers in the rest of the United States. Classic rock artists like Elvis achieved Roseburg status; rhythm and blues (R&B) greats like Big Joe Turner did not. Soul artist Aretha Franklin crossed over to the popular (white) music charts; fellow soul artist Solomon Burke barely touched them.

## Eleven: There Just Isn't Enough Room

This work contains limitations in both scope and depth. If we tried to address every important artist, the book would be burdensome and unwieldy. Choices had to be made, and some successful and talented artists are absent from this narrative. For those that do appear, the book focuses upon the years and accomplishments that we consider to be historically and creatively significant. Some commercially successful and popular releases—generally produced during later years of normalization—are left for the reader to discover. It is hoped that the reader will come away with a sufficient understanding of the rock/pop genre to want to explore it further.

## Twelve: Objectivity and Bias

Some historians claim objectivity; none achieve it. The best an author can do is to alert the reader to personal biases—to let the reader know where you're coming from. I grew up in New York City, exposed to the world's wonderful music. My father taught me guitar and sang folk songs from Woody Guthrie and the Weavers. Pete Seeger was the music counselor at my summer camp and taught us how to sing from our hearts. A few years later, my friends and I hung out on street corners in Queens, hitting doo-wop harmonies. Our a cappella group, the Chapters, serenaded captive hospital and nursing-home audiences.

The late 1950s saw a surge in the popularity of bluegrass music in, of all places, New York City's Washington Square Park. There I learned to play the banjo and to sing falsetto. After college I found an apartment near Greenwich Village and joined in the sixties folk boom. We later went electric, and I said hello to the seventies on bass, playing original rock music. For the next seven years, it was life on the road in rock's medium-fast lane. Following a few years in "the business," I ascended the ivory tower. There I remain—although I never have hung up my rock and roll shoes.

This musical odyssey has helped to shape my rock/pop musical tastes. I trust that rockermortis has yet to set in. However, I do especially enjoy certain things: singers who can control their voice and exhibit some emotion, vocal harmony, rhythmic diversity, and lyrics of substance (the human condition, humor, politics, and so on), sweaty performers, and new musical horizons. I also believe that rock/pop music listeners should have access to a range of musical styles. Musical and cultural diversity and pluralism must be maintained at all costs.

## A Brief Overview of Our Journey

Before we begin our story, we offer the following brief overview of rock's first thirty years. It is intended to light the way and make your journey more comfortable.

Rock music exploded on the American scene in the mid-1950s. However, its musical ancestry can be traced back many centuries to the musical traditions of both Africa and Europe. We hear, in the same music, the call-and-response patterns from an African village mixed with classical music harmonies of eighteenth-century Europe. It is these and many other elements that contribute to the African-American styles of blues, gospel, jazz (and, subsequently, rhythm and blues), and elements from folk and country music that form the foundation of rock and roll.

At the same time that pop music's "hit parade" dominated the midfifties American musical mainstream, teens had the opportunity to listen to a new, vibrant, underground music called rock and roll. This music unfolded in two generations. The first, predominantly Black, consisted of Fats Domino, Chuck Berry, Little Richard, and Bill Haley. They scored significant popular chart success between 1953 and 1955, breaking ground as rock and roll's pioneers. Their music, a synthesis of Black and white styles and dominated by a strong, drum-generated backbeat, sported lyrics celebrating this postwar generation's teenage life experiences of romance, dance, a hint of sex, and rock and roll itself.

Classic rock's second generation garnered even more commercial success than the first, erupting with Elvis Presley in early 1956. This group was all white, had grown up listening to the pioneering country music of Hank Williams and, later, blues, rhythm and blues, and classic rock's first generation. Presley's chart success was followed in 1957 by the Everly Brothers, Jerry Lee Lewis, and Buddy Holly. This generation ensured rock and roll's succession to the popular music throne with a style that, although a bit less raucous than earlier rockers and often favoring teen romance over teen angst, was enthusiastically embraced by the era's youth.

Rock and roll shared commercial success with pop artists and a vocally oriented rhythm and blues called doo-wop until the end of the decade, when this "classic" rock all but faded from view. In its place records from female vocal groups (who became known as the "girl groups") and young clean-cut men (teen idols), a budding California "surf" sound, and a developing folk revival became popular, all unknowingly awaiting the impending onslaught of the British invasion.

In 1964 the United States awakened to the sound of the Beatles, with their variety of classic rock styles combined with touches of pop and rockabilly. This British invasion, which included music from the Rolling Stones, the Dave Clark Five, the Who, and others, reawakened America's rock and roll urges. Their success would cause the young American folk singers, like Bob Dylan and others, to "go electric," adding the power of rock and roll to "serious" lyrics and strummed acoustic guitars. Some would move to Los Angeles and the folk-rock scene of the Byrds, Buffalo Springfield, and others, and some ended up in San Francisco as a part of the budding counterculture musical community.

Meanwhile, two African-American genres were born at the beginning of the sixties. Soul music, and its transcendent concept of essential "Blackness," grew out of the Memphis-based Stax studio (as well as some other studios) with artists like Otis Redding, James Brown, Aretha Franklin, and Sam and Dave. Motown showcased talented Detroit youth and became a brilliant success story choreographed by Berry Gordy Jr. With writer-producers like Holland/Dozier/Holland, Smokey Robinson, and Norman Whitfield directing virtuosic vocalists like the Temptations, Marvin Gaye, the Miracles, the Four Tops, and the Supremes, the Motown story was a Black economic civil rights parable for the sixties.

The pace of change, in popular music as in society itself, accelerated near the end of the 1960s. Experimentation by the Beatles and other British invasion groups helped to redefine the nature of rock music, lyrics, and the surrounding culture. Musical boundaries were sufficiently expanded to include the sitar, an Indian string instrument, and tapes of guitars played backwards; lyrics quoted interpretations of the Tibetan *Book of the Dead*.

A major innovation at this time was an increased role for the electric guitar; solo improvisation became a focal point and organizing quality for many new bands. Guitar pioneers Eric Clapton (with the groundbreaking band Cream) and Jimi Hendrix (with his Experience) soared in extended "jams" during concerts, where some of the audience came only to hear these "guitar gods" play their instruments. These efforts led to the development of hard rock and its most commercially successful proponent, Led Zeppelin. Their music—composed of a power trio (the three-instrument attack pioneered by the Who) plus lead vocalist Robert Plant—typified the brash, male, teen-oriented sound that was later purveyed by bands like Aerosmith, AC/DC, and Grand Funk Railroad and dominated a formidable segment of pop music during the seventies.

By the early 1970s the rock music audience had grown to such an extent that a new, younger generation of listeners sought different sounds than their older contemporaries, who still clung to their sixties favorites. New artists emerged, like singer-songwriters Elton John, Paul Simon, and Neil Young, the popular California band the Eagles, and pop icons like Chicago, Fleetwood Mac, the Doobie Brothers, and Linda Ronstadt. As the decade progressed and recording technology became highly sophisticated, most popular music moved toward a studio-oriented perfectionist aesthetic (typified by Boston and Steely Dan). If you didn't record in a state-of-the-art studio and overdub every note until it was perfect, you just weren't "in"—or you would be placed on an increasingly constricted radio playlist.

In reaction to this prevailing techno-oriented pop era, punk music burst out of the garage, art school, and pub and thrust itself on to the British scene in the mid-seventies. Sporting torn t-shirts and blasting a bare-bones, frantic un-music, the purveyors of punk attempted to offend everyone. They succeeded beyond their wildest dreams and in the process helped to revitalize a sagging rock music market. The pioneering Sex Pistols self-destructed, but others like the Clash found a way to survive and thrive in the commercial scene.

The most commercially palatable elements from punk found their way into an offspring called new wave. British artists such as the Pretenders, Elvis Costello, and Generation X, and Americans such as Talking Heads, Blondie, and Devo, among others, adopted some of the frantic and aggressive musical elements and eclectic actions and image of their punk predecessors. Concurrently, industry entrepreneurs initiated a music video channel for cable television, MTV, which found an inordinate proportion of videos available from the burgeoning new wave genre. Songs and artists, unable to get radio airplay on increasingly restricted radio formats, were aired on MTV and achieved significant record sales. Thus, by the early 1980s, a wide variety of rock styles were flourishing simultaneously—hard rock, rock/pop, new wave, singer-songwriters, cool funk, and others—each supported by a share of the radio and record-buying markets divided by age, ethnicity, and cultural characteristics.

Music from the Black community had also taken significant evolutionary steps. Sixties pioneers Sly and the Family Stone, Isaac Hayes, and James Brown contributed innovative musical ideas to the next generation's funk. Successes ranged from George Clinton's eclectic dual identity Parliament/Funkadelic (a syncopated, groove-laden, lyrically creative, costumed story-song) to the hot and smoother Earth, Wind, and Fire and the lasciviousness of Kool and the Gang and the Ohio Players. Although not wholly derived from the Black tradition, disco nevertheless maintained the focus on the Black rhythm and dance traditions, and artists like K. C. and the Sunshine Band, Chic, and Donna Summer had successes with the genre. In addition, during those years, pop stars like Stevie Wonder, Michael Jackson, and Diana Ross maintained their ascendant positions on the charts.

The Black dance tradition, cultural verbal jousting of the "dozens," and deterioration of the urban ghetto led to the emergence of rap, a new synthesis of styles for the eighties. As a part of the larger cultural/musical mix of hip hop, including break dancing, language, fashion, and graffiti art, rap began with elemental beats from portable turntables and pilfered lamppost power during the hot summers in New York's South Bronx. The "DJ" was the artist, orchestrating a dexterous dance of mixes and cuts punctuated by the syncopated "scratching" of needle against vinyl. Rap's first top-40 hit—"Rapper's Delight" (Sugar Hill Gang)—was followed by early rappers Kurtis Blow, Grandmaster Flash, and Afrika Bambaataa.

In the ensuing decade rap expanded geographically from New York and flourished commercially by assuming a variety of stylistic poses. Musically, it stretched from elementary rhythms to more sophisticated and complex instrumental or-chestration. Early rappers Run-DMC (from Queens), L. L. Cool J, and the white Beastie Boys were followed by the political activism of Public Enemy, the gangsta rap of N.W.A., sexually explicit lyrics of 2 Live Crew, and extraordinary main-stream success of M. C. Hammer.

The fragmentation of the rock marketplace continued throughout the eighties. Fans embraced dinosaurs like the Rolling Stones, the Grateful Dead, Led Zeppelin, and even Elvis Presley as oldies radio formats proliferated. Madonna, Michael Jackson, Prince, and Billy Joel dominated the pop end of the charts. Hard rock spawned its dominant sibling, heavy metal, a broad spectrum of bombastic, male-centered, guitar-oriented, distorted music including bands Judas Priest, Iron Maiden, Def Leppard, Mötley Crüe, Metallica, and many others.

In a Western political environment dominated by Thatcher-Reagan conser-vatism, musicians, the music industry, and political activists created a partnership of volunteerism to promote humanitarian goals. Monumental concerts and tours traveled and were broadcast worldwide—Amnesty International Human Rights Now! Tour (1988), Live Aid Concerts (1985), Farm Aid, and the recording of "We Are The World" during the Grammy Awards in 1985 are some examples.

You now have an idea of where this journey will take you and the general na-ture of the rock and roll terrain. Our narrative will begin in the pre-rock era, where the styles of blues, gospel, big band jazz, folk, country, and rhythm and blues provide the essential elements for the music that we will call rock and roll. Please fasten your seatbelts.

# 2· The Roots of Rock and Roll: I Went Down to the Crossroads

*Oh Lawd, I'm tired, oh Lawd, I'm tired a' dis mess. . . .*

**Traditional rural blues lyric**

*Folk music is my music. Folk music is sincere, there ain't nothin phony about it. When a folk singer sings a sad song, he's sad. He means it.*

**Hank Williams**

EARLY ROCK AND ROLL WAS PRIMARILY African-American music. The syncopated rhythms, raw vocal emotionalism, and work-chant "call and response" are all part of an African musical heritage and became building blocks for rock and roll. This chapter provides an overview of rock's musical roots, both Black and white. We begin with early-twentieth-century rural blues and describe the nature and development of urban blues, gospel, and jump band jazz. The fusion of these four African-American styles would become the pivotal form of the early-1950s Black music called rhythm and blues—rock and roll's major musical foundation. The traditional white styles of folk and country music, themselves a synthesis of Black and white forms, also provided important ingredients for early rock and roll. Rockabilly, a midfifties, white southern fusion of country music, blues, gospel, and rhythm and blues, provided the musical and emotional catalysts for many white musicians to move past the boundaries of traditional country music and on to early rock and roll.

## Black Musical Roots

In the early and mid-twentieth century, blues existed in a number of different forms. The popular blues style, with vocalists like Ma Rainey and Bessie Smith, was performed in theaters, tents, and concert halls, primarily east of the Mississippi River. The artists sold millions of records, achieving significant commercial success even in the white community. Unemployed Black men, carrying battered guitars, crisscrossed the South during the bitter days of the depression singing about their lives of hardship and pain. This rural blues contained very specific stylistic elements: Most songs were twelve measures (or bars) in length, contained only three chords (a I-IV-V harmonic progression), and repeated the first line of the verse twice before offering a different third line (A-A-B lyric structure).

Blues lyrics were about struggle, adversity, and, on occasion, celebration. Most singers accompanied themselves on the steel-string acoustic guitar, occasionally using a burnished bottleneck (or slide) to mimic the emotive wail of the vocal style. Sometimes one or more companions joined in on harmonica (commonly referred to as a "harp"), a second guitar, or percussion sticks called "bones." Many prominent rural blues artists came from the Mississippi Delta, the fertile lowland region formed by the confluence of the Yazoo and Mississippi Rivers in the northwest part of the state. Delta blues stylists Son House and Robert Johnson, Texan Blind Lemon Jefferson, and Louisiana-born Huddie Ledbetter (or Leadbelly) were especially influential.

Southern rural blues performances on the back porch, in the roadhouse, or in the town square diminished in importance in the decade following World War II—to be replaced by its northern and western counterpart, urban blues. The venues became smoke-filled bars of Chicago's South Side, as well as other urban centers and theater stages. A massive Black migration during the depression and the World War II years created numerous large African-American communities in the country's northern urban centers by war's end in 1945. The newness and alienation of urban existence, and removal from the rural homestead, extended family, and its emotional and nutritional support, helped to create the context in which urban blues flourished.

The late Muddy Waters (born McKinley Morganfield), a former cotton picker and rural blues artist from Mississippi, formed a seminal Chicago-based blues band in the late 1940s. Drums, string bass, electric rhythm guitar, and piano made up the basic rhythm section, or "core," of the band. A lead electric guitar and harp were added as solo instruments. This core band became the model for the modern rock band, and, later, many classic rockers adopted this ensemble (or group) format. The urban blues vocal style maintained the emotionality, slurred lyrics, and bent ("blue") notes of its southern predecessor; however, the lyrical topics were expanded to include the urban landscape and some positivity and boastfulness to go along with rural depression and catharsis. Its line pattern often transcended the rural three-line A-A-B format (the Muddy Waters recording of "Hoochie Coochie Man" is an example).

Other urban bluesmen rose to prominence. In Chicago bass player Willie Dixon wrote songs that were recorded by Howlin' Wolf ("Spoonful") and harmonica great Little Walter ("My Babe"). Elmore James was known for his bottleneck-style guitar playing and John Lee Hooker created and recorded storysongs about the "hard life." In other locations guitarists Riley "B. B." King (Memphis), Aaron "T-Bone" Walker (Los Angeles), and Lightnin' Hopkins (Texas) represented regional blues efforts. Urban blues, with its expanded core ensemble, heightened role for the electric guitar, and departure from solely depressing topics, represented a major step toward the birth of rock and roll. Subsequent rock generations, including pioneer guitar players such as Eric Clapton, Jimi Hendrix, and Keith Richards, would turn to urban blues for inspiration.

A focus on emotionality and a harmonically complex vocal style characterized a second vital Black root of rock and roll, the religious music called gospel. Gospel had roots in the "invisible church" of the late slave era and was a form that included hand clapping, call and response, rhythmic complexities, persistent beat, melodic improvisation, and percussive accompaniments. All of these stylistic roots would find their way into rhythm and blues, many eventually into rock music itself. In the early twentieth century, composers like Thomas Dorsey created a contemporary version of gospel that we can easily recognize today.

Groups like the Soul Stirrers and the Swan Silvertones became popular, emphasizing interpretive phrasing, emotional expressiveness, and vocal excellence. Singers would soar into falsetto one measure and emit a bass growl the next. Highly syncopated rhythmic improvisation on the melody was common. Call and response—rooted in the African work-chant—featured a song leader and congregation response. Gospel also inspired enthusiastic and uncensored body movements by both performers and congregation. Each of these elements also became components of R&B and, later, rock and roll.

Jump band jazz, as epitomized by Louis Jordan and his Tympani Five (or Six), was the third style that contributed significantly to rhythm and blues, and thus to rock and roll. It emerged at the tail end of the big band era after World War II, a cheerful style with a small five- or six-piece ensemble and prominent saxophone solos. Its size belied its power; this small jazz band really "swung." The generally upbeat swing feeling and tenor saxophone instrumental solos were two elements that young players carried over from jazz to R&B.

In the late 1940s Black music visionaries transformed elements of blues, gospel, and jump band jazz into the style known as rhythm and blues. This fusion later became the basis for rock's first era, classic rock and roll. R&B's musical synthesis consisted of the core blues band plus jazz's tenor saxophone soloist. Like jump band jazz, the feeling was predominantly upbeat. The gospel-generated emphasis on the second and fourth beats of the measure (or "backbeat"), played primarily on the snare drum, created a body movement that excited the listener. Vocal virtuosity and onstage showmanship, both gospel legacies, were important components of R&B—displayed by stylish tenor lead singers like wailer Clyde McPhatter and crooner Sonny Till. Vocal emotion, slur, and blue notes were carried over from the blues. The instrumental solo, most often by the tenor saxophone, combined the improvised fluidity of jazz with the long slurs and repetition from the blues.

The worldview of rhythm and blues was more optimistic than its predecessor, depression-era blues, although it was still firmly rooted in uncensored, real-life experiences. Some classic R&B artists were hard-drinkin' (like Stick McGee, "Drinkin' Wine Spo-Dee-o-Dee," 1948), were hard-partyin' (like Roy Brown, "Rockin' at Midnight," 1948), or, like Ray Charles, celebrated women, as in his 1954 classic "I Got a Woman." Life could still contain the blues' struggles, but romance and sexual innuendo were more common subjects—much to the chagrin of most whites and many Blacks. R&B's musical power, rhythmic emphasis on the backbeat ("the beat"), and lyrical authenticity attracted a burgeoning audience of post–WWII young Black listeners.

## Country and Folk Music

Some forms of classic rock and roll also had significant roots in white folk and country music. Coincidentally, two major contributors to both styles, Jimmie Rodgers and the Carter Family, were discovered in the space of two days in August 1927 by talent scout Ralph Peer. Rodgers, dubbed "the father of country music," wrote ballads and blues about his wanderings as a railroad brakeman. Many of his lyrics followed the traditional A-A-B blues pattern, and Rodgers even titled tunes "Blue Yodel #1" (or "T for Texas"), "Blue Yodel #2," and so on. He was this country's first recording star, selling more than 20 million records in the six-year period between 1927 and his death in 1933. Rodgers's music, actually a synthesis of folk and rural blues, was eventually labeled as country and western (C&W).

The Carter Family, who began recording at the same time, mixed traditional Anglo-Saxon ballads, hymns, and other church melodies with harmony and acoustic guitar and autoharp accompaniment. They left a legacy of string-band accompaniment to songs of a wholesome and religious nature. Interestingly enough, even these legends of traditional American folk music recorded an occasional blues tune (for example, "Worried Man Blues").

While America enjoyed the big band era (the late 1930s and 1940s), country music formed its own equivalent, the western swing band. Texas and Oklahoma were the homes for this style—which included the genre's most popular adherent, Bob Wills and His Texas Playboys. Wills, a fiddler steeped in both country and blues, formed a dance band with a basic lineup that included fiddle, electric guitar, bass, drums, steel guitar, piano, and tenor sax (at times, more horns and fiddles were added). His repertoire, a mix of blues, country, and traditional fiddle tunes, was innovative—as was his use, in country music, of steel guitar (from Hawaiian music) and drums.

By the mid-1940s the stage was set for Hank Williams, the father of modern country music. He grew up in Alabama, listened to and played with blues artists, learned guitar from a Black street musician, and finally left home to perform as a country singer. Williams's songs cataloged the spectrum of experiences and emotions in the everyday lives of ordinary people. His forthright accounts of lost love, sexual infidelity, and hard drinking were atypical of the song subjects then available to white audiences—typically positive love-struck fantasy tales. This "modern" country music, like blues and R&B, provided an alternative to the "June, croon, spoon" worldview of contemporary popular music. Although Williams's audience was generally perceived to be southern and white, he also had a substantial Black audience.

During live performances, Williams would hunch over the microphone and deliver stories with that fabled trembling sincerity in his voice; his country string band featuring fiddle, acoustic and electric guitars, steel guitar, and bass conveyed the songs with great emotionality. During his short, six-year recording career—Williams died on January 1, 1953—the proliferation of the radio and increased record sales catapulted Williams and country music in general to great commercial success.

Hank Williams

By the mid-1950s some youngsters, influenced by Williams, yearned for more. Conscious of the power and emotionality of rhythm and blues, they sought to add "the beat" to authentic country music. Mississippi-born Elvis Presley, then living in Memphis, entered Sun Records one July evening to record a rural blues tune entitled "That's Alright Mama." Recording with only an acoustic guitar, electric guitar, and bass and singing with tremulous, reckless abandon, Elvis created the country/blues/R&B synthesis known as rockabilly. Later, drums were added to the ensemble, and rockabilly became a transitional genre for some white performers, attracting stars like Jerry Lee Lewis, Johnny Cash, Carl Perkins, and Roy Orbison to Sun Records before the decade was out. After recording five rockabilly songs at Sun, Elvis signed with RCA Records. In January 1956 he recorded "Heartbreak Hotel." In the wake of Elvis's success, classic rock's commercial future was assured.

## The Fifties, Kids, and Rock and Roll

The story of classic rock and roll is not only about the evolution of musical styles and their acceptance by the young American mainstream. It is also about the growth of small independent record companies and their success in producing underground music. In addition, it is another tale of how R&B and early rock music practically saved radio from its seemingly inevitable destruction by the new technological behemoth, television. And, finally, the story must describe how some youth, emboldened by the rising expectations of America's economic and political successes, sought and found a life different than the one portrayed on television's "Father Knows Best" and "Leave It to Beaver."

Rock/pop music was adopted by a generation of teenagers who eventually came to question some tenets of the dominant culture. During a slow process of disillusionment, this newly recognized age group—adolescents—formulated the questions that would become rallying cries a decade later. But, as Don Hibbard and Carol Kaleialoha point out, the cries were still only whispers in the 1950s. "In essence, rock and roll provided its predominantly middle-class audience with a vent for its discontent, a form of excitement, and a sense of group identity, while it pursued socially prescribed goals."[1]

Some models of dissent existed, but in the era of McCarthyism and the Cold War, they were much maligned and not very popular. Activity in the peace and civil rights movements was at a low ebb. The Committee for a SANE Nuclear Policy protested against the bomb and a few activists came out against U.S. involvement in the so-called police action in Korea. The U.S. Supreme Court's *Brown v. Board of Education* decision (1954) held unconstitutional separate-but-equal school segregation and helped to spur the civil rights movement. The next year citizens in Montgomery, Alabama, organized a successful boycott to desegregate the municipal bus system. One of the boycott's leaders was the young Reverend Martin Luther King Jr.

On both coasts, counterculture types—in this case, the "beat generation"—lived out free-love alternatives to the prevailing repressed sexuality, embraced daring poetry, and, in general, criticized the rigid, uptight, and restrictive environment that was the fifties. Still, however dynamic and creative, these movements were still marginal and did not touch the lives of most young Americans.

What did concern young America was leisure. For the first time, many teenagers did not have to work to support their families. Besides school, teens had few burdensome responsibilities, and with the advent of allowances they acquired some disposable income. American business, recognizing the existence of a new consumer group, rushed to fill the void, providing "essential" items such as clothes, cosmetics, fast food, cars—and music. Teens proved an especially malleable consumer group, spending money in predictable conformity. The record industry, however, produced a "Hit Parade" that was banal and bland; it lacked any identifiable reference to the everyday lives of this new consumer class.

However, on small Black radio stations, and in increasing frequency on larger popular music stations in major urban markets, rhythm and blues and its progeny, classic rock, were being programmed. This music, excited by a throbbing backbeat and often offering a daringly suggestive treatment of romance, appealed to this generation of teens who had been taught by their parents to want and expect more than they were getting.

In the summer of 1954 "Little Things Mean a Lot" by Kitty Kallen dominated the pop charts. This syrupy ballad played in stark contrast to "Work with Me Annie," the suggestive, up-tempo counterpart #1 on the R&B (Black music) charts. Teens in major urban centers like Cleveland, Philadelphia, and New York could choose to tune in to either song on their radios. By 1955 young people were listening to, and buying, R&B in record numbers. Steve Chapple and Reebee Garofalo point out that in 1952, at the Dolphin Record Store in Los Angeles, 40 percent of R&B music customers were white, a complete departure from a few months earlier.

The major record companies, who controlled the prevailing pop music, were agitated by the growing young white interest in Black music; their pop music–oriented sensibilities were severely disturbed. For one thing, not only were these new styles musically simplistic, but they were also perceived as being overtly sexual in both lyrics and performance—and this bordered on immorality. Second, the "majors" (the big-three record companies RCA, Columbia, and Decca and other film industry–based labels like Paramount and Capitol) didn't own the sound. Having abandoned Black (or "race") music and country music as unprofitable during World War II, the majors had no R&B artists on their labels.

Rhythm and blues, blues, and subsequently classic rock were left to small regional independent record companies, called "indies." These small one- or two-person operations recorded, pressed, and distributed Black blues and R&B artists in the late 1940s. By 1954 many had gone national, with major artists and million-selling records. A few of the best-known examples are Atlantic from New York with Ray Charles, Chess from Chicago with Muddy Waters, Imperial from Los Angeles with Fats Domino, and King/Federal from Cincinnati with Hank Ballard.

At first, the majors ignored R&B. By 1953 R&B record sales and radio airplay provoked them to "cover" R&B hits. For majors, the cover phenomenon meant paying royalties for the rights to record a song, often cleaning up lyrics and softening the music's harder edges, and releasing their own version recorded by a pop artist that they held under contract. For approximately three years (1953–1955), this practice had the effect of smothering the original Black versions. The indies simply could not press enough records and lacked the network to distribute them nationwide—and they did not have the necessary friendly relations with radio station personnel to ensure radio exposure.

Thus, while the original "Sh-Boom" by the Chords failed to be listed on the top-40 popular charts, the cover by the white Crewcuts was successful enough to become #1. Similarly, Ivory Joe Hunter had an R&B hit with "I Almost Lost My Mind," but it was Pat Boone, a notorious cover artist, that had the pop #1. The McGuire Sisters, Gail Storm, Perry Como, and many more singers used R&B covers to maintain pop-chart prominence.

Following the lead of the independent record companies, small radio stations in urban areas with sizable Black populations started to regularly program blues and R&B. Young white teenagers, hearing these exciting new sounds over the airwaves, began to search for them in local record stores. This created a demand in white retail outlets for rhythm and blues and, accordingly, on radio stations where these stores advertised. Reeling from competition with television, radio station managers were forced to compromise their personal reticence over playing "low-class music" in favor of potential economic salvation. Stations in major markets, using both Black and white disc jockeys, began to program rhythm and blues.

The best known of the white disc jockeys who programmed rhythm and blues was Cleveland's Alan Freed. Originally a classical musician, he was persuaded, after seeing a crowd of white teens purchasing rhythm and blues discs at a local record store, to offer an afterschool R&B show called "Alan Freed's Moon Dog Rock and Roll House Party." His 1951 WJW broadcasts were syndicated to other stations, and in March 1952 his Moon Dog Coronation Ball attracted 18,000 fans to the 10,000-seat Cleveland Arena.

Freed moved to New York City, and lowly station WINS, in 1954. For four years he held down the 7–11 PM slot and his "Rock and Roll Party" quickly became New York's top popular music show. "Cousin Brucie" Morrow, later New York's top evening DJ, once said of Freed: "Alan Freed became one of the bravest men ever to be a part of the radio industry. There can be no question that it was a kind of integrity that led him to play the R&B music that no one else would touch."[2] This popularization of R&B on radio stations took hold nationwide. Hunter Hancock in Los Angeles, "John R" Richbourgh in Nashville, and George "Hound Dog" Lorenz are a few examples of white DJs who promoted R&B.

By 1955 radio airplay of R&B and classic rock gave young listeners a choice of versions. Although their music was condemned by local PTAs, government committees, and church leaders, American teens chose the authentic, the original. Viewing rock as a passing fad, some majors, like RCA and Decca, signed only one artist—Elvis and Bill Haley, respectively. They then chose to wait out the inevitable demise of rock and roll. Instead, the classic rock and roll artists described in Chapters 3 and 4 reshaped American popular music. Rock and roll was here to stay.

# 3· Classic Rockers—the First Generation: Just Give Me Some of That Rock and Roll Music

*Rock and roll in the 1950s attacked, often indirectly, many of the institutions that helped to control young people. . . . During the otherwise silent years of the Eisenhower administration's authoritarian attitudes, rock and roll's suggestive stage manner, guttural vocals, double entendre lyrics were seen as attackers of sexual decency and the stable family. Rock and roll fostered the separation of youth from parental control.*

**Steve Chapple and Reebee Garofalo, Rock and Roll Is Here to Pay**

*Rock and roll is poison put to sound.*

**Cellist Pablo Casals**

*Combine a traditional European ballad form with an irregular Afro-American rhythm, a vocal and/or instrumental ejaculation to break up or distort the melody, and in 1955, you have a new sound.*

**Rock historians Don Hibbard and Carol Kaleialoha, The Role of Rock**

*Rock and roll is just rhythm and blues. It's the same music I've been playing for 15 years in New Orleans.*

**Fats Domino, from an interview on "Heroes of Rock and Roll," a 1981 ABC-TV special**

## I Found My Thrill

In 1954 teens growing up in Springfield—whether in Maine, Missouri, Oregon, or Illinois—had probably never heard of rock and roll. The local radio station and television's "Your Hit Parade" were playing the same old pop songs—conformist, fantasy-oriented lyrics and soporific, beatless music. This popular music appealed to both parents and their kids and featured a mixture of artists: older song stylists like Perry Como, Frank Sinatra, and Nat "King" Cole, newcomers like Eddie Fisher, Patti Page, and Rosemary Clooney, and the slightly more emotional singers like Frankie Laine, Guy Mitchell, and Johnnie Ray.

Public awareness of rock and roll grew slowly. While rhythm and blues was becoming popular in cities with large Black populations, also developing a "cult" following among some white teens, most young white Americans were unaware of their impending musical liberation. Once rock and roll did emerge, it so threatened the prevailing societal equilibrium that Columbia University's Dr. A. M. Meerio was moved to conclude at the time, "If we cannot stem the tide of rock and roll with its waves of rhythmic narcosis and vicarious craze, we are preparing our own downfall in the midst of pandemic funeral dances."[1]

Rock and roll music was not musically complex—it contained elements from rhythm and blues, blues, and gospel mixed with varying amounts of country music and pop. There were emotion-laden vocals. There was an emphasis on the two and four beats of the measures (one-TWO-three-FOUR); listeners rocked on the one and three and rolled on the TWO and FOUR. Young people reacted emotionally to the music, moving their bodies in sympathetic vibration as the performers moved theirs. The lyrics told teen tales about romance, dance, school, music, and sex—just simple stories about everyday life.

In an era of the organization man, when dutiful parents strove to belong and conform, rock music became a catalyst for teens to form their own group identity—a comradeship of those who felt good about, and identified with, the music. Many youth of the fifties viewed rock and roll as an expression of both rebellion and a growing uneasiness against the perceived rigidity and banality of an era dominated by conservative Republican politics and Mitch Miller musicality. It gave them a sense of community, as would the antiwar protests of the next generation.

To most adults, however, there was something unnerving about the music. To parents, many of whom were socialized by training in the military, the hierarchical structure of workplace and home, and the conformist societal climate, this music produced a frighteningly spontaneous and sensual reaction in their children. Their offspring reacted in an unauthorized manner. And adult antagonism toward rock music also reflected the inherent racism of the era. Having correctly perceived rock music as fundamentally Black in both origin and nature, most white parents judged it bestial and subhuman. For example, the Alabama White Citizens Council announced a campaign to rid the country of this "animalistic, nigger bop." Many government, religious, and educational spokespersons echoed those sentiments, characterizing the music as immoral and sinful—and its purveyors as lazy and shiftless juvenile delinquents.

So young people had a problem. Father, teacher, and parson all said that rock and roll was bad for them. But, lying in bed cuddling their radios or after school at a friend's house, young people knew that listening to rock music made them feel good. Dad and Mom, if they talked about it at all, said that songs with double entendre lyrics about sex and romance were wrong. However, since parents seemed to be involved in the sexual activity that they prohibited for their teenage offspring, it appeared like a "do as I say, not as I do" scenario. Life for teens was beginning to lose its safe predictability. The infallibility of the family and the honor of society was at stake, and maybe, just maybe, father didn't know best.

Like their audiences, the classic rockers sought musical and emotional outlets. Having been exposed to both Black and white musical roots, these rock pioneers forged a fusion of styles. There emerged two distinct generations: predominantly Black artists who became popular before 1956; and the Elvis-led, white, country-rooted group who parlayed the genre into its extraordinary commercial success. The first generation of classic rockers—Fats Domino, Bill Haley, Chuck Berry, and Little Richard—rose to prominence between 1953 and 1955. They led the rock and roll explosion, establishing the classic rock genre as a viable commercial force in popular music. Their music remained close to its roots in rhythm and blues, blues, and, in Haley's case, country, creating mostly upbeat rock songs about dance, romance, and teen lifestyles. Yet their stories show how they were just ordinary folks who exhibited an abundance of creative talent and a passion for their music.

## Antoine "Fats" Domino

*He was a performer of great charm but little charisma . . . (his musical style) was dominated by a warm vocal style and a thick, chunky, boogie-woogie bass New Orleans piano.*

**Rock historian Peter Guralnick,** Feel Like Goin' Home

In 1949 Antoine "Fats" Domino recorded his first rhythm and blues hit, "The Fat Man," which sold 1 million copies by 1953. Yet Domino didn't become rock and roll's first superstar. Though he was an accomplished pianist and he co-composed most of his hit songs, his stage show, and consequently much of his public persona, lacked the explosive rebelliousness of Elvis or Little Richard. Domino and his music were too easygoing. White America would have to wait for its king of rock and roll.

One of nine children, Domino was born in New Orleans on February 26, 1928. His family spoke mostly French-Creole at home and was steeped in the rich musical tradition of the city. His father was a well-known violinist, but Domino learned to play mostly from his uncle, jazz guitarist Harrison Verrett. Verrett, who had worked with jazz pioneers Kid Ory and Papa Celestin, taught the nine-year-old Domino by writing note letters on the white piano keys with black ink.

Within a few years the youngster was playing in local honky tonks for tips, working during the day mowing lawns for $1.50 a day.

In December 1949 New Orleans bandleader and trumpeter Dave Bartholomew suggested to Lou Chudd (president of Los Angeles-based Imperial Records) that they go see Domino perform. Chudd was impressed, and Domino, with Bartholomew's band, went into the studio to record "The Fat Man." This began a collaboration that lasted into the sixties. The combination of performer-composer Domino and bandleader-arranger-producer-composer Bartholomew is credited with more charted rock/pop hits than any classic rock artist except Elvis Presley.

The studio, in this case, was J&M Studios, located behind a furniture store at the corner of Rampart and Domaine in New Orleans. Like many other studios (Sun and Stax in Memphis, Motown in Detroit, Chess in Chicago, and Atlantic in New York), J&M was a place that captured the sound of a region—the New Orleans R&B sound. It featured a specific group of musicians, led by Bartholomew, the studio sound was engineered by owner Cosimo Matassa, and local recording stars like Domino, Lloyd Price, and Huey "Piano" Smith charted new waters.

By today's standards, recording conditions at that early J&M location were primitive. Producer Robert "Bumps" Blackwell once described it this way: "The studio was just a backroom in a furniture store, like an ordinary motel room, for the whole orchestra. There'd be a grand piano just as you came in the door. I'd have the grand's lid up with a mic in the keys and Alvin Tyler and Lee Allen (saxes) would be blowing into that. Earl Palmer's drums were out of the door, where I had one mic as well. The studio bass man would be over on the other side of the studio. You see the bass would cut and bleed in, so I could get the bass."[2]

"The Fat Man" entered the R&B charts in April 1950 and rose to #6. The title was no anomaly; although only five-foot-five, Domino weighed 224 pounds. He released five more gold (million-selling) records before 1955. In July 1955 "Ain't It a Shame" (#10) reached the top-40 popular music charts, allowing Domino his first major access to teenage America. Pat Boone's cover of the same tune hit the charts simultaneously and eventually climbed to #1.

Throughout the 1950s and into the early 1960s, the team of Domino, Bartholomew, and the "Cosimo" sound created a series of thirty-five top-40 hits. Based on the traditional R&B ensemble of drums, bass, piano, electric guitar, and saxophone(s), Domino's sound, called rhythm and blues in 1954, was heralded as rock and roll by 1956. Although Domino never had a #1 hit, his ten top-10 hits included: "Blueberry Hill" (1956; #2); "Blue Monday" (1957; #5); "I'm Walkin'" (1957; #4); "Whole Lotta Loving" (1958; #6); and "I Want to Walk You Home" (1959; #8).

Like most classic rockers, Fats Domino came from humble beginnings in the South. The rich musical tradition of New Orleans provided him with a variety of influences. His piano style drew from boogie-woogie players such as Meade Lux

Lewis, Albert Ammons, and Pete Johnson. Domino's recording band (Dave Bartholomew's group) contained some of the finest R&B players available in New Orleans. His musical blend included Domino's own Creole-accented lilting vocal style—"I found my three-ill on Blueberry he-ill"—strong drums and bass, jazz-flavored, melodic saxophone solos, and that syncopated honky-tonk piano.

Despite Domino's failure to score a #1 hit on the pop charts, he was still one of the most commercially viable of the classic rockers. Early in his career, Domino took his uncle's advice and retained the songwriting royalties to his compositions. Thus, Domino received substantial sums of money (via songwriting royalties), whether songs he penned gained popularity through his own recording or covers by other artists.

Rock and roll artists who achieve a top level of commercial success do so not only because of individual talent, but also because they are surrounded by a team of gifted, highly motivated individuals working in support. Fats Domino had such a team. Co-composer Dave Bartholomew was a skilled musical director and record producer; Cosimo Matassa's studio and engineering blended perfectly with the "New Orleans sound"; and Lew Chudd's Imperial Records was one of the largest independent record companies in the nation—with sufficient resources, motivation, and talent to market its stable of artists. Although Domino didn't have an influential manager the caliber of Elvis's infamous "Colonel" Tom Parker, Harrison Verrett provided him with sound business advice and direction. This "team" of support personnel is absent for many of the less successful artists of the era.

Fats Domino's legacy is a musical smile—the sound and feeling that come with his "good time" rock and roll. His music was bouncy, attributable in part to that wonderfully syncopated honky-tonk piano. His lyrics, which portrayed an unspoiled, romantic lifestyle and were reinforced by his relaxed delivery and stylish drawl, presented a relatively asexual, nonthreatening vision for youth and parents. Domino fostered this safe image by remaining seated at the piano during his live performances. Although he lacked the charisma and sexual energy of Little Richard and Elvis, Domino was the era's second most successful recording artist—collecting eighteen gold awards and selling more than 30 million records. He has survived rock's first three decades and continues to perform into the nineties.

## Bill Haley

In the spring of 1955 Bill Haley had everything going for him. His third top-20 hit, "Rock Around the Clock," had gone #1, he fronted an exciting rock and roll band, and he had an entré into mainstream success because he shared the same skin color as his (mostly) white audiences. Yet Haley would fail to emerge as rock and roll's first teenage heartthrob. At 28, he lacked the youthful charisma and sexual swagger to become the king of rock and roll. The world would have to wait for Elvis Presley. Haley was, however, one of rock and roll music's pioneers.

Incorporating his intuitive feel for, and experience with, country music, blues, jazz, and rhythm and blues, Haley consciously created a collage of up-tempo, beat-driven dance music chronicling the rocking and rolling of fifties teens.

William Haley was born in Highland Park, Michigan, on July 6, 1925. His father had moved from Kentucky to the Detroit area to find work, but when the depression hit he settled his wife and two children near Chester, Pennsylvania. Haley senior found steady work in the Sun Shipyards, which gave his family a reliable income at a time when rural neighbors barely got by.

When Bill was seven, he taught himself guitar and entered amateur contests in an outdoor country and western park near his home. Haley came from a musical family—his mother taught piano and his father played mandolin. Starting out as a country and western singer, he soon met Hank Williams: "Hank taught me a few chords and he did influence me. He was a great blues singer and he stimulated my interest in rhythm and blues music, race music as it was called then."[3] Haley was also listening to the jump band jazz of Louis Jordan, Lionel Hampton, and Lucky Millender.

By age fifteen Haley had joined Cousin Lee, a group with a regular radio show on WDEL in Wilmington, Delaware. Haley became a professional country and western musician and traveled widely in the Midwest, but he eventually quit the road, got married, and returned to Chester, where he worked at WPWA as disc jockey, sports announcer, and emcee of his own live music show. Onstage, the yodeling, guitar-strumming singer was shy and reserved, which stemmed from the self-consciousness of being blind in one eye.

Chester, Pennsylvania, contained a thriving music scene. Not only did the Four Aces and Frankie Avalon hail from that area, but Haley also worked clubs in the Black section. "Back then, we worked colored nightclubs and there was no problem with either the musicians or the patrons. And I worked on the same bill at Pep's Music Barn with B. B. King, Fats Domino, Lloyd Price, Ray Charles, Nat King Cole—no hang-up whatsoever."[4] Haley was a visionary, in that he made a conscious effort to integrate his country roots with rhythm and blues. "I felt that if I could take, say, a dixieland tune and drop the first and third beats, and accentuate the second and fourth, and add a beat that the listeners could clap to as well as dance, this could be what they were after."[5]

Thus Bill Haley was a sideburned, cowboy-booted country and western singer when, in 1952, he recorded an R&B tune entitled "Rock This Joint" on the small independent Essex label. His band, the Saddlemen, was a country band that contained an accordion and a steel guitar, along with bass, drums, guitar, and piano. Haley had written "Rock-a-Beatin' Boogie" for another group and found out that disc jockey Alan Freed was using it to open his radio show in Cleveland. The words "Rock, rock, rock everybody/ Roll, roll, roll everybody" were infectious.

The time for Haley's personal transformation was clearly at hand; off came the sideburns, boots, and country name, out came the tuxedos. Bill Haley and the Saddlemen became Bill Haley and His Comets. The country group became a powerful rock and roll ensemble consisting of drums, bass, two electric guitars, piano, steel guitar, and tenor saxophone. Haley began to instill more emotion in his vocals, and Rudy Pompelli's saxophone solos and R&B-derived "down on your knees" stage antics drove the audience wild. They recorded "Crazy Man Crazy," which sold over 1 million and reached the Billboard top 20 in 1953. The group garnered interest from all three majors (Columbia, RCA, and Decca); it signed with Decca.

In April 1954 the group assembled at New York's Pythian Temple for their first Decca session. Rarely has there been a more auspicious first session. They recorded "Rock Around the Clock," a song written by a pair of white middle-aged music-business veterans.[6] Although it sold a healthy 75,000 copies, the record failed to make much of an impact. The band also recorded their musically and lyrically sanitized cover version of Big Joe Turner's R&B hit "Shake, Rattle and Roll" and it reached #12. The decision to use "Rock Around the Clock" behind the opening credits of the 1955 movie *Blackboard Jungle* secured the song, and Bill Haley, a place in the history books. Teens acquired an anthem of rebellion, as they added the words "whether you like it or not" to the title—and parents found a target. The song rose to #1 and stayed there for an incredible eight weeks. It has since sold 30 million copies, more than any other rock single.

Haley became the first white rock and roll star. He toured with the major package shows, headlined concerts, and became a rock idol in Europe. At the end of 1955, Haley was named *Downbeat* magazine's Rhythm and Blues Personality of the Year, which evidenced that Haley was also popular in the Black music community. He reached the top 20 once more in early 1956 with "See You Later, Alligator" (#6). But America was still looking for a teen idol, and the slightly balding, pudgy, somewhat shy Haley didn't fit the bill. Consequently, other white artists, including Elvis Presley, surged past him in popularity. Haley continued to tour for the next two decades, becoming a star in the rock nostalgia movement of the late 1960s. By the late 1970s he was in severe physical and financial distress. His sax player and musical director, Rudy Pompelli—who had stayed loyal through it all—died in 1976. Bill Haley lived his last years in Harlingen, Texas. He drank heavily, slipping in and out of reality. On February 9, 1981, he died alone.

Bill Haley was the first white musician of the fifties to synthesize Black and white musical styles and have a major impact on popular music. He combined a strong backbeat with a clear forceful vocal style, Rudy Pompelli's outstanding tenor saxophone solo work, and a lyrical content that reinforced the joys of dancing to rock and roll. Before Elvis, Chuck Berry, and Buddy Holly, there was Bill Haley, who introduced teenage America to classic rock and roll.

# Chuck Berry

---

*Berry was the first performer to demonstrate that rock and roll could be philosophically and artistically worthwhile as well as good to dance to. . . . [Berry put] a measure of quality into rock and roll.*

**Rock historian Loyd Grossman, A Social History of Rock Music**

*Hail, hail rock and roll/ Remember it from the days of old. . . .*
*Long live rock and roll/ The feelin' is there, body and soul.*

**Chuck Berry's "School Days" (Chess Records, 1957)**

---

Charles Edward Anderson Berry was the father-poet of classic rock and roll. He chronicled the fifties teenage experience with a literacy and musical creativity unmatched by his contemporaries. His stories of struggle, romance, and dance provided the listener with a lyrical pastiche reflecting the first stab at self-sufficiency by the era's youth. Chuck Berry the person, however, remains somewhat of an enigma. His struggles with the law have left him embittered and uncommunicative—so much so that, until the release of his autobiography in 1987, even the year and place of his birth were in doubt. Now we know that Berry was born on October 18, 1926, in St. Louis, Missouri, the second of three boys in a family of six children. Although these were the depression years, his father was a building maintenance contractor, ensuring his family a relatively comfortable existence. Both parents were active in the Baptist Church and young Charles sang in the choir at age six.

In addition to his church music, Berry's vocal interests lay in the era's popular music: "My favorite singers . . . are Nat [King Cole] and Frank [Sinatra], in that respect, because I'm moody, and Nat sang moody music."[7] His clear enunciation on his material reflects these pop vocal influences. St. Louis was perfectly positioned, geographically speaking, as a musical crossroads. It was close to Kansas City, the jazz mecca of the big band era, and astride the Mississippi River; the city also was an important waystation for the railroad and river traffic that brought southern blues musicians to the industrial North. Making his home along these routes, Berry was inundated with various styles of music throughout his youth.

Berry was a self-taught musician, proficient in guitar, saxophone, and piano. As the father of rock and roll guitar, he would fuse elements from the blues (repetition, choke, and bend), with country-derived speed and slides. His developing guitar style was clearly influenced by regional Black jazz and blues artists as well as by the country and western music that he followed avidly on the radio. When asked about his guitar influences, Berry cited "a person named Charlie Christian, guitarist for Benny Goodman, T-Bone Walker, and Carl Hogan (Louis Jordan's guitarist)."[8] One important innovation, often overlooked in chronicling the development of rock guitar, is Berry's rhythm-guitar style. Using E-fingering bar chords, Berry would strum an eighth-note pulse on the bass strings of the guitar while alternating with his pinkie every two beats four frets above the bar. This created a forceful, driving foundation to Berry's material that continues to be used by modern rock guitarists.

Berry's first brush with the law occurred in 1944. He and two companions were arrested for auto theft and robbery and Berry spent nearly three years in reform school. Later, Berry obtained a job at the General Motors plant while he and his sister studied to become hairstylists at the Poro School of Beauty Culture. In the early 1950s, with a wife and two children to support, Berry supplemented his income by leading a small blues combo. A local piano player named Johnny Johnson invited guitarist Berry to replace a departed sax player, and the quartet eventually became popular enough to rival larger local combos such as Ike Turner and the Rhythm Kings.

Berry's rise to fame is steeped in legend. Mythology has it that Berry, ostensibly in town for vacation, stepped onto a Chicago stage to join blues great Muddy Waters during a jam session. Berry disputes this but acknowledges that Waters did recommend Berry visit Chess Records head Leonard Chess. By 1954 Chess Records was the premier proponent of the Chicago urban blues sound; its artist roster included Waters, Howlin' Wolf, Willie Dixon, and many others. Berry viewed himself as a blues artist, but Leonard Chess was more interested in a medium-tempo song named "Ida May" (also identified as "Ida Red"). He instructed Berry to rework the tune at a faster pace and change the name.

Returning to Chicago, Berry recorded the song, now titled "Maybellene," on May 21, 1955. Leonard Chess rushed "Maybellene" to New York and disc jockey Alan Freed. The country's most prominent rock and roll disc jockey gave it his enthusiastic support—and Chess gave Freed one-third of the songwriter's royalties. With the assistance of New York airplay, "Maybellene" reached #1 on the R&B charts and #5 on the pop charts that summer.

While most classic rockers wrote tales of love, Berry wrote tales of teen existence that exhibited a freshness, humor, and literacy reminiscent of Tin Pan Alley professionals. It is paradoxical that a man who was already thirty years old by the time "Roll Over Beethoven" was a hit in 1956 could so accurately speak for a generation of teens that was tasting rebellion for the first time. Perhaps the indelibly etched experience of being a Black youth from the Border South gave Berry insight into the oppression and frustration felt by a new generation of adolescents. A man with a high school education became rock's first poet laureate.

Chuck Berry recorded eight more top-40 hits during the next four years. "Roll Over Beethoven" (#29, May 1956) alerted the nation to the excitement of the new sound, chiding classical music composers Beethoven and Tchaikovsky to vacate the scene and make way for rhythm and blues (that is, rock and roll). In 1957 "School Days" (#3) chronicled a typical school-day experience from "Up in the morning and out to school" to day's end at the local gathering place, where they all "hail, hail rock and roll." Of special note in "School Days" is the call and response between the vocal and the guitar during the verses. In an era of live recordings, this almost perfect call-and-response synchronization of the guitar to the meter and pitch of the vocal melody and phrasing was a marvelous accomplishment.

Berry once again celebrated the new sound with "Rock and Roll Music" (#8, November 1957) and introduced his audience to their first teenybopper in "Sweet Little Sixteen" (#2, February 1958). "Johnny B. Goode" (#8, May 1958) was one of rock and roll's first biographies—the story of a young Louisiana guitarist out to make it big. I don't know of another song that has permeated live rock and roll to a greater extent. Request "Johnny B. Goode" at any rock and roll club and you're likely to get it played on the spot; its anthemic "Go, Johnny, go!" has become a rallying cry for the entire genre of rock and roll.

Berry developed a performance style that excited his audiences (though he was not as wild onstage as Jerry Lee Lewis and Little Richard). Bent over in a crouch, his head bobbin' and weavin', Berry would strut across the stage doing his famous duckwalk. Down through the years, this and other Berry performance practices have been emulated by rock guitarists.

Berry's strong sense of artistic and personal integrity was challenged the first time he appeared on Dick Clark's network TV show, "American Bandstand." Like all other performers, Berry was expected to lip synch (move his mouth without singing) the words to his song while the record played on the air. Berry balked. Luckily for Berry, Leonard Chess was present to point out the potentially cataclysmic results of a stand-off with Dick Clark. Berry eventually saw the economic wisdom of this argument, lip synched, and later even named his St. Louis club Chuck Berry's Bandstand.

Movies were another medium where rock music received additional exposure. With the success of "Rock Around the Clock" in *Blackboard Jungle*, Hollywood jumped on the rock and roll soundtrack bandwagon. Berry's first movie effort was *Rock, Rock, Rock,* which was followed by *Mr. Rock and Roll* and *Go Johnny Go*. During this era, approximately twenty-five major movies were devoted to the subject of rock and roll.

As with many of the other classic rockers, Berry's career and financial security were illusory. In December 1959 Berry was charged with a violation of the federal Mann Act, which prohibited transporting a minor across state lines with intent to commit prostitution. According to Berry, he added a twenty-one-year-old woman to his entourage during an El Paso tour date and gave her a job as a cigarette girl in his club. She began turning tricks as a prostitute, was assaulted by a customer, and possibly traded testimony against Berry in exchange for the goodwill of the authorities. The prosecution contended she was only fourteen years old.

The first trial verdict (a conviction) was vacated on appeal due to the blatant racial prejudice of the presiding judge. The second trial sealed Berry's fate. Again convicted, he entered federal prison in Terre Haute, Indiana, in February 1962. By the time of his release in the fall of 1963, he had lost his club and found his career in shambles. The experience changed him. Carl Perkins noted that the man who had once seemed so friendly and easygoing was now terse and moody. In Patrick Salvo's 1972 *Rolling Stone* magazine interview, Berry even denied that he went to jail.

In 1964 Berry went head-to-head with the British invasion. Although he had three top-40 tunes—"Nadine," "No Particular Place to Go," and "You Never Can Tell"—it was a losing battle. Many sixties groups recorded Berry's songs and often cited him as a major influence in their development, but he never again achieved his previous popular status. Ironically, in 1972, a live recording of the suggestive "My Ding-a-Ling" became Berry's only #1 chart hit. Forty years after his first hit record, he continues to perform, thrilling fans with his masterful version of classic rock and roll.

Chuck Berry created the most literate, stylistically innovative, and original music of the era—he was a complete musician who was not only a vocal stylist like Elvis, but also a composer, instrumentalist, and bandleader. While most other performers limited their scope to various permutations of boy-girl romance formula, Berry's songs dealt with the important adolescent concerns such as romance, sex, work, school, cars, dancing, parents, and rock and roll music. As a guitarist, he created the baseline for the genre. But Berry, the era's "brown-eyed, handsome man," fell from grace, as did many other classic rockers. However, his massive legacy and the man himself are still a vibrant part of the rock and roll community.

## Little Richard

*When Jerry Lee [Lewis] hits the piano keyboard with his butt, bangs the keys with the boot of his heel of an outstretched leg and leaps on top, it's Little Richard. When Presley chokes-gasps-gulps his words and swivels his pelvis, it's Little Richard. When the Beatles scream "yeah, yeah, yeah" and gliss into a high falsetto, it's Little Richard.*

**Pop music scholar Arnold Shaw, The Rockin' '50s**

Richard Pennimen has always wanted to be acknowledged as the king of rock and roll. He had exploded into the first era of rock and roll with a string of top-40 hits. His unique stage appearance and live performance style were imitated by many of his contemporaries. His persona and penchant for a controversial lifestyle were unmatched. But Richard was simply too outrageous, too raw, and too Black to capture the crown he so desperately wanted. America would await another's ascendance to the throne.

Little Richard was born on December 5, 1932, at his home in the comfortable Pleasant Hill neighborhood of Macon, Georgia. He was the third child, and second boy, in a family that eventually numbered twelve children. His father, the son of a preacher, was a brickmason and sold moonshine on the side. His mother, Leva Mae, was probably being kind when she stated once that "Richard was the most trouble of any of them." Richard was rambunctious, a practical joker, and uncontrollable into his teens. As an adolescent, he claims to have been "experienced" with men, boys, women, and girls.

At age thirteen, Richard's wild behavior landed him on the streets. He hit the road as a vocalist for Dr. Hudson's Medicine Show selling "tonic." Upon his return

Little Richard

to Macon, Richard was taken in by a white couple, Ann and Johnny Johnson, who ran a nightclub called the Tick Tock Club. From this point on, Richard set his sights on a career in music.

The outstanding feature of Little Richard's music was his unique vocal style. This highly emotive singing, soaring falsetto, and screams of praise all came from his gospel background—singing in choirs, contests, and revival and camp meetings. Whether it be the pentecostal, AME Methodist, or Holiness Temple Baptist Church, the gospel style was emotional and musical. Richard was apparently good enough to become lead vocalist in a number of church-affiliated singing groups, including Ma Sweetie's Tiny Tots. These roots are evident not only in his vocal style, but also in his active performance style.

In 1951 at the age of eighteen, Richard won a recording contract with RCA records in a talent contest. The eight sides that he cut had little impact but enabled Richard to assemble a fine rhythm and blues band, the Upsetters. The core rhythm section and powerful saxophones created a potent sound that later included Georgia natives James Brown and Otis Redding as Upsetter vocalists. Richard recorded additional tunes with the Peacock label in 1953 while developing a regional following.

According to rock legend, Little Richard was washing dishes in Macon's Greyhound bus terminal when "the call" came from Art Rupe of Los Angeles-based Specialty Records. What the legend omits is that Richard was already an established regional artist with a top-notch band who had pestered Rupe unmercifully about the demo tape he had submitted seven months earlier. Specialty sent Little Richard to J&M Studios in New Orleans to record with producer Bumps Blackwell (the musical mentor of Quincy Jones and Ray Charles). Blackwell described the session this way: "When I walked in, there's this cat in this loud shirt, with hair waved up six inches above his head. He was talkin' wild, thinkin' up stuff just to be different, you know. I could tell he was a mega-personality."[9]

Richard's first time through "Tutti-Frutti" left Blackwell in a quandary; the music and feeling of the song were explosive but the words were beyond suggestive: "Tutti frutti, good booty/ If it don't fit, don't force it/ You can grease it, make it easy." New Orleans blues writer Dorothy La Bostrie was called in to rework the lyrics and Richard, with backing from Bartholomew's studio band, recorded the tune in fifteen minutes. By January 1956 the song was #2 on the R&B charts and #17 on the pop charts. During the next two years, Little Richard had eight more top-40 hits. His chart success was followed, like that of Chuck Berry and others, by inclusion on the star-laden package tours that crisscrossed the United States.

If the lyrics of Richard's song were any indication of his life, it was pretty unidimensional. He simply enjoyed "rocking," "rolling," and "balling" with his coterie of R&B belles. They ranged from Sue and Daisy, representing the sanitized version of "Tutti Frutti," to Miss Molly, Long Tall Sally, Lucille, Jenny, and more. Either white society was oblivious to the sexual double entendres in these songs or relished the thrill of those intemperate references.

The Hollywood Little Richard of "Don't Knock the Rock," "The Girl Can't Help It," and "Mr. Rock and Roll" was fairly sedate. Live audiences were treated to his mega-personality on stage. His appearance was outlandish. There were silver lamé or multicolored suits, boots, and capes. His processed hair (straightened and shaped) stood anywhere from six inches to a full foot above his forehead. He wore pancake makeup, mascara, and eyeliner. Charlie Gillett describes a Richard who was "Dressed in shimmering suits with long drape jackets and baggy pants, his hair grown long and slicked straight, white teeth and gold rings flashing in the spotlights, he stood up, and at times on, the piano, hammering boogie chords as he screamed messages of celebration and self-centered pleasure."[10]

During the fall of 1957, at the peak of his career, Little Richard announced that he was giving up secular music and enrolling in Oakwood College in Huntsville, Alabama. At this Seventh Day Adventist school he would pursue a course of bible study to ready himself for the ministry. He had reached this conclusion, according to rock mythology, while on tour in Australia. The details are cloudy, but Richard saw, heard, or felt a sign from God. According to legend, this sign came in the form of an apocalyptic vision, an engine fire on a tour charter aircraft, news that the Soviet Union had just launched Sputnik, a fireball over the concert stadium, or some or all of the above.

This abdication from rock/pop took Specialty Records by surprise. They weathered the storm by releasing previously recorded sessions, including "Good Golly Miss Molly," well into 1958. Richard studied, sang, and recorded gospel music. But while on tour in England in 1962, he reversed his direction, performing many of his old hits to the delight of his fans (who included another group on the bill, named the Beatles). This jumping between two genres (classic rock and gospel) continued into the eighties.

Little Richard attempted a major comeback in the late 1960s, recording soul-flavored material on the Okeh label. He later cracked the top 100 twice on Reprise in 1970. This was the time of mirrored costumes, talk-show tiffs, and the revelations of Richard's bisexuality. However, no matter how outlandish his behavior became, Richard maintained that the effect of his music was a healing one: "I believe my music is healin' music . . . because it inspires and uplifts people."[11]

Although his song catalog didn't have as much impact on subsequent rock generations as those of Berry and Holly, Little Richard's live performance style and emotive vocal style were major building blocks of sixties rock and roll. Richard's androgynous stage persona is reflected in the performance styles of Mick Jagger, David Bowie, Jimi Hendrix, Prince, and others. Teens of the fifties may not have been ready for a scabrous Black rock messiah, but, even in the 1990s, Richard is still making the congregation rock.

❋　　　❋　　　❋

Between 1953 and 1955, the first classic rock and roll generation (Fats Domino, Bill Haley, Chuck Berry, and Little Richard) appeared on the popular music charts. Three of the four were Black, and all played a music that reflected primary roots in blues or rhythm and blues. Domino's lilting visions of courtship and dire straights were driven by a pulsating piano and the beat of a forceful rhythm and blues band. Haley shouted his calls of dance and romance over his own driving country- and R&B-rooted ensemble.

Chuck Berry was an exceptional innovator. Firmly rooted in blues, Berry defined certain elements of rock/pop music. He focused the instrumental solo on guitar, then created its stylistic parameters. His lyrical vision included most of the major concerns of the adolescent audience. Finally, Little Richard brought the most bawdy parts of the rhythm and blues legacy—the howl, the harem, the musical power—to his rock audience.

As a group, they were pioneers of rock and roll. Each paid his dues in another style before crossing over to the popular charts—their average age was twenty-six at the time of their first pop hits. Staying close to their Black musical roots, they maintained that unrestrained, rebellious exhortation in their lyrics. In addition to songs about romance, there were also some about sex, school, dancing, and rock and roll music itself.

Though some of the lyrics were subliminally "wicked," few songs were overtly critical of the system. It wasn't until the sixties that some rock/pop lyrics called decisively for change. Lyrics and music of the classic rock era redefined adolescent lifestyles. They opened a Pandora's box—filled both with a spontaneous, emotional response to this essentially Black music and an evolving sense of teen identity and community. Rock and roll was here to stay.

By 1955 young, white, country-rooted musicians populated the South, listening to rock's first generation and adapting those sounds to their own creative visions. Soon, these men—Elvis, Buddy Holly, Jerry Lee Lewis, and the Everly Brothers—would explode on the scene. As classic rock's second generation, they would bring guitars to the forefront, return to an almost exclusive emphasis on romance, and reap commercial success and economic rewards beyond their wildest dreams.

# 4· Classic Rockers—the Second Generation: There's Good Rockin' Tonight

T HE SECOND GENERATION of classic rockers—Elvis Presley, Jerry Lee Lewis, Buddy Holly, and the Everly Brothers—forged to the forefront of rock and roll by 1957. Their particular brand of country-rooted rock and roll placed more of an emphasis on the guitar-oriented string band, the electric guitar instrumental solo, and a worldview that was almost exclusively focused on romance. As opposed to rocking around the clock with Bill Haley and dancing in the "juke joint" with Chuck Berry and his "School Days" characters, this generation chose mostly to "Love Me Tender," as with Elvis, and yearn for "True Love Ways," with Buddy Holly.

## Elvis Presley

*This cat came out in red pants and a green coat and a pink shirt and socks ... and he had a sneer on his face and he stood behind the mic for five minutes I'll bet before he made a move. Then he hit his guitar a lick and broke two strings. ... So there he was these two strings a-dangling, and he hadn't done a thing yet, and these high school girls were screaming and fainting and running up to the edge of the stage, and he started to move his hips real slow like he had a thing for his guitar.*

**Bob Luman describing Elvis at Kilgore, Texas in 1956**

*When Elvis turned forty, the media had a field day, he was fat, depressed about it, and didn't get out of bed all day. It seemed to be a continuing battle against creeping mortality, and Elvis was not winning.*

**Peter Guralnick, Lost Highway**

*From the beginning I could see he had a different outlook on things, just the way he dressed, the way he wore his hair. He was a rebel: really without making an issue out of it.*

**Scotty Moore, Elvis's guitarist**

Elvis Presley was a poor white kid from northeastern Mississippi who lived the American dream. One moment he was singing in a school talent show, the next he was appearing on nationwide television. One moment he was strumming his battered acoustic guitar in the school lunchroom, the next he was recording in Nashville with the best backup musicians money could buy. Like other classic rockers, Elvis was on the creative cutting edge of the era. What separated him from the rest was that he became the vehicle for the mass popularization of the genre. He became the King of Rock and Roll. Endowed with a pleasing voice, the innate ability to select the right material, and an abundance of charisma, Presley ascended to, and for most Americans has since personified, the pinnacle of classic rock and roll.

Yet many other rockers had similar combinations, plus more instrumental and songwriting talent. But they didn't have "the moment"; and they didn't have "the team," which made all the difference. The moment was a brief period during which white teens were becoming increasingly exposed to rhythm and blues and the early classic rockers through the medium of radio. Excited by its beat and suggestive lyrics, they were ready to recognize and embrace a rock messiah. The team—brilliant promotion and management by Colonel Tom Parker and the big recording sound and clout of RCA Records—perceived the moment, captured it, and sold it to America.

Elvis's music went through three developmental periods in the forties and fifties. First, Presley spent his youth listening to a wide variety of musical styles. Following high school graduation, Elvis began to mold elements from these roots of blues, R&B, gospel, and country into the style known as rockabilly. Finally, upon his signing to RCA Records, Presley created his unique version of classic rock and roll. Developmentally, it was the three R's: roots, rockabilly, and rock and roll.

Elvis Aaron Presley began life amid humble surroundings. He was born at home—a two-room shotgun shack—in Tupelo, Mississippi, on January 8, 1935. His twin brother, Jesse Garon, died at birth. Elvis was doted upon by his mother, who continued to walk him to school until his freshman year in high school. His mother's feelings were reciprocated; Elvis worshipped her. The Presleys were active church members, and Elvis grew to love gospel music: "We were a religious family, going around together to sing at camp meetings and revivals."[1]

Presley never lost his love of gospel vocals and harmonies, and later, in Memphis, he would spend days at the "sings" where many of the best white gospel quartets, such as the Blackwood Brothers and J. D. Sumner and the Sunshine Boys, performed. For a short time he even became a member of the Memphis-based gospel group the Songfellows. Two Black radio stations in the Memphis metropolitan area, WDIA and KWEM, broadcast blues, gospel, and R&B, and Elvis claimed to have been an avid listener. Many famous Black artists—B. B. King, Sonny Boy Williamson, and Howlin' Wolf, for example—even broadcast live from Memphis at the time. Radio also provided Elvis with a rich variety of country artists. He was particularly fond of Jimmie Rodgers, Bob Wills, and radio station WSM's "Grand Ole Opry" from Nashville featuring Roy Acuff and Ernest Tubb. At age eleven, young Presley performed the song "Old Shep," which he learned from an Opry broadcast, and won second prize at the Mississippi-Alabama Fair and Dairy Show during the "Kid's Day" talent contest.

In 1948, with hopes for a better life and steady employment, parents Vernon and Gladys Presley packed all their belongings into their car and drove to Memphis. Vernon, who hadn't been able to find steady work in Tupelo, took work driving a truck. The Presleys upgraded their housing, moving to a federally funded housing project, Lauderdale Courts. Elvis enrolled in L. C. Humes High School, the white school, but did little to distinguish himself, majoring in shop and trying out for the football team. By his senior year, the once-shy Elvis began to bloom. He brought his guitar to play at school and eventually won the talent show in the schoolwide musical review. He also adopted an appearance just this side of outrageous; his hair was styled in a DA (duck's ass, that is), kept in place with a generous application of palmade. At Lansky Brothers, a clothing store on Beale Street, Memphis's Black Broadway of music, Elvis picked out a multicolored array of finery.

Given his previous economic condition, Elvis was quite happy to secure a truck-driving job for Crown Electric after graduation. One Saturday in mid-1953, Elvis stopped at Sun Records/Memphis Home Recording Service. For $3.98, he recorded two sides of a 45-rpm disc, "My Happiness" and "That's When Your Heartaches Begin"—two songs by the popular Black vocal group the Ink Spots. According to Marion Keisker, an administrative assistant at Sun Records, "Over and over . . . I remember Sam [Phillips, Sun owner] saying 'If I could find a white man who had the Negro sound and the Negro feel, I could make a billion dollars.'"[2] Keisker jotted down Elvis's name and a neighbor's phone number, but when Phillips returned to hear the end of the session, he was not impressed.

Phillips recommended that Elvis get together with two other musicians, guitarist Scotty Moore and bassist Bill Black. On the night of July 5, 1954, the trio met at Sun studios. Scotty Moore describes the scene:

> Well, we tried three or four things. . . . Then we were taking a break, I don't know, we were having cokes and coffee, and all of a sudden Elvis started singing a song, jumpin' around and just acting the fool, and then Bill picked up the bass and he started acting the fool too, and you know I started playing with them. Sam, I think had the door to the control booth open—I don't know, he was either editing some tape or doing something—and he stuck his head out and said, "What are you doing?" And we said, "We don't know." "Well back up and try to find a place to start and do it again."[3]

The song was "That's All Right (Mama)," written by Black Tupelo bluesman Arthur "Big Boy" Crudup. It was not only Elvis's first commercial recording, but more importantly, it was that synthesis of blues and country music that would come to be called rockabilly. Essentially it was an Elvis Presley construction, combining the raw, emotive, and slurred vocal style and emphasis on rhythmic feeling from the blues with the string band and strummed rhythm guitar from country. Scotty Moore's guitar solo, a combination of Merle Travis-style country finger-picking, double-stop slides from acoustic boogie, and blues-based bent-note, single-string work, is a microcosm of this fusion. The style became a musical magnet for rebellious white southern youths wanting to combine the raucous emotionality of Black music with their country roots. As Elvis became more popular and the music spread, future stars like Jerry Lee Lewis, Carl Perkins, Johnny Cash, and Roy Orbison flocked to Memphis in search of the Sun sound.

"That's All Right (Mama)" created a stir in Memphis, went to #1 on the local country charts, and enabled the group to start touring. The record earned Elvis an appearance on Nashville's "Grand Ole Opry," where he was advised to go back to driving a truck. The band toured the South, appeared regularly on country music's second most popular radio show, "Louisiana Hayride" on Shreveport's KDKH, and released four more singles before November 1955. Elvis added "Hayride"'s staff drummer, D. J. Fontana, to his band, making it a quartet.

Elvis's live performances provided a major impetus to his career. "Everybody was screaming . . . my manager told me it was because I was wigglin'," he once said. "Well, I went back for an encore and I did a little more."[4] Elvis was impelled to move to the music. He ascribed it, in part, to his experiences with Black gospel revival meetings. "The preachers cut up all over the place, jumpin' on the piano, movin' every which way. . . . I guess I learned it from them."[5] Seeing the effect Elvis had on his audience, former circus huckster and country-artist manager Colonel Tom Parker (it was an honorary title) signed him to a management contract. Parker was extremely shrewd, hardworking, and a promotional genius; for a sizable cut of the gross (reports vary between 50 and 20 percent) Parker devoted himself exclusively to Elvis's career. Major labels, grudgingly acknowledging classic rock's early success, began searching for their own rock artists. RCA outbid Atlantic and Capitol and paid Phillips the considerable sum of $35,000 for the year left on Elvis's contract.

The stage was set, the cast of characters was in place, and "the Moment" was about to arrive: The rock artist, the major label, the crafty manager, the quality studio, and its legendary musicians were about to deliver the first rock deity. On January 10, 1956, Elvis entered RCA's Nashville studios—they shared them with the Methodist Church—to record "Heartbreak Hotel" and "I Want You, I Need You, I Love You." In an incredibly daring move, the label allowed Elvis to begin his first release without instrumentation, singing "Well since my baby left me." The gamble paid off as both songs went to #1 and Elvis scored ten more #1s and twenty more top-40 hits during the next four years.

The RCA Elvis was qualitatively and quantitatively different from Sun's earlier incarnation. At Sun, three kids spun loose, spontaneous renditions of blues and country songs drenched in echo. At RCA, the rock band grew to include drums (complete with a forceful two-plus-four backbeat), piano (studio master Floyd

Cramer), backup vocalists (the Jordinaires) singing harmonies, carefully crafted arrangements, and a crispness of sound that was characteristic of a major-label studio. RCA even attempted to duplicate the Sun echo, but the stairway they used as an echo chamber was just not the same. The energetic sensuality of Elvis combined with the polished professionalism of RCA, Chet Atkins's production, and Steve Sholes's organizational abilities fashioned a sound that obviously appealed to the broadest cross-section of the rock audience. It became some of the best-selling popular music in history.

Colonel Parker's promotion plan called for media saturation. Presley appeared on national TV at least twelve times in 1956, with many teenagers viewing the visual power of rock and roll for the first time. After Elvis appeared twice on "The Ed Sullivan Show," CBS censors prohibited camera shots of Elvis below the waist—none of Elvis's pelvis for America's youth. Detractors, a group that included most parents, hoped the tide was turning. Jack O'Brien's comments in a New York daily were typical of parental feelings at the time: "Elvis Presley wiggled and wriggled with such abdominal gyrations [on "The Milton Berle Show"] that burlesque bombshell Georgia Southern really deserves time to reply in gyrating kind. [Presley] can't sing a lick, makes up for vocal shortcomings with the weirdest and plainly planned suggestive animation short of an aborigine's mating dance."[6] The criticism, however, did not deter Presley's expanding audience—it may have even enhanced his status with teens.

By the end of 1956 Presley had garnered a string of five #1 hits and seven more in the top 40. He literally dominated the charts. "Don't Be Cruel" and "Hound Dog" were a double-sided #1. "Love Me Tender," the title track from his first film, also topped the charts. Unlike Haley and Berry, who recorded anthems to teen life and rock music, Elvis stuck with a tried-and-true pop music formula. He sang about romance—crying "Love Me," you "Hard Headed Woman," because I'm your "Teddy Bear" and "A Big Hunk of Love," and if you don't I'll be "All Shook Up." Elvis rarely wrote his own material, instead choosing from demonstration records (demos) sent him by his publisher and others. He selected a subject matter that was of utmost concern to his teen audience—the ebb and flow of youthful infatuation. Some of the era's best songwriters contributed hits for Elvis, including Jerry Lieber and Mike Stoller, Otis Blackwell, and Boudeleaux Bryant.

Another element in Colonel Parker's master plan was the movies. Elvis starred in four films—*Love Me Tender, Loving You, Jailhouse Rock,* and *King Creole*—before entering the army in March 1958. The films became vehicles to keep Elvis in front of his fans and also served as showcases for sets of new songs. Sandwiched between recording sessions and filming was a full schedule of touring. On the road and elsewhere, a large male entourage made up of high school friends and other assorted "good ole boys" accompanied Presley and serviced his every wish. They were dubbed the "Memphis Mafia." Whatever he did, they did—just a good old gang on salary.

In the late 1950s the only thing bigger than Elvis was Uncle Sam. Colonel Tom and Elvis decided that a compliant Presley was a rich Presley. Thus Elvis reported for induction and dutifully had his hair—one symbol of a rocker's masculinity—shorn; he served as an eight-to-five jeep driver in West Germany. Elvis lived off-post and his cronies waited on him and chauffeured him around in a Mercedes sedan. Many music-business prognosticators speculated that Elvis's two-year hitch would have a deleterious effect on his career. However, buoyed by the image of Elvis-as-patriot, his appeal actually broadened to include some post-teens. His music softened somewhat as RCA kept up a steady stream of releases.

During this period, Elvis lost his mother and met his future bride. Author Albert Goldman, in his psychologically oriented 1981 biography *Elvis*, contends that Presley never got over his mother's death. Goldman speculates that "sexually, Elvis was fixated at precisely the age of his typical fan: thirteen or fourteen." Thus, it is not surprising that when Elvis met Priscilla Ann Beaulieu, the fourteen-year-old daughter of an army major, in Germany, he was captivated.

They spent many evenings sequestered in Elvis's bedroom, and when it came time to return stateside, Presley invited Priscilla along. She lived at his Graceland mansion, ostensibly under the watchful eye of Presley's father and grandmother. While Presley dated numerous starlets and had a series of steady girlfriends, Priscilla attended school and waited. Seven years later, they were married. Nine months later to the day she gave birth to their only child, Lisa Marie, who would marry Michael Jackson in 1994.

By the early 1960s classic rock had run its course. Elvis chose to move closer to the nonrock mainstream. His #1 hits included the syrupy ballads "It's Now or Never" and "Are You Lonesome Tonight?" Presley appeared nationwide in a made-for-TV welcome-back special hosted by Frank Sinatra. Loyd Grossman comments, "Rock and roll was becoming mere entertainment and abandoning its social and artistic role as interpreter of the world for teenage America." Elvis no longer dominated the charts but became simply a major recording artist. He lost his penchant for rebellion and bowed to the will of his manager and to commercial considerations. Between 1961 and 1967, Presley gave no public performances, though he appeared in two to three movies per year, the soundtracks containing his pop hits. The King had abdicated his throne.

On February 1, 1968, Elvis returned to the stage. Exhausted and uninspired by his film schedule, the King appeared in a live TV special from Las Vegas. With old pals Scotty Moore and D. J. Fontana, and accompanied by studio greats Tommy Tedesco and Hal Blaine, Elvis rekindled the spark. Rock journalist Jon Landau reported, "He sang with the kind of power that people no longer expect from rock and roll singers." In January 1969 Elvis returned to Memphis to record *From Elvis in Memphis*. The hometown atmosphere produced a number of critically acclaimed cuts including the poignant and timely "In the Ghetto."

In the 1970s Elvis's professional life consisted of concentrated touring, Las Vegas shows, and periods of inactivity. It was during this time that some of his old gang became concerned with his self-destructive behavior. Presley's weight fluctuated wildly; he would go on crash diets in order to make public appearances. Drug use became a problem. Three former members of the Memphis Mafia have described how Presley was unable to leave his bed certain days. "He takes pills to go to sleep. He takes pills to get up. He takes pills to go to the john and takes pills to stop him from going to the john. There have been times he was so hyper on uppers that he has had trouble breathing, and on one occasion he thought he was going to die. His system doesn't work any more like a normal human being's. The pills do all the work for him. He's a walking pharmaceutical shop."[7] On August 16, 1977, at his Graceland mansion, Elvis's tormented body simply gave out.

❋      ❋      ❋

Elvis was white and handsome, had charisma, a rich, expressive baritone voice, and a sneer that seemed to symbolize growing teen uneasiness. His sensual/sexual performances, a direct copy of Black tradition, thrilled his adolescent audiences. He had an innate ability to fuse musical elements from Black and white forms, creating a commercially viable synthesis. Elvis was not the first nor the most talented classic rocker. When the prevailing racism of the day prohibited a Black artist from appearing as the rock messiah, Elvis seized the chance—and the moment.

His ascendance took place in two stages: the Sun rockabilly era and his mass, commercial, classic rock success at RCA. The first stage followed normal patterns of the regional artist: a record, airplay, public appearances, and an outward spiral of popularity. His conquest of the national market utilized not only outstanding raw talent, but also incisive management, brilliant promotion, and music-industry clout. The marketing plan, which included radio, television, print, films, and paraphernalia, proved to be a blueprint for later pop music careers. The end result was commercial domination. His 107 top-40 singles is still a record; the Beatles are second with 48.

Only twenty-six months passed between his first RCA hit and his induction into the army. During that time, he succeeded in carrying rock and roll to all corners of the United States, thus helping to solidify rock's permanence as a popular music form. Even as critics chastised rock as a form of nonmusic by and for subhuman juvenile delinquents, Presley's success called these views into question. To his fans, Elvis symbolized rebellion, sexuality, and youthful vitality; these could be ingested in small doses that provided a thrill but no real threat. On the Sun release "Milkcow Blues Boogie," Elvis expressed it this way: "That don't move me, let's get real, real gone for a change."

## Jerry Lee Lewis

---

*Lewis wasn't like any of the others. . . . If they were wild, he was ferocious. If their music was sexy, his was promiscuous. Presley shook his hips; Lewis raped his piano. He would play it with his feet, he would sit on it, he would stand on it, he would crawl under it and he would leap over it.*

*Rock journalist Andy Wickham*

---

They called him "the Killer." Onstage, he pounded the piano with any part of his anatomy that was handy. His private life was a never-ending rock and roll soap opera: three wives by the time he was twenty-two, alcohol and drug abuse, a personality that was a "mixture of brash egotism and bubbling irrepressible charm," and a constant battle with his personal devil. In the tradition of Elvis and Little Richard, Jerry Lee made audiences rock with his music.

In early 1958, at the peak of his career, Lewis was successful enough to challenge all previous comers for the crown. But then he stumbled, as his secret marriage to thirteen-year-old Myra Brown—Lewis's third cousin—was exposed during a British tour. Without the public relations machinery and clout of a major label or a Colonel Tom Parker to smooth things over, Lewis floundered in a sea of bad ink. The scandal was all the establishment press needed to assail rock and roll, and Lewis's rock career never recovered.

Like most classic rockers, Lewis was raised among the working people of the South. Jerry Lee was born near Ferriday, Louisiana, on September 29, 1935. His father, Elmo, was a carpenter by trade, who went to jail for selling moonshine. Elmo played the piano and guitar, and Lewis's mother, Molly, was an avid pop and country music fan. Lewis grew up in the rural South during the depression; his parents scratched out a living on a small piece of land, surrounded by a large extended family. His family history also included a fundamentalist interpretation of religion and episodes of hard drinking and violent behavior.

The Lewis family attended the local Assembly of God Church, traveled to many revival meetings, sang psalms, and danced to receive the Holy Spirit. Young Jerry Lee intended to become a preacher and for a short time attended Southwestern Bible School near Dallas, Texas. Instead he chose to become a secular musician—a decision that would condemn Lewis to an inner conflict between righteousness and Satan's music. Jerry Lee's religious upbringing was manifested in his expressive vocals and stage activity. When Jerry Lee performed, he testified—an unrepentant, bawdy, rebellious alternative to the constraints of many organized religions.

Lewis mythology has him picking out a passable version of "Silent Night" on his aunt's piano at age eight. His family deemed him a child prodigy and his father mortgaged the family home to purchase a new piano. Jerry Lee's musical roots are similar to other classic rock piano players. He said, "When I was a young man, I used to go to Haney's Big House, a local dance hall, where Negro bands and combos played. Afterward, I'd try and do the songs I heard and pick up on their styles."[8] Famous blues artists Muddy Waters, Tampa Red, and Sunnyland Slim were among those billed at Haney's. Lewis also listened to recordings of country-boogie artists Moon Mullican and Merrill Moore, jazz-era blues players Albert Ammons and Pete Johnson, and the New Orleans piano of Fats Domino. With typical bravado, Lewis stated, "Well I can't see how anyone influenced me. God, man, I just got with it, you know. I created my own style."[9]

Upon returning from bible school—where his raucous versions of sacred music offended the administration and he experienced a bit of "woman trouble"—Jerry Lee sold sewing machines, led prayer meetings, and established a reputation as a performer. Sometimes, with cousins Jimmy Swaggart and Mickey Gilley, Lewis played a mixture of country music and piano-oriented blues at local functions. He worked in clubs in nearby Natchez, Mississippi, and even traveled to Nashville for a stab at the big time. Like most white southerners, Jerry Lee was raised on a substantial dose of country music. His first record was a country song, and he subsequently recorded a series of Hank Williams songs for Sun. Lewis revered Williams and considered all others as just pretenders.

Meanwhile, the Sun rockabilly sound was becoming popular throughout the South. Lewis headed for Memphis but was advised to return with a more upbeat repertoire. Jerry Lee's first Sun recording was a rockin' version of Ray Price's country hit "Crazy Arms." For his next release, Sun mortgaged itself to the hilt, gambling that Lewis's appearance on Steve Allen's network TV show would spark national interest in the record, entitled "Whole Lot of Shakin' Going On" (#3, July 1957). The show rocked and the single went to #3, eventually selling 3 million copies. Sun felt Lewis was ready to challenge Elvis for his crown.

In November 1957 Lewis released "Great Balls of Fire," which was cowritten by Otis Blackwell and punctuated by "kiss me baby," and "oooh, feels goood." It climbed to #2, and the Blackwell-penned follow-up, "Breathless," went to #7. In May 1958 Lewis, his band, and his new bride, Myra (who was also the daughter of his bass player, J. W. Brown) left for an English tour.[10] The British press, a conservative-yet-sensationalist institution in contrast to its American counterpart, crucified Jerry Lee. Myra was his third cousin, merely a child of fourteen years, and Lewis had somehow neglected to secure a legal divorce from his second wife. None of these matters would have caused much of a stir in his rural South, but they outraged the British establishment. One paper sniffed, "We say that the baby-snatching antics of this bigamist are very much the affair of British teenagers and their parents."

Lewis was unrepentant. He paraded Myra onstage and protested his love for her to the audience. The rest of the tour was canceled and Jerry Lee returned stateside with his career in disarray. The Killer lacked the public-relations skills, insightful management assistance, and label clout to forestall a full-scale assault on him by the church and the press. He tumbled from the upper echelons of the rock world, soon playing one-nighters in clubs and roadhouses throughout the South. After "High School Confidential" (#21, June 1958), he never again had a major rock hit. In the early 1960s, with his career at its nadir, Lewis signed with Smash Records and started to record country music. He had a series of hits and for the past twenty-five years has been a country music star—sprinkling his live performances with rock and roll hits from the past.

Lewis embodies a struggle common among early southern rockers—that of the rock musicians with deeply ingrained ambivalent feelings about their own rock music due to a fundamentalist religious upbringing. Many church-goers—especially among the fundamentalist sects in the South—viewed rock and roll, along with blues and R&B, as the devil's music. Thus rockers, as the purveyors of this music, were condemned to lives of sin and eternal damnation. Little Richard jumped between styles, unable to make the final decision whether to stay within the flock or abandon it. Lewis, resigned to the secular choice, embraced sin with a gusto—he abused his body with drink and drugs, was a notorious womanizer (in addition to his six-plus marriages), and often raged out of control.

*     *     *

Jerry Lee played with an incredible intensity—fueled by his internal battles—that made his records and live performances so exciting. Paradoxically, on record he was able to accomplish that same intensity with a very small ensemble that consisted, at times, of only piano and J. M. Van Eaton's drums. On other cuts, Roland Janes's guitar and Brown's bass were added to the mix. Lewis's expressive vocals, pounding piano, and the not-so-subtle, sexually oriented lyrics gave the records that spark. Jerry Lee Lewis, like his piano-playing predecessor Little Richard, was one of classic rock's most active performers. Some promoters actually provided Lewis with two instruments, knowing one would get trashed. His shakin' usually started on the ground, but by the end of his set Jerry Lee was on top of the piano, hair flying in front of his face, wiggling his butt and shouting into the microphone.

Blues historian Robert Palmer illuminates Lewis's behavior in describing the generational reaction to the rural southern background: "There was a rebellion in the new music—rebellion against the double standards that allowed consenting adults to pick each other up at honky tonks while teens were taught to stifle their sexual desires, rebellion against the long furrowed faces and the beat-up cars and dilapidated farm lives of the white-trash south." Lewis's legacy was this rebellion: an outrageous personality, a reckless performer, and raucous musical predilection. He didn't leave a large catalog of material and his piano virtuosity was difficult to emulate. Nevertheless, the Killer will always survive as an authentic rebellious alternative to the antiseptic pap of the era.

## Buddy Holly

*Buddy Holly's life was an enactment of the American dream, and his music mirrored its spirit. What we long for, we never quite obtain, and yet we keep reaching; and if we have no reason to be sure of the outcome, we cling to our faith that the effort will not go unrewarded.*

**Holly biographer John Goldrosen**

Buddy Holly was a homely kid from western Texas who, in the short space of two years, produced a catalog of songs that had a major impact on subsequent rock generations. Holly was a synthesist and an innovator, melding country and Black music roots with rockabilly and early classic rock. His lyrics painted a picture of a world populated by young lovers embroiled in various stages of clean teen romance. The brushstrokes were broad, bursting with musical bravado, and delicate, capturing the whispered beat of a vulnerable teenage heart. The masterpieces remain, the artist swept away in a gust of wind.

Charles Hardin Holley (the "e" was excised as he took to the stage) was born in Lubbock, Texas, on September 7, 1936. His father worked as a tailor and later a salesman at a local clothing store. The youngest of four children, Holly grew up in a stable nuclear family and economic environment—what might later be pictured as the white all-American family. Holly's family attended the Tabernacle Baptist Church, where his father and brothers were church officers. This religious music was void of the emotionalism found in pentecostal sects. Thus, Holly's vocal style lacks the soaring leaps and slurred lyrics of his Black contemporaries. Holly was serious enough about his faith to donate 10 percent of his first record's earnings to the church.

Buddy Holly's earliest interests were in country music. Surrounded by a family that played guitars, a fiddle, and piano, Holly sang with them in his first talent show at the age of five. At eleven Buddy studied piano, but he soon switched to guitar. Buddy began his professional career singing songs by country artists like Hank Williams and bluegrass greats Bill Monroe and Lester Flatt and Earl Scruggs. He also imitated the high tenor harmonies of the bluegrass artists.

Radio was the medium through which most people discovered new music, as high-powered radio stations from Nashville, Shreveport, and Dallas blanketed the South with live variety shows like "Grand Ole Opry" and "Louisiana Hayride." Holly began to listen to Black music shows from Shreveport's KWKH, where he heard the seminal blues figures Muddy Waters, Lightnin' Hopkins, and Little Walter. There was not much contact between Blacks and whites in Lubbock, and Holly's interest in Black music was probably atypical for the area.

In junior high school Buddy met Bob Montgomery; for the next six years The Buddy and Bob Show played to local audiences. Their career together progressed from parties to their own Saturday-night radio show on Lubbock's KDAV. By 1955 they were opening for touring national acts like Bill Haley and Marty Robbins. Buddy and Bob's repertoire came essentially from country music songs

Buddy Holly

by Hank Williams, bluegrass pioneer Bill Monroe, and blues artists like Muddy Waters. They recorded a series of mostly original material at local radio stations and recording studios.

In early 1955, when Elvis Presley appeared in Lubbock, Buddy and Bob opened the show, and they became friends with rock's messiah. The Sun Sound found a receptive audience in Holly and he went on what a friend once called "an Elvis kick." His vocal range fell from bluegrass-influenced nasal to Elvis-style crooning. He began to play Scotty Moore-style rockabilly lead guitar and the group added more bounce to the sound. (These Elvis-influenced elements can be heard on his Decca releases.) Holly's big break came when they opened a Lubbock show for Bill Haley in October 1955. A talent scout recommended that Haley's label, Decca, offer Buddy a contract alone, and Bob bowed out gracefully. The local hero left for Nashville and anticipated stardom.

Decca released five singles from three 1956 recording sessions. The records have that distinct Sun Sound rockabilly flavor, and at times Holly's vocal timbre resembles that of early Elvis. The band, Buddy Holly and the Three Tunes, toured with rising country stars George Jones and Hank Thompson, but meager record sales left Decca unimpressed. Holly returned to Lubbock at the end of 1956. Early in 1957 Buddy visited Norman Petty's Nor Va Jak recording studio in Clovis, New Mexico. As biographer John Goldrosen points out, "Petty had the equipment, musical training and ability and technical competence to make good records."[11]

In Clovis Petty gave Holly and his new group, the Crickets, unlimited studio time, allowing Holly the chance to put ideas into practice and learn about the technical side of music production. Buddy set about to create his masterful synthesis of three styles: the heartfelt stories, vocal harmonies, and guitar-oriented instrumentation from country; the strong backbeat from Black roots and early classic rockers; and the overall freshness and spontaneity of rockabilly.

Between February and July 1957, Holly recorded and Norman Petty produced most of his early hits at Nor Va Jak. "That'll Be The Day" (#1, August 1957) took three months to enter the rankings, but when it did, it climbed to the top of the pop charts and #2 in R&B. The Crickets (bassist Joe B. Mauldin, drummer Jerry Allison, and third cousin Niki Sullivan on rhythm guitar) left for their first big gig at New York's Black music showcase, the Apollo Theater.[12] Because of their success on the R&B charts, the Crickets had been hired sight unseen. When they arrived at the theater, the management was shocked; it was unheard-of for a white group to play that venue. For the first two days the audience sat on its hands. Niki Sullivan describes the scene: "Buddy turned around and said 'Let's do Bo Diddley.' ... [We were] cutting up and working our buns off. I was dancing around in a big circle, going through a bunch of gyrations and Buddy was all over the stage, and Joe B. was bouncing that bass back and forth and laying it down. . . . And when we finished that song people went bananas."[13]

During the classic rock era, most audiences saw their favorite rock and roll performers as a part of package-show tours. Promoters would contract with the current stars for lengthy cross-country tours by bus. For two or three dollars fans could see ten or more acts in medium-sized venues in or near their hometowns. Each artist would sing three or four songs—a few more for the headliners—backed by their own groups or the package-tour's rock and roll big band. (This variety-show concept contrasts sharply with the past twenty-five years, where one- or two-act shows go on the rock and roll circuit.)

In the fall of 1957 the Crickets were signed to a package tour called The Biggest Show of Stars for 1957.[14] Many of the era's major artists went, including Fats Domino, Chuck Berry, the Everly Brothers, the Crickets, Frankie Lymon and the Teenagers, the Drifters, Clyde McPhatter, La Vern Baker, Paul Anka, Eddie Cochran, and Jimmie Bowen. The tour lasted two-and-a-half months without a single day off. All participants traveled by bus; if they were lucky, they grabbed a few hours of sleep at a hotel before the show. An example of 1957's version of life in the not-so-fast lane can be found in a single week's schedule for the tour: Sunday, Spokane, Washington; Monday, Pullman, Washington; Tuesday, Calgary, Alberta; Wednesday, Edmonton, Alberta; Thursday, Regina, Saskatchewan; Friday, Denver, Colorado; Saturday, Wichita, Kansas.

Musical and personal cross-pollination occurred continuously. Niki Sullivan describes his experience: "My whole life or education seemed to occur, right there on that eighty day tour. The most outstanding to me was the camaraderie—everybody living and working together. Color just didn't come up. The Drifters treated me like a kind of white sheep of the family. If I had trouble, or worry, or loneliness, they would always sit down and talk to me. After we got back to New York, we had our farewell party, and when they all got out of the bus to leave, I cried." Holly appeared on national television and, in early 1958, toured England and Australia. Buddy was becoming enamored with New York City, where he was exposed to a smorgasbord of musical styles. While in New York he recorded the unique R&B-flavored "Early in the Morning" (featuring a searing sax solo) and "It Doesn't Matter Anymore" using a lush orchestra. Upon his death, critics would point to his use of strings as a sign that Holly had lost his rock and roll soul.

At the time Holly the lyricist yearned for "True Love Ways" and expected to find "a love so rare and true," Holly the person was living the dream. In June 1958 Buddy met, fell in love with, and proposed to Maria Elena Santiago—in one day. They were married in August. Maria worked for Peer-Southern Publishing, one of New York's largest publishing houses; her aunt was the head of its Latin American publishing division. Maria helped to ground the idealistic Holly in the real-world practices of the music business.

Holly realized that his loose business arrangements with Petty, which included allowing Petty's name on the band's material, needed renegotiation. As their manager, Petty had turned down movie offers, underpromoted the latest material, and treated the band without much trust. Holly decided to terminate his relationship with Petty, but the Crickets, homesick and alienated by New York, feeling the loss of camaraderie caused by Buddy's marriage, and tantalized by Petty's promises of continued stardom using the band's name, broke with Holly. Both sides were regretful, but each trudged off in a different direction.

By the end of 1958 Buddy became concerned about the advancement of his career. His initial songs were million-sellers, but he hadn't had a top-20 hit since the previous spring. The record company and his wife urged him to get back out in front of his fans. Buddy acquiesced, agreeing to headline the three-week Midwest Winter Dance Party tour. Included in the small package were Dion and the Belmonts, Richie Valens, and the Big Bopper. The weather conditions for this tour were typical for the time of year—frigid temperatures, snow, ice. Leaving Green Bay, Wisconsin, after the February 1 show, the party drove 350 miles southwest, to Clear Lake, Iowa. The bus broke down that night, not an uncommon occurrence, and arrived at 6 PM, just before showtime. Desperate for a good night's sleep and carrying a laundry bag filled with dirty clothes, Holly chartered a private plane for the band's 430-mile leg to the next night's venue, in Morehead, Minnesota.

J. P. Richardson (the Big Bopper) convinced Buddy's bass player, Holly protégé Waylon Jennings, to relinquish his seat on the plane. Valens flipped a coin with Holly guitarist Tommy Allsup, called heads, and won his seat. The tour's in-house drummer was hospitalized with frostbite incurred during the previous night's breakdown, so Buddy played drums for the opening acts. Holly played his headline set and Buddy, Valens, and Richardson left for the airport. Just before 1 AM on February 3, 1959, the three artists and the pilot boarded the four-seat Beechcraft Bonanza at the Mason City, Iowa, airport. The wind was gusting, temperature eighteen degrees, and a light snow was falling. The plane lifted off the runway and headed over the horizon to the northwest. The next morning, the plane was found nestled against a snowfence, eight miles from the airport.

\*     \*     \*

Holly's legacy is enormous, especially in light of the brevity of his two-year classic rock career. Not only did many groups follow his two-guitar, bass, and drums format, but they duplicated the ambiance of the songs themselves. The perky simplicity of the early Beatles work bears more than a passing resemblance to Holly songs like "It's So Easy" and "I'm Gonna Love You Too." Buddy was the master scribe of clean teen romance. Instead of romantic fulfillment, however, many protagonists were consumed by yearning and anticipation (expressed in "Maybe Baby," "Heartbeat," "Oh Boy," and many others). One can imagine the shy boy leaning against the gym wall at a school sock-hop staring at his secret love, who is dancing with the quarterback, thinking, "If she only knew how much I loved her."

Holly was also technologically advanced for the time. With Petty's assistance, Buddy spent considerable time acquainting himself with the recording studio. They used multitrack techniques, pioneered by guitarist Les Paul, on "That'll Be the Day" for guitar and vocal harmony overdubs. Holly was also the first classic rocker to popularize the Stratocaster, a classic guitar manufactured by Fender that would become the guitar of choice for many modern artists. Bruce Springsteen reflected on Holly's legacy this way: "I play Holly every night before I go on, it keeps me honest."[15]

## The Everly Brothers

*Darling you can count on me, till the sun dries up the sea./ Until then I'll always be, devoted to you.*

*The Everly Brothers, "Devoted to You" (1958)*

Imagine first a sound reminiscent of the caress of teenage heartstrings, where shimmering notes of a tremoloed electric guitar enchant the listener. Then, as if called forth from on high, two tenor voices chime in, entwined in celestial close-interval harmony. Like love-struck minstrels, they croon of endless love and devotion, "Until then I'll always be, devoted to you." It is the Everly Brothers.

Don and Phil Everly, the last of the classic rockers that we will examine, developed a unique country-rooted vocal style. Their music combined sensational harmonies, crisp production, and a string band dominated by a blend of acoustic and electric guitars. Their hit songs, usually from the pens of husband-and-wife songwriting team Boudleaux and Felice Bryant, painted a masterful portrait of teen concerns, including romance and school and a sometimes humorous look at adolescence. The unique emotion and uncanny oneness of their singing enhanced the intensity of these portraits and gave us one of the most commercially successful sounds of the late 1950s.

The Everly story is unique. Elvis, Buddy, and Jerry Lee listened to country and bluegrass music and were deeply influenced by it. Don (who was born in Brownie, Kentucky, on February 1, 1937) and Phil (Chicago, January 19, 1939) were born into it. Their parents, Ike and Margaret Everly, were well-respected country and western singers who had their own radio show and toured extensively. The family performed together; the boys made their radio debut at ages eight and six. Ike was also a fingerpicking guitar pioneer who had an impact on contemporaries like Merle Travis.

Intent upon their own career, the boys headed for Nashville, wrote songs, and recorded unsuccessfully for Columbia Records. With the help of family friend Chet Atkins, the Everlys acquired manager Wesley Rose (the son of publishing giant Fred Rose of Acuff-Rose fame) and signed with Cadence Records. Although an independent label, Cadence was large enough to have produced hits for pop musicians Julius La Rosa, the Chordettes, and Andy Williams. They were well on their way to assembling their own version of the "team," and the last addition turned out to be the Bryants. Boudleaux (the husband) was a former violinist for the Atlanta Symphony who had turned to writing country songs.

The Bryants were asked to submit material for the boys. Boudleaux recounts: "One of our biggest songs was shown over thirty times before it was ever cut. . . . It was even shown the very morning of the same day the Everlys heard it in the afternoon . . . the fella said in rejecting it, 'Why don't you show me a strong song.'"[16] The song, "Bye Bye Love," was cut with producer Chet Atkins on guitar and Floyd Cramer on piano, released in May 1957, and climbed to #2 on the charts. The successful formula of vocal virtuosity and teen tales was established.

"Wake Up Little Susie" (September 1957) provided them not only with the first of three consecutive #1s, but also a bit of controversy. It describes an adolescent's comic nightmare: a teen couple falls asleep at the drive-in movies until 4 AM. How could one explain the situation to suspicious parents and snickering pals? Due to its suggestive nature, the song was banned on Boston radio—a fact that probably aided its ascent to #1. Musically, "Susie" is more forceful than its predecessor, featuring an accentuated backbeat (even if only with brushes on the snare), and some tasty electric guitar fills (probably by producer Atkins).

"Dreams" (April 1958) and "Bird Dog" (August 1958) followed this classic at #1, and the Everlys became headliners on the package tours. Dressed in matching suits and strumming identical Gibson acoustic guitars, they looked enough alike to be twins. Their live performances were not the active, raucous, sensual stage shows of most of their contemporaries. Like their vocal delivery, their onstage act was joyous but not rough or aggressive. Their camaraderie with other classic rockers extended into the studio; in 1959 "Till I Kissed You" was recorded in Nashville with Crickets Jerry Allison on drums and Joe B. Mauldin on bass.

The Everlys also had hits with their own material; "Till I Kissed You" (#4, August 1959) was Don's creation and Phil penned "When Will I Be Loved" (#8, June 1960). By 1960, with confidence bolstered, they decided to leave the womb and sign with Warner Bros. Records—leaving Cadence, their production team, and the Bryants behind. Their first single for Warner, "Cathy's Clown" (May 1960), stayed at #1 for five weeks, further emboldening the duo. However, they never again hit the top 5. Classic rock was on the wane and the Everly sound had become diluted by ornate arrangements and strings. Although they scored a few more top-10 hits, their career never recovered.

A hitch in the U.S. Marine Reserves and personal problems took them out of the limelight. Don fought with substance abuse and spent some time in a sanitarium. The Everlys had a resurgence with the nostalgia craze of the late 1960s, but by the early 1970s their relationship had deteriorated. In a July 1973 concert in California, Phil Everly smashed his guitar and walked off the stage—leaving Don to finish the show. There is a happy ending. In September 1983 the Everlys played a reunion concert at London's Royal Albert Hall and released an album of new material.

\*     \*     \*

The Everly Brothers, like Little Richard, became popular with a style that remained essentially true to their roots music. Their acoustic-oriented country music favored by their parents provided the foundation. Copying bluegrass pioneers Bill and Charlie Monroe, the Everlys developed a close bluegrass duet style. The two important unique musical elements of their classic rock—the acoustic guitar-led string band and precisely phrased harmony vocals—are direct, undiluted descendants from country roots.

Their repertoire of lyrics centered on "malt-shop scenarios." The lighthearted cameos presented feelings of infatuation, romance, and even helplessness. As victims of circumstances beyond their control—not unlike the era's teens, caught in parental and societal expectations—song characters often stand helplessly by, as when the police cart off "Poor Jenny" while she's on her first date with the singer.

The Everly Brothers were musical innovators who had a major impact on rock's next generation. Their symbiotic vocal relationship was unique to a genre that was usually more spontaneous. Musicologist Terence O'Grady credits the Everlys as a major foundation of early Beatles music: "Both the vocal harmony style . . . and the rich acoustical accompaniment, are clearly found in the Beatles' early music."[17] Their catalog of songs has been recycled often since (James Taylor and Carly Simon's version of "Devoted to You," Simon and Garfunkel's "Wake Up Little Suzie," and Dylan's "Take a Message to Mary"). Chuck Berry gave this evaluation: "I didn't think Presley was as good as the Everly boys."[18]

## More Shakin' Goin' On

A number of successful and innovative artists have yet to be mentioned in this discussion. Bo Diddley (born Elias McDaniel) capitalized on a syncopated beat—which was called "shave and a haircut," "sham-poo" in the forties—for his 1955 R&B hit "Bo Diddley." A guitarist with a penchant for odd-shaped instruments, the youngster McDaniel came to Chicago from Mississippi and played violin in grade school. With percussionist Jerome Green, he formed a street band around 1950. Bo Diddley was signed to Chess and became a major performer in Black theaters and clubs during the classic rock era. He never made a significant impression on the popular music charts, although many classic rockers covered his songs and penned their own in the same rhythmic style (Holly's "Not Fade Away" is an excellent example).

Gene Vincent and the Blue Caps had a major hit (#7) with "Be-Bop-A-Lula" in 1956. Vincent came from the "reckless abandon" school of living and performing; hard drinking and active stage movement were limited only by a leg mangled in a motorcycle accident. After his last U.S. top-40 hit in 1958, a wild, adoring English audience made him a major star there in the early 1960s. In 1960 Vincent's best friend was American rocker Eddie Cochran. The Oklahoma-born Cochran had moved with his family to Los Angeles and eventually signed with Liberty Records. Cochran's early music included the rockabilly-influenced "Twenty Flight Rock," an early Rolling Stones demo tune.

Eddie Cochran's later material, including the hard-driving "Summertime Blues" (#8, August 1958), "C'mon Everybody" (#35, January 1959), and "Somethin' Else," as well as his songwriting, active stage performance, and good looks portended a promising career. However, while returning from a Bristol, England, tour date, on the way to London's Heathrow Airport, the car carrying Vincent and Cochran went out of control and smashed into a telephone pole. The twenty-one-year-old Cochran was killed; Gene Vincent sustained broken ribs and reinjured his already lame leg. Close friends claim Vincent never recovered emotionally. Vincent died in 1971 at the age of 36.

Ricky Nelson stood somewhere between the raucous classic rocker and the tepid teen idol. His commercial success spanned both periods. Nelson's early material and accompanying band (which included seventeen-year-old master guitarist James Burton) were reminiscent of rockabilly and classic rock, but his weak voice and clean looks resembled the teen idols. From 1949 to 1966, Ricky starred on radio and TV with his parents and older brother in "The Adventures of Ozzie and Harriet."

Rock legend has Ricky responding to a date's swoon at a Presley tune by claiming, "I can do that." The musically inclined Nelson responded with twenty-nine top-40 songs between 1957 and 1962, including "Poor Little Fool" (#1, July 1958), "Travelin' Man" (#1, May 1961), and its flip side, "Hello Mary Lou" (#9). In 1972 Rick Nelson returned to the charts with the original composition "Garden Party," a critical retort to nostalgia-show audiences. On tour in Texas, Nelson died in an airplane crash in December 1985.

## Classic Rock at Decade's End

The classic rock era, which began with a group of primarily Black artists creating reconstituted blues and R&B, ended with white artists playing a mixture of rockabilly, early classic rock, and R&B. The first group, reflecting its proximity to Black musical roots, presented a relatively uncensored view of life around them—songs of a rebellious and of a sexual nature. The second generation's songs of courtship and rejection lacked the seditious and libidinous edge of their precursors. However, the live performance styles of Little Richard, Elvis, and Jerry Lee were sufficiently scandalous—at least in the eyes of critics—to provide their teen audiences with projected rebellious gratification. The first generation fashioned the music, forging the music's crossover to the popular charts. Elvis and his second generation progeny appeared, capitalized on the previous inroads, reframed the musical form, and collected the fruits of classic rock's labors.

By 1960 the classic rock era was over. The players were victims of fate as well as pressure from the government (in the form of "payola" investigations, addressed in the next chapter), the major labels, and church and civic leaders. Artists fell by the wayside or were neutralized: Berry was indicted, Lewis scandalized, Little Richard got religion, Holly crashed, Elvis enlisted, and Haley just quietly faded. Fats Domino and the Everlys continued to release material, but none with prolonged commercial success. America would have to wait for the British invasion and the Beatles to listen again to the strains of classic rock. A similar dynamic of ascendance in the midfifties, a shift to white performers, and fade in the early 1960s occurred to the vocal-based R&B style called doo-wop. In Chapter 5, we start listening to four or five guys singing on the street corners and go on from there.

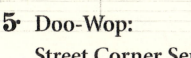

# 5· Doo-Wop:
## Street Corner Serenade

*Bay Doom-boppa Doom-boppa Doom-boppa Doe-doe*

*Sherman Garnes's bass vocal introduction to "Why Do Fools Fall in Love,"*
*by Frankie Lymon and the Teenagers (1956)*

---

In the midfifties young Black men often gathered on front steps and street corners in New York and other northern urban centers to "hit some notes." In clusters made up of four or five guys, they would practice harmonizing to rhythm and blues songs, hoping to be discovered by a talent scout for one of the many small independent labels that dotted their city. Some made it to school talent contests, others even farther, to local theaters and dance halls, but most never got past the street corner. Not discouraged, they filled their cities with music.

They sang a style of music that has subsequently been labeled doo-wop (in all probability due to the nonsense syllables favored by the background vocalists). Doo-wop's roots can be found in the emotional vocal stylings of gospel combined with the beat-driven music of rhythm and blues. The lead singer, usually in an expressive tenor voice, would pledge his love to a listener or audience member as the rest of the group responded to these urges with close harmonies. Although most songs were created in an informal setting without instrumentation, they were recorded in a studio with a band that normally included drums, bass, piano, guitar, and tenor saxophone.

Doo-wop's earliest proponents, pioneering groups typified by the Ravens and the Orioles, were stylistically close to earlier Black popular music groups, such as the Mills Brothers and the Ink Spots. Sonny Till of the Orioles and Maithe Marshall of the Ravens carried on the high tenor virtuoso tradition of Bill Kenny of the Ink Spots. Raven Jimmy Ricks radiated subsonic bass sounds similar to those of Inkspot Hoppy Jones. The Ravens, and later the Orioles, scored hits on the race music charts (pre-R&B Black music charts) in the late 1940s with a wide variety of material that included gospel-flavored ballads and covers of popular songs.

In 1953 the Orioles crossed over to the popular music charts with a #14 hit, "Crying in the Chapel." This opened doors for vocal-oriented R&B to break into the pop music scene. It is also interesting to note that the popularity of the Ravens and the Orioles hatched other groups with bird names: the Flamingos, the Swallows, the Crows, the Cardinals, the Robins, and the Penguins all had major doo-wop hits and many other bird groups, such as the Larks, the Pelicans, the Swans, the Wrens, and the Sparrows, also spread their wings and began to flourish.

By 1955 the Penguins (with "Earth Angel"), the Moonglows ("Sincerely"), the Crows ("Gee" and "I Love You So"), the Platters ("Only You" and "The Great Pretender"), and a few others had crossed over and achieved pop-chart success. Yet in the early days of doo-wop success was typically only regional—a group recorded on an independent label, received airplay on the local radio station, and developed a regional following. Sometimes the same song was a local hit for two different groups in two different cities. Nevertheless, doo-wop was on its way to becoming the most popular form of Black music for the late 1950s.

As the genre flourished, individual vocal groups frequently formed and disbanded. The transient nature of the small independent record labels was one contributing factor. These labels were usually one- or two-person operations, and their fortunes rose and fell with the successes and failures of their local artists—no hit, no label. As was the case with some of the other independent labels, the ones that eventually did succeed did so because they became large enough to compete in the national popular music marketplace.

The first group to achieve lasting pop-chart success was the Platters. Having previously recorded for the independent Federal Records, their manager and songwriter, Buck Ram (really!), secured a contract for the group in 1955 with major-label Mercury Records. Beginning with two famous Ram originals, "Only You" (#5, October 1955) and "The Great Pretender" (#1, December 1955), the group scored eighteen top-40 hits through 1960. A major factor in their success was lead singer Tony Williams, a brilliant tenor in the Bill Kenney tradition. The group continued its climb with three more #1 hits: a cover of the Ink Spots' "My Prayer" (July 1956), "Twilight Time" (April 1958), and Jerome Kern's "Smoke Gets in Your Eyes" (December 1958). In a story typical of this genre, the charismatic frontman left to pursue a solo career, and neither he nor the Platters garnered much success after his departure.

Doo-wop recordings generally fell into two categories: up-tempo numbers that emphasized the beat, saxophone solo, and, at times, humorous lyrics; and slow, romantic ballads with lyrics featuring idealized adolescent yearnings. Some groups, like the Platters with their ballads, and the Coasters with their up-tempo selections, recorded predominantly in one style or the other. Sometimes the same group of musicians recorded songs in both styles, adopting a different band name for each, as in the case of the Cadets (with "Stranded in the Jungle," a humorous rocker in the controversial Amos 'n Andy style), and the Jacks ("Why Don't You Write Me," a ballad).

In February 1956 Frankie Lymon and the Teenagers made the charts with "Why Do Fools Fall in Love" (#6). Accounts differ as to the origin of the lyrics and the path the group took to the New York offices of Gee Records, but the reality of a thirteen-year-old singing a major hit sent ripples throughout the industry. Other junior high school kids rushed to start groups and cut records. This included

Frankie's brother, Louie, who with his group, the Teenchords, recorded "I'm So Happy." Frankie Lymon's personality, projection, and movements served as models for later child stars, such as Michael Jackson. The Teenagers flourished, touring Europe and the United States, starring in package shows, and scoring several more chart successes.

In predictable fashion, in 1957 Lymon left the Teenagers to pursue a solo career. He had only limited success, in part because his crystalline, expressive young voice took its expected hormonal plunge into the deeper registers. Lymon, whose reported allowance had been only $27 per week in his heyday, then asked for access to his trust fund, which supposedly contained his past royalties and performance fees. Like many doo-wop artists, Lymon collected little of that accumulated cash. In 1968 at the age of 25, the destitute Lymon died in a Harlem tenement, having overdosed on heroin.

The Coasters were the other doo-wop group able to sustain popular chart success. Their material was written and produced by white creative wizards Jerry Lieber and Mike Stoller. In their youth lyricist Lieber and pianist-composer Stoller moved from the East Coast to California. Each grew up in an integrated neighborhood, listening to both Black and white music. They started collaborating in the summer of 1950; by 1953 they had penned R&B hits "Hound Dog" for Big Mama Thornton and "K.C. Lovin'" for Little Willie Littlefield.

In 1953 Lieber and Stoller started Spark Records and produced "Smokey Joe's Cafe" for the Robins in 1955. The song contained a humorous lyrical style, which would later become successful in hits by the Coasters. It also brought Lieber and Stoller an offer from Atlantic Records for an independent production contract—normal by today's standards, but quite innovative for the time. The terms called for Lieber and Stoller, who were not on the Atlantic staff, to independently write and produce records by the Robins. Atlantic would then manufacture and market the records.

Only two of the Robins agreed to travel east for this new arrangement, so the new band was renamed the Coasters for the singers' West Coast origins. Lieber and Stoller polished the comic, Black idiomatic formula and hit big with their second release, the double-sided "Searchin'" (#3, May 1957)/"Youngblood" (#8). In the latter tune the writers introduced another device that served them well in the future—the music stopped to make way for a vocal line spoken in dialect: each singer, starting with the highest pitch, repeated the phrase "Looka there!" during the break.

Like Chuck Berry, Lieber and Stoller covered a broad range of adolescent experiences. They also chronicled some of teen life's absurdities. The Coasters attained their commercial peak with "Yakety Yak" (#1, June 1958) and its follow-up "Charlie Brown" (#2, February 1959). "Yakety Yak" contains the threat "You ain't gonna rock and roll no more" as punishment for not completing banal household chores (sweeping the floor and taking out the garbage). The music is punctuated with the staccato blasts of King Curtis's tenor saxophone—a style later described as "Yakety Sax." The subject in "Charlie Brown" is a schoolhouse troublemaker who innocently pouts the phrase "Why's everybody always pickin' on me?" The Coasters continued to score chart successes into the early 1960s. And Lieber and Stoller built upon their earlier successes by writing and producing for Elvis (the entire movie score for *Jailhouse Rock*, including the title cut), the Drifters ("There Goes My Baby," among others), and Ben E. King ("Stand By Me" and others).

Doo-wop also produced hundreds of artists who were often acclaimed by fans but who enjoyed varying amounts of commercial success. Tenor great Clyde McPhatter, for example, left Billy Ward and His Dominoes (a gospel group turned secular), to form the Drifters. After some initial chart success for his group, McPhatter was drafted and returned to a solo career in the late 1950s. His flair and vocal mastery influenced many later singers. Another early doo-wop pioneering work was the Chords' 1954 hit "Sh-Boom"; it was whitewashed by the Crewcuts and became a #1 pop hit. Other examples of midfifties groups with up-tempo hits are the El Dorados with "At My Front Door" (they were one of the "car" groups, along with the Cadillacs, the Fleetwoods, the Impalas, the Edsels, and the Imperials); the Cadillacs with "Speedo"; the Cleftones with "Little Girl of Mine" (some of my homefolks from Queens); the Dell-Vikings with "Come Go with Me" (one of the few integrated groups); and the white group Danny and the Juniors with "At the Hop" (#1, December 1957).

During this period slow-tempo, head-on-the-shoulder dance tunes were equally popular. Some of these dreamy numbers included the Five Satins with "In the Still of the Nite"; the Dells with "Oh, What a Nite"; the Heartbeats with "A Thousand Miles Away"; the Chantels with "Maybe"; Lee Andrews and the Hearts with "Teardrops"; Little Anthony and the Imperials with "Tears on My Pillow"; and Harvey and the Moonglows with the classic "The Ten Commandments of Love." For each of these selections hundreds of songs on the pop or rhythm and blues charts go without mention.

By late in the decade white youths had entered the field. Whereas white groups had previously recorded almost exclusively as cover artists, new younger performers such as Danny and the Juniors (from Philadelphia), Dion and the Belmonts (named for Belmont Avenue in the Bronx), Vito and the Salutations (New York underground favorites), and the Fleetwoods (from the Northwest) emerged. White kids began to hang out on the street corners in major urban centers and harmonize together. This author's own group, the Chapters, formed in the stockroom of an engineering firm one summer. We practiced in high school stairwells and bathrooms (these places had wonderful acoustics!) and sang to captive audiences in hospitals and nursing homes in the New York metropolitan area.

*　　　*　　　*

By 1960 doo-wop, like classic rock, was beginning to fade. The sounds had become softer as the faces became whiter. Still there were some late successes: the Drifters hit with "Up on The Roof" (#5, December 1962) and "On Broadway" (#9, April 1963), the Marcels cut a remake of "Blue Moon" that went to #1 (March

1961), and the Regents introduced us to "Barbara-Ann" (#13, May 1961). The genre was sufficiently aged to have Little Caesar and the Romans ultimately pine "Those Oldies but Goodies (Remind Me of You)." Groups like the Four Seasons and even the Beach Boys upheld the tradition.

The doo-wop branch of rhythm and blues established vocal virtuosity and background harmonies as commercially viable elements in popular music. Having coexisted with classic rockers of the middle and late fifties, it too faded at decade's turn. Like classic rock, doo-wop also had a major impact on music of the sixties; it provided the vocal foundation for Motown and, to a lesser extent, soul music. Doo-wop should be remembered as a highly accessible form of music, a style available to anyone willing to sing aloud with friends. Large numbers of urban youth tried it, enjoying varying degrees of success. Some even found the path to the neon lights on Broadway—which is where our next chapter begins.

# 6. The Early Sixties:
## The Calm Before the Storm

*Many followers of rock 'n' roll history believe that the true spirit of the music died in the late fifties, and that the first few years of the sixties were filled with mechanized and bleached pap heralded by the arrival of the so-called "teen idols."*

**Alan Betrock, Girl Groups: The Story of a Sound**

*Those records had a Wagnerian power and intensity. Phil got so wrapped up in those recordings. Then everything got bigger, and bigger, and bigger until there was no more record. But he wanted to go further, get bigger and bigger, but there was no bigger.*

**Ellie Greenwich, talking about Phil Spector**

*I hear the neon lights are bright on Broadway/ I hear that dreams come true there every day.*

**"On Broadway," Barry Mann, Cynthia Weil, Jerry Lieber, and Mike Stoller (1963)**

T HE YEARS BETWEEN 1959 and 1963 were a time of transition for popular music. Classic rock and roll and doo-wop rhythm and blues formulations had essentially faded from the scene. They were replaced on the popular charts by a variety of styles that had little in common besides the absence of a strong beat and a worldview and performance style that contained more clean teen romance and less sexuality. These newer pop styles ranged from the highly successful efforts of so-called teen idols and girl groups to newer strains of an emergent folk music, "ethnic" Calypso and other pre-reggae Caribbean instrumentals (mostly featuring electric guitar), California-based surf sounds, and early successes of soul and Motown artists.

Powerful pressure from a combination of religious and secular leaders, governmental officials, and major-label interests within the music industry had combined to hasten the demise of fifties rock. The major record labels and their Los Angeles-based movie-industry counterparts (ABC-Paramount, MGM, and

Capitol) had strong self-interest in seeing rock and roll and doo-wop fall; not il-logical, given that they owned only a relatively small piece of that action. With the advent of less objectionable music, the majors once again had a chance to domi-nate the charts. Although the majors didn't immediately regain control of popular music (however, they did garner a much larger piece of the pie) the process of cre-ating and recording the product returned to a more familiar arrangement.

For a brief moment in the mid- and late 1950s, classic rockers had wrestled artistic control away from the music-business establishment. They had written a majority of their hits, cut them with their own bands, and were responsible for the overall artistic interpretation. However, by the early sixties, the "music estab-lishment" had reasserted its control over the process. According to this new model, recording artists had relinquished their power and returned to the early 1950s role of song interpreters. The process now reverted to the prerock, assem-bly-line model, in which songs were crafted by office-based professionals, recorded by seasoned studio musicians, and produced by major-label or big inde-pendent producers.

The music of the teen idols was the most representative example of this turn away from classic rock. The performers, mostly cute and nattily attired young men, sang ersatz rock music that contained little or no beat, saccharine string arrangements, and a multitude of nonsexual, romantically safe messages. The epi-center of this sound was Philadelphia, where the big-three indies—Cameo-Parkway, Chancellor, and Swan—produced pop for new teen audiences. Cameo produced Bobby Rydell while Chancellor countered with Frankie Avalon and Fabian. Displaying varying degrees of vocal proficiency, these three idols courted audiences with a combined thirty-nine top-40 hits. Parkway's major act was dance king Chubby Checker (Ernest Evans). His cover of Hank Ballard's "The Twist" created a national dance craze in the summer of 1960. Subsequently, Checker popularized a multitude of new dances, including the Pony, the Fly, the Limbo Rock, and the Freddie.

The cause was promoted by Philly TV personality Dick Clark. The now-leg-endary Clark, whose afterschool show "American Bandstand" was viewed nation-ally on the ABC network, became pop-rock music's most prominent cheerleader. America watched as popular music favorites lip synched their hits while regular "Bandstand" dancers (some of whom even had their own fan clubs) strutted the latest steps. "Bandstand" sold America the well-dressed, well-behaved side of rock music. Clark was also deeply involved in the Philadelphia music business, having an interest in three record companies, music publishing firms, a management company, and a record pressing plant.

The inside interest represented by Dick Clark caused some consternation, and in 1959 the U.S. House of Representatives Legislative Oversight Committee, which had been investigating cheating on TV quiz shows, turned its attention to pay-for-play practices on rock music radio. Payola, as it was called, had been com-monplace—radio station program directors and DJs often supplemented their in-comes with "consultant fees," Christmas TVs, and musical credits on records (putting them in line for songwriting royalties). As former WABC DJ Cousin Brucie Morrow wrote, "'Booze, broads, whatever you want'—this was a standard offer."[1]

Convinced that radio stations played rock music only because they were paid to do so, congressional investigators held hearings to determine the truth. They found a practice that was common but not illegal at the time. Conflicts of interest such as Clark's—he was known to have promoted artists that he managed, played songs that he carried publishing rights in, and played up record companies in which he owned stock—were nothing new. Clark admitted to having a personal interest in 27 percent of the records he promoted on his show. ABC asked Clark to divest himself of his music-business holdings or quit the show. Clark chose to stay with the show, and in the process of cleaning up cleared tidy sums on his earlier investments (in one case over $31,000).

Whereas Clark was eventually congratulated by the investigating committee chairman—he was called "a fine young man"—others, like pioneer DJ Alan Freed, continued to be hounded. In 1960 Freed was charged with commercial bribery, which he eventually pleaded guilty to in court. The loyal defender of original rhythm and blues and rock's most successful promoter, Freed was targeted again in March 1964, this time for 1957–1959 income tax evasion. Unable to find work and in financial distress, Freed died in January 1965.

Many other disc jockeys were called before the committee, but this did not impede the success of popular music. Teen idols, the early 1960s less-rebellious version of rock music, continued their chart prosperity. Paul Anka, a talented Canadian who recorded for ABC-Paramount, also wrote hits for other artists (including "It Doesn't Matter Anymore" for Buddy Holly). Others of the genre included Bobby Vee, Bobby Vinton, Tommy Sands, and TV's Edward "Kookie" Byrnes.

Female artists were also successful during this period. They were not usually categorized as teen idols, but their music followed the same pallid formula. Former Mickey Mouse Club Mouseketeer Annette Funicello recorded "Tall Paul" for the Disneyland label. Brenda Lee scored two #1s in 1960 with "I'm Sorry" and "I Want to Be Wanted." Seventeen-year-old Leslie Gore told tales of heartbreak in the Quincy Jones-produced "It's My Party" (as in, "And I'll cry if I want to . . . ") and revenge in "Judy's Turn to Cry." Most popular was Connie Francis, who claimed thirty-five top-40 records between 1958 and 1964. Recorded for MGM, these hits included "Lipstick on Your Collar" (#5, 1959) and "Everybody's Somebody's Fool" (#1, 1960).

In a sign of the times, the most prominent female artists of the period were known simply as the girl groups. These groups produced some of the most memorable and best-produced songs of the era. They include the Crystals ("He's a Rebel" and "Da Doo Ron Ron [When He Walked Me Home]"), the Shirelles ("I Met Him on a Sunday" and "Will You Love Me Tomorrow"), the Chiffons ("One Fine Day"), the Ronettes ("Be My Baby" and "Walkin' in the Rain"), the Shangri-

Las ("Leader of the Pack" and "Walkin' in the Sand"), the Cookies ("Chains" and "Don't Say Nothin' Bad About My Baby"), and many others.

Though the success of these groups increased both Black and female prominence in popular music, the songwriting, production, and financial rewards still rested with the production companies and labels. As in the case of the teen idols, girl groups were simply song stylists. Some of the era's most talented songwriting teams created the material, producers like Phil Spector directed production, and indies like Philles, Red Bird, Scepter, and Dimension pressed the hits. Many of the genre's creative forces were sequestered in office buildings near the corner of 52nd Street and Broadway in New York City. The Brill Building at 1619 Broadway listed 165 music businesses in its lobby directory. Across the street, 1650 Broadway housed the headquarters of Aldon Music and Scepter Records. On Seventh Avenue and 48th Street songwriters could get demos cut at Associated Studios. Songs were written, demoed, shopped, signed, and recorded within a few blocks.

From a creative standpoint, two players stand out: Phil Spector and Aldon Music. Spector, in addition to being a successful songwriter and producer, started a number of prosperous record companies. He is best known for his sonic creation known as the "Wall of Sound"—a layered production style heard on many of the era's hits. His first hit, "To Know Him Is to Love Him" (#1, 1958), was written and recorded with his own group, the Teddy Bears, one month after high school graduation. At the age of nineteen, Spector moved back to New York from Los Angeles and wrote "Spanish Harlem" and "Stand by Me" for Ben E. King. Within four years, Spector was a millionaire, having produced hits by a multitude of artists, including the Crystals, Darlene Love, and the Ronettes.

The impact of Spector's wall-of-sound production techniques on the industry was tremendous, and he was one of the early pioneers of multitrack recording. His multitracking called for use of a three-track tape machine and several instruments to a track. For instance, on track one, Spector would typically record three to five rhythm guitarists, two or three pianos, two electric basses, a horn section of two trumpets, two tenor saxophones, and two trombones, a drum kit, and additional percussion instruments. Track two contained all the vocals, and strings were recorded on track three. The three tracks would then be mixed down to a one-track (monophonic) final product. This "wall" of instrumentation was so steeped in reverberation that Spector once commented, "I want my records to sound like God hit the world and the world hit back."

The second creative player was Aldon Music, which was formed in early 1958 by two musician-songwriters named Al Nevins and Don Kirshner. They employed a stable of pop music songwriters that crafted some of the era's most memorable songs. Early arrivals Neil Sedaka and Howard Greenfield penned hits for Connie Francis, the Shirelles, and Sedaka himself. Carole King, who worked with husband Gerry Goffin, had a #1 hit ("Will You Love Me Tomorrow," by the Shirelles) at age nineteen. The King-Goffin string of successes continued with "Take Good Care of My Baby" (Bobby Vee), "The Loco-motion" (Little Eva, the couple's babysitter at the time), "Up on the Roof" (the Drifters), "Chains" (the Cookies), "One Fine Day" (the Chiffons), and even "Pleasant Valley Sunday" by the made-for-TV quartet known as the Monkees.

Other successful songwriting teams of the era include two other couples who eventually married, Jeff Barry/Ellie Greenwich and Cynthia Weil/Barry Mann, who wrote songs sometimes independently and sometimes as couples. Between them they wrote many big hits for the genre's major groups: the Crystals, the Ronettes, the Dixie Cups, the Jelly Beans, Darlene Love, the Shangri-Las, the Righteous Brothers, and the explosive duo of Ike and Tina Turner. Eventually Aldon was sold, and the youthful collective of songwriters disbanded. They moved on to write hits for other artists as the girl groups were swamped and then pushed aside by the incoming wave of the British invasion.

Because of the commercial success of the girl-group sound, female artists in general returned to prominence in popular music. This did not, however, change their financial or artistic status—women as a rule remained in their role of song interpreter and continued to be relatively low-paid performers. As Shangri-La drummer Joe Alexander describes it: "Nobody knew from royalties. It was just from doin' what we were doin'. And, when it came right down to it, what else could we do?"[2] Should a group have a million-seller, at a 3–4 percent royalty rate, they were grossing $30,000–40,000. Contracts specified percentages and costs for the manager, producer, studio, arrangers, musicians, and money lost on non-hit records. Thus, many individual members of the groups made very little money, even though they might have had a series of hit records. Ellie Greenwich's perspective was different: "The girls gave and the girls took. . . . It was just fun, and better than their alternatives."

Other vocally oriented styles were also enjoying some chart success. Berry Gordy's Motown label was developing its roster and producing the first hits by Smokey Robinson, Marvin Gaye, the Marvelettes, and Mary Wells. Soul artists like Otis Redding followed Booker T. & the M.G.s to the Stax/Volt studios in Memphis as people began to climb aboard the "soul train." Some Caribbean sounds became popular. Harry Belafonte's calypso/latin recordings of "Jamaica Farewell" and "Banana Boat Song" were followed by Jamaican Millie Small's 1962 hit, "My Boy Lollipop."

American folk music, having recovered from the McCarthy-era stigmatization as un-American, was now experiencing a revival. Traditionalists such as Joan Baez toured college campuses, and button-down groups like the Kingston Trio and the Highwaymen had refined top-40 folk hits with "Tom Dooley" and "Michael (Row Your Boat Ashore)" respectively. Another trio, Peter, Paul, and Mary, entered the charts with a tune called "Blowin' in the Wind," penned by the then unknown Bob Dylan. Guitar and banjo sales soared as folk music became another seminal style of sixties percolating pop.

On the West Coast, sun, sand, and suburban lifestyles were reflected in a style termed surf music. Its musical roots lay in guitar-oriented classic rock with a driv-

ing beat, but its worldview contained an affluent, white, suburban, male-dominated society preoccupied with the common adolescent concerns of girls, cars,
and surfing. Early proponents were groups like Dick Dale and the Deltones (with
their regional hit "Let's Go Trippin'") and the Surfaris. The duo of Jan and Dean
covered "Barbara-Ann" and then recorded a string of hits including the #1 "Surf
City"—where one could find "two girls for every boy."

The Beach Boys—a name foisted upon the group by a record company executive—were the most popular and talented of the genre. Sporting a lineup that included the three Wilson brothers, Brian, Dennis, and Carl, cousin Mike Love, and
neighbor Al Jardine, this suburban Los Angeles combo created one of the few
original sounds of the early 1960s that was derived from classic rock. Their vocals
reflected an early obsession with the Four Freshmen, with tenor leads and close
complex background harmonies.

Although he didn't actually surf, Brian Wilson wrote or cowrote paeans to
"surfer girls" and to just having "fun, fun, fun." As he became more self-assured as
a producer, Brian created a layered production sound similar to that of his favorite producer, Phil Spector. All of this creativity and success initially flourished
in a household that one friend described as "like walking into twelve soap op-
eras."[3] Their father, Murray, was an overbearing manager who often hit his boys in
the heat of an argument. Their Capitol Records liaison called Murray "a maniac."[4]

The band overcame their turbulent personal history, though not without consequences. Brian eventually stopped touring, teetering on the brink of emotional
instability. Dennis engaged in a variety of self-destructive behaviors for years before he finally drowned in 1983. Creatively, the Beach Boys rarely strayed from
their initial formula. They transformed Chuck Berry's "Sweet Little Sixteen" into
"Surfin' USA." Their odes to local girls included "Surfer Girl," "Help Me, Rhonda,"
"California Girls," and "Barbara-Ann." However, this light-hearted mood was occasionally broken by the introspective and vulnerable Brian, as in the 1963 hit "In
My Room."

The critical high point of their career came in 1967, with the painstakingly layered "Good Vibrations." It reportedly required six months, twenty recording sessions, four studios, and $50,000 to create this single, a classic tribute to "good
vibes." The band has survived despite many personnel changes and the pendu-
lum-swings of Brian's mental health. One of the few American groups to remember the classic rockers, they built on that foundation and continued to perform
into the 1990s.

\*　　　\*　　　\*

This period of transition—roughly the first half of the 1960s—contained a variety of new popular music styles. The music of the girl groups and the teen idols,
although popular, left little legacy. Production techniques developed by the duo of
Lieber and Stoller and the innovative Phil Spector, and the catalog left behind by

Aldon Music's master songwriters, have not only survived but continue to have a significant impact. The "ethnic" rhythms of Caribbean music would eventually make their mark in the form of reggáe and salsa. Folk music, soul, and Motown would withstand the British invasion and would even emerge in their own right later in the sixties. The Beach Boys and the rest were swamped by the first tidal wave of the British invasion, which carried a good many English groups to commercial victory and popular dominance on American shores. That story is next.

# 7. The Beatles:
## Because the World Is Round
## It Turns Me On

*"How do you find America?"*
*"Turn left at Greenland."*

**Question and answer at Beatles press conference, Dublin, 1964.**


*There was more good than evil being a Beatle. But it was awful being on the front page of everyone's life, every day.*

**George Harrison, 1980, quoted in Rolling Stone**


*They [the Beatles] were doing things nobody was doing.*

**Bob Dylan, 1964**


*Whatever wind was blowing at the time moved the Beatles too. Maybe the Beatles were in the crow's nest shouting "land ho" or something like that, but we were all in the same boat.*

**John Lennon, 1980, quoted in Playboy**


As the last strains of classic rock rang through the American music scene, British youth across the Atlantic, who had been listening all along, became keepers of the beat. In homes and in dance halls, the music thrived. Eventually, a new music—a fusion of classic rock, rockabilly, blues, and pop—returned to the United States. It became the most commercially and critically successful genre of music in popular music history. Both the music and its transatlantic crossing were called the British invasion, and the band that led the charge was the Beatles.

The Beatles followed a road that was unlike any taken before. Their music and lyrics took off in uncharted directions and were closely followed by a procession of other musicians. Their impact on Western culture was enormous. Hair grew to the shoulder (and past) and a multitude of new cultural and political questions were asked and answered. The group's massive commercial success rewrote the artist's relationship with the record label and pointed the way to untold record-industry profitability.

The Beatles didn't unilaterally cause these societal and music-industry changes. However, their massive commercial success, combined with the concurrent explosion in communication and marketing technologies, allowed them to transmit their musical, lyrical, and cultural messages to more people than ever before. And, because of the Beatles' status as cultural deities, young people listened and, much of the time, believed.

There is little to indicate that, in the beginning, there was anything special about the four boys from Liverpool, a coastal city in western England. They were each born during World War II and most of their childhoods reflected the turbulence of the war. John Lennon (born October 9, 1940) had a dad who deserted the family, and his mother, Julia, gave up five-year-old John to her older sister, Mimi. Although raised in comfortable and loving surroundings, John carried scars from his abandonment, and his school years were characterized by an increasing propensity to find trouble. As the charismatic leader of his young cronies, he exercised his caustic, inventive, and quick wit on friends, enemies, teachers, and administrators alike.

Within a year of entering Quarry Bank High School in 1952, his beloved Uncle George died, and his mother, Julia, became a more important part of his life. She and John exchanged regular visits. She taught him a few banjo chords, which he transposed to the guitar, and Julia's house became a refuge from his periodic fights with Aunt Mimi. John adopted his mom's mercurial philosophy of "live for the moment and let the rest take care of itself." As suddenly as their friendship blossomed it ended. On July 15, 1958, Julia was run down and killed by a drunken off-duty policeman.

Richard ("Ringo") Starkey Jr. (born July 7, 1940) began life under similar circumstances. Ringo's dad, Richard Sr., and his mom, Elsie, split up when Ringo was young. Where John's legacy was emotional turmoil, Ringo had to overcome poor health and impoverished surroundings. A burst appendix and pleurisy kept him in the hospital for three of his first fifteen years. Describing his neighborhood near the docks, Ringo replied, "There's a lot of tenements in the Dingle. A lot of people in little boxes all trying to get out." At the age of eighteen, while apprenticing as a fitter, Ringo was given his first regular set of drums. They became his ticket out of Dingle.

Jim McCartney, a cotton salesman, and his wife, Mary, a visiting nurse, had two sons, James Paul (born June 18, 1942) and Michael. Paul, having easily passed through his early school years, finally enrolled in the prestigious Liverpool Institute. When Paul was fourteen Mary McCartney died suddenly from cancer. Michael believes Paul turned to his guitar for solace: "It became an obsession. . . . It took over his whole life." While preparing in school for a career as an English teacher, Paul started slicking his hair back and dressing like a rocker. In the summer of 1956 he auditioned for a skiffle group called the Quarrymen, which was led by John Lennon.

The boyhood of George Harrison (born February 25, 1943) lacked the trauma of his Beatles compatriots. He was the youngest of four children and grew up in a close-knit family environment. Whereas John's classroom rebellion took the form of sharp-tongued boisterousness, George wore his long hair slicked back and dressed outrageously. Rebellion didn't stop George from entering Liverpool Institute and he, too, pursued the guitar with a passion. With mom's help George purchased a new electric guitar, and he soon formed his own group, the Rebels. He also started jamming with Paul McCartney, who rode the same bus to the Institute.

In the summer of 1956 McCartney auditioned for the Quarrymen with the Eddie Cochran tune "Twenty Flight Rock" and his Little Richard imitation on "Long Tall Sally." The intoxicated, sixteen-year-old Lennon didn't say much. A week later, because of his guitar proficiency, McCartney was invited to join the band. Sometime in 1958 George Harrison, who had been tagging along with the Quarrymen, was invited to become a regular member. Although quite a bit younger than John—and slightly in awe of the elder leader—George knew more about the guitar than all the others.

The Quarrymen were originally an informal gathering of friends playing music and having a good time. By 1959 the lineup had solidified to include John, Paul, and George on guitar, with John's art college mate, Stu Sutcliffe, playing bass. A talented and respected art student, Sutcliffe had been coaxed by John to spend the sixty-five pounds that Sutcliffe had earned in a national painting competition to buy a bass guitar. Protesting that he had little musical talent, Stu was nevertheless installed as the regular bass player. He spent much of the next year with his back to the audience, doing his best to pick out the correct notes.

In 1960 the Quarrymen, as informal arrangement, ceased to exist; the Beatles, a "professional" rock and roll band, took their place. This process included an evolution in names, from the Moondogs (named after Alan Freed's Moondog Rock and Roll House Party radio show) to Long John and the Silver Beatles, to the Silver Beatles, and finally to the Beatles. The name was derived from their love affair with Buddy Holly's Crickets—thus the insect beetle—combined with the common name for rock music of the day, which was known as "beat" music.

Barely out of the garage, the band's early work was sporadic; they played art college dances, backed Johnny Gentle on a Scottish tour, accompanied Shirley the Stripper, and made some appearances at local clubs such as the Casbah. Then, in August 1960, the Beatles were sent by club manager Alan Williams to work at the Indra Club in Hamburg, Germany. At the last moment, Paul McCartney asked drummer Pete Best whether he still had his drums. Pete said he did, played a few tunes, and became the regular drummer.

The Beatles' four and a half months in Hamburg transformed the band in many ways. Required to play six to eight hours per night, their repertoire expanded considerably. Playing clubs located in "Reeperbahn," Hamburg's red-light district, the boys were intimidated by their potentially dangerous audiences. Club owner Bruno Korschmeier implored them to "mak schau," or make a show. Slowly the group learned the skills befitting professional entertainers. The crowd enjoyed the beat, and John would occasionally regale them with his impressions and his costumes that utilized underpants and a toilet-seat necklace.

To a group of teenage rock and rollers—John, the oldest, was almost twenty—Hamburg was a garden of delights. In this and successive trips, the lads made friends with the working girls, created a new favorite breakfast (cornflakes and beer with a glass of milk on the side), and swallowed increasing quantities of "prellies," a diet pill with remarkable stay-awake qualities. They also progressed in status from the Indra Club to the Kaiserkeller, the Top Ten Club, and finally the Star Club. Their accommodations progressed in kind, from a room behind the screen of a ramshackle moviehouse to barracks above the Top Ten Club.

Hamburg was the beginning of the end for Stu. At the Kaiserkeller he met and fell in love with an art student and photographer, Astrid Kirchherr. She redesigned the group's hair and took their picture on the rooftops of Hamburg. Stu left the band during the group's spring 1961 stay, married Astrid, and enrolled in art school. Rather than add another member to the group, Paul moved over to bass. On April 10, 1962, Stu Sutcliffe died of a brain hemorrhage in Hamburg. The next day, the Beatles arrived for a seven-week engagement.

Upon returning to England from Hamburg in December 1960, the Beatles sought to increase their local popularity by playing the Cavern Club. This former fruit-and-vegetable warehouse became the home of beat music in Liverpool, and the Beatles became its most famous resident band—they appeared there 292 times between March 1961 and August 1963. For all its notoriety, this basement club left much to be desired. Down seventeen steps, three rooms with vaulted ceilings and sawdust on the floors hosted lunch-time and evening crowds. When the audience danced, moisture would condense on the ceiling and rain on the floor.

During 1961 the Beatles developed a strong following in Liverpool and the surrounding environs. They also returned to Hamburg, where they recorded their first sides as a backing group (using the name the Beat Brothers) to British singer Tony Sheridan. During those sessions, which were produced by Polydor A&R (artist and repertoire) man Burt Kaempfert, the Beatles recorded two songs, the pop classic "Ain't She Sweet," sung by John, and the Harrison-Lennon instrumental "Cry for a Shadow." Beatle legend has it that "My Bonnie," a song from those sessions, was the catalyst for Brian Epstein to sign as the group's manager. Ostensibly, a young man named Raymond Jones walked into the North End Music Store (NEMS) branch at Whitechapel on October 28, 1961, and asked for "My Bonnie" by the Beatles. By coincidence, NEMS manager Brian Epstein was behind the counter. Unaware of the record or the band, Epstein promised to look into the matter. Nearly two weeks later Brian went to see a Beatles gig at the Cavern. In December he signed the group to a management contract.

A more likely scenario is that the record-customer inquiry alerted Epstein to the importance of the Beatles as an emerging local musical force. At the time, Epstein was intrigued by the local music scene. He even wrote a music review for *Mersey Beat*, a biweekly popular music newspaper started by art college student and Beatle friend Bill Harry. It seems highly unlikely that Epstein was not already aware of the Beatles; their picture and a story were on the front page of the July 20 issue of *Mersey Beat;* Epstein's reviews and numerous Beatles stories appeared concurrently in subsequent issues.

With Epstein aboard, the Beatles were beginning to build their version of "the Team"—that group of talented, motivated professionals that surround most ultrasuccessful popular musicians. Epstein brought intelligence, upper-class taste, organizational skills, and money to the Beatles. Epstein's parents owned a large furniture-store chain that was headquartered in Liverpool. Brian had spent some time at England's Royal Academy of Dramatic Arts and had parlayed NEMS record stores into one of the largest in northern England. He was ready for a new project, and the Beatles were it.

As a major retailer, Brian had some clout with the record companies. Decca Records agreed to tape a series of songs designed to demonstrate the talents and capabilities of the Beatles, and the band drove through the snow to London for a January 1, 1962, recording session. They were quite nervous but recorded three originals and a dozen pop and rock tunes, including "Besame Mucho," "The Sheik of Araby, " "Till There Was You," Chuck Berry's "Memphis," the Coasters tune "Searchin'," and Phil Spector's "To Know Her Is to Love Her."

Decca A&R head Dick Rowe instead chose to sign a London group known as Brian Poole and the Tremeloes. Proximity, and perhaps the knowledge that few successful groups came out of the provinces, were the deciding factors, and Rowe was marked for life as the man who passed on the Beatles. Epstein made the rounds of the record labels; EMI, Pye, Philips, Columbia, and HMV were not interested in the band. Finally, George Martin, the head of Parlophone Records, expressed a slight interest in Paul's and John's singing and the band's raw energy. Arrangements were made for an audition for Martin in June 1962 at EMI's Abbey Road studios.

Martin signed the band to a recording contract in July and entered the inner circle. Martin's background and talents were to later prove invaluable to the band's professional growth and musical maturation. Trained as an oboist and arranger, Martin had started out as an assistant A&R man for Parlophone, EMI's "junk label" subsidiary. At the age of twenty-nine, Martin had become the chief at a label that produced the assortment of nonmainstream acts assigned by the parent company as well as a series of successful comedy albums by Peter Sellers, Peter Ustinov, and Beyond the Fringe, featuring Peter Cook and Dudley Moore.

During the Beatles audition Martin mentioned in an aside to Epstein that, should the band record for his label, he would use a studio drummer. Commenting on Pete Best's drumming, Martin concluded that "it isn't good enough for what I want. It isn't regular enough." Some group members already had strong feelings about sacking Pete, and Martin's opinion sealed the drummer's fate. In August the band asked Epstein to fire Pete—a hypocritical procedure not unusual in the music business. After two years of paying his dues and on the eve of the group's first big record deal, Pete was out and Ringo Starr was in.

Ringo was available, acknowledged as a steady, driving, classic rock drummer, and already a Beatles crony from the Hamburg days.

Finally, on September 11, 1962, the Beatles assembled at Abbey Road studios for their first Parlophone recording session. The band and Martin felt some closeness right away. During a playback of their first take, Martin commented "If there's anything you don't like, tell me, and we'll try and do something about it." When Harrison rejoined, "Well for a start, I don't like your tie," Martin learned about typical Beatle humor. The Beatles recorded Lennon-McCartney originals "Love Me Do" for the A side and "P.S. I Love You" for the B side. Leaving nothing to chance, Martin hired studio drummer Andy White to join the session. Ringo played drums on one version of "Love Me Do," tambourine on another (the U.S. and album cuts), and maracas on the second song.

"Love Me Do" was released on October 5, 1962, and to George Martin's chagrin the tune was only lightly promoted by parent-label EMI. Brian guaranteed the record's availability in Liverpool, and he cleverly assured it a position on the British *Billboard* charts by purchasing 10,000 copies for his stores. The Beatles continued to perform in northern England and returned to Hamburg in December, and "Love Me Do" reached a peak of #17. As their second single, "Please Please Me," moved up the charts on its way to #1, the band recorded their first album (of the same name) in a single, wearying, thirteen-hour session. The album also went to #1 and remained there for thirty weeks.

The stage was set for the Beatles to explode upon the British pop scene. Like Presley before them, they had "the moment" and they had "the team." Their brand of safe, classic rock-derived rebellion appealed to both girls and boys; the girls found them cute enough to take home, and the boys identified with them as they might a popular athletic squad. The team consisted of the band (who filled the roles of singers, musicians, soloists, and talented songwriters); Brian Epstein as manager; Dick James, who headed their publishing firm, Northern Songs; George Martin as producer, musical consultant, and label head; and the clout of the EMI organization.

Till this point their live performances relied on a repertoire of covers that included classic rock numbers from Chuck Berry, Little Richard, and Buddy Holly; rhythm and blues tunes from Ray Charles, Larry Williams, the Isley Brothers, and Lieber and Stoller; several Carl Perkins rockabilly songs; early 1960s American pop tunes from Carole King and Motown; and an assortment of British pop tunes. Now that the Beatles started recording, they determined to focus on mostly original material.

The Beatles shaped an original sound that fused elements from these musical roots. They adopted Holly's two-guitar/bass/drums format, as well as his generally asexual adolescent vision of romance. Their dexterous manipulation of rock lyrics was reminiscent of Tin Pan Alley and Chuck Berry; Berry's rhythm- and lead-guitar styles were also well represented. Vocal influences were Little Richard (a fusion of R&B and gospel energy and falsetto) and the Everly Brothers (close tenor harmonies and strummed acoustic rhythm guitar). George Harrison's electric-guitar solos were especially derivative of the rockabilly/classic rock stylings of guitarists Carl Perkins and Scotty Moore.

Throughout 1963 the Beatles' popularity rose to such heights in England that by the fall audiences were totally out of control. This phenomenon was soon labeled Beatlemania. Starting out the year with extensive touring in England—first as an opening act and finally as the headliner—the Beatles ended it with national television spots and an invitation to appear on the 1963 Royal Variety Show. Upon returning from a Swedish tour for the Royal Command Performance, they were met by thousands of screaming fans at London's Heathrow Airport, delaying the prime minister and forcing the band to fully realize the extent of their massive popularity.

Their Royal Variety Show performance gave them credibility with a broad cross-section of the British population. John Lennon introduced "Twist and Shout" with a now-legendary quip: "Those in the cheap seats can clap your hands. The rest of you can rattle your jewelry." The Queen Mother's response to this witty remark at royal expense? "They are so fresh and vital. I simply adore them."[1] A band that was mobbed by teenage fans and praised by the Queen Mother could have few detractors. The Beatles were also heralded by most major British newspapers as good clean fun. Fleet Street (a synonym for the mainstream London press) went into a journalistic frenzy, falling over itself reporting the next chapter in the ongoing saga of Beatlemania.

Numerous explanations have been offered for the intensity of Beatlemania—a delirious response that surpassed the excitement generated by American pop idols Frank Sinatra and Elvis Presley across the ocean. One has it that England, as with the United States, experienced a baby boom following World War II. The surge of popularity reflected an inordinately large number of teenagers coming of age. Another has it that the country was trying to discover a way to recover from some unusually tumultuous months, which included the Profumo Affair (a sex scandal involving the highest government officials), the subsequent resignation of Prime Minister Harold Macmillan, and the Great Train Robbery. The happy-go-lucky Beatles were a positive diversion, an antidote.

In addition, some credit rests in Brian Epstein's master plan. In the tradition of his pop predecessor, Colonel Tom Parker, he scheduled important national-TV exposure. The Beatles' October 13 appearance on TV's top-rated "Sunday Night at the Palladium" was seen by 15 million viewers and caused newspapers to report, incorrectly, that the band was forced to escape from 1,000 screaming fans following the show.

The Beatles, through the combination of musical ingenuity, sound management, Tory Party high jinks, and zealous promotion by the fourth estate, captured the imagination of a nation. By December 1, 1963, they had released their fifth single, "I Want to Hold Your Hand," and second album, *With the Beatles,* and were turning their attention across the Atlantic, to the United States. Epstein had already tried twice to convince EMI subsidiary Capitol to release the early singles in America. With no British group having ever made a substantial inroad into the

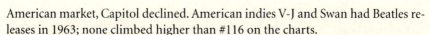

American market, Capitol declined. American indies V-J and Swan had Beatles releases in 1963; none climbed higher than #116 on the charts.

Pointing to the rising tide of Beatlemania, Epstein and Martin finally convinced EMI (and thus Capitol) to release Beatles records in America. The savvy record company allocated a phenomenal $50,000 for a promotional budget. Major DJs in America received all the Beatles releases and an interview record and script, which gave listeners the appearance of live interview conditions. Capitol printed and distributed in New York, Chicago, and Los Angeles 5 million bumper stickers with the phrase "The Beatles Are Coming" printed in black block letters on a simple white background. That winter, I can remember walking up Sixth Avenue in New York City and seeing the plywood walls surrounding skyscraper construction sites plastered with these stickers. Not having heard the music, I assumed a new horror movie was about to hit town.

When Capitol released "I Want to Hold Your Hand" backed by "I Saw Her Standing There" on December 26, 1963, the American music-industry pump was fully primed. The following week the record entered the American charts at #83, moved the next week to #42, and climbed to #1 on January 15. The lads (as they came to be known), who were struggling through three weeks of lukewarm response in Paris, celebrated with Epstein (who even donned a chamberpot fedora) and Martin. Besides the record company blitz, Brian had planned other appearances. He convinced Ed Sullivan—who had become stuck in the same October airport traffic jam as England's prime minister—to book the Beatles on his top-rated variety show. They received headliner billing but little recompense (under $10,000 total) for three shows (two live, one taped). Also scheduled were three live concerts: one at Washington Coliseum and two at New York's Carnegie Hall.

The Beatles' conquest of the United States began in earnest on February 7, 1964, when Pan Am flight number 101 landed at New York's Kennedy Airport and the "Fab Four" descended to American soil—to the screams of about 10,000 fans. The hysteria of Beatlemania was obvious from the start. Nearly 200 members of the press poised to deliver judgment on the Fab Four, but the Beatles were their usual charming, irreverent selves. When asked about a movement in Detroit to stamp out the Beatles, Paul replied "We've got a campaign of our own to stamp out Detroit." When it got too noisy, John told everyone "Shurrup." Everyone laughed.

Two days later, on February 9, 1964, a record 73 million TV viewers watched the Beatles perform five songs on "The Ed Sullivan Show." The next day's press was awash with Beatles stories and the follow-up February 16 Sullivan performance was watched by even more viewers. As Ringo was to later comment, it was just like before only ten times bigger. The conquest of the hearts and minds of America's youth was made easier by the recent loss of the charismatic President John F. Kennedy. The American press would, like the British press before it, be able to focus upon something less weighty. The Beatles' personalities, wit, and mostly upbeat, romance-oriented music offered positive distraction from the grief.

A country that had easily forgotten the beat, rebellion, and authentic emotion-ality of the classic rock era was now faced with four young Englishmen in their early twenties who dressed in collarless Pierre Cardin suits and bounced happily to the music while giving the occasional nod, wink, or headshake to the audience. For effect, the lads punctuated their performances with falsetto ooohs and breathy yeah, yeah, yeahs. Epstein had successfully transformed the four raw, side-burned, bluejeans-wearing rockers into a professional team of polished, nattily at-tired, and safely rebellious rock and roll artists.

Epstein had already planned the next move, and the band returned to England to appear in its first motion picture. *A Hard Day's Night* (originally titled *Beatlemania*) broke from the typically fabricated rock-movie mold. The Beatles would be themselves. Liverpudlian Alan Owen tagged along on tour, then wrote the script. Director Richard Lester sandwiched the six-week shoot—on the London streets, live in concert, and while touring by train— between the United States and pending dates in Europe, Asia, and Australia.

The Beatles life was chronicled as a circus, traveling to a show, evading crowds, playing a show, evading crowds, evading management, horsing around, and re-peating the process the next day. Some movie critics dubbed them the Marx brothers of the sixties. The movie reinforced the already popular concept that the band did not consist of one leader and three followers, but rather as four separate people with individual personalities. John was the witty extrovert, Paul was cute and smart, George was quiet, and Ringo was the vulnerable, cuddly teddy bear. Female fans had four potential heartthrobs to chose from.

The thirteen Lennon-McCartney compositions on the British *A Hard Day's Night* made up their first all-original album. The strummed opening chord of the title cut introduced the world to the sound of George's twelve-string Rickenbacker guitar. Many later artists, including Roger McGuinn of the Byrds, became enamored with and adopted it. Upbeat tunes like "Can't Buy Me Love" and "Tell Me Why" continued in the "She Loves You" tradition, driven even harder by McCartney's pulsating bass lines. "If I Fell," a ballad written primarily by John, shows off an exotic introductory chord progression. "And I Love Her" was Paul's first in a series of outstanding romantic ballads, which would later include "Michelle," "Yesterday," and "Here, There, and Everywhere." While the thirteen-cut British version of *A Hard Day's Night* was available to most of the world's lis-teners, Americans received a very different twelve-cut album—the eight songs from the movie were joined by four George Martin-orchestrated instrumentals. Although this album was on the United Artists label, the practice of marketing different versions for stateside consumption was indicative of a larger distortion of the Beatles' creative efforts. Each time Capitol released an early Beatles album it removed a number of cuts to be used at some later date.

Most of Capitol's U.S. releases, therefore, contain only eleven or twelve songs. The unreleased songs, which were then released out of sequence and delayed up to six years, can be found on different compilation albums such as *Yesterday and Today* and *Hey Jude*. Thus, "Yesterday," which appeared in the summer of 1965 on the British version of *Help,* wasn't released on an album in the United States until the summer of 1966, on *Yesterday and Today.* Capitol also distorted the artistic balance of the Beatles' album releases. The original (British) *Revolver* contains five John Lennon compositions; the Capitol (American) *Revolver* contains only two. (The other three appear on the compilation LP *Yesterday and Today.*) Some critics became appalled at the Beatles' lack of artistic control over the product.

The Beatles extracted a modicum of revenge against Capitol's taking of these liberties, when the lads submitted a somewhat grotesque photo for the cover art on *Yesterday and Today.* The Fab Four were pictured in butcher smocks and Liverpudlian smirks, with raw meat and decapitated baby doll parts strewn about. After American DJs railed against the photo, Capitol spent $200,000 to replace it with a different photo. Not surprisingly, most British and American releases, starting with the Capitol release of *Sergeant Pepper's Lonely Hearts Club Band,* were identical.

Concert audiences all over the world received the same treatment. Between June and November 1964 the band played England, Europe, Australia, New Zealand, Hong Kong, and twenty-four North American cities. Unlike Elvis, who never performed in Europe, the Beatles purposely and personally spread their rock and roll message worldwide. The shows included local or regional stars as opening acts (in England that meant the Yardbirds and Freddie and the Dreamers, in the United States, Jackie De Shannon and the Righteous Brothers, the latter duo recorded by close Beatles friend Phil Spector).

One only has to listen to a tape of a concert to get a real feel for the experience. Intermittent screams throughout the warm-up acts would grow in intensity until a din had been achieved by the time the Beatles were introduced. From that point on, it was literally impossible to hear anything but the high-pitched wail of adolescent girls. For their own amusement, the band often toyed with the audience; a wink by Paul or offhand remark by John sent sound meters off the scale.

Not that the Beatles were onstage for very long (in a format similar to the package shows of an earlier era, they played only briefly). Typically, on the U.S. leg of their tours they played twelve songs, lasting a total of approximately thirty-five minutes. The set normally opened with John singing "Twist and Shout" and closed with Paul's version of "Long Tall Sally." Sandwiched between were mostly original songs; George and Ringo each sang a song and John and Paul split the rest.

This format remained constant throughout the rest of their touring career—a period lasting a scant two years. Their first major American tour started at the Cow Palace in San Francisco on August 19, 1964. Their last performance before a paying audience was at Candlestick Park in San Francisco on August 29, 1966. Between, the band played to audiences each year in England, on the Continent, and in North America. At New York's Shea Stadium in August 1965, they sold an unheard-of 55,000 tickets. In the summer of 1966, while on their final tour, they played Tokyo (where 3,000 security personnel kept order over 9,000 audience

members), and Manilla (where they barely escaped beatings administered by en-
raged Marcos officials and supporters).

Life on tour for the Beatles became an insane parody of the parody in *A Hard
Day's Night.* Having finally attained deification, the Beatles themselves became
Mecca for fans. And as fans fought to be in their presence, the Beatles tried to keep
from being despoiled. Days were spent holed up in hotel rooms surrounded by security officers, who tried to invent ingenious ways to transport the band from
plane to hotel to show to plane.

Life on the road was not, however, without its rewards. Their choirboy image
didn't impede their ability to pursue nightly dalliances with specially selected
women. John described Beatle tours "like the Fellini movie *Satyricon* . . . [women
were organized by] Derek and Neil, that was their job."[2] To Ringo, touring was the
best of times and the worst of times. The music and excitement were fun, but "it
was like 24 hours without a break: press people fighting to get into your hotel
room, climbing 25 stories up drainpipes. It never stopped."[3] In August 1966 it did.
Although the decision was spontaneous, they had known for some time it would
end soon. The Beatles heaved a collective sigh of relief and went on to pursue individual interests.

One of the reasons the band stopped touring was the difficulty in performing
their increasingly complex music on stage. Their songs had changed since the
days of *A Hard Day's Night.* Musically, the Beatles had embarked on a continual
expansion of the boundaries of rock and roll. They had added new instruments to
their recording ensemble, starting with the piano and then extending to flute
("Hide Your Love Away"), fuzz bass ("Think For Yourself"), sitar ("Norwegian
Wood"), French horn ("For No One"), and strings ("Yesterday" and "Eleanor
Rigby"). Soon other British and American groups were adopting similar instrumental flexibility in rock music recordings.

The Beatles didn't stop at creative use of instruments; various unidentifiable
sounds began to creep onto their recordings. John Lennon recorded feedback on
"I Feel Fine" in 1964, claiming to be the first modern musician to do so. *Revolver*
contained some "scratching" and coughing on the "Taxman" introduction, and
biographer Terence O'Grady describes "the most elaborate and well-developed
use of electronic sounds and concrete musical effects" on "Tomorrow Never
Knows."[4] Returning home drunk one night, Lennon played a tape backwards in
his Kenwood music room and was delighted with the effect—so he introduced
backwards sounds on the 1966 single "Rain." The Beatles continued to distance
themselves from the I-IV-V blues-based harmonic progression, favoring instead a
variety of chord changes and unusual rhythmic syncopations ("Good Day
Sunshine" and "She Said She Said," for example).

Beatles lyrics were undergoing a concurrent topical evolution—enhanced by
friends and acquaintances, especially those from the arts, who were experimenting with alternative cultural lifestyles. Like their American counterparts, Britons
pursued a philosophical and political examination of the status quo, also offering
a solution that consisted of varying degrees of change or escape. The Beatles par-

ticipated in these changes, reflecting those experiences musically with shifts in both form and subject. Bob Dylan was an early catalyst to these changes. In a legendary August 1964 meeting in the Beatles' suite at New York's Delmonico Hotel, Dylan offered them their first psychoactive experience—a marijuana cigarette. By 1965 their pot intake had increased to such an extent that during the filming of their second movie, *Help,* as Lennon pointed out, "We were smoking marijuana for breakfast. . . . Nobody could communicate with us because it was all glazed eyes and giggling all the time. In our own world."[5] In 1967 they would call for its legalization.

Dylan not only contributed a chemically expanded consciousness, he also pointed out the importance of using its vision in creating consequential lyrics. As Lennon once recalled: "I wasn't too keen on lyrics in those days. I didn't think they counted. Dylan used to say 'Listen to the words, man.' And I'd say 'I don't listen to the words.'"[6] Within a year, Beatles lyrics took on a psycho-philosophical cast. The *Help* soundtrack contained nuances of introspection and vulnerability. The title cut, which Lennon later described as a depressed cry for assistance, portrays a psychological awareness rare for that era. "Hide Your Love Away" even sounded like Dylan.

A metamorphosis was taking place, transforming the band of happy-go-lucky pop musicians into cultural pied pipers. Rock music, a genre that not even its most serious proponents could call philosophically important, was acquiring a "serious" dimension. And the Beatles were among the pioneers. The turning point came with their December 1965 release of *Rubber Soul.* Gone were the formula songs of simple boy/girl romance; they were replaced by abstract references ("Norwegian Wood"), social commentary ("Nowhere Man"), a Lennon favorite about friendship and love ("In My Life"), and the weighty "The Word," intoning the message, LOVE.

This experimental edge to Beatles music was enhanced by an incident that took place in the spring of 1965. While attending a dinner at the house of George's dentist, John, George, and their wives were dosed with another form of consciousness expansion; unbeknownst to them the sugar cubes that were ceremoniously placed in their coffee were laced with the drug LSD-25. The four spent an evening traipsing around the elite rock clubs of London, vacillating between revelation and insanity. In a later interview Lennon recounted, "God, it was just terrifying, but it was fantastic."[7] George commented, "It was like opening the door . . . it just opened up this whole other consciousness."[8] Lennon became a frequent tripper; the rest of the band joined in, though to a far lesser degree.

*Revolver,* released in August 1966, confirmed the shift toward more meaningful material. Focusing both inwardly on travails of the psyche and outwardly on contemporary society, this was hailed as music of inner and outer vision. On the album, George Harrison emerged as a major contributor—offering more classical Indian coloring from his sitar ("Love to You") and the political commentary on the British revenue system ("Taxman"). In "Eleanor Rigby," a song often dissected by high school English classes, Paul sings a poetic vision of loneliness and alienation to the accompaniment of a string octet. By the time of *Revolver,* except for the occasional collaboration for a song for Ringo, the Lennon-McCartney songwriting team had essentially dissolved. From that point forward, the vocalist generally wrote the entire song.

From the oblique "And Your Bird Can Sing" (which contains pre-Allman Brothers twin-guitar harmony lines), to the acid tale "She Said She Said," Lennon's material continued to reflect his personal pilgrimage past the outer boundaries of rock music. "Tomorrow Never Knows" was the most eclectic, combining a collage of odd syncopation, backwards and forwards music, and a message inspired by the philosophies contained in the Tibetan *Book of the Dead.* To an anguished sixties Lennon urged, "Turn off your mind, relax, and float downstream/ It is not dying." To ensure that no one took themselves too seriously, the British *Revolver* also contained the universal sing-along "Yellow Submarine."

With the release of *Revolver* and their decision to stop touring, the band was faced with a unique quandary. Having recorded, toured, and filmed constantly since 1963, they now had newfound leisure time. This would not be the first time they were called upon to find answers to new situations. To some situations, like the role of popular musician as cultural guru, the Beatles adjusted creatively. Other band situations, like the struggle for individual interests within a group context, would remain unresolved for some time.

The band dispersed in many directions. Paul McCartney decided to continue his arts education. The Beatle who had worked so closely with producer George Martin to add a string section here, and brass there, studied music theory and composition, wrote a film score, produced other artists, and went on safari in Africa. George Harrison returned to India for two months to study philosophy and sitar with guru Ravi Shankar. His use of the instrument would prompt similar sounds by the Rolling Stones ("Paint It Black"), Traffic ("Paper Sun"), and Donovan ("Sunshine Superman"). Of equal importance, George had finally developed a strong public persona and an identifiable territory within the band. He became the rock aesthete, adding a sprinkling of Eastern spiritual flavor to popular music.

John Lennon was struggling; he would go through periods of creativity and then sink into depression. John spent days at a time staring at the television, bored and not knowing why. In November 1966 John was invited to attend an exhibition at the Indica Gallery, Unfinished Paintings and Objects, by Japanese artist Yoko Ono. Yoko handed John a card that said simply, "breathe." John returned home to wife Cynthia and son Julian. It took eighteen months for the seed planted at the Indica to germinate and bear fruit. Meanwhile, the band regrouped in November for a unified effort to produce an album of artistic and social consequence.

*Sgt. Pepper's Lonely Hearts Club Band,* designated by many rock critics and radio programmers as the greatest rock and roll album in history, took an unheard-of four months to produce at a cost of $100,000. Band members cited it as a peak group effort inspired, in part, by the experiences of Paul's trip to the West Coast of

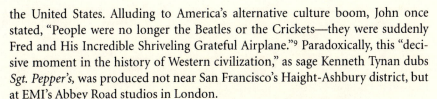

the United States. Alluding to America's alternative culture boom, John once stated, "People were no longer the Beatles or the Crickets—they were suddenly Fred and His Incredible Shriveling Grateful Airplane."[9] Paradoxically, this "decisive moment in the history of Western civilization," as sage Kenneth Tynan dubs *Sgt. Pepper's,* was produced not near San Francisco's Haight-Ashbury district, but at EMI's Abbey Road studios in London.

Aptly termed a hallucinatory cabaret revue by Beatleologist Nicholas Schaffner, the album is suggestive of a live concert—crowd noises and the introductory title cut are followed by a full complement of songs, a final *Sgt. Pepper's* refrain, and the encore, or epilogue, "A Day in the Life." The album is a collage, each song presenting, in form and content, innovative representations of some of the era's social and artistic concerns. In "Strawberry Fields" and "Penny Lane," originally intended as part of the album, John and Paul, respectively, return to childhood haunts and memories. McCartney explores the lack of generational communication in "She's Leaving Home." Drawing from the images of Lewis Carroll and the dreams of son Julian, John paints pictures of "plasticine porters . . . looking-glass ties . . . and the girl with kaleidoscope eyes" in "Lucy in the Sky with Diamonds." John's clever acronym notwithstanding, he always denied the song was inspired by LSD.

The musical innovations were striking. The Beatles used the technology of the recording studio as if it were another instrument—another instance where the invaluable contributions of producer-arranger George Martin were evident. On "Strawberry Fields," Lennon recorded two versions of the song, using different keys and tempos. Deciding that he wanted the beginning of one version and the end of the other, John asked Martin to meld them together. The ingenious use of a variable-speed tape recorder accomplished the task. Typically, numerous Beatles musical innovations relied upon the flexibility and inventiveness of producer Martin.

But Martin contributed even more to *Sgt. Pepper's.* At John's behest, the producer contracted with forty-two classical musicians to provide an orchestral transition between the two sections of "A Day in the Life." Martin then wrote scores for each of the instruments, climbing chromatically from the lower reaches of each instrument's range to a higher note in an E-major chord. The effect of this collaborative effort was a powerful tension-producing crescendo to the album.

Other Martin contributions included the Eastern-sounding score written to accompany Harrison's Indian musicians on "Within You, Without You"; the Grammy Award-winning chicken cluck-to-guitar note transition at the end of Lennon's ode to Kellogg's Corn Flakes, "Good Morning"; and the backwards-playing, spliced-together strips of organ music appearing on John's "For the Benefit of Mr. Kite," similar to the classical "music concrete" style. All of this was fashioned with the elementary technology of four-track recording. By dubbing from one machine to another Martin was able to utilize nine tracks. This manipulation of the studio technology transported the Beatles light-years ahead of contemporaries.

The innovative package was wrapped in a novel album cover and the lyrics were printed on the back of the album sleeve. On the front cover art the band pictured a mixture of boyhood heroes, cult figures, and persons whose names had a creative ring to them. Comedians (W. C. Fields, Laurel and Hardy, and Lenny Bruce), gurus (Karl Marx, C .J. Jung, Einstein, and Huxley), artists (Stockhausen, Beardsley, William S. Burroughs, and G. B. Shaw), and buddies like Dylan, Stu Sutcliffe, and the Rolling Stones populated the picture collage just above the marijuana garden (missed by EMI executives). The Beatles' creativity had spread even to the album art.

Having been showered with critical praise for *Sgt. Pepper's,* the Beatles turned their attention in August 1967 to spiritual growth and the transcendental meditation (TM) of the Maharishi Mahesh Yogi. The Indian guru promised that if one practiced TM for fifteen to twenty minutes twice per day one could escape from the stress of everyday life—a process that could lead to a state of pure consciousness. During one weekend in August the band traveled to Wales to attend a workshop with the Maharishi.

While the Beatles sought spiritual regeneration, an event took place that foretold the band's demise. On Saturday night, Brian Epstein took some Carbitrol, a sleeping bromide, and never woke up. Those who interpreted his death as a suicide could point to many reasons for his anguish. Epstein's contract with the band would expire in a few months and his leadership role, once the band stopped touring and needed no promotion, had diminished severely. He wondered whether his unswerving loyalty would be enough to ensure renewal of his contract. He had also previously attempted suicide. Finally, Epstein's homosexuality and his choice to lead a turbulent, physically damaging lifestyle had caused him grief and turmoil in an era that lacked understanding and acceptance in such matters.

The coroner's inquest handed down a finding of accidental death due to incautious self-overdoses; toxicity built up from three days of use caused a drowsy Epstein to take a little too much. There were also suggestions of a murder contract taken out on behalf of American businessmen slighted in negotiations for a licensing deal for Beatles paraphernalia. Whatever the cause, Epstein's absence became a formidable problem. Without an unswervingly loyal and competent business representative, the Beatles' business situation would destabilize, and the band would eventually become engulfed by controversy surrounding their business dealings. Brian Epstein's death was the first step in this deterioration.

The significance of this event was probably lost on the Beatles at the time. Told by the Maharishi that this was simply a matter of the flesh, they continued to pursue their career, with Paul attempting to pick up the organizational slack. "Magical Mystery Tour" had been written for the *Sgt. Pepper's* sessions but had been rejected for the album. Paul suggested a tour of their own, patterned after the bus-tripping odyssey of San Francisco-based Ken Kesey and his band of Merry Pranksters (chronicled in Tom Wolfe's *The Electric Kool-Aid Acid Test*). The Beatles version was a modern touring coach adorned in day-glo paint.

In September and October the Beatles, accompanied by over forty actors, midgets, and relatives and a film crew—collectively described in one publication as a bunch of weirdos—spontaneously arrived on southern England without script, director, or direction.[10] Although the score contained several well-received numbers (John's Lewis Carroll-inspired "I Am The Walrus," Paul's philosophical paradox "Fool On The Hill," and the hard-driving title cut), many reviewers considered the film to be a self-indulgent bomb. The scathing critical reaction to the December 26 showing appears to have been, in part, a zealous bombardment of a heretofore untouchable target. Neil Aspinall (their road manager) was later to comment that had Epstein been alive the tour would not have been such a disorganized disaster, nor would he have allowed the release of such a poor-quality product.

In another flirtation with TM, the Maharishi welcomed the Beatles to the mountains northwest of New Delhi, India, in mid-February 1968. At his Rishikesh Ashram (spiritual retreat), the entourage set about to meditate, sightsee, and write songs. Ringo and wife Maureen left after two weeks, citing missed children and spicy food. Paul and girlfriend Jane Asher had enough after two months. George and John returned to England disillusioned with the Maharishi's apparent interest in self-promotion and his alleged dalliance with a Swedish airline stewardess. Paul commented, "We thought there was more to him than there

The Beatles (Late)

was. He's human." In an allusion to the Maharishi, in "Sexie Sadie" John was to record "Sexie Sadie, what have you done/ You made a fool of everyone."

Upon their return to the United Kingdom the band turned to business. They had started an umbrella firm called Apple in April 1967, designed to handle the Beatles' marketing business. The band set about to consolidate various business ideas under Apple Corps, Ltd., Apple Electronics (established to market state-of-the-art technology), Apple Retail (established as a boutique to sell designer goods), and Apple Publishing (which actually already existed). With a $2 million budget earmarked for Apple, rather than the tax collector, Apple Records and Apple Films rounded out the roster. Apple headquarters moved to a white Georgian townhouse located on an exclusive block at 3 Saville Row, London.

In May 1968, while aboard a Chinese junk in New York harbor, John and Paul held an Apple press conference. Included was an appeal to talented, unknown artists to cease prostrating themselves before the altars of record companies and to send a tape and picture to Apple. Apple headquarters, of course, received an avalanche of every sort of "art" imaginable. At a press party a few days later, rock and roll "girlfriend" and photographer Linda Eastman managed to slip her phone number to Paul. He called her that night. The next day, Linda accompanied Paul and John to the airport.

Back in England, John packed wife Cynthia off to vacation in Greece and rang up his longtime friend, Pete Shotten. He then rang up Yoko Ono. John had become increasingly tantalized by this kindred spirit; Yoko was blazing a similar trail at the outer fringes of her own field. That evening he shared his experimental tapes with her, music the Beatles would find hard to accept. At dawn, they made love. When Cynthia returned a few days later she was greeted in the kitchen by John and Yoko, who were wearing bathrobes. In November 1968 Cynthia was granted a divorce on the grounds of John's adultery.

John's traditional "chauvinist" Liverpudlian upbringing was sorely tested by his infatuation with Yoko. "I just realized that she knew everything I knew and more probably, and that it was coming out of a woman's head. . . . It was like . . . exactly the same relationship as any mate in Liverpool you'd ever had. But you could go to bed with it, and it could stroke your head when you felt tired or sick or depressed."[11] They became inseparable, moved into an apartment in London, and began to collaborate on musical and artistic projects. Those who later blamed Yoko for the breakup of the Beatles appear to have minimized John's avant-garde personal and artistic propensities, his marital boredom, and the experiences and education that Yoko had to offer.

The Beatles wrote thirty-four songs during their Indian pilgrimage, and these provided the basis for the band's next foray into the recording studio. The thirty songs that compose *The Beatles* were recorded between May and October 1968; the two-disc set is nicknamed the *White Album* because of its stark white exterior. Whereas *Sgt. Pepper's* had reflected a sense of teamwork—virtuoso performances by one Beatle on another's song and dialogue between members on song structure and arrangements—*The Beatles* reflected a growing gulf between John and

Paul as personal and artistic interests headed in divergent directions. In an inflammatory *Rolling Stone* interview in 1971, Lennon comments "It was just me and a backing group, Paul and a backing group, and I enjoyed it. We broke up then."

The individualized efforts produced an album that displayed a broad stylistic diversity. Numerous styles were represented: the simple beauty of John's folk memorial to his mother and Yoko, "Julia," and Paul's visionary ballad "Blackbird"; the raucousness of Paul's "Helter Skelter" and "Birthday" and John's "Yer Blues"; the Berry-style rock of McCartney's "Back in the USSR"; the Caribbean-flavored "Ob-la-di, Ob-la-da"; and songs reminiscent of vaudeville, country music, and doo-wop. George's songs finally began to receive critical acclaim, especially "Piggies," his swipe at the establishment, and "While My Guitar Gently Weeps," with a guitar solo by George's good friend, Eric Clapton. Ringo, the drummer who had once almost emigrated to Texas to become a country musician, sang his first original composition, the down-home "Don't Pass Me By."

This album dispels the notion that Paul was simply a purveyor of unidimensional, formulaic, pop love songs—most of the driving rock and roll numbers are his compositions. Ringo also had to contend with criticism. Rock drumming styles had changed drastically in the past five years, departing from the metronomic, simple-fill, classic rock approach toward the more complex and fill-dominated styles of Keith Moon (the Who), Ginger Baker (Cream), and Mitch Mitchell (Jimi Hendrix Experience). In comparison to this hard-edged, technically demanding approach, Ringo's sparse, straightforward drumming was seen as simplistic, even bordering on incompetent.

The pressure became so great that during one of the sessions Ringo walked out on the band. One week later he was welcomed back to flowers strewn over his drums and a vote of confidence from the other band members. It is easy to see why Ringo and, at times, each of the other members weren't feeling needed. As John observed about "Why Don't We Do It in the Road," "[Paul] recorded it by himself in another room. That's how it was getting in those days. We came in and he'd made the whole record."[12] Even with this individualistic approach to recording—which was duplicated by other band members—*The Beatles* was released in November 1968 and became the fastest-selling album in history.

Dissonance was replacing harmony in the band's lives. It was not simply different interests, such as Paul's now flowering relationship with Linda or John's more flamboyant partnership with Yoko. It wasn't only the differing musical directions, which precluded a teamwork approach to their music. The bottom line was getting in the way; enormous business problems were beginning to surface and lead to conflict. They would eventually provide the most important tangible reason for the band's demise.

The Beatles controlled neither their management company, Nemporor Holdings (also known as NEMS), nor their publishing company, Northern Songs. In earlier years this wasn't considered problematic; the controlling interest in each company rested in sympathetic hands. In 1968 Clive Epstein, Brian's brother and successor at NEMS, was proposing its sale to an aggressive investment firm, Triumph Investment Trust. This sale would gain Triumph NEMS's 25 percent share of Beatles royalties. Paul, sensing the Beatles' lack of business acumen, called upon the well-respected New York copyright attorney (and future father-in-law) Lee Eastman to help the Beatles purchase NEMS themselves. In a move that proved disastrous, Eastman sent Linda's brother, John, to negotiate. Clive Epstein later commented, "He [John Eastman] loaded the offer with so many conditions and warranties that he ended up talking himself out of the deal. In my opinion, he was a little too young to be negotiating at that level."[13]

In a drama worthy of a daytime TV soap, the negotiations were further complicated by the arrival of Allen Klein, former Rolling Stones manager. With a reputation as a vicious infighter during record contract negotiations, Klein approached John with an offer. Punctuating his detailed account of John's finances with John's own song lyrics, Klein guaranteed he would acquire NEMS for the Beatles without cost. Lennon felt a certain affinity toward this slightly pudgy accountant, who had lost his mother and spent part of his childhood in an orphanage. Whereas the Eastmans were high-society types, Klein was an epithet-flinging "street-fighting man." John, George, and Ringo lined up behind Klein; Paul stayed with Lee Eastman. NEMS was eventually lost, and the finger-pointing started.

The next round featured Northern Songs, the publishing firm originated for the purpose of collecting Beatles song royalties and finding other artists to record Beatles material. Former singer Dick James (who recorded the "Robin Hood" TV show theme) and Brian Epstein began Northern Songs in 1963. In early 1969, fearful of the Beatles' increasingly entangled business affairs, James secretly sold over 31 percent to entertainment mogul Sir Lew Grade. John discovered this by reading about it in a newspaper; Paul learned about it during his honeymoon in the United States. Thus, for the second time in recent history, an important part of the Beatles' business empire had been sold to the business establishment. After months of internal wrangling and negotiations, the Beatles' 30 percent share of Northern Songs proved insufficient to stop Grade's company, ATV, from gaining decisive control of Northern Songs.

In the midst of this turmoil, Paul once more provided the impetus for a team effort. On January 2, 1969, at Paul's prodding, the band repaired to a soundstage at Twickenham Film Studios, where they were filmed recording an album. Dubbed the "Get Back" sessions, the Beatles played all or part of hundreds of songs, some even dating back to their Hamburg days. The eclectic mix included classic rockers like Domino's "Whole Lotta Loving," Holly's "It's So Easy," and Guy Mitchell's "Singin' the Blues"; music from the early 1960s such as Dylan's "Blowin' in the Wind," the Drifters' "Save the Last Dance for Me," and the Crystals' "Da Doo Ron Ron (When He Walked Me Home)"; and contemporary tunes like Janis Joplin's "Piece of My Heart" and Jimi Hendrix's "All Along the Watchtower."

Some sessions began at 8 AM, definitely not a good time for nocturnal rock musicians, and McCartney's calls for discipline and organization were resented by other band members. The soundstage was cold and drafty, the emotional environment tense. George, after particularly strong prodding from Paul about a guitar solo, became the second Beatle to temporarily quit the band. He reappeared at the next regularly scheduled Beatles business meeting. Yoko's presence at the sessions was also an irritant. Never one to stifle artistic suggestions, Yoko's attempts to become a functioning member of the world's most exclusive boys club—a pursuit that had dated back to the *White Album* sessions—only worsened the situation. The final product, *Let It Be* (the movie soundtrack album), included an old Quarrymen chestnut, "One After 909," a second version of John's "Across the Universe," the classic title cut, and Paul's intended follow-up to "Yesterday," the ballad "Long and Winding Road."

Then one day the band, along with keyboard player Billy Preston, took to the roof of their Apple headquarters, set up their equipment, and played five songs for the cameras. To the delight of the assembled Apple staff and a small crowd that listened from the street, the Beatles played what proved to be their last live performance together. Even though the band had recorded hundreds of numbers, neither the group, producer Martin, nor engineer Glyn Johns considered the tunes worthy of further consideration. They were stored away and forgotten as the band became engrossed in the aforementioned business squabbles.

The "Get Back" tapes followed their own odyssey. With the consent of the band, the recordings were offered to producer Phil Spector by Allen Klein in the hopes that he might salvage an album of songs for the movie soundtrack. Spector sequestered himself in California, added his usual Wall of Sound complement of strings, percussion, and background vocals to a number of tracks, and sent a test pressing to each band member. In a sequence of events still cloaked in controversy, Paul claims to have been stifled in his attempts to remove the grandiose orchestration from "Long and Winding Road." In May 1970, one month after the Beatles breakup, *Let It Be* was released. It was even less of a group effort than the *White Album,* was not produced by George Martin, and was not polished by the band—questionably a Beatles album at all.

Soon after the "Get Back" sessions, two Beatles married their respective lovers. On March 12, 1969, Paul married Linda Eastman in London. Numerous female fans, including the group that camped each night outside his home, mourned the "passing" of the Beatles' holdout bachelor. On March 20, 1969, John married Yoko in a quiet ceremony at Gibraltar, attended by Apple chief Peter Brown. Few people found this union acceptable; the era's racism and the couple's avant-garde antics did not endear them to many. For their honeymoon, John and Yoko arrived at the Amsterdam Hilton's presidential suite to begin their "bed-in" for peace. A dialogue raged in the press as to whether these symbolic efforts were at all effective. No one accused the Lennons of having a realistic assessment of effective political organizing or of the efficient use of their power and money. To their credit, they did speak their minds.

In a strange turn of events given this tumultuous atmosphere, the Beatles returned to their recording home in Abbey Road's newly refurbished, sixteen-track Studio B to collaborate for the last time on record. Recorded in the spring and summer of 1969, *Abbey Road* proved to be one of the finest technological accomplishments of the decade. Although some of the instrumental timbres and equalization settings today sound archaic, the polish and crispness, forged by Martin and engineer Geoff Emerick, come close to contemporary standards. Although Lennon described the material, like that on *Sgt. Pepper's*, as a group of unfinished songs, the variety and quality of tunes exhibited by the primary songwriters (John, Paul, George) were well received. Most importantly, the band played at their motivated, musically mature best. Paul's bass-playing exhibited a tasteful choice of melodic passages, adding yet another dimension to what had historically been a more rhythmically oriented style. In 1980 Lennon stated that "Paul was one of the most innovative bass players . . . and half the stuff that's going on now is directly ripped off from his Beatles period."[14]

George's songs were singled out for praise. "Something," which was called by none other than Frank Sinatra the best love song in the past fifty years, exhibited newly developing teamwork between Harrison and Martin. The tune's guitar solo was, not surprisingly, quite similar in tone and melody to Clapton's *White Album* cameo. It also was Harrison's first A side Beatles single release, a fact that only slightly mollified his long-simmering resentment on the subject. "Here Comes the Sun," Harrison's other contribution, has turned into one of those shared-experience songs—on a hypothetical day, when the sun breaks through the cloud cover, one can imagine people the world over beginning to hum "Here comes the sun, Da-da, Da-da."

Along with Lennon's stream-of-consciousness powerhouse "Come Together," side one contained the two romantic screamers, Paul's "Oh, Darling" and John's weighty, repetitive "I Want You (She's So Heavy)." On side two, John's often-overlooked cosmic reminder "Because" was followed by eight song fragments linked by musical transitions. Here we are introduced to Lennon's tongue-in-cheek characters "The Sun King," "Mean Mr. Mustard," and "Polythene Pam."

The album concluded with four sections that, in the light of subsequent events, proved to be their recorded swan song. The musical interlude after "Carry that Weight" contains Ringo's first and only drum solo. Considering the previous discussion of Ringo's shaky reputation, this simplistic solo would appear to have been a courageous undertaking. Then, reverting to the Silver Beatles' three-guitar lineup of the late fifties, George, Paul, and John alternate two-bar guitar solos for eighteen measures.

Like a musical prophet, Paul intones the band's final message to the congregation: "And in the end/ The love you take, is equal to the love you make." It is unclear as to whether the Beatles realized this would be their final message to the world, but it certainly reads as such. And to remind listeners that the band should never be taken too seriously, Paul inserted an irreverent, folk-style fragment, "Her Majesty," just as the vinyl grooves were about to end. Although the album would be released out of creative sequence, appearing before the compilation *Hey Jude* and *Let It Be*, this was their last collective effort.

*Abbey Road* was released in late September (in the United Kingdom) and sold phenomenally well, but the unity forged in the studio didn't last. Returning from his appearance with the Plastic Ono Band (which included Lennon, Yoko, drummer Alan White, Hamburg pal Klaus Voorman on bass, and Eric Clapton) at September's Toronto Rock and Roll Revival show, John communicated his desire to leave the Beatles. Having already experienced the exhilaration of recording three albums independent of the band and performing live with Yoko, Lennon no longer wanted to be saddled with the outdated Beatles format. Allen Klein and Paul pointed out the potentially disastrous economic ramifications this announcement would have on Klein's ongoing royalty negotiations with Capitol. John kept quiet and Klein closed the deal, but the band was all but formally dead.

In the ensuing six months tension abounded. John and Paul barely talked. Phil Spector worked on the "Get Back" tapes. Ringo recorded his solo album of timeless pop favorites, *Sentimental Journey*. And Paul single-handedly recorded his first solo effort, *McCartney*. Paul's requested April release date was vetoed by Klein and the rest of the band, fearing a conflict with *Let It Be*. Although he eventually won that argument, it was obvious to McCartney what others had felt for a long time: The Beatles were dead. On April 10, 1970, Paul's departure from the band was made public.

In a strategy he was later to regret, Paul included in the British *McCartney* release an insert containing a hypothetical interview with the artist. When asked about the break, he cited "personal differences, musical differences, business differences, but most of all because I have a better time with my family." Paul described the feel of the album as "Home. Family. Love." And he included snide swipes at the rest of the band. The public blamed Paul for the breakup of the world's most successful rock and roll band. John was furious at McCartney's self-serving tactics, considering the pressure Paul had exerted on him to stay with the Beatles just six months earlier. It took John years to get over his anger.

For the next few years, John and Paul traded barbs in word and song. Yet each Beatle remained a prolific artist. John went through primal therapy, freeing his feelings of love, fear, and pain—all of which he revealed on record with a unique honesty and forthrightness. He continued to plumb the boundaries of his genre, creating both mainstream and avant-garde music. He later pointed to predecessors such as Vincent van Gogh, Lewis Carroll, and Dylan Thomas and stated, "Surrealism to me is reality. Psychedelic vision to me is reality and always was."[15] Yet his eclecticism was tempered with spiritualism. In reference to "Imagine," he commented "It is the concept of positive prayer. . . . If you can imagine a world at peace then it can be true."[16]

Lennon's odyssey took him through a burst of creativity in the early 1970s, a lost weekend that turned into a year (including a separation from Yoko), an attempt by the United States to deport him because of his political activity, the birth of son Sean, and five years as a househusband. In 1980 John and Yoko returned to music, releasing *Double Fantasy* and the single "(Just Like) Starting Over." On

December, 8, 1980, John Lennon was assassinated by a crazed fan at the doorway to his New York apartment building.

Paul, stung by the criticism surrounding the breakup as well as his first two albums, decided to return to the simple life of a rock and roller. Forming the band Wings with a guitarist, drummer, and neophyte Linda McCartney on keyboards, he set off to tour the English countryside in a van. McCartney and Wings achieved consistent popular success with three #1 Capitol albums from 1975 to 1976. In 1970 Paul instituted the lawsuit he would eventually win, an attempt to extricate himself from the Beatles partnership and the control of Allen Klein. As the suit dragged on dirty laundry was aired and Paul was again painted as the Beatle-killer. McCartney continues to create, and through purchases of the Holly song catalog and other significant publishing properties he has solidified his position as an astute businessman.

George continued on a roll following the band's demise. His album *All Things Must Pass* went to #1 and was critically well received. On August 1, 1971, George produced the Concert for Bangladesh at New York's Madison Square Garden. Dedicated to the relief effort for the victims of Pakistan's civil war, the group of friends Harrison collected for the all-star show included Ravi Shankar, Ringo, Leon Russell, Eric Clapton, and Bob Dylan. George's reputation for Beatle-like idealism remains intact, and he continued to release albums through the eighties. Ringo continued both his recording career and followed up on his interest in acting. Some albums were more popular than others; none approached the critical acclaim given to the Beatles.

❃     ❃     ❃

The band that had come together in Hamburg in 1960 ended acrimoniously ten years later. During this period, rock music evolved from its roots in the classic rock era to the golden age of the late 1960s and early 1970s. The Beatles explored the creative cutting edge, becoming major catalysts in rock music's maturation. They made important musical innovations and helped to reshape the record industry. The themes and ideas contained in their songs reflected the consciousness not only of individual band members, but also the growing counterculture of the era. The Beatles' commercial success ensured the distribution of these ideas to the largest possible audience.

Whereas most bands strive for one unique musical idea, the Beatles developed many, consistently rewriting rock's musical boundaries. Their material contained increasing harmonic and rhythmic complexity, more and different instrumentation (sitar, orchestra, piccolo, trumpet, and so on), a highly advanced understanding and use of studio technology, and the ability to make their songs sound as varied as are the styles of Chuck Berry and Ravi Shankar. Other musicians listened to these innovations and tried for themselves.

The Beatles also helped transform the record industry. What had started in the teen idol era as pop music written in office buildings by Aldon songwriters ended with rock and roll stars as performers, songwriters, producers, and businessmen. The Beatles were dominant artistic forces in a record industry that almost tripled its gross sales between 1960 ($600 million) and 1970 ($1.66 billion). The rock album replaced the single as the medium of exchange as profits skyrocketed. Whereas albums previously had been a compilation of a few hit singles and filler cuts, British Beatles albums contained fourteen cuts of similar quality. This encouraged other artists to do the same.

The group's phenomenal record sales were a catalyst for many other changes. Artists, the product's creators, gained power at the bargaining table. The Beatles' record royalty rates rose from 3 percent in 1962 to 17.5 percent by 1970. Record companies, envisioning enormous profits to be made by the sales of popular music, rushed to sign almost any band with a British accent. At era's end, record sales had surpassed all other areas of entertainment, including movies and sports.

The Beatles, like Elvis, were part of a moment. Their popularity coincided with the vast expansion of communications technology. The "All You Need Is Love" broadcast was seen by 200 million people worldwide. Beatlemania thrived on six continents. Due to the band's deification, as well as its momentous impact on British and American culture, the subsequent marketing and proliferation of Western popular culture throughout the world made the Beatles the most potent musical force in history.

The Beatles proved once again a fitting axiom: You can't remove rock music from its societal context. Young people in the sixties, building on rebellious behavior of the previous decade, created their own lifestyle, challenged the prevailing morality, and initiated an era of creativity and experimentation. The Beatles concurrently drew from a classic rock foundation and blazed a trail that continuously expanded the boundaries of rock music. Their creative integrity, idealism, and spontaneity posed the challenge to leading critics—to evaluate rock music's form and content seriously. The Beatles enabled the discussion of rock and roll as art. They also taught a lot of people to sing "yeah, yeah, yeah." In Western popular culture's journey through the sixties, the Beatles were in the crow's nest, calling "Land ho!"

# 8· The Rolling Stones: It's Only Rock and Roll but I Like It

*"Are the Stones more satisfied today?"*
*"Sexually, do you mean, or philosophically?"*
*"Both."*
*"Sexually—more satisfied, financially—dissatisfied, philosophically—still trying."*

**Mick Jagger, at a 1969 New York press conference**

*You go out every time roaring drunk. After five years you're a fucking wreck. . . . It used to be booze. It used to be . . .*

**Keith Richards, 1971, quoted in** Rolling Stone

*The best rock and roll encapsulates a certain high energy—an angriness— whether on record or on stage. That is, rock and roll is only rock and roll if it's not safe.*

**Mick Jagger, 1988, quoted in** Rolling Stone

ALONG WITH THE BEATLES, there were a number of British bands poised on the cutting edge of midsixties rock and roll. These contemporaries were led by the Rolling Stones. In February 1963, as the Fab Four were making their way to the top of the British charts, the Rolling Stones were starting their first regular Sunday appearances in the backroom of a London pub. The band, named after the Muddy Waters blues tune "Rollin' Stone," capitalized on aggressive, unpolished versions of predominantly Black American music to propel it to the forefront of the fledgling British blues movement.

By the middle of the decade the Rolling Stones had achieved commercial success on both sides of the Atlantic. When the Beatles self-destructed, the Stones emerged from the shadows to create their own brief golden age. This is the story of four young London suburbanites (singer Mick Jagger, guitarist Keith Richards, bassist Bill Wyman [née Perks], and drummer Charlie Watts) and one well-off provincial (guitarist Brian Jones) who went beyond the classic rock music of their youth to discover and follow its blues and R&B antecedents.

Mick grew up in a household of moderate means in suburban London: "My mum is very working class, my father bourgeois, because he had a reasonable good education, so I came from somewhere in between that." His father, Joe, was a physical education teacher, and Mick was both intellectually and athletically gifted. His mother was sure Mick would become a politician, especially after the young Jagger enrolled in the prestigious London School of Economics (LSE) to study accounting. Indicative of his cautious nature, Mick didn't quit LSE until he was sure that the Rolling Stones had become a commercially viable group.

Jagger's musical history included the stereotypical introduction to American rock and roll via the classic rockers. Labeled "jungle music" by his father, Mick was crazy about Little Richard, Jerry Lee Lewis, Bo Diddley, and to a lesser extent Buddy Holly. From there he followed a musical progression back in time, discovering bluesmen Big Bill Broonzy (who toured England before his death in 1958) and Muddy Waters. These roots took hold of young Jagger, who had already demonstrated a propensity toward show business pursuits, appearing as a model on his father's physical-fitness TV show. A boyhood friend described the strangely remote Mick as giving his friends "the idea he'd sooner be somewhere else than with us, doing far more glamorous things."[1]

Keith Richards played with Mick in the same Dartford primary school playground until the age of six or seven, when the Richards family moved to a housing development on the rougher side of the tracks. Keith was sufficiently talented as a boy to appear at Westminster Abbey and Royal Albert Hall, but the onset of puberty lowered his vocal range and he turned to rock and roll. Keith wore tight-fitting jeans, violet shirts, and pink socks, practiced air guitar, and listened to Chuck Berry and Little Richard records.

In 1958 Doris Richards purchased a guitar for her son. Soon thereafter, Keith was expelled from Dartford Technical School; as a last resort he enrolled at Sidcup Art School. The art school environment proved to be musically enlightening for Richards: "I learned from all these amateur art school people . . . Broonzy first. He and Josh White. . . . Then I started to discover Robert Johnson and those cats. . . . The other half of me was listening to all that rock and roll, Chuck Berry."[2]

Lewis Brian Hopkin Jones, who went by the name Brian, was raised in the elegant surroundings of Cheltenham, a spa-resort town in western England. Brian excelled in his grammar school studies and learned to play piano (from his mother), clarinet (which he played in an orchestra), and saxophone. Adolescence brought rebellion; rebellion brought him a child out of wedlock and a premature departure from school. Brian became enamored with jazz saxophone, working day jobs and playing with jazz and rock bands at night. He was graced with a good ear for music—the ability to hear and reproduce music easily—and his next infatuation was with blues-style guitar. After the birth of his second child (with a second girl) Brian left Cheltenham for London. Billing himself as Elmo Lewis, a take-off on slide guitarist Elmore James, Brian joined Alexis Korner's seminal blues band, Blues Incorporated.

One day in 1960 Keith boarded a commuter train to London. "So I get on this train one morning and there's Jagger and under his arm he has four or five albums. . . . We haven't hung around since we were five or six. We recognized each other straight off . . . and under his arm he's got [albums by] Chuck Berry, and Little Walter, Muddy Waters."[3] Their common interest in music deepened and eventually developed into a symbiotic relationship similar to that of Lennon and McCartney (somewhat odd, given the natures of the rough, teddy-boy Richards and the cautious, middle-class Jagger). Along with Keith's school chum, Dick Taylor, they formed a short-lived trio called Little Boy Blue and the Blue Boys.

In March 1962 Blues Incorporated, including Charlie Watts on drums and Elmo Lewis on guitar, played its first night at the Ealing Club, a rented room behind the ABC bakery. A few weeks later, Mick and Keith traveled to London to see them. They were astounded by Brian's playing. Richards says of that night: "Suddenly it's Elmore James, this cat man, and it's Brian . . . playin' bar slide guitar. . . . He's really fantastic and a gas. . . . He'd been doin' the same as we'd been doin' . . . thinkin' he was the only cat in the world doin' it."[4] Although Brian continued to play with Korner (Mick occasionally sitting in as vocalist), the nascent Stones now numbered three, as Brian started playing with Mick and Keith.

In July the three were joined by Dick Taylor, Ian Stewart (on piano), and a drummer to play a gig at London's new blues center, the Marquis Club. Billed as the Rolling Stones, they acquitted themselves well but found few other bookings. Brian, Keith, and Mick moved into a rundown flat in London's Chelsea district, living and jamming together and exhibiting the craziness of young musicians on the loose. Bill Wyman, who was about six years older than most of the band and had already served a stint in the Royal Air Force, answered their add for a bass player. In addition to a love of classic rock and a feeling for the blues, Wyman arrived with a large amplifier and proffered extra equipment, cigarettes, and a round of drinks; he was welcomed into the band.

Their next task was to find a regular drummer. They tried to persuade Charlie Watts to join to no avail. Watts had little reason to join the Stones, a band without an assured future. He already had security, having attended Harrow Art School and then being employed as a graphic artist with an ad agency. He also had a regular gig with a popular blues band at night. Charlie's first love was jazz, but his experience with Blues Incorporated acclimated him to the blues and started his friendship with the Stones. After many evenings at the Chelsea flat and encouragement from Korner, Charlie accepted their offer. In January 1963 all five members were in place and the Rolling Stones were born.

In 1963 the first wave of popular music mania took hold in England and the Stones were swept up in the tide. Within the year, they established a residency at the Crawdaddy Club and recorded and released their first single—Chuck Berry's "Come On" backed by Willie Dixon's "I Want to Be Loved." That same year they toured as a support act for American rockers Little Richard, the Everly Brothers, and Bo Diddley. One night the Beatles, Britain's most popular rock and roll band, came down to the club to listen. Both groups spent the rest of the night carousing at the Chelsea pad; a few days later the Stones returned the favor, catching the Beatles show at Royal Albert Hall.

In the spring of 1963 Andrew Loog Oldham saw the Stones at the Crawdaddy. He was a public-relations man already at the age of nineteen, having worked as a publicist for Brian Epstein during the release of "Please Please Me" and for Mary Quant and her line of hip designer clothing. What impressed Oldham about the Stones was "Music. Sex. The fact that in just a few months the country would need an opposite of what the Beatles were doing."[5] Oldham recognized the raw emotion and sexual rebelliousness generated by the band and its music, and so he set about to package and sell that image. Early attempts to dress the Stones in matching outfits were sabotaged by band members, who left assorted uniform parts in dressing rooms and hotels across England.

One evening, George Harrison mentioned to Decca's Dick Rowe (the man who passed on the Beatles) that he ought to see about signing the Rolling Stones. Rowe wasted no time in catching them at the Crawdaddy and signing them to a contract. As a record producer, Oldham was strictly laissez-faire; he simply arranged for the recording sessions and turned the band loose in the studio. He couldn't do much more, as his knowledge of music and recording technology was less than elementary. Without much in the way of direction, the recordings reproduced an unpolished authenticity reminiscent of the American originals.

The Rolling Stones of early 1964 were still being led by their most talented musician, Brian Jones. Much like John Lennon, Brian experimented with and explored the frontiers of permissible behavior offstage. "He was the first one that had a car," describes Jones's former partner, Anita Pallenberg. "He was the first into flash clothes and smoke, and acid. . . . It was back then when it seemed anything was possible."[6] Once he tasted success (by hanging out with the Beatles), Brian wanted to be the one on top. Mick concurs: "The driving force [of the Stones] was to be famous, get lots of girls and earn a lot of money, that and the idea of just getting our music across as best we could."[7]

The Stones released their second single, the Lennon-McCartney composition "I Want to Be Your Man," in November 1963 and saw it climb into the top 20. Slowly their music was changing; a few original tunes sneaked into their repertoire of covers. The first Stones album, *The Rolling Stones,* was released in April 1964; it paid homage to their roots while hinting at a new direction. Lead singer Jagger growled and slurred blues favorites like "I'm a King Bee" and "I Just Want to Make Love to You" in a style dripping with sexual innuendo. Up-tempo classic rock favorites like Holly's "Not Fade Away" (with Hollies Graham Nash and Alan Clarke singing backup and friend Phil Spector on maracas) and Chuck Berry's "Carol" were joined by Memphis soulman Rufus Thomas's "Walkin' the Dog."

But the Jagger-Richards original "Tell Me" had a distinctly different feeling. Jagger sang with crisper pronunciation and the feel was dominated by a twelve-string acoustic rhythm guitar. Of their early writing experiences, Keith comments, "The first things, usually I wrote the melody and Mick wrote the words . . . every song we've got has pieces of each other in it."8 Both the covers and the original material presented a worldview consistent with its blues roots—men and women struggling for a few moments of satisfaction.

These were years of nonstop touring. Says Keith: "We worked our asses off from '63 to '66. Right through those years non-stop, I believe we had two weeks off."9 As with the Beatles shows, playing onstage was not always a pleasant experience for the band. Crowds screamed and yelled and, at least in the case of the Stones, were moved by the scene to express themselves physically. "There was a period in England," Keith recalls, "when we couldn't play ballrooms anymore because we never got through more than three or four songs every night, man, chaos, police, and too many people in these places fainting."10

In June 1964 the Stones arrived in New York for their first U.S. tour. "Not Fade Away" had barely made the charts, so the band had to be content with the acclaim of musical friends and some popularity on each coast. Typical of their midwestern gigs, 600 fans squeezed into a 15,000-seat Omaha venue. The tour's highlight proved to be a recording session at Chicago's Chess Records. The engineer, Ron Malo, had recorded Chess greats Chuck Berry, Bo Diddley, and Howlin' Wolf; Muddy Waters, Willie Dixon, and Berry stopped in to chat. Female fans caused a near riot and the Chicago police told the Stones to get out of town, which they did. Though generally ignored by the mainstream press, a piece in the fashion magazine *Vogue* hinted at their future success: "The Stones have a perverse, unsettling sex appeal with Jagger out in front of his team-mates. . . . To women, he's fascinating, to men a scare."

To this Mick added his mimicry of moves by James Brown and other Black artists. In October the Stones had the good fortune to appear as headliners at the T.A.M.I. show—a video of this show is available—along with Brown, Chuck Berry, Motown artists Marvin Gaye, the Supremes, and Smokey Robinson, and the Beach Boys. Jagger stepped off the return flight to London doing the James Brown shuffle and incorporated these and other moves into his performances.

As the Stones became more popular and accumulated a series of chart hits, their live shows, and the responses to those shows, became more raucous. A 1965 Dublin concert "was stopped when part of the second show Adelphi Theater audience leapt over the orchestra pit onto the stage. Mick was dragged to the floor; three boys were throwing punches at Brian while two others were trying to kiss him. Wyman was crushed against a piano at one side of the stage. . . . In Belfast, the audience tore up the seats and threw them at the stage. As the Stones tried to leave, fans covered the car, but they got away with another collapsed roof."11 Although most top groups now had difficulty moving about in public, the Stones had reached a point where they weren't even safe while onstage.

Even though "Time Is on My Side" and "The Last Time" had reached the top 10 and the band was scheduled for an October appearance on "The Ed Sullivan Show," the Stones had yet to conquer the United States. The May 1965 release of the Jagger-Richards composition "(I Can't Get No) Satisfaction," which mocked the superficiality of life on tour in America, changed all that. (The story goes that

Keith woke in the middle of the night at a Florida motel to write the legendary guitar-riff introduction, immortalizing him in rock music annals.) To this Mick added a stream of themes chronicling men on TV, advertising detergent, and voices on car radios giving out useless information and the headwhirring emptiness of "drivin', doin' this, and signin' that." Although the song is generally misinterpreted as a diatribe on the inability to achieve sexual satisfaction, only the next-to-last chorus and last verse allude to the frustration of not finding a willing sexual playmate. "Satisfaction" hit the charts in June and stayed at #1 for four weeks. In the next eighteen months the Stones would score six more top-10 hits, including three #1s, and each of their three studio albums would achieve top-5 status.

The band had finally achieved mass commercial success. They would boast to the Beatles that with the addition of Allen Klein in 1965 as their business manager and record contract negotiator, they would make more money from records in one year than the Beatles had made since the beginning of their career. This success was further enhanced by Oldham's ability to sell the Stones as the bad boys of rock and roll, the antithesis of the Beatles' positive pop-star image. The Stones body-based music also helped. The Wyman/Watts rhythm section accentuated the Black-rooted two and four backbeat and sometimes even emphasized a 1-2-3-4 quarter-note snare and bass pulse. These driving pulses evoked a physical reaction that was perceived by some as a threat to the status quo, much in the same manner as during the classic rock era. When kids moved uncontrollably, parents got uncomfortable.

Jagger's vocal style and onstage performance reinforced this visceral, sensual reaction to the band. Like his blues predecessors, Jagger slurred, growled, and screamed his delivery. Onstage, he sweated, pouted—with those luscious and world-famous lips—and undulated his way across the stage. As in previous eras, physicality could be interpreted as sex, and sex usually meant rebellion. To varying degrees, the audience was moved to react, to rebel. In addition, R&B and blues covers meant Blackness, and in the midsixties identification with Black forms still carried with it a dark or unwholesome connotation.

Writing about a 1965 Stones press conference, columnist Pete Hamill reflects some of these reactions: "There is something elegantly sinister about the Rolling Stones. They sit before you at a press conference like five unfolding switchblades, their faces set in rehearsed snarls, their hair studiously unkempt and matted . . . and the way they walk and the songs they sing all become part of some long mean reach for the jugular."[12] Something was happening, but you didn't know what it was, did you, Mr. Hamill?

The reaction to the Stones occurred predominantly on emotional and physical levels. Yet much of the activity in "swinging London" surrounding the Stones was located in the mind; many of popular music's leading figures were preoccupied with consciousness expansion and its chemical catalysts. The Stones were slow to join this pilgrimage and never fully embraced its direction, but they dabbled sufficiently to allow their repertoire and worldview to grow.

Following the Beatles' lead, the Stones experimented with exotic and orchestral instrumentation. Brian learned to play the sitar for "Paint It Black" and then discarded it. He also played dulcimer on "Lady Jane," flute on "Ruby Tuesday," marimba on "Under My Thumb," and mellotron on "2000 Light Years From Home." This new experimentation in musical coloration, which also included other players on brass, strings, and double bass, gave Rolling Stones songs a musical depth that their earlier material lacked. They were changing along with the times.

Lyrics occasionally strayed outside the usual romantic parameters. "Paint It Black" and "As Tears Go By" were pictures of sadness and depression. "Mother's Little Helper" dug at the hypocrisy of antidrug sentiments while the societal mainstream abused tranquilizers in a struggle to cope with "meaningless," pressure-filled lives. However, Jagger was later to remind us "that for every one song that took some serious social view, like say 'Mother's Little Helper'—there were lots of others that were just teenage bullshit."[13]

There were relationship songs that, along with the romantic fare of "Ruby Tuesday" and "Lady Jane," drew the ire of numerous parties. Ed Sullivan and the CBS censors required the band change the words "the night" to "some time" in "Let's Spend the Night Together" for their TV appearance. And Jagger's reputation as a male chauvinist was sealed with the release of "Under My Thumb" and "Stupid Girl." Keith later rationalizes that "it was all a spin-off from our environment . . . hotels, and too many dumb chicks. Not all dumb, not by any means, but that's how one got."[14]

Concurrent with these artistic changes was a shift in the power relationships within the band. Brian, who in the early days had been the organizer, spokesman, and equal arbiter of artistic choice, was relegated to second-class status. Artistic direction and power gravitated to the songwriters, Jagger and Richards. Brian attempted to write and failed—he was once locked in a room with American rocker Gene Pitney and a piano—leaving him feeling paranoid that his usefulness to the band was over. Brian did continue his quest for different life experiences. His affinity for costumes, including dressing in silk and satin, gave him some notoriety. Brian and the stunning actress Anita Pallenberg descended into an intense and bizarre relationship. In a stormy partnership characterized by spontaneous acts, sexual experimentation, a profusion of drug use, and Brian's jealous rages and physical abuse, they lived the lives of rock royalty.

Life on the edge eventually caught up with Brian, who from then on rode an emotional roller coaster dominated by downhill plunges. The Jagger-Richards friendship and writing alliance left him depressed and helpless. His close friend, Guinness heir Tara Browne, died in an auto accident, and his relationship with Anita became combative. Brian sought chemical refuge. His drug intake, as described by supplier and friend Tony Sanchez, was a regular morning assortment that might include amphetamines, cocaine, morphine, LSD, and mandrax. This left him "a scrambled wreck"—many times incapacitated for the rest of the day.[15]

Lacking the constitution to withstand the pressures and rigors of the road, his refuge in drugs only made things worse.

If Brian's personal problems were not enough, the February 12, 1967, police raid on Keith's Redlands home also had serious ramifications for the Stones' ascent to the top. The previous Sunday, sensationalist tabloid *News of the World* had printed an article incorrectly identifying Mick as the Stone who displayed hashish (an Eastern cannabis-based product that is usually smoked) in front of a reporter. Mick readied a libel suit and went to Redlands for a party with friends. That morning Mick took his first LSD trip, and the party, which for a time included George and Patti Harrison, traipsed around the Sussex countryside. Most participants returned to the house for an evening of records and television.

At 8 PM, nineteen police, including three policewomen, pounded on the door. Mick was arrested for possession of four prescription amphetamine tablets long ago placed in his jacket pocket by his girlfriend, Marianne Faithfull; Keith was charged with allowing drug use on the property. Police conveniently overlooked a briefcase, filled with LSD and other exotic drugs lying out in full view. It belonged to a notorious American "acid king" who slipped out of the country that night. Keith would later claim that *News of the World* had hired the drug dealer to inform the paper of a party in progress so that it could tip off the police. The police didn't miss Marianne, who was wrapped only in a fur rug. During the trial, she was referred to as "Miss X," and accounts of her dropping the rug while standing before a female officer scandalized the nation.

In a remarkable coincidence, Brian was arrested in his London flat the same day that Mick and Keith were scheduled for a court hearing, having been found in possession of cocaine, methedrine, and cannabis. Drugs and the Rolling Stones remained on the front page. In July Mick and Keith were convicted and sentenced to serve time in jail. In response to the overly severe penalty, the editor of the prestigious *Times* wrote a scathing editorial taking the judge to task. On appeal, Keith's conviction was quashed, and Mick was given a lecture and an unconditional discharge. Brian eventually pleaded guilty to cannabis possession; the other charges were not pressed.

These episodes left a mark on the band. Brian would continue to be harassed, and he was arrested again by corrupt members of the vice squad. He would pay them off, but he became increasingly paranoid and insecure. Mick and Keith were truly frightened by the brutal reality of their nights in jail. At times, it seemed, even the Stones were at the mercy of the fates. Brian's drug conviction made touring difficult, as many countries, including the United States, did not grant visas to persons with drug records. Thus, the Stones touring train ground to a halt. Between October 1966 and July 1969, the band played only one three-week European concert tour (March–April 1967).

Aside from an expedient trip to Morocco to avoid further unpleasantries with the authorities, the Stones turned their efforts to defending themselves in court and recording their next album. Nobody was more surprised than I when, while sitting in the marketplace in Marakesh one afternoon watching the Gnawa dancers, I looked up to see Mick, Keith, and Brian walk by. The Rolling Stones in Morocco? Oh well, here's to good health! In the summer of 1967 the Beatles released *Sgt. Pepper's.* Mick, who had traveled with the Beatles to Wales in the search for transcendental enlightenment, suggested a similarly styled effort for the Stones. Brian argued against it, and his viewpoint proved to be correct. The Stones' predictable attempt at creating psychedelic musical collage, *Their Satanic Majesty's Request,* was released in November 1967, but it was clearly not a natural outgrowth of the band's creative nature—in fact it was out of character for the more sexually oriented band. Even if their ideas were creative and focused, the band lacked a producer like the Beatles' George Martin to translate their inspiration into reality.

However, their spring 1968 sessions at London's Olympic Studios produced a music that sent reverberations throughout the music world. It was innovative, the sound was crisper, and the musical ideas more sophisticated. Their lyrical worldview had expanded its previous focus on romantic/sexual involvement to include topics of social and political concern. Yet the rhythm section still throbbed, Jagger still growled and howled, and danger and taboo still lurked among the lyrics. The maturing Rolling Stones were anything but tame. They produced a classic quartet of albums—*Beggars Banquet, Let It Bleed, Sticky Fingers,* and *Exile on Main Street*—that ensured the Rolling Stones would forever be considered one of rock and roll's greatest groups.

One can point to producer Jimmy Miller as a reason for the musical maturation and the new sophistication in arrangements and sound. An American percussionist, Miller had already produced albums by Spooky Tooth and Traffic when he was invited to these Stones sessions. A working relationship was established, and Miller went on to produce the next five albums, the first four of which are the artistic peak of the band. One of the trademarks of this period (thanks, perhaps, to Miller's studio savvy) is the layering of percussion instruments at the beginning of hits such as "Sympathy for the Devil" and "Gimme Shelter."

"Jumping Jack Flash," the song that alerted the public of things to come, was released as a single in May 1968. Keith's memorable guitar hook proclaims a remarkably strong presence, followed by Jagger's autobiographical maelstrom, which begins "I was born in a crossfire hurricane/And I howled at my ma in the drivin' rain. But it's awww riiight noww—in fact it's a gas!" The song hailed a new Stones era—one that included deeper, more symbolic lyrics and sophisticated musical arrangements. It was also a time when the Stones' artistic and commercial focus shifted from singles to albums. Each of the next four studio albums placed in the top 5, including two #1s; from those albums only three top-10 singles emerged.

The first album in the golden quartet, *Beggars Banquet,* was originally scheduled for an August 1968 release. It was issued in time for Christmas, as the band wrangled with Decca over the album cover, which the label considered offensive.

The original cover pictured a toilet surrounded by graffiti that offered album information and some choice phrases. The final cover is plain white with black lettering. Inside, however, the Stones reached for and achieved a new quality of artistic consistency.

"Sympathy for the Devil," the first track on side one, continues the trend of layered, percussion-oriented arrangements begun by the breakthrough single "Jumping Jack Flash." Introductory drum, conga, hi-hat, maracas, guero, and syncopated vocal sounds, in layered steps, precede Jagger's vocals. Lyrically we are treated to an autobiographical stroll through some of the devil's more celebrated carnage. This song in particular reinforced the band's negative image, which was already peaking as a result of bad-boy antics, violence at concerts, and drug trials. They now paid homage to the devil, singing in the first person. Although there is little (if any) evidence that the band practiced the occult, regular critics painted them as satanists.

The Stones were also not immune from the political turmoil existing in 1968. Antiwar demonstrations occurred in front of the American Embassy in Grosvenor Square and Mick attended one such event. Students took to the streets on the continent, and Mick and Keith spent time in America, enveloped as it was by the political and cultural maelstrom. (It was also their favorite place to write songs due to the incredible infusion of stimuli.) These experiences seeped into their new material. Still, Mick's involvement in political causes was limited: "I was much more involved with politics before I got into music. At the London School of Economics, I was always in arguments."[16] However, given songs like "Street Fighting Man," a rallying anthem for the day's youth, it was obvious the Stones didn't completely insulate themselves from the surroundings. Mick continues: "But you're always involved in what's going on around you. There is, I suppose, a certain political content to that song."[17]

Unlike Lennon's (and later Harrison's) penchant for activism, Jagger and Richards counseled resignation in "Street Fighting Man": "But what can a poor boy do/ Except to sing for a rock and roll band." Keith states more explicitly: "We're not saying we want to be in the streets, but we're a rock and roll band, just the reverse. Those kids at the press conferences want us to do their thing, not ours. Politics is what we're trying to get away from in the first place."[18] Nevertheless, two other songs contained obvious political references: "Factory Girl," the folk-flavored tribute to a female working-class hero; and the proletarian anthem "Salt of the Earth," which concludes "Let's drink to the hard working people/ Let's drink to the salt of the earth."

Mindful of a lack of visual footage capturing the energy of the band, the Stones decided to create their own magical event, The Rolling Stones Rock and Roll Circus, in December 1968. It was a forty-eight-hour happening featuring authentic circus acts (tigers, acrobats, fire-eaters), bikers, Merry Prankster Ken Kesey, schoolteachers, and a major musical agenda. The circus acts were scattered between performances by Jethro Tull, Taj Mahal, the Who, the Rolling Stones, and the so-called Supergroup (John Lennon on vocal and guitar, Eric Clapton on lead guitar, Keith Richards on bass, and Mitch Mitchell of the Jimi Hendrix Experience on drums). All the Stones were costumed and Mick acted as ringmaster. The film, intended for a BBC special, was short-circuited by the band itself and never aired—the band was apparently displeased with their performance.

Brian and the band were more estranged than ever by this time; his tenuous grip on reality only worsened. He wasn't contributing to the band in the new studio sessions, and his drug conviction still impeded the band's touring plans. Brian finally agreed to leave the band in return for two years' compensation at 100,000 pounds per year. Frustrated by the Stones' new musical direction and encouraged by contemporaries like Creedence Clearwater Revival, Brian renewed contact with old pal Alexis Korner. He retreated to his new abode (Cotchford Farm, the former home of *Winnie the Pooh* author A. A. Milne) to cleanse himself and prepare a return to his roots.

By most accounts Brian was indeed on the mend. But on July 3, 1969, he drowned in his swimming pool. Although he had consumed alcohol and prescription sedatives, Brian was a strong swimmer and had been left alone for only a few moments by friends. The coroner's inquest ruled "death by misadventure"; a number of unanswered questions remain about the circumstances of his death. Keith feels that "some very weird things happened that night, that's all I can say." Pete Townshend, once asked to comment on Brian's death, replied, "Oh, it's a normal day for Brian, like he died every day you know."

"Peace, peace! He is not dead, he doth not sleep." Those were the words recited by Mick at the first live Stones performance in more than two years. Two stanzas of Shelley's "Adonais," recited in homage to Brian, greeted the 250,000 fans at London's Hyde Park on July 5, two days after his drowning. New to the Stones was twenty-one-year-old Mick Taylor, former lead guitarist for John Mayall's Blues Band. (Eric Clapton, the Stones' first choice, had reportedly declined an offer.) The set showcased current music, opening with "Honky Tonk Woman" and closing with "Sympathy for the Devil." Although timing was off, cues were muffed, and Mick Taylor appeared stiff and nervous, the Stones were back and looking forward to a new album and planned U.S. tour.

At the Stones' Olympic Studios base in London, with producer Jimmy Miller and engineer-friend Glyn Johns teaming up in the control room, the band recorded *Let It Bleed*, which was greeted with effusive praise. Writer Greil Marcus intoned, "*Let It Bleed* is not only one of the most intelligent rock and roll albums made, but also one of the most visceral and exciting." The music continued the now-familiar trends of layered introductions ("Gimme Shelter" and "Let It Bleed"), increased diversity (the London Bach Choir on "You Can't Always Get What You Want"), and throbbing rhythmic feel.

Jon Landau had written "the Rolling Stones are violence" in referring to *Beggars Banquet*. This effort was even more saturated with angry, violent, and sometimes bloody references. Typical of the lyrics were images of bleeding men ("You Can't

Always Get What You Want"), rape and murder (being just a shot away, as in "Gimme Shelter"), and smashing windows and rape ("Midnight Rambler"). Jagger and Richards refused to ascribe any cause and effect between their music and the highly charged atmosphere of the era. Critic and musician Lenny Kaye chose to focus on the audience's use of the band: "Through a special community alchemy, we've chosen the Stones to bring our darkness into light, in each case via a construct that fits the time and prevailing mood perfectly. . . . If you can't bleed on the Stones, who can you bleed on?"

Amid the swirling controversies of violence, satanism, and Mick's androgynous stage persona, the Stones excitedly prepared for their first American tour in three years. Jagger was not oblivious to societal changes taking place: "I see a great deal of danger in the air. . . . Teenagers are not screaming about pop music anymore, they're screaming for much deeper reasons . . . about the world and the way they live. I see a lot of trouble coming in the dawn."[19] The tour's violent finale would prove him right. When the fifteen-city tour stopped at New York's Madison Square Garden, *New Yorker* magazine exalted, "The Stones present a theatrical musical performance that has no equal in our culture. . . . Listening to Mick Jagger is not like listening to Jasha Heifetz. Mick Jagger is coming in on more circuits than Jasha Heifetz. He is dealing in total undefined sensual experience of the most ecstatic sort."[20] However, the Grateful Dead's Jerry Garcia noted at the time that there was danger in adding a little bit of sadism to their sexuality, and the Stones did add a combustible touch of leather.

Sensitive to charges of price gouging and befitting the Bay Area's concert-in-the-park tradition, the band had planned to stage a free concert in San Francisco's Golden Gate Park as their final gig. Turned down by the park commission, Stones tour management, with help from friends in the Grateful Dead organization, decided on nearby Sears Point Raceway as an alternative. A large stage and light towers were constructed, but just days before the concert a disagreement over exclusive film rights eliminated that site. Less than twenty-four hours before concert time, the crew dismantled the stage and equipment and moved it sixty-five miles south to a new site, Altamont Raceway.

On December 6, 1969, a warm overcast day gave way to a cold evening. Facilities for performers and concert-goers were almost nonexistent; there were few rest rooms and little food. The stage, a low temporary affair that would be used by the acts during the show, was surrounded by members of the Hell's Angels Motorcycle Club, who were hired to provide a secure buffer between the audience and performers. As the day progressed, chaos reigned. Santana opened, followed by the Jefferson Airplane—lead singer Marty Balin was knocked unconscious by an Angel after trying to stop them from beating an audience member—the Flying Burrito Brothers, and Crosby, Stills, Nash, and Young. Waves of violence, provoked mostly by the brutality of the Angels, rippled through the crowds—onstage and offstage.

The Stones, who had sauntered slowly through the camped masses late the previous night, were now being sequestered in a well-stocked, well-secured backstage trailer. In a sinister omen earlier in the day, a teenage boy punched Mick in the face as he stepped from the shuttle helicopter. The evening turned cold and the Stones lounged in their trailer, delaying the show until darkness provided better lighting conditions. They struggled to reach the stage, which at the moment was a war zone nominally under the control of the Hell's Angels. Mick, after asking the bikers for more space to perform, launched into "Jumping Jack Flash." Drunk, LSD-sotted Angels set upon similarly drunk and drugged concert-goers who strayed across the imaginary boundary of the war zone. No one, not even performers, promoters, or photographers, was exempt from biker violence.

During the fourth song and in front of the cameras (the shot is included in the video entitled *Gimme Shelter*), Meredith Hunter was stabbed to death by Hell's Angels. The Stones finished the set, afraid that stopping would only trigger more violence. They sprinted to their helicopter and took off. *Rolling Stone* magazine, in a major story, crucified the Stones as most responsible for the tragedy. Columnist-editor and rock elder Ralph J. Gleason called Altamont the end of rock innocence. Promoter Bill Graham, whose warnings of impending doom had been ignored, lashed out at Jagger: "What right do you have to leave the way you did, thanking everyone for having a good time and the Angels for helping out? . . . What did he leave behind throughout the country? Every gig he was late, every fucking gig he made the promoter bleed. . . . But you know what is a great tragedy to me? That cunt is a great entertainer."[21]

With the exceptions of a European tour in 1970 and an abbreviated English tour in 1971, the Stones stopped performing for a time. In a move that reflected their musical roots, they hired Marshall Chess, the son of Chess Records founder Leonard, as president of their new label, Rolling Stone Records. For their manufacturing and distribution deal they again made a choice with historical significance, signing with Atlantic, the R&B and soul major. In response to the British tax laws, which George Harrison assails in "Taxman" as 95 percent for the government and 5 percent for the rich musician, the entire band moved to southern France.

The classic *Sticky Fingers,* recorded in Muscle Shoals, Alabama, at Olympic Studios, and at Mick's Stargroves mansion, is a musically tight and emotionally gritty journey through drug-plagued existence. The listener encounters needles and spoons, Sister Morphine and Cousin Cocaine, a demon life, a head full of snow, and Brown Sugar (in reference to either heroin or a female slave or both). Also included is "Wild Horses," Mick's haunting ballad to Marianne—first recorded by Gram Parsons's band, the Flying Burrito Brothers. The "scandalous" Andy Warhol-designed front cover features men's pants with a working zipper, and the disc label contains Warhol's famous lips logo.

The fourth Miller-produced album, *Exile on Main Street,* closed out the first decade. The sessions, captured by the band's mobile recording unit parked outside Keith's French villa, eventually filled four sides. Of this record, Jagger comments: "It's a wonderful record but I wouldn't consider it the finest Rolling Stones work. I think that *Beggars Banquet* and *Let It Bleed* were better records."[22] Like the Beatles' *White Album, Exile* contains a variety of sounds, and some contemporary reviewers considered its length to be a drawback. However, the double album captures Keith's creative genius. During the sessions, however, Richards was continuing to struggle with his heroin addiction. He later quipped: "While I was a junkie, I still learned to ski and I made *Exile on Main Street.*"

During the seventies the Stones toured the United States about every three years ('72, '75, '78). The self-contained Stones tour party was an all-consuming juggernaut, becoming more extravagant with each successive tour. Reflecting in part a societal shift toward individual gratification, the newer Stones music ran back to the familiar hedonistic themes of sex, drugs, and rock and roll music. Mick Taylor, perhaps the most technically gifted guitarist in the band's lineup, left in 1974, depressed at the music's narrow focus and his own involvement with heroin. Ron Wood, Faces guitarist and light-hearted Richards crony, filled in for the 1975 tour; he never really left. In the late 1970s some band members continued to struggle with the debilitating effects of drug addiction.

As of this writing, the Rolling Stones have survived the rock and roll fast lane for more than three decades. Their music over the last twenty years has been flavored by contemporary popular styles like disco and new wave. Their records continue to sell, although they do not receive the artistic acclaim of earlier efforts. Their current portraits show some graying hair and lined faces, but these rock and roll dinosaurs still crank out that gritty, emotional, arrogant, Black-rooted music that brought them to the dance in the first place.

*　　*　　*

Whereas the early Beatles attracted a spectrum of fans entranced by their safely rebellious mixture of classic rock elements, the Stones initially appealed to Black music fans and those who were titillated by aggressive, crude, and sexual behavior. The music throbbed, pushed by the emphasized quarter-note pulse of Watts and Wyman. Mick replicated many stylistic attributes of contemporary Black music, illustrated by his choice of blues and R&B material; the slurred pronunciation and emotive, sliding growl of his vocals; and his onstage sexuality and physicality. And Keith kept up a barrage of sparse, bent-note licks and classic rock/blues-derived phrases.

In the midsixties the Stones, like many contemporaries, tempered these early stylistic elements with musical experimentation and an expanded worldview. Brian Jones added the coloration of nontraditional rock instruments and songwriters Jagger-Richards composed airy ballads filled with orchestration to complement their sensual, driving rockers. As the band matured, their adolescent sexual orientation broadened to include introspection and societal examination.

These trends of musical expansion and intellectual growth burst forth in the late 1960s and early 1970s—the "golden era" of the Stones.

As the sexual revolution of the sixties spread, and talking about and participating casually in sex became more acceptable, the Stones were able to move closer to the cultural mainstream. An undulating Jagger, now stripped to the waist, was no longer a pariah, but an androgynous visage tempting the masses with tangible delights. Satisfaction was now in, as Madison Avenue reinforced the notion of immediate sexual gratification. The addition of an intellectual level to the band's lyrics also moved the band nearer to the center. Even the Stones were listening to the words, attempting to communicate stories ("Jumping Jack Flash"), ideas ("Gimme Shelter"), or personal feelings ("Wild Horses").

During this golden era, the Stones matured as musicians, arrangers, and lyricists, creating multilevel works that rank as some of the period's best. Even with the critical raves over the more fully developed material, they were unwilling to abandon the sexuality, raw creativity, and aura of danger that had carried them this far. For each new accessible "Honky Tonk Woman" (#1, June 1969), there was a sinister and controversial "Sympathy for the Devil." They sold themselves as the bad boys of rock. Long after they ceased to evolve in any significant musical or lyrical fashion, or to create a meaningful amount of quality material, younger generations treat the Stones as pretenders to the title. The Rolling Stones—who created the most artistically ingenious and commercially successful white fusion of blues and R&B-rooted rock and roll in pop history—continue into the nineties, assured that, although it's only rock and roll, we'll like it.

# 9· The Who:
## People Try to Put Us Down

*Basically . . . [guitar smashing is] a gesture which happens at the spur of the moment. I think with guitar smashing, just like performance itself, it's a performance, it's an act, it's an instant. And it really is meaningless.*

**Pete Townshend, 1968, quoted in Rolling Stone**

*What was important at the time [Tommy], and continues to be important, is that the human individual accepts the fact that he or she is capable of being spiritually swayed. And in order to make the best of that, they really have to listen to what's being said.*

**Pete Townshend, in a 1987 interview**

*Adolescent Townshend smashed his guitar and his teenage fans cheered. Young adult Townshend dabbled in drugs and Eastern religion and his college age fans grooved along. But as he approached his thirties, Townshend publicly became torn between writing to create songs about the difficulties of adulthood—marriage, being a parent, shaky health, fear of growing old, and the silence of God—and the demands of a youthful rock audience for loud, raunchy celebration.*

**Rock journalist Bill Flanagan, 1986**

P ICTURE LEAD SINGER Roger Daltrey, resembling a perpetual-motion machine, commandeering the stage for a two-hour athletic romp. Guitarist Pete Townshend swings his right arm in a gigantic windmill motion, striking his guitar to produce loud, crashing, ringing power chords that saturate the hall. Sometimes these blasts are accompanied by agile leaps as Townshend vaults across the stage. Drummer Keith Moon frantically thrashes at his drum kit, occasionally launching one of his drumsticks off a drumhead and toward the audience. This whirlwind surrounds bassist John Entwistle, who stands as if anchored to the stage, motionless except for the blur of finger attack on the bass fretboard.

This hypothetical set climaxes with the song "My Generation." After an extended solo, Townshend raises his guitar above his head and smashes it to pieces against the stage, jamming the remaining skeleton through the protective grill-cloth and into his speaker cabinet. Squealing, tortured feedback wails from the speakers, sounding the instrument's death rattle. Daltrey swings his microphone by its cord in an ever-increasing arc until it too smashes into the stage. Moon's bass drum has been set with a small charge of smoke-producing explosive and it erupts as he kicks it off the raised drum podium onto the stage. Standing behind his kit, Moon laughs maniacally at the smoldering pyre. Finally, Entwistle's throbbing bass ceases and the Who straggle offstage, just another day in the life.

The Who have always been considered one of the most energetic and entertaining live bands in rock/pop music history. Even when compared to 1970s hard rock performances, with their displays of athletic prowess, explosive charges, and frantic energy, the Who hold their own. At the same time, the Beatles bobbed their heads and the Rolling Stones sold sex and spectacle. But the incredible power of the Who's live performances has overshadowed the extraordinarily thoughtful and musically interesting material that songwriter-guitarist Pete Townshend composed during the Who's twenty-five-year existence. Of the three major British invasion groups—the Beatles and Stones being the other two—the Who most directly and thoughtfully confronted the philosophical and political issues of the day. To Townshend, good rock music reflected important societal concerns and was a powerful vehicle for ideas.

Of the major British invasion groups, the Who were initially the most musically competent. They developed and used the power trio format (using only one guitar, drums, and bass) long before Cream, the Jimi Hendrix Experience, and Led Zeppelin made it popular. Their definitions of the instruments' respective functions were different than traditional classic rock definitions—typified by the rhythm guitar, lead guitar, bass, and drums used by the Beatles and Stones. The Who's relatively complex harmonic structure, regular use of three-part vocal harmonies, and development of the "rock opera" format were innovative and sometimes overlooked.

In addition to the quality of the contributions, they also had a significant impact on subsequent rock generations. The rebellious fury of their 1965 teen anthem "My Generation" sowed the seeds of two major musical forms that sprouted later in the seventies, hard rock and punk. Townshend's power-chording, Moon's active drumming style, Daltrey's aggressive lead vocalist image, and the band's volume and overall stageshow were all precursors to hard rock; punk roots are visible in the music's frantic driving pulse and its reactive get-out-of my-face sentiment. Thus the Who, known primarily for energy and opera, made many important contributions.

The Who's story is not unlike our previous tales. Roger, Pete, and John grew up in the Shepherd's Bush district of London and went to the same grammar school. Roger was, in many ways, similar to John Lennon. He was rebellious, dressed as a teddy boy, formed a musical group with friends, and had a reputation in school. For the aggressive five-foot five Daltrey, prone to settling disputes with his fists, his band, the Detours, was seen as a way out of Shepherd's Bush. Pete and John were best mates. They went through school together, one grade behind Roger, and started their own first band, the Confederates. After playing in a series of rock and trad-jazz bands, both eventually joined forces with Roger in the Detours.

Initially, Pete's mom, Betty, acted as their booking agent and van driver. Rounding out the band were drummer Doug Sandom (ten years older than the rest) and a series of lead singers (as Roger then played lead, with Pete on rhythm guitar). During these years their repertoire included classic rock, country and western, traditional jazz, and current English pop by bands such as the Shadows and the Beatles.

The Detours, like the early Stones, was a group comprising well-trained as well as untrained musicians. John's parents were musicians, and as a youth he learned piano and trumpet, played in an orchestra, and studied jazz. His initial interest in rock and roll was as a lead guitarist, but John's primal urges led him to bass (bass being a fundamental part of the rhythm in rock). In addition to lead guitar, Roger played some trombone before switching to vocals. Pete's dad played the clarinet, and Pete learned the banjo, playing in jazz bands. Townshend's shift to guitar was motivated by the instrument's growing popularity and by his insecurity about his appearance. In Pete's mind, his large nose dominated his features, and attention focused on power chords and leaps shifted the spotlight away from the guitarist's facial features.

Much like McCartney and Hendrix, both of whom compensated for the loss of their respective mothers with a single-minded pursuit of music, Townshend used music as a retreat from his self-perceived physical handicap. Keith Moon was another who possessed innate musical talent; he learned trumpet and started drums by age fourteen. His idols were big band drummers Gene Krupa and Buddy Rich and Hollywood session player Hal Blaine, the man who played on many of the early surf music hits. Dave Marsh, in his creditable Who biography, *Before I Get Old*, notes that Moon not only tried to emulate their technique, power, and flamboyance— Krupa's twirling drumsticks, for example—but also copied their large drum sets, which at times included double kickdrums.

But musical training wasn't the only formal education that helped the Detours. In 1961 Pete started studies at Ealing Art College; this turned out to have a major impact on the Who. Many rockers found in art school a stimulating refuge from the sometimes dead-end English educational system. Challenged by a new generation of art educators, Pete was impelled to think about how and why people create and about what forms creations might take. When Pete began to smash his guitar, Gustav Metzker's lectures on "auto-destructive" art offered a fitting rationale.

While attending Ealing Pete entered a social circle that introduced him to the blues, rhythm and blues, modern jazz, and marijuana. (Also attending Ealing were future band biographer Richard Barnes, future Small Faces and Stones guitarist Ron Wood, and budding Queen vocalist Freddie Mercury.) Soon the Detours were incorporating Black American roots music into their show and by 1963 were popular enough to play on the same bill with the Rolling Stones,

Manchester's Hollies, and Liverpool's Searchers. One day, however, they spotted a band on national TV that was also calling itself the Detours. The final choice for the band's new name was between the Hair and the Who; they chose the latter.

Pete Meaden, an intense, fast-talking, pill-popping publicist who had just left Oldham's Stones organization, sought a band that he felt could represent the growing Mod subculture. He changed the band's hair, clothing, demeanor, and name. Meaden preferred the High Numbers, a term combining allusions to the "high" induced by the Mod penchant for amphetamines with a popular Mod t-shirt that was emblazoned with numerals.

With the addition of drummer Moon to the lineup in the summer of 1964, the intensity of the band's music soared. In an incident resembling Pete Best's departure from the Beatles, the Who (not yet the High Numbers) auditioned for Fontana Records. The A&R man suggested the band might benefit from a different drummer. Doug Sandom, who was not enjoying the new focus on blues, opted to leave the band. According to rock mythology, a slightly drunk Keith Moon auditioned for the band by performing a bashing rendition of "Road Runner" and then breaking the temporary drummer's kickdrum pedal and hi-hat.

This story omits the fact that Moon had been following the Detours, knew their music well, and had come to the pub for the sole purpose of making the lineup. After the audition Moon returned to his drink, steeling himself for anticipated retribution over the damage to the drum set. Instead, the band offered to pick him up on Monday for a gig. Years later, Keith would contend that he was never formally asked to join the Who but was only asked, "What are you doing on Monday?"[1]

Moon joined a band in transition. The High Numbers bought vented jackets and button-down shirts on Carnaby Street, played at the hip Mod Scene Club, and recorded the Meadon blues clone "I'm the Face/Zoot Suit" on Fontana Records (released in July 1964). Pete and Keith followed Meaden into the speed-laced Mod world of amphetamine abuse, becoming more combative in a band that already had its share of verbal and physical conflict. Roger and Pete vied for supremacy; Roger could win with his fists, but Pete had a sharp and brutal tongue. John had seen his straightforward drummer traded in and was not sure he relished the idea of playing with a maniac. "The wiry, high strung and anxious nature induced by taking pills made them touchy," states biographer Barnes. "Anything could spark them off and usually did." Pete would later comment "We were four 'orrible unpleasant little bastards."[2]

In late 1964 the High Numbers were working steadily, touring and playing clubs six and seven nights per week. Still, their record wasn't being promoted by the label and wasn't selling. One evening movie producer Kit Lambert caught their act. Lambert and partner Chris Stamp were searching for a rock and roll band for a movie; after catching the act live they were convinced to forget the movie and manage the act. Meaden had no legal hold, so the band, attracted by Lambert's upper-class demeanor and industry connections, jumped ship. The High Numbers toured that summer with such notables as Tom Jones, the Kinks, and the Beatles and then dropped the name, reverting back to the Who.

Different managers offer different areas of expertise to their bands. Epstein contributed style and organization to the Beatles, and Oldham was an image-maker for the Stones. Lambert, whose father was well known in British music circles, became mentor and confidant to Pete. Although not a trained musician, Lambert provided encouragement and critical thinking when Pete was just beginning his songwriting career. It was Lambert who would later suggest that Townshend string works together into lengthier pieces (he even helped with the libretto for Tommy). In late 1964, however, management's job was to keep the Who working and secure another recording contract. Chris Stamp went back to work on the set of the film *Heroes of Tellemark* in Norway just to pay the bills.

The band survived on gigs such as their weekly dates at the Railway Tavern. One night, during the set, Pete accidentally bumped the neck of his guitar on the ceiling. He recalls that "it broke and it kinda shocked me cause I wasn't ready for it to go. . . . I was expecting everybody to go 'Wow, he's broken his guitar,' but nobody did anything which made me kind of angry in a way and determined to get this precious event noticed by the audience. I proceeded to make a big thing out of breaking the guitar. I pounded all over the stage with it and I threw the bits on the stage."[3] The next week fans arrived expecting another guitar-smashing spectacle. Pete declined, but "Moonie" obliged, capping off the evening by beating up his drums.

Smashing instruments produced consequences. For one, it was costly; Lambert urged Pete to do it only on special occasions. (In fact, the penchant for trashing equipment kept the band in the red for a number of years.) It also created audience expectations as well as a stir in the entertainment community. To some, the Who's destructive finale became the hit song the band was expected to play every show. Some fans experienced a vicarious thrill, the symbolic act of rage and rebellion carried out by their surrogates on stage. According to Moon, they destroyed things because they were just "pissed off."[4]

The next logical step for the Who was to seal a recording contract. EMI passed, citing the lack of original material. So Townshend, with Lambert's encouragement, pursued this challenge with a vengeance; songwriting became his passion. It turned out that Kinks producer Shel Talmy was so entranced by a demo of Townshend original "I Can't Explain" that he signed the Who to a contract and scheduled a recording session. When Talmy insisted on using his trusted studio guitarist, future Led Zeppelin legend Jimmy Page, Townshend balked and played the lead solo. Page churned out the choppy Kinks-style rhythm-guitar chords. "I Can't Explain" sold over 100,000 copies, peaked at #8 (U.K.), and earned the band nationwide TV appearances. Guitar feedback characterized their follow-up, "Anyway, Anywhere, Anyhow," in an attempt to simulate and capture the live Who on record. It was adopted as a theme song for pop-music TV show "Ready, Steady, Go" but reached only #10 (U.K.) on the charts.

Despite its mounting success, the band was embroiled in turmoil. They were torn apart by conflicts over lifestyle, leadership, and creative differences. Pete, Keith, and even John were dedicated to life in the fast lane, fueled by amphetamines and alcohol and, in Pete's case, marijuana and hashish. Each night, when the supercharged band hit the stage, sparks flew and anything could happen, and it often did. Thus it is not surprising that the Who's live show was described as pure energy and that the mixture of drugs, adrenaline, loud music, and a rebellious psyche produced a climax of destruction.

Roger and Pete were also locked in battle over band leadership, a task for which neither was naturally suited. Both were argumentative, especially toward one another, and neither Roger's fists nor Pete's tongue helped in leading the band or mediating disputes. Finally, in Denmark, Roger, who was furious at Keith's constant partying and inconsistent playing, dumped out a box of pills. When Keith protested, Roger knocked him out. Ejected from the band, Daltrey—who wasn't considered to be a very good lead vocalist at the time—found himself staring at a future as a sheetmetal worker. Making an about-face, Roger promised to exchange his combative personality for that of a peaceful team player. This solution gave Pete creative carte blanche and challenged Roger with the role of interpreting Townshend's material.

His first chance came with "My Generation." In retrospect this song is a successor to Chuck Berry's "School Days"—a musical and lyrical adolescent anthem. In the fifties Berry criticized his era's mores by favoring romance and rock; Townshend's sixties were a time of more forthright rebellion. So to *his* older generation, Pete cries "People try to put us down/ Just because we get around." And also, "Why don't you all f-f-f-f-fade away/ Don't try and dig what we all say." Townshend would later comment that "'My Generation' was very much about trying to find a place in society. I was very, very lost."[5]

Musically, the Who attack the song—guitar and bass pound out a quarter-note pulse, Roger shouts the lyrics, and Keith rides a percussive roller coaster of fills and cymbal crashes. Halfway through the song, the listener is treated to a unique guitar-bass call-and-response solo. The finale degenerates into drummed frenzy and feedback-filled guitar barrages. Thus "My Generation" is hard rock before its time. But Townshend's 1970 description of the song's effect also anticipated punk rock: "It repulsed those it was supposed to repulse, and it drew a very thick line between the people that dug it and the people that wouldn't dig it."[6] Some certainly didn't dig the song's retort "Hope I die before I get old."

Released in late 1965, "My Generation" quickly rose to #3 on the British charts but barely even placed in the United States (#74). Yet it was a definitive moment for rock and roll. The Who were laying the groundwork for the two important musical streams of the 1970s, hard rock and punk, in a single, driving, chaotic song—through the power trio, screaming singer, and distorted, pounding guitar on the one hand, and in-your-face lyrics and brash, thrashing music on the other. It was no wonder that Moon and Entwistle nearly quit and formed a band with Jimmy Page in 1966 or that, in 1977, Paul Cook and Steve Jones of the Sex Pistols were to praise the Who as one of their favorite bands.

During the years 1966 and 1967 the band consolidated its popularity in England with its auto-destruct live shows and a series of top-10 British singles:

"Substitute" (#5), "I'm a Boy" (#2), "Happy Jack" (#3), "Pictures of Lilly" (#4), and "I Can See for Miles" (#10). During this time there was a distinct stylistic shift in Townshend's writing. Whereas "I Can't Explain" and other early tunes had musical and lyrical similarities to the early Beatles and other period hits, Pete was now electing to craft compositions in accordance with the emerging trend toward musical complexity and deeper lyrical meanings.

"I Can See for Miles," the Who's only American top-10 hit (#9, September 1967), lyrically addresses romance (in this case, retribution), but musically it functions on a different level. The song offers a brilliant example of the power trio cruising on all cylinders. Moon is in delightful synchronization with Townshend's power-chording during the verse as he provides the section with brash but tasteful dynamic coloration on his cymbals and tom-toms. A sustained E note by the guitar—the song is in E-major—rides on top of the chorus as the voices and chords change underneath from the tonic I to bVII, IV, VI, IV, and back to the I.

Certainly powerful but also musically interesting, "Miles" was part of a conceptual expansion that included the EP *A Quick One While He's Away* and the pop-art album *The Who Sell Out*. With songs tied together by original commercial jingles and on-air material from pirate radio station Radio London, *Sell Out* featured "I Can See For Miles" and an inside jacket adorned by advertising photos of each band member. (In fact Roger contracted pneumonia from the shooting, having been submerged in a tub of baked beans.)

In 1967 the Who, frustrated by their inability to crack the American market, finally made a number of major concert appearances in the United States. They were on the bill at Murray the K's Easter Show in New York City along with Cream, the Blues Project, Wilson Pickett, and Mitch Ryder and the Detroit Wheels. During eleven destructive Easter shows the band totaled twenty-two microphones, five guitars, four speaker cabinets, and one sixteen-piece drum kit.

In June the Who appeared at the Monterey International Pop Festival, rock's first megaconcert (see Chapter 14 for a more detailed account). The group opened a monumental closing-night set, followed by the Grateful Dead, Jimi Hendrix, and the Mamas and the Papas. The Who completed their show with their usual demolition; Hendrix, who had resided in England for a year and felt quite competitive, not only smashed his guitar but burned it as well. As relative unknowns in America, the Who gained notoriety with this appearance and toured with countrymen Herman's Hermits—a classic mismatch, but not as bad as the one pairing Jimi Hendrix with top-40 idols the Monkees.

Later in the year the Who toured America once again and also appeared on CBS's "The Smothers Brothers Comedy Hour." Richard Barnes describes the havoc caused by what Pete terms "the destruction bit": Moon, who was drunk on brandy, "secretly added extra flash powder to the special effects. The explosion at the end of 'My Generation' was enormous. Pete temporarily lost his hearing and singed his hair, a fragment of flying cymbal embedded itself in Keith's leg, and show guest [movie star] Bette Davis fainted into Mickey Rooney's arms." In Michigan Moon celebrated his alleged twenty-first birthday (really only his twentieth) by trashing rooms in the local Holiday Inn. While being chased by the authorities he filled all available cars with fire-extinguisher foam and then leaped into an empty swimming pool.

Experimentation with legal, recreational, and psychoactive drugs fueled the frantic nature that characterized the band's work. Use of alcohol and speed kept some members intemperate and overly aggressive. Townshend and Moon also ingested LSD and other psychedelics. Like the Beatles, Pete was also entranced by the teachings of an Eastern mystic, in this case Meher Baba—a man who wrote prolifically but who had not spoken in forty years. In 1968 Townshend reduced his drug intake and began to follow Baba's life philosophy. He would later say, "I think at the end of the day all religions are based on finding a reason why people should act in a caring, compassionate and humanitarian way. But, most of all, that they should act."

Reflective of this message of individual moral responsibility, Townshend set about to write rock and roll that was in some way illuminating to audiences. With the assistance and encouragement of manager Kit Lambert, he sketched out a storyline that worked in both the symbolic and real worlds. Townshend explained: "The thing is, we wanted it to work on lots of levels. . . . We want to turn on the spiritually hip, we want to turn on the fuckers and the street fighters. . . . We want to turn on the opera lovers and we succeeded in turning on a lot of people that weren't reached before."[7]

Early titles for this project included *Amazing Journey* and *Brain Opera* before settling on *Tommy,* after the central character. The fact that an actual story was being told through song, without accompanying narrative, was then unique in rock music and most closely resembled the opera form. This story, or libretto, begins with young Tommy witnessing his father's death at the hands of his mother's lover—the father, having been thought dead, returns years after the war. Tommy is traumatized and becomes deaf, mute, and blind. Tommy's mother attempts to find a cure for her son, after which he is administered LSD by the Acid Queen; eventually he is miraculously cured after smashing the mirror into which he has been looking.

While in his sense-deprived state Tommy becomes famous for excelling on pinball machines. And even though Tommy is finally cured, his Uncle Ernie still tries to merchandise the boy's achievements, at summer camps. Once Tommy's normalcy and the fraud of his returned senses are revealed, the campers (representing the public) revolt, and Tommy is left alone, pleading for compassion.

On a symbolic level Tommy represented a person who through suffering achieved a God-realized state, without senses yet in tune with the cosmic pulse of all life that surrounds us—in this case represented by electromagnetic impulses of the pinball machine. When the commercialized Tommy and his gifts—rock and roll, spiritual enlightenment, furtherance of humanity—are revealed to have been sold on a fraudulent basis, humanity revolts. Don't sell us false prophets! they cry. "We're not gonna take it!" A rejected Tommy cries "See me, hear me," still capable of offering spiritual enlightenment.

In his masterwork Pete, following the tenets of Meher Baba, attempts to engage important issues surrounding the search for morality: "It [that era of pop music] was its strong connection with the roots of spiritual theosophy and the language that rang with it—the idea that pop music was about spiritual uplift, human potential, solidarity, unification."[8] The response to Tommy was near-universal acclaim. Mainstream British magazine *Melody Maker* named it LP of the Year; Albert Goldman in the *New York Times* called it a "work of innovative power and philosophical profundity." It rose to #7 in the United States after its summer release in 1969 and reascended to #4 one year later.

The Who finally made it, achieving the kind of critical and commercial success that eluded them for so long. No longer relegated to the role of auto-destruct kings, the band took their place at the head of the creative/artistic class. Townshend received accolades as a composer and songwriter, Daltrey's stature as a rock vocalist and song interpreter was at its zenith, and the rest of rock and roll finally caught up with rhythm-section pioneers Entwistle and Moon. Hard rockers looked to the Who as a prototype. And, as if to thumb their noses at the music aristocracy, the Who arranged for a *Tommy* tour of opera houses in Europe, ending with two shows at New York's prestigious Lincoln Center.

The Who's appearance at Woodstock in August 1969 was filled with brilliant images, but it was in fact a personal nightmare for the band. The golden-maned Daltrey wowed 'em, resplendent in his white-fringed leather and bathed in blue-white light; Townshend windmilled his guitar; Moon and Entwistle drove the runaway train. However, they waited all night and had been dosed with LSD and had to follow an explosive set by Sly and the Family Stone at 3:30 AM. Said Pete of the experience: "Woodstock wasn't what rock was all about. . . . *Tommy* wasn't getting to anyone. Sly and the Family Stone had just whipped everyone into a frenzy and then kind of walked off."[9] After a long medley of *Tommy* songs, the exhausted bandmates performed a lengthy regular set that included the "My Generation" climax. During this set, an irritated and disoriented Pete swatted Yippie activist Abbie Hoffman into photographers' row—the penalty for hijacking one of the Who's microphones—during the set—to harangue the crowd with a political speech.

Many artists, having paid their dues and subsequently achieved high critical acclaim and commercial success, would dance the so-called dinosaur dance, content to rest on aging laurels. Pete Townshend paused for a moment and then began work on another major undertaking, a science-fiction film project entitled *Lifehouse*. The major character, Bobby, another God-realized guru, leads a small band of freethinkers against the totalitarian rulers of the land. Bobby's faith consists of a kind of biorhythmic, transcendental mythology. Each follower, in touch with individual biorhythms and concomitant notes or sounds, would, at nirvana's gate, dance themselves into a whirling-dervish state—to the strains of the guru's band.

However, the forces of control find the location of worship and break down the energy barriers protecting the church. They shoot Bobby, but before he dies the congregation achieves an ecstatic state, the mythological lost chord is sounded, and they are all transformed into the innocence as if in a Garden of Eden. Pete wrote the songs for this project and set about writing a screen treatment to sell to film studios anxious to capitalize on the Who's previous success. In the end none was willing to risk the investment necessary for a contract and Pete eventually found himself in a state of nervous exhaustion.

With their record company clamoring for a follow-up to *Tommy* and a release of live material, the Who recorded 240 hours of shows on their American tour. Nobody had the patience to cull the acceptable cuts, so the band booked a university concert in Leeds, England. Pete recalls, "We got a Pye 8-track and we said take it to Leeds, and we went to Leeds and it just happened to be like one of the greatest audiences we ever played to in our whole career."[10] Released in May 1970, *Live at Leeds* includes cover favorites "Summertime Blues" by Eddie Cochran and Mose Allison's "Young Man Blues"; it also contains extended renditions of "My Generation" and "Magic Bus." Not only did it showcase the vibrancy and vitality of their live act, but it also showcased Pete's talents as both a rhythm and lead guitarist functioning within the structure of a power trio.

*Lifehouse* was simply not to be and the task of compiling the band's next studio album fell to acclaimed producer and engineer Glyn Johns. He assembled four *Lifehouse* songs along with three other Townshend cuts and Entwistle's "My Wife." The result album, the critically acclaimed *Who's Next*, was released in the summer of 1971. The *Lifehouse* cuts exhibit compositional brilliance, pioneering use of the synthesizer in rock music, and further synchronicity in play among the band members.

The first song, "Baba O'Reilly," named for Meher Baba and electronic music composer Terry Reilly, would have opened *Lifehouse*. The ARP-2600 synthesizer was programmed with approximations of physiological attributes of Meher Baba and thus the repetitive phrases at the beginning reflect the story's interest with an individual's sonic representation. At one point in the song, Townshend describes the future (and perhaps current) environment as a "teenage wasteland." The acoustic opening of "Behind Blue Eyes" is a form that parallels the Led Zeppelin mega-hit, "Stairway to Heaven," released the same year. Daltrey's plaintive opening is followed by Moon's explosive entrance at midsong in a number that attempts to engender sympathy for the leader of the oppressive forces.

"Won't Get Fooled Again" uses another repetitive underlay from the synthesizer to set off the explosive ensemble. As they are in "I Can See for Miles," Townshend and Moon are marvelous at creating a broad and rhythmic dynamic range by their synchronized playing. Entwistle adds bass slides to the mix during the chorus. The lyrics leave plenty of room for interpretation. If one neglects the verses, the song can easily be seen as "We're not gonna take it" redux. Paradoxically, the verses actually discourage political interest or activism by suggesting that any change in leadership will produce new leaders just as bad as the old.

Townshend recanted in 1987, telling an interviewer, "It was dumb to deny the political role of the individual. The political responsibility of the individual. . . . It was an irresponsible song. It was quite clear that during that period that rock musicians had the ear of the people."[11] "The Song Is Over" rounded out the four *Lifehouse* cuts. The *Who's Next* cover was graced by their own science-fiction obelisk, in the process of being adorned by band members, who appear to be peeing on it.

The band's early greatest-hits package, *Meaty, Beaty, Big and Bouncy,* kept fans busy while Pete worked on his third parable, *Quadrophenia.* Centered around Jimmy, another hero, it chronicles the Mod experience in midsixties England and features a frustrated, inarticulate, confused, and violent young man who feels betrayed by all elements in his life. Townshend had always felt that rock, at its essence, was "the music of the frustrated and dissatisfied" and that the Mod subculture represented its purest, working-class audience.

The Mod was represented by four distinct personality characteristics, each with a theme song that also represented characteristics of a member of the band. Roger was the tough guy/"Helpless Dancer"; John the romantic/"Doctor Jimmy"; Keith the lunatic/"Bell Boy"; and Pete the philosopher/"Love Reign O'er Me." Feeling discouraged and disillusioned, our hero Jimmy returns to the Brighton coast, the scene of past glories from the gang fights between Mods and Rockers. During this return he spies the Ace Face, the former general of the Mod troops, working as a hotel bellboy. In the final scene Jimmy clings to a rock in the coastal surf in a final reevaluation of life's meaning.

Townshend called *Quadrophenia* "a study in spiritual desperation. The fact that all desperation and frustration leads somebody to the point where the first time in their life they realize that the only important thing is to open their heart. It wasn't about blood and guts the way that the film turned out to be." The album represented the highest chart success for the band, peaking at #2 in November 1973. The film version, released six years later, didn't garner the same acclaim, in part due to the distinctly British experience of the Mod subculture.

In 1978 the Who released *Who Are You,* which questioned the relevance of rock dinosaurs in the era of punk and metal creativity and the seemingly simultaneous death of Keith Moon, who died from an overdose of pills. Into the nineties Townshend continues to write and release solo projects, and the surviving bandmates periodically go on tour.

As one of rock's most accomplished and dedicated composers, Townshend continues to address issues he considers important: "[What] continues to be important is that the human individual accepts the fact that he or she is capable of being spiritually swayed. And in order to make the best of that, they really have to listen to what's being said."[12] Although he considers the music business to be "financially, spiritually and morally corrupt," Pete believes that rock still is a "key" to freeing the person to be themselves.[13]

*　　　*　　　*

Having played in the shadows of other British invasion groups during the mid-sixties, the Who began to receive the recognition they deserved at the time of Woodstock. Musically, and in their live-performance style, they pioneered the hard rock form. Because of their musical aptitude, talent, and social proclivities, they redefined instrumentalist roles and functions, creating a daring and more sophisticated rock. Drums became more than timekeeper, the bass more than harmonic and rhythmic foundation, and guitar became both lead and rhythm.

As rock composer Townshend is one of the best. He wrote alone, not as a part of a team like Lennon-McCartney or Jagger-Richards. And he wrote about the broadest scope of topics, whether it be through in-your-face rock and roll or thoughtful, philosophical, and sophisticated commentary on the human condition. What's more, this was accomplished as audiences and critics focused on the high-volume, high-energy, destructive bombast of their live shows. Rarely does one band successfully combine such essential rock elements with such complex and sophisticated musical and lyrical components.

In Chapter 10 we will return to the United States to chronicle the folk revival of the early 1960s, the emergence of Bob Dylan as a singer-songwriter, and the genre's response to the rock and roll success of the British invasion.

# 10· Bob Dylan: Somethin' Is Happening, but You Don't Know What It Is

*The poet makes himself a seer by a long, prodigious, rational disordering of the senses.*

*Rimbaud*

*I'm just one person, doing what I do. Trying to get along . . . staying out of people's hair.*

**Bob Dylan, 1969, in a** Rolling Stone *interview*

*The point is that Dylan's songs can serve as metaphors, enriching our lives, giving us random insight into the myths we carry and the present we live in, intensifying what we've known and leading us towards what we never looked for, while at the same time enforcing an emotional strength upon those perceptions by the power of the music that moves with his words.*

**Rolling Stone** *magazine, 1970*

---

Bob Dylan, an itinerant nineteen-year-old folksinger, wandered through the streets of New York's Greenwich Village one cold day in December 1960. Recently arrived from Minnesota, he was on a pilgrimage to the bedside of his idol, American folk hero Woody Guthrie. Within a few years this scruffy, curly-haired Midwesterner would turn the folk community, and later the rock and roll world, upside down. For now, he was just another kid come to see Woody Guthrie.

## Digression: The American Protest Song Tradition

Folk music has always been an important part of the American music tradition, and topical songs—personal stories linked to current political and cultural events—are an essential part of that heritage. Supporters of the American Revolution sang songs in praise of their heroes; Jeffersonian Democrats issued a scathing attack on the Federalist Party with the tune "Jefferson and Liberty"; abolitionists railed against slavery and both sides—Union and Confederate—created sad songs of a country ravaged by the Civil War.

The twentieth century, with the growth of the trade-union movement, saw a shift in the nature of topical songs. Many songs focused on events rather than the more personalized stories of earlier eras. International Workers of the World (IWW) union organizer Joe Hill took a song about train engineer Casey Jones and made it into a pro-union protest song about Casey Jones the strikebreaker.

The depression and the concurrent expansion of union organizing efforts became topics for songs dealing with injustice and inequality in American society. Woody Guthrie, a boy from Oklahoma whose family was decimated by tragedy, saw dust storms destroy the land and banks evict his neighbors. Guthrie became convinced that only if the common people banded together, via unions and other associations, could they successfully fight for their rights.

Woody had a talent for attaching topical lyrics to traditional folk and religious melodies. In a country where most resources were in the hands of a rich few, Guthrie pointed out that "This Land Is Your Land," or that it could be, should you choose to struggle for it. His "Pastures of Plenty" and "Deportees" painted poignant portraits of migrant farm laborers. Among his 1,400 songs were the Dust Bowl Ballads, as well as songs about the Northwest's Bonneville Power Authority (including "Roll On, Columbia"), humorous children's songs, "hard-travelin'" ballads, and numerous union songs (including "Union Maid").

Although Guthrie would point out that he was just one guy singing about life as he saw it, others found him a figure of heroic stature. Woody crisscrossed America, a hobo riding the rails or thumbing a ride on the nation's highways. He turned his back on fame and commercial success, opting instead to perform in union halls and on strike picket lines. Acting on these beliefs earned him more than a few bruises. But Guthrie's persistent idealism, coupled with a talent for reflecting the attitudes and hopes of working-class America with simple, direct songs, established him as a poet-prophet of the era.

After World War II Guthrie began to experience the first symptoms of Huntington's Chorea, the degenerative nerve disease to which he would ultimately succumb in 1967. Groups like the Almanac Singers (of which Guthrie was a member) and the Weavers carried on the topical song tradition. Pete Seeger, the son of musicologist Charles Seeger, left Harvard, collected folk songs in the South, learned to play the banjo, and traveled with Woody before the war. With Lee Hays, Ronnie Gilbert, and Fred Hellerman, Seeger formed the Weavers, a folk group dedicated to preserving the political-activist protest song tradition. The Weavers also added a spectrum of international folk songs to their repertoire.

Discovered by Decca arranger and bandleader Gordon Jenkins, the Weavers reached #1 on the pop charts with their version of blues singer Leadbelly's "Goodnight Irene." The Hebrew folk song on the flip side, "Tzena, Tzena, Tzena," reached #2. They appeared on television, had further hits, and toured clubs and concert halls nationwide. As the Cold War and the McCarthy era's Red Scare hysteria reached its peak, an important and meaningful pop music career was destroyed by accusations of left-wing leanings. Apparently, a repertoire containing international folk songs, Negro spirituals, and pro-union broadsides was considered too subversive for the guardians of American morality. The Weavers were relegated to playing union halls, civil rights and peace benefits, and college concerts.

By the late 1950s the popularity of the Weavers was again on the rise and a new era in folk music was beginning. Seeger left the group, hounded by right-wing patriots such as the House Un-American Activities Committee (HUAC), and pursued a successful solo career. He achieved commercial success in spite of his politics, recording for Columbia Records and releasing albums that included the songs "We Shall Overcome," "Turn, Turn, Turn," and the Cuban patriotic anthem "Guantanamera."

Smooth-sounding button-down folk groups, inspired by the Weavers legacy and Seeger's banjo playing, performed on college campuses and had popular chart successes. The Kingston Trio reached #1 with the folk ballad "Tom Dooley" and had a hit with Seeger's "Where Have All the Flowers Gone." The Highwaymen, with a lineup of Connecticut college students, had a #1 with Weavers original "Michael, Row Your Boat Ashore." Even the Beach Boys recorded the Bahamian folk song "Sloop John B," introduced on record in the United States by the Weavers.

## Back to Greenwich Village

This topical folk song tradition of Woody Guthrie, Pete Seeger, and the Weavers influenced the new generation of folksingers, including Bob Dylan, who were drawn to Greenwich Village in the early sixties. Blues-based singers like Dave Van Ronk mingled with Guthrie cohorts Cisco Huston and Ramblin' Jack Elliot; traditionalists such as Joan Baez; emerging topical balladeers such as Tom Paxton, Phil Ochs, and Bob Gibson and groups like Peter, Paul, and Mary; and bluegrassers the Greenbriar Boys. During that chilly winter day Bob Dylan came to New York to find Woody and stayed, one day to change the face of American popular music.

This story begins in America's heartland, the open-pit iron-ore mining town of Hibbing, in northern Minnesota. Bob's father, Abe Zimmerman, was a partner at Zimmerman Furniture and Electric, on Hibbing's Fifth Avenue. His uncle owned the local movie theater, where Bob swept up popcorn to images of the American dream. Young Robert Zimmerman grew up in the Jewish mercantile middle class of America's Midwest.

Bob was something of a loner, a condition enhanced by the prevailing local attitude toward Jews. He had a few close friends but also spent increasing amounts of time in his room reading, writing poetry, and later composing lyrics to songs. Bob had an early interest in the piano, rejecting lessons and opting instead for the I'll-do-it-myself school of learning. He also picked up the guitar. In 1955 Haley's "Rock Around the Clock" and the music of Little Richard reached northern

Minnesota—not, of course, on Hibbing's WMFG, but at night, from stations in Little Rock, Arkansas and Shreveport, Louisiana.

At the age of fifteen and with images of Brando and Dean in mind, Zimmerman purchased a leather jacket and a Harley-Davidson motorcycle. He formed a rock band, the Teen Chords, with friends, emulating the brash aggressive style of Little Richard on the piano. Like high school bands everywhere, Bob and friends were plagued by the authority's attitude toward rock and roll. At one performance, the vice principal simply pulled the plug, literally. The ensuing loss of face impelled Bob to move away from rock and the piano toward the guitar and folk music.

Bob listened to bluesmen Muddy Waters and Jimmy Reed and classic rockers Elvis Presley and Buddy Holly. Three days before Holly died, Bob was in the front row at Buddy's Duluth, Minnesota, concert. But it was folk music that grabbed his attention most. Zimmerman enrolled in the University of Minnesota, having graduated from high school in 1959 and spent the summer playing music. Bob began to haunt the folk clubs of Minneapolis's bohemian section, Dinkytown, anxious to perform. Here, "Zimmerman" was exchanged for "Dillon." Some cite "Gunsmoke" TV hero Matt Dillon, or even the Hibbing family of the same name, as influences in the name change. Others note his later appetite for the works of Dylan Thomas in explaining Bob's last legal name change, to Dylan in 1962.

In Minneapolis Dylan developed that single-minded pursuit of success that one sees in many of the artists discussed in this work. This zeal was matched by the recently acquired enthusiasm for Woody Guthrie. Introduced to the Guthrie myth through the autobiography *Bound for Glory*, Dylan learned his songs, phrasing, vocal inflections, and guitar style. He telephoned Guthrie in the hospital, telling him that he would be East soon to visit. After a year's apprenticeship in Minneapolis, Dylan began his own guru quest. His subsequent success surprised many of those he left behind—some embittered by the feeling that they had given much more to Dylan than they had received in return.

The Bob Dylan who reached New York was very different from the Robert Zimmerman who had left Hibbing. Dylan had built a fantasy life-history to replace discarded pieces of the real one. Zimmerman transformed himself into Dylan. In one version Dylan had no living parents. In another young Bob had run away from home on numerous occasions, hitchhiking or riding the rails to South Dakota, California, New Mexico . . . wherever. Dylan claimed to have met Woody as early as 1954 while on the run from home.

Bob dove into the burgeoning Village folklife, visiting Woody in the hospital and arriving on the Guthrie family's Queens doorstep, to the delight of young Arlo and dismay of the baby-sitter. Invited to the weekly get-together at an apartment near the hospital, Dylan initially sat quietly at Guthrie's feet as the era's folk cognoscenti swapped tales and tunes. Eventually, Bob got up the nerve to sing his "Tribute to Woody," a song that moved the master to comment, "That boy's got a voice. Maybe he won't make it by his writing, but he sure can sing it."[1]

Dylan was by no means a polished performer at the time. But what he lacked in experience he made up for in enthusiasm, a confidence bordering on arrogance, and a nervous energy that proved contagious to an audience. Oscar Brand, a well-known folksinger, reflects, "I thought Bob was pretty crummy. He was a pale version of Woody. . . . He was like Woody in that he wrote bad and he wrote good. When he wrote good, he was a genius."[2] Noting that success took a year and a half to happen, folksinger Bob Gibson's initial impression was that by contemporary standards Dylan had nothing going. "He couldn't play real good. He couldn't sing real good. . . . But you were drawn back."[3]

Much of the commentary about Dylan the person was also ambivalent. He appeared so vulnerable at times that many performers and supporters took it upon themselves to take care of him. He arrived in the Village unkempt, a folk urchin—reportedly wearing the same hat and jacket for years (they appear on the cover of his first album). In short the folk community put him up, fed him, and took care of him. Some would later feel discarded, no longer needed, no longer cultivated as friends. As Dylan became more popular, he became more aloof and sometimes cruel. During legendary drinking sessions, Dylan would unleash brutal sarcastic attacks, putting down friends and other performers. Some left; others returned for more.

Success comes to different performers in different ways. For Dylan, it began with a laudatory column, about his September 1961 Gerde's Folk City performance, by *New York Times* reviewer Robert Shelton. In it Dylan was touted as a "bright new face in folk music" whose career was going "straight up." The day the Shelton review appeared, Columbia Records A&R genius John Hammond Sr.—the man who had signed Bessie Smith, Billie Holliday, Miles Davis, and Aretha Franklin and would later sign Bruce Springsteen—signed Dylan to a record contract. Hammond had seen Dylan in concert months before, pegged him as a rebel, and decided that he wanted to record the spirit of protest. Dylan embodied that spirit.

The initial album, the self-titled *Bob Dylan*, hints at flashes of future brilliance. Dylan, with guitar and harmonica, sped through traditional blues and folk tunes, offering only two originals. His voice, phrasing, and harmonica style were called unique by some, just plain bad by others. Record sales were minimal, and in the halls of Columbia Records Dylan was being referred to as "Hammond's Folly." But, in the absence of artistically viable rock music, the commercial importance of folk music was growing. Dylan was learning quickly, soon to outdistance the pack.

In the early 1960s Greenwich Village continued as the center of bohemian culture in New York—folk music and jazz were the music of choice, art and literature the common pursuits. Dylan inhaled the atmosphere: Rimbaud and the beat poets, a wide variety of musical and performance innovations by fellow artists, and the nascent political and social upheaval of the sixties. Dylan fell in love with Suze Rotolo, a budding sculptor and artist, and her activities with the civil rights and peace movements exposed him to a variety of new political and literary experiences. She also became everybody's folk sweetheart as she appeared arm-in-arm with Dylan on the cover of his next album, *The Freewheelin' Bob Dylan*. To Suze, Bob's genius was the depth and detail of his vision and his ability to synthesize the information and express it in words.

The May 1963 release of *The Freewheelin' Bob Dylan* unveiled Bob Dylan, poet-prophet, to the world. A new era in politics was reflected in "Masters of War" and "Hard Rain's a-Gonna Fall." Warm reminiscences of "Girl from the North Country" clashed with the first of his acerbic tirades against the real and imagined transgressions of Dylan's lost lovers, "Don't Think Twice, It's Alright." Suze's unwillingness to act as a Dylan appendage, and her subsequent flight from the relationship, would provide the wounded Dylan with an easy target for his bittersweet sarcasm.

The album's first cut, "Blowin' in the Wind," is the rough jewel that reveals Dylan's potential songwriting genius. Dylan uses the poetic devices of allusion, symbol, metaphor, and imagery within an abstract framework of questions about issues of war and peace, justice and injustice. The answers to these questions are "blowin' in the wind." Does that mean they are tangible, surrounding us like the wind? Or that they are amorphous and indistinct like the wind? Dylan frames the questions, challenging listeners to draw their own conclusions. This ability to confront issues of both political and personal consequence in an artistically creative and abstract manner proved to be one of Dylan's major contributions to folk music and, later, rock music.

Dylan's version of the support-system "team" came together at this time. This brilliant and unique performer and songwriter now commanded the services of Albert Grossman, a dedicated, business-minded, and powerful folk music manager. With the addition of the clout offered by Columbia Records and the production talents of Hammond and, later, Tom Wilson, Dylan was poised to rise as high as his artistic growth would merit.

One of Grossman's clients was the folk trio Peter, Paul, and Mary. Already nationally known entertainers with hit records of the Seeger-Hays anthem "If I Had a Hammer" and "Puff the Magic Dragon," their popular version of "Blowin' in the Wind" gave Dylan some overdue national recognition. At the August 1963 civil rights march on Washington, D.C., Dylan sang "Only a Pawn in the Game" and Peter, Paul, and Mary sang "Blowin' in the Wind." Dylan's career also received a significant boost from the queen of traditional folk music, Joan Baez. Mesmerized by Dylan's performances and struck by the understated brilliance and timeliness of his songs, Baez took Dylan on tour, exposing him to her adoring college audiences. He opened her shows, they sang duets, and they eventually became lovers. At the 1963 Newport Folk Festival, the queen introduced the new crown prince to the elite folk audience. When asked in a *New York Daily News* interview in October 1963 about the subject of folk music, Dylan replied, "The times cry for the truth . . . and people want to hear the truth and that's just what they're hearing in good folk music today."

Dylan, who experienced the artistic creativity and political activity of the New York Greenwich Village folk scene firsthand, crafted that vision of the truth throughout his next album, *The Times They Are a-Changin'*. In it Dylan's notion of the inevitability of change proved illuminating for his growing audience, causing converts to hail Dylan as a prophet. Dylan's late-1963 America, as represented in this historic recording, was full of people struggling against the tide of injustice. There are poignant reproductions of true stories: a disconsolate farmer choosing the murder of his family and suicide over the loss of his farm and slow starvation ("The Ballad of Hollis Brown"); the beating death of a Black servant woman by a rich young tobacco baron ("The Lonesome Death of Hattie Caroll"); "One Too Many Mornings" and "Boots of Spanish Leather" find the weary lover at the end of a relationship; civil rights leader Medgar Evers's assassin appeared as "Only a Pawn in the Game," the larger game being racism and oppression. The title cut ties these vignettes together in a prophetic vision regarding the inevitability of change and the resultant turmoil should the powerful of the United States continue to resist democratic change. He calls upon politicians, journalists, and critics to become part of, instead of obstruction to, this new wave of human rights activism. Finally, Dylan calls on parents to refrain from criticizing their children and to get out of the way if they can't lend a hand.

The civil rights movement rejoiced at this poetic expression of imminent change. Young people discovered a spokesperson for their generation. The twenty-two-year-old Dylan found himself in the role of seer, a position in which he was not altogether comfortable. Then, just as people were beginning to discover the prophetic Dylan and as the country was getting caught up in political activism, Dylan began one of his many creative course corrections. Having started his career singing traditional folk and blues, Dylan had evolved into a topical singer. Now, having briefly experienced the dangers of civil rights activism during a trip to the South, Bob turned his focus away from the sociopolitical landscape. Fear was one motivation. Struck by the sudden death of President Kennedy and cognizant of possible involvement of the radical right, Dylan feared he was next on the assassins' list of liberal ideologues. Beyond this paranoia, Dylan was reacting to new vistas opened by his use of mind-expanding drugs. They helped create a more personal, metaphysical orientation. After all, nobody has ever accused psychoactive drugs of enhancing political activism. Time slowed to a microscopic crawl as the poet examined his relationship to the forces of the cosmos.

In March 1965 Columbia released the album *Bringing It All Back Home*. The distorted cover contains a dressed-up, no-nonsense Dylan, a sultry woman in red (manager Grossman's wife, Sally), and a gray cat named Rolling Stone. One can imagine the surprise when a listener placed the record on the turntable and "Subterranean Homesick Blues," the record's first cut, exploded from the speakers. Accompanying the now-famous stream-of-consciousness lyrics, which warn listeners to beware of those in authority, pulses an electric rock and roll band with a new musical energy. Many fans enamored with Dylan the folksinger, those who venerated him as a political visionary and learned to accept the personal focus of his transition period, were stunned by the first side's electric instrumentation. To most followers of serious protest or traditional folk music, rock and roll was still considered a simplistic, romance-dominated, adolescent-oriented pop music.

However, Dylan's turn toward and eventual embrace of the rock and roll idiom was not such a radical departure but instead a return to his musical roots. Dylan came from a generation that worshipped the classic rockers. He had recorded the single "Mixed-Up Confusion" with an electric band back in 1962. What's more, his friendship with the Beatles pushed him toward rock. Aware of both the limited commercial potential of acoustic folk music and the astounding success of the British invasion bands, "going electric" proved a natural progression for an artist who was not restrained by convention. The Beatles and Dylan participated in a process of cross-pollination: Dylan suggested that the Fab Four pursue poetic lyrics of social and political consequence; the Beatles countered with the power of rock and roll.

It is interesting to note that throughout the 1960s Dylan made a series of artistic course corrections. The journey that started in traditional folk music followed a path through protest, psycho-social folk, folk-rock, and country-flavored folk-rock. Dylan seemed aware of the commercial potential of each shift in direction, as each brought increased record sales. Dylan seemed able to sense the shifting commercial pulse of the nation.

Though abandoning societal polemics in *Bringing It All Back Home*, Dylan nevertheless maintained his individual rebellion. He wasn't "gonna work on Maggie's Farm no more" and he led an estranged life in "Outlaw Blues." This rebel was also a wanderer, and the trip taken by "Mr. Tambourine Man" that opens side two is one of his most famous songs. In it Dylan is at his abstract best, telling a tale of a weary, disillusioned, and smoke-blurred existence, pleading for escape and a new morning. Listening to this surreal plea at the 1964 Newport Folk Festival, I was not the only one to experience both confusion and enlightenment. The song contained something indefinably marvelous. What was it?

On "Bob Dylan's 115th Dream," the listener is treated to a glimpse at Dylan's famous spontaneous recording process. Whereas most artists took great pains to create exacting versions of their songs in the studio, Dylan was notorious for his casual approach—"Here's the song, let's wing it." Gathering musicians whom he considered artistically trustworthy, Dylan describes the process: "I play it, and everyone just sort of fills in behind it."[4] On "115th Dream" we hear the band forgetting its cue to start the tune, laughter, and then the successful second try.

In April 1965 Joan Baez accompanied Dylan on his return to England. The seven dates sold out within an hour. Whereas Baez had introduced Bob to her folk audiences, immediately garnering him the status of folk music's crown prince, she hoped for some reciprocity as to Dylan's English fans. The call to join him onstage never came. Hurt and miserable, Baez left for the continent. It was only after many years, and then through a cathartic song of retribution called "Diamonds and Rust," that she communicated with him again. They eventually performed together on the Rolling Thunder Review of 1975 (discussed later).

The 1965 English tour's essence was captured in a cinema verité documentary by D. A. Pennebaker entitled *Don't Look Back,* now available on video. It chronicles not only Dylan's stage performances, but his jousting with the press, his verbal demolition of a student reporter, Grossman in no-holds-barred negotiation mode, and informal song sessions. We are treated to Dylan the hero and Dylan the boor. By tour's end Dylan had become the object of affection of former model Sara Lowndes, a Pennebaker assistant and Sally Grossman's friend. Bob and Sara were secretly married in November 1965.

The live debut of the electric Dylan was scheduled for the 1965 Newport Folk Festival. *Bringing It All Back Home* had reached the top 10 and his new single, "Like a Rolling Stone," was headed up the charts to #2. (It was blocked from the top spot by Sonny and Cher's "I Got You, Babe.") In anticipation of the show, Dylan corralled members of Chicago's Paul Butterfield Blues Band, including guitarist Mike Bloomfield, plus Al Kooper on organ and Barry Kornfeld on piano, for an all-night jam and practice. Dylan hit the stage in an orange shirt and the band started into "Maggie's Farm." The audience's hostile reaction was divided between folk purists who felt betrayed by electrification and less purist concert-goers who couldn't distinguish Dylan from the surrounding noise due to the terrible sound balance.

The furor over Dylan's new direction continued into the following autumn. Some contended that he had given up his search for a "universal sound" and thrown in his lot with the forces of top-40 radio. In short Dylan had gone commercial. Other critics were quick to point out that this fusion of poetry and consequential lyrics with the guitar-based rock and roll band produced a hybrid of monumental artistic and commercial potential. By June 1965, before Dylan's ascendance to the top 10 with "Like a Rolling Stone," a California-based group named the Byrds electrified "Mr. Tambourine Man" and scored a #1 hit—and the folk-rock genre was now off and running.

The demanding and debilitating 1965–1966 schedule continued with the release of *Highway 61 Revisited,* the second in Dylan's folk-rock trilogy. The opening cut was "Like a Rolling Stone," which was listed as the best rock and roll song of all time by the British magazine *New Musical Express;* the song became his most popular work. Like much of Dylan's best, the lyrics can be interpreted in various ways. It can be interpreted as the latest diatribe against the lost lover. Dylan might also be empathizing with young people leaving home—either to escape or to search for a better life—by asking, "How does it feel, to be on your own?" Even the basic "How does it feel?" brought a new, feelings-oriented perspective to a tightly controlled emotional environment.

Dylan also reached a musical peak with "Like a Rolling Stone"—the opening drum shots signal its power while the large ensemble climbs harmonic steps to the chorus, crowned by Bloomfield's slashing guitar fills. The refrain rides on top of Al Kooper's broad organ chords (see Kooper's autobiographical *Backstage Passes* for a hilarious account) while Dylan shouts "How does it feel?" The song was Dylan's first to receive significant radio airplay and remained in the top 40 for nine weeks. For the first time, Dylan had achieved mass commercial success and mass popular penetration. He had achieved Roseburg status.[5]

The rest of this album, which is considered his best by some critics, continues the themes of anger and rebellion. Musically it contains his hardest-driving rock and roll yet, played by a variety of New York and Nashville session musicians. Lyrically, Dylan introduces us to the stereotypical "Nowhere Man"—Mr. Jones in "Ballad of a Thin Man." Reflecting the feelings of a younger, more active generation, Dylan confronts this representative of straight society: "Because something is happening here/ But you don't know what it is/ Do you, Mister Jones?" Dylan's other topics (or targets) include a selection of real or imagined female companions, materialism, and a variety of places visited aboard his magic swirling ship.

Having now entered the world of popular music, Dylan occupied a peculiar and exalted position. Although he had not achieved the mass commercial success of the British invasion rockers, he was viewed, even by some of them, as a man whose songs contained magic and wisdom. This perception made contact with the press problematic. Press conferences were bound to include questions about the meanings of his songs, to which he would inevitably reply, "What do they mean to you? I don't know, I just write them." Thus, there existed the paradox of a man perceived to know "the truth" acting like a hostile boor when asked for the one-thousandth time what it all meant. Dylan simply didn't want the responsibility.

Dylan's increased popularity also meant an exhausting international tour, which included periodic stops for recording sessions in Nashville. His backup band consisted of the Hawks, four Canadians and an Arkansas-born drummer (that was Levon Helm, who missed most of the ensuing tour when he returned to his native Arkansas). With roots in country music, blues, and classic rock and roll, and exhibiting both musical mastery and great instrumental versatility, the band (later to become known simply as the Band) proved to be a perfect complement to the bard. Guitarist-songwriter Robbie Robertson roamed the stage, punctuating Dylan's jabbing lyrics with simple melodic riffs.

The tour encompassed dates in the United States, Europe, and Australia, sometimes three to four nights per week. Although Dylan denied that his songs were drug-oriented, he candidly admitted that drugs (speed, marijuana, and others) kept him up there to pump 'em out. While the band slept, Dylan wrote. Friends felt Dylan was not well, exhausted, even close to death. Response to the electric sets ranged from acceptance, mostly in the United States, to massive walkouts, booing, and even violence. This lack of audience acceptance, the constant bickering with the press, and pressures for a new product exacted a telling emotional toll on the artist.

In May 1966 Columbia released an album with no identification on the front jacket, the two-record set *Blonde on Blonde*. From the cover gazed a deliberately out-of-focus Dylan with disheveled hair and a perplexed look. (A 1977 poll of critics rated the album #2 on the all-time rock list.)[6] Some reviewers felt it would have been a brilliant one-disc album and that the two-disc format stretched the quality of the material. This was the first double album by a major artist, predating Frank Zappa's *Freak Out* by several months. The album's first cut, "Rainy Day Women #12 & 35," sounds as though it were recorded at a party. The lyrical hook, "Everybody must get stoned," does nothing to dispel the druggie image. A barrage of disclaimers about the lyrics was ineffective as radio stations on both sides of the Atlantic banned the tune from the airwaves.

*Blonde on Blonde* showcases the fine musical tastes of Dylan's studio players interpreting his broadest range of music. Lyrically the songs generally fall along a continuum of love relationships—from the negative, nasty, sarcastic portraits of women loved and lost ("Just Like a Woman" and "Leopard Skin Pillbox Hat") to the glowing portrait of his new love Sara ("Sad-Eyed Lady of the Lowlands"). Sandwiched between are a variety of visions, some unobtainable, some in the blues mode of loved and lost, and some, of course, incomprehensible.

That summer, with the album and single "Rainy Day Women #12 & 35" having reached the top 10, Dylan's Columbia record contract expired and he faced a new series of concert dates. The exhausted Dylan retired to the upstate New York countryside to rest with his family, near the artist colony of Woodstock. There, on July 29, 1966, Dylan crashed his Triumph motorcycle. Whether Dylan broke his neck, as was reported in the press, or sustained less serious injuries, he remained out of the public eye until the January 1968 release of his next album. Everybody worried and wondered whether his head injury would prevent him from writing his next chapter of existential angst. In hindsight Dylan was probably due for another course correction, and the injury and subsequent period of slowing down and recuperation possibly saved him from becoming another casualty of life in the fast lane.

Throughout the summer of 1967 Dylan turned on the tape recorder while he and the Band jammed in the basement of their pink tract house in nearby West Saugerties, New York. The songs, released as *The Basement Tapes* in July 1975, show a man midtack in yet another artistic course correction. He continues the quest for answers yet at the same time seems more satisfied, surrounded by friends–co-composers (the Band), a growing family, and a nurturing physical environment. During this hiatus, Dylan-penned compositions were recorded by other artists ("The Mighty Quinn" by Manfred Mann and "Wheels of Fire" by Brian Auger).

At a time when many artists were creating more musically complex, studio-oriented music, Dylan surfaced in January 1968 with the sparse, simple sounds of *John Wesley Harding*. Recorded in Nashville with top studio session men Charlie McCoy on bass, Kenny Buttrey on drums, and Pete Drake on pedal-steel guitar, this album showcases a Dylan come full circle—to strummed acoustic guitar, harmonica, and vocal. With one exception the songs are short, and generally the tone is less ominous than his most recent efforts. Biblical allusion of repentance and salvation creep into the mix in his relentless pursuit of solutions to life's dilemmas.

The devoted family man and Woodstock country gentleman returned again to Nashville in February 1969 to solidify this latest musical change of course. With an expanded cast that included Charlie Daniels, Norman Blake, and Johnny Cash, Dylan recorded *Nashville Skyline*, released in April 1969. It was an immediate commercial success (the album hit #3), and the single "Lay Lady Lay" went to #7. Dylan's newest incarnation featured a relatively smooth vocalist (in part, as a result of his quitting smoking) who is crooning positive, and even sometimes playful, tunes about love gained and sometimes lost.

Dylan garnered an even larger audience with this album. His metamorphosis into a country-flavored folk-rock artist won him increased sales and added country music listeners to his stable of fans. Dylan even appeared as a special guest star on Johnny Cash's network TV show, where the duo played the record's dissonant duet "Girl From the North Country." However, the appeal to a wider audience—fashioned by creating less abstract and symbolic lyrics, more songs featuring just plain romance, and identifiable country music instrumentation (use of pedal-steel guitar, fiddle, and dobro)—gave reviewers ample ammunition to label Dylan a sellout pandering to Nixon's "silent majority."

To many antiwar protesters, Dylan's timing for his journey into country music appeared inopportune. While protest music—and even Dylanesque folk-rock—could be interpreted as philosophically and politically progressive, country music, including its "redneck" proponents, conservative orientation, and lack of social conscience, were red flags to former supporters. Many wrote off their prophet as no longer relevant, a Judas.

In his defense, Alan Rinzler points out that Dylan was only doing what he had always done—writing from experience reflecting a happy relationship and home life and a long-standing love of country music.[7] Here we have an ordinary man, without the crown of thorns. Dylan's next release, *Self Portrait* (June 1970), garnered such negative criticism that *Rolling Stone*'s Greil Marcus was driven to comment, "What is this shit?"[8] Although many felt he had returned to form with his October 1970 release *New Morning*, Dylan had finally fallen from the ranks of rock's vanguard—that special group at the apex of their artistic and commercial careers, whose every release is scoured for its musical essence and lyrical truths.

As with many rock dinosaurs, Dylan's future releases would, for the most part, be compared to the faded image of the demigod. Still, some efforts of the next fifteen years ranked among his creative best. Dylan concert appearances were especially legendary. In August 1971 he performed a series of oldies while accompanied by Leon Russell, George Harrison, and Ringo Starr (at Harrison's Concert for Bangladesh benefit). A dynamic 1974 tour with the Band was chronicled in *Before the Flood*. In the fall of 1975 Dylan set out with an assortment of singers (Joan Baez, Jack Elliot, Roger McGuinn, and others), acoustic and electric musicians, poet Allen Ginsberg, and over seventy other members, on an odyssey called the Rolling Thunder Review. Playing in venues ranging from New England college campuses to Madison Square Garden, this "floating musical crap game" of folk pranksters reminded the world that one of music's major puppeteers was back, pulling the audience's strings.

From time to time, Dylan releases alerted critics that he was still a contemporary songwriter worthy of note. *Blood on the Tracks* (January 1975), a document of romantic dissolution, contains gems like "Tangled Up in Blue" and "A Simple Twist of Fate." A year later, *Desire* presented a musically entrancing collage of lost romance ("Sara," the song to his former wife), mythic fantasy ("Isis" and "Mozambique"), and a return to the political broadsides of an earlier age ("Hurricane," an appeal for justice on behalf of former middleweight boxing champion Reuben "Hurricane" Carter).

In a startling 1979 course correction, Dylan converted to born-again fundamentalist Christianity, recording *Slow Train Coming* (which contained the Grammy-winning "Gotta Serve Somebody"); he also refused to perform any classic material while touring with his new band and gospel-flavored vocal backup group. This brief incarnation stirred further controversy, as Dylan gained a new group of fans and renewed popularity. Dylan would assert that biblical allusion was not new to his work, that he was simply more fully exploring a different direction.

Who knows how many more directions we can reasonably expect from this troubadour, this self-described song and dance man? Dylan has contributed so much already. His fusion of the folk/protest heritage with abstract lyrical style had an extraordinary impact on the form and content of 1960s folk and rock music. His political and personal visions contained within that often-copied artistic form compelled artists and audiences to ask What does it all mean? Never complacent, the bard would then slip off in new directions, chronicling his experiences in ways that, although seeming to make sense, no one claimed to understand.

# 11· Folk-Rock: So You Want to Be a Rock and Roll Star

*You had to be a little nuts to want to take folk music changes and put 'em to rhythm and blues beats and sing Dylan Thomas sort of words to 'em.*

**David Crosby of the Byrds**

*We sang our asses off. Our sound could have filled a cathedral. It is the first time we had ever achieved what Denny [a bandmate] and I called the Fifth Voice: the ringing, resonant overtones that vibrate throughout the harmonies and into your limbs and chest when they are perfectly tuned. . . . We were flying.*

**John Phillips of the Mamas and the Papas**

*Tin soldiers and Nixon coming, we're finally on our own/ This summer I hear their drumming, four dead in Ohio.*

**"Ohio," Neil Young (1970)**

IN THE EARLY 1960S SALES of acoustic guitars skyrocketed as young men and women strummed along to the era's latest folk melodies. Those that were good enough found their way to New York's Greenwich Village and other urban folk music centers, performing in the streets for tips or, if they were lucky, in clubs and coffeehouses. Stephen Stills came to the Village from Florida, Richie Furay from Ohio, Jim McGuinn from Chicago, John Phillips from Virginia, John Sebastian just stayed close to home, and on and on.

Some were attracted to folk by its accessibility; all one had to master was a simple melody and some lyrics, plus a few chords on the guitar. Others were drawn to its sociopolitical heritage and the timeliness of its meaningful outlook, as society surged into the socially relevant sixties. Folk music during the early 1960s achieved some commercial success. Young, white, predominantly male groups recorded smooth versions of generally nonpolitical songs for popular consumption. This music reached the radio airwaves, filling in for classic rock while the nascent British invasion waited in the wings.

When the Beatles hit big, pre–folk-rock artists felt torn between the two genres. Purist folk wisdom regaled rock as simplistic pop pap. However, most of these players grew up listening to and loving classic rock and roll. Those that remained acoustic, Phil Ochs and Tom Paxton for example, stayed in New York. Many others, citing the sun and fun promise of California dreamin', headed to Los Angeles. There they found a relatively affluent, white youth culture that venerated individual freedom, cars, beaches, and the opposite sex. Homeboy David Crosby described it as "blasting down the road with the wind in your hair, listening to the radio turned up."

Los Angeles became the Mecca for early electric folk. Although Dylan is generally acknowledged as folk-rock's foremost pioneer—fusing acoustic guitar and topical lyrics from folk with the electric guitar-based rock and roll band—members of the L.A. scene also deserve similar credit. In the summer of 1964, while Dylan played an acoustic "Mr. Tambourine Man" at the Newport Folk Festival, Jim McGuinn, a former accompanist with the Limeliters and the Chad Mitchell Trio, was strumming his twelve-string guitar singing Beatles songs at the Troubadour folk club. Gene Clark (recently of the New Christy Minstrels) made it a duo, and David Crosby (formerly with Les Baxter's Balladeers) joined them to form Jet Set. This group became the Beefeaters, an anglicized name inspired by the Beatles movie *A Hard Day's Night*. In October 1964, with the addition of bassist Chris Hillman and drummer Michael Clarke, they became the Byrds.

This two-guitar, bass, drums, and tambourine lineup had already recorded an album, titled *Preflyte,* before their manager received a copy of "Mr. Tambourine Man" featuring Dylan, with an attempted harmony by Ramblin' Jack Elliot. With Dylan's permission, the Byrds recorded the song in the spring of 1965. That June, at the same time Dylan released "Like a Rolling Stone," the Byrds' version of "Mr. Tambourine Man" had reached #1. They followed with Dylan's "All I Really Want to Do" and the Pete Seeger composition "Turn, Turn, Turn," which also hit #1. McGuinn's vision of finding the gap between Dylan and the Beatles had paid off. The Byrds' particular folk-rock formula of droning electric twelve-string guitar—McGuinn's use of the Rickenbacker electric twelve-string was inspired by George Harrison's sound from *A Hard Day's Night*—three-part harmonies, a driving rhythm section, and meaningful lyrics set the tone and geographic location for the new genre.

The success of the Byrds, coupled with Dylan's 1965 Newport electric conversion and release of "Like a Rolling Stone," unleashed the dormant rock and roll spirit in many folk musicians. In early 1966 a legendary encounter took place that led to the formation of a band called Buffalo Springfield. Folkie Stephen Stills left the Village for L.A. to form a rock and roll band. Stills telephoned singer-guitarist Richie Furay, inviting him to L.A. to join the as yet unformed group. Fate placed them in a traffic jam on Sunset Strip, behind a 1953 Pontiac hearse with Ontario license plates; they had been on the lookout for Canadian friend Neil Young. Believing that they recognized the vehicle, they discovered Young and bassist Bruce Palmer inside. With the addition of drummer Dewey Martin, Buffalo Springfield (named after a steamroller) was formed.

Stills once described the band's inspiration, saying "He [Young] wanted to be Bob Dylan and I wanted to be the Beatles." The band contained three prolific songwriters in Stills, Furay, and Young, whose early compositions clearly show flashes of later greatness. Stills wrote the group's only top-40 hit "For What It's Worth" (#7, February 1967), inspired by a Sunset Strip police riot against teenagers protesting a 10:00 PM curfew. The sparse, airy feeling (especially the chimed harmonics) is typical of his later work in Crosby, Stills, and Nash (CSN). Neil Young's compositions tended to be more driving and hard-edged. "Mr. Soul" even contains the signature riff from "Satisfaction," perhaps a reflection of the band's earlier experience as an opening act for the Rolling Stones.

Buffalo Springfield lasted only two years. They performed sporadically, due to an absence of hit records and the turbulent personal and musical relationships within the band. Although their live performances were legendarily energetic, they were not enough to keep the band together. In 1968 Neil Young left for the last time, replacement bassist-producer Jim Messina compiled the final album, and the band dissolved.

In typical L.A. musical-chairs fashion, as soon as the music stopped for Buffalo Springfield, three different bands emerged. Furay and Messina went on to form Poco, the seminal, country-flavored, folk-rock band. Stills busied himself with numerous projects until he and Crosby visited John Sebastian, former leader of the Lovin' Spoonful. The Hollies were in town and member Graham Nash came over to Sebastian's pad to sing. Within months Crosby, Stills, and Nash began rehearsals and recorded the self-titled, critically acclaimed album that shook the music world to its foundation. Meanwhile, Neil Young settled down in Topanga Canyon to write and record his first solo effort. He employed the band Crazy Horse (formerly the Rockets), who became Young's regular backup band.

The progeny spawned by Buffalo Springfield added important elements to the growing genre now known as folk-rock. Poco was a trendsetter, fusing country and folk-rock stylings. Instrumentalist Rusty Young added a country-flavored texture to the band through his pedal-steel guitar, banjo, mandolin, dobro, and Fender Telecaster electric guitar. Poco's high, close harmonies and generally romance-oriented lyrics were also reminiscent of country and bluegrass roots. Jim Messina left Poco after two years, intending to become a CBS staff producer. Label chief Clive Davis prevailed upon Messina to produce songwriter Kenny Loggins's first solo album, then asked him to appear on the album and finally to play with Loggins on the road. Messina found himself a creative partner for the next four years in the widely heralded Loggins and Messina. The addition of four excellent session players ensured that this group's live shows cooked.

Although there have been numerous incarnations of CSN and, later, CSN and Young (CSNY), their first album firmly established the group and their unique sound in the rock and roll pantheon. CSN proved that essentially acoustic folk-rock could be effective, moving music, and their mellifluous, celestial harmonies became a stylistic trademark. Stills's paean to Judy Collins and their lost relation-

Crosby, Stills, Nash, and Young

ship, "Suite: Judy Blue Eyes," exemplifies both these qualities, with his bass and occasional electric-guitar fills being the only electrified sounds.

In the summer of 1969 Ahmet Ertegun, president of Atlantic Records, facilitated Neil Young's entry into CSN. Unwilling to give up his solo career, yet interested in attaining the superstar status and monetary rewards that had eluded Buffalo Springfield, Young decided to pursue both careers. He recorded CSNY's only studio album, *Deja Vu* (#1, April 1970), and went on tour with them (including the historic appearance at Woodstock) while writing and rehearsing with Crazy Horse. Young's second solo album, *Everybody Knows This Is Nowhere* (#34, August 1970), is his favorite album and contains early versions of "Cowgirl in the Sand," "Cinnamon Girl," and "Down by the River." It is one of the era's gems that rarely gets the mention it deserves.

In subsequent years the loosely knit fabric that held together the careers of Crosby, Stills, Nash, and Young frayed and Neil Young emerged as the most critically acclaimed and commercially successful of the four. His next two albums *After the Gold Rush* and *Harvest* (#1 with the #1 single "Heart of Gold"), cemented his place in rock-music history. Although Young is perceived as a brooding loner, and his songs of the period chronicled desperate times, he has proven to be a creative and durable artist. As many of his friends succumbed to life in L.A.'s fast lane (including Crazy Horse guitarist Danny Whitten), Young somehow survived—epilepsy, bad back, and all.

After the closure of CSNY, Stephen Stills went to England. In early 1970 he purchased Ringo Starr's mansion and recorded his first solo album with a host of friends, including Eric Clapton, Jimi Hendrix, and "Mama" Cass Elliot. Having always wanted to play bass for Hendrix, Stills hung out with the guitar master in an attempt to learn the secrets of Jimi's artistry. Although Stills never achieved that level of virtuosity, his solo and group permutations (the solo Stills, Manassas, and CSN) have produced some well-received material. At the same time, Stills wove in and out of the inebriated high life, which he termed the "rock and roll circus."

Working as a duo, Crosby and Nash continued to tour and release albums throughout the seventies. Nash appeared physically and spiritually healthy, assuming leadership roles among the music industry on social and environmental issues; Crosby fought legendary bouts with substance abuse, eventually served time in jail, and rose again to sing, record, and tour while battling serious health problems. This genre of folk-based rock, as practiced by Byrds/Buffalo Springfield alumni, retains its importance today among musicians and fans. Its legacy of recorded material and its stylistic effect (strummed guitar style, harmonies, consequential lyrics, and its counterculture image and dress) had an impact.

The Flying Burrito Brothers, led by the talented and mysterious Gram Parsons, were another influential L.A. band with a cult following similar to Springfield's. Parsons joined the Byrds in early 1968 and, befitting his Deep South roots, infused them with his vision of the country-flavored rock and roll that appeared on *Sweetheart of the Rodeo*. This seminal country-rock album features banjo, fiddle, and pedal-steel guitar and a lyrical motif of liquor, love, and loves lost. Parsons refused to join the Byrds on their South African tour and spent the summer of 1968 in London with the Rolling Stones before returning to L.A. to form the Burritos.

The Burrito Brothers, with Byrds compadre Chris Hillman and pedal-steel player Sneaky Pete Kleinow, became L.A.'s resident musical cowboys. The band graced the cover of their first effort, *Gilded Palace of Sin*, in flowery rhinestone cowboy suits from Nudies of North Hollywood. Although they never achieved much commercial success, elements of their country chic/folk-rock fusion paved the way for later L.A. cowboys. One first-album highlight, "Sin City," aptly describes the debauchery rampant in the L.A. music scene. Parsons, ever the wanderer, left the Burritos and struck out on his own with a band that included the young Emmylou Harris as backup vocalist. He died of a drug overdose in 1973, another rock casualty. Gram had asked to be cremated out in the desert. His manager Phil Kaufman hijacked the body from an airport terminal, drove to the desert, and burned the casket.

The Burritos, Byrds, and Poco carried on. Meanwhile, four members of Linda Ronstadt's backup band formed a group that parlayed the various stylistic elements of their L.A. predecessors into major artistic and commercial success. The summer of 1971 proved to be the right time for the L.A. sound to mature. At the suggestion of Ronstadt producer John Boylan, former Burrito guitarist Bernie Leadon, Motown émigré Glenn Frey, former Poco bassist Randy Meisner, and

The Eagles

Texas-born drummer Don Henley sequestered themselves in a room and just played music together. Thus the Eagles were born.

This was a two-guitar band containing country instrumental inflections (with Leadon adding pedal-steel and banjo), a driving rhythm section, and high, tight harmonies. Their songs contained personal stories of what Henley has called "looking for it . . . whatever it is." The time was right, as were the combinations of talent. The "team" the Eagles put together included prolific songwriters within the group plus outsiders like Jackson Browne and J. D. Souther. Management was handled by feisty Irv Azoff, they recorded on a potent new label, the David Geffen-run Asylum, with stablemates Browne and Joni Mitchell, and utilized the production skills of veterans Glyn Johns and Bill Szymczyk.

Paradoxically, the first two albums of this new-era American folk/country-rock prototype were recorded not in America, but in London with English producer Glyn Johns. The first album, *The Eagles,* had three top-40 hits ("Peaceful Easy Feeling," "Witchy Woman," and "Take It Easy"), and included a logo and album art that reflected the contemporary fascination with Native American religion and the teachings of the Indian brujo Don Juan. The day the Eagles photographed the cover, the band drove into the desert, built a fire, ingested peyote tea, and then faced the camera. Their second release, *Desperado,* was thematic, a symbolic representation of the rock and roll band as a band of outlaws in society.

Subsequent albums were characterized by two trends, a movement away from acoustic-oriented music and toward more driving rock, hastened by the addition of guitarists Don Felder in 1974 and Joe Walsh, who replaced Leadon in 1975. This incorporated a harder-edged, distorted-guitar sound (featuring Les Paul guitars rather than Leadon's Telecaster) that reached its peak with the album *Hotel California* and the harmony guitar solo contained in the title cut. At the same time, Eagles lyrics reflected the hedonistic lifestyle of a large segment of the Los Angeles rock community—some of whom dwelled in the not-so-mythical, snow-filled Hotel California. Having achieved megastardom, sellout concerts, and gold and platinum records, the band expired in 1982 as individuals went on to pursue solo careers.

There are numerous singer-songwriter members of the L.A. music community during these years that deserve more than the simple mention they receive to this point in our story. Jackson Browne was a local songwriter who started writing at age seventeen, moved to New York at nineteen, and returned for a successful performing career during the midseventies. He has created a broad range of material, including poignant, introspective ballads, such as "These Days," and stinging social and political commentaries. Browne is one of the few committed activist-musicians in the Guthrie tradition, who actively supported social justice and antinuclear movements well before they became fashionable.

Canadian Joni Mitchell, another extraordinary songwriter, began writing in a folk vein in the midsixties, moved to L.A., and became one of the "Ladies of the Canyon." She first received notoriety when artists like Judy Collins ("Both Sides Now") and CSNY ("Woodstock") recorded her songs. In addition to the obvious quality, personal awareness, and sociopolitical relevance to her songs, Mitchell's distinctive lilting soprano voice and unusual open guitar tunings further prompted her own success. An extraordinary breadth of vision allowed Mitchell to later combine folk and rock with jazz players and compositions.

Not all music from the folk-rock genre originated in Los Angeles. Since New York retained its folk prominence, some electro-acoustic artists originated there. The Mamas and the Papas straddled both coasts. Founder John Phillips, who had migrated to the Village in 1957, married his California dream girl, Michelle Gilliam, in 1962. They were joined by former Mugwumps Cass Elliot and Denny Doherty, retired to a campsite in the Virgin Islands, and created the Mamas and the Papas. Instead of returning to the inclement environment of New York, the band headed for Hollywood, where they signed to Dunhill Records and recorded "California Dreamin'" (#4, February 1966). The song set the tone for the rest of their hits, with strummed acoustic guitars, rich harmonies (featuring the unusual two men-two women alignment), and strong songwriting. Studio session musicians filled in the rest.

Phillips and Dunhill label head Lou Adler were the prime movers for the June 1967 Monterey Pop Festival (see detailed description in Chapter 14). They arranged for artist participation (the board of directors included Smokey

Robinson, Paul Simon, Paul McCartney, Brian Wilson, Roger McGuinn, and others) and sparked record industry interest. Scheduled to close the show on Sunday, the Mamas and the Papas found themselves in the unfortunate position of following torrid performances by the Who, the Grateful Dead, and Jimi Hendrix. That same year they also had hits with a superior version of the Shirelles' "Dedicated to the One I Love" (#2, March 1967) and the autobiographical "Creeque Alley" (#5, May 1967). Within a year of the Monterey festival the band disintegrated, having fallen victim to interpersonal friction and life in the fast lane. John and Michelle (divorced in 1970) and Denny and Cass attempted solo careers; none were able to achieve much commercial success.

The other two members of the fabled Mugwumps, John Sebastian and Zal Yanovsky, remained in New York City to pursue folk-rock careers. Sebastian came from a musical household—his father was a classical harmonica player, his mother the administrator for Carnegie Hall. With Steve Boone (bass) and Joe Butler (drums), Sebastian and Yanovsky organized the Lovin' Spoonful, a name taken from Mississippi John Hurt's "Coffee Blues." Their debut album, *Do You Believe in Magic*, and the title cut (#9, September 1965), were typical of the bouncy style that they dubbed "good-time music." On the single, Sebastian, the group's major creative force, strummed the electric autoharp while waxing ebulliently over love and rock and roll.

For the next two years, these striped-shirted Manhattan moptops released a series of smile-inducing songs, including "Daydream," "You Didn't Have to Be So Nice," and "Nashville Cats." Atypical of this fare was their only #1 hit, "Summer in the City" (July 1966). Catchy lyrics describe the Big Apple, brought to a standstill by the stifling summer heat; the singer dreams of the cool nights dancing on the rooftop with his girl. The music is dominated by driving rhythms and city sound effects. After "two glorious years and a tedious one," Sebastian left and the band disintegrated. Sebastian's solo career was sporadically successful, including an appearance at Woodstock and a #1 single, "Welcome Back" (April 1976), the theme for the hit TV series "Welcome Back Kotter."

The Band was the most musically interesting and varied folk-rock group based in the New York area. They originated in the late 1950s in Canada as a backup band for Arkansas-cum-Canadian rocker Ronnie Hawkins. Arkansan Levon Helm (drums, mandolin) and Canadians Jaime "Robbie" Robertson (guitar), Rick Danko (bass), Richard Manuel (keyboards, drums), and Garth Hudson (keyboards, sax) left Hawkins after a number of years and moved to New York. They interrupted their career quest to tour as Dylan's band in 1965 and 1966 (Helm chose not to go). The Band moved to Woodstock in upstate New York near Dylan, recorded hours of material with him after his motorcycle accident (released as *The Basement Tapes* in 1975), and released their first album, *Music from Big Pink* (#30, October 1968). The album was named for their large pink residence and contained a Dylan painting as the front cover. The sound was distinctive and included Dylan tunes like "I Shall Be Released" and Robertson originals like "The Weight."

Their second album, *The Band* (#9, October 1969), became an era classic. Pictured on the cover in sepia tones, the group looked more like rural laborers than rock musicians. Inside were sketches (mostly Robertson's) of Americana: the decimation wrought by the Civil War on a family in the poor rural South ("The Night They Drove Old Dixie Down"), the paean to a country lass ("Up on Cripple Creek"), and hard times as a sharecropper ("King Harvest"). The rural nature of this music was further accentuated by the drawl of lead vocalists Levon Helm and Canadians Manuel and Danko.

These vignettes were transported by an inventive and multilayered rock/pop music. The ensemble included the normal drums, bass, acoustic guitar, and electric guitar, plus concertina, fiddle, mandolin, and a full complement of keyboards (organ, piano, and electric piano). The music contained more syncopation than most folk-rock; bassist Danko played a fretless bass, allowing him to slide, and he emulated the playing of his heroes, Motown's James Jamerson and session player Chuck Rainey. The few instrumental solos were generally taken by Robertson in a minimalist blues and rockabilly-derived style. Three-part harmonies predominated, but they were rough and wailing compared to the celestial and crisp harmonies of CSN.

The Band never again achieved the critical acclaim given their second album. Among others, they released a live album with a horn section *(Rock of Ages)* and an album of classic rock-era material *(Moondog Matinee)*. They went out in style, at San Francisco's Winterland on Thanksgiving Day 1976. Among the guest performers were Dylan, Clapton, Muddy Waters, Neil Young, and Ronnie Hawkins. Martin Scorsese captured the event, released on film as *The Last Waltz*. One of the era's best bands was gone and one of the era's best folktale tellers, songwriter Robbie Robertson, continued to go unnoticed.

I would like to mention two marvelous but unheralded bands, Seatrain and Pure Prairie League. Seatrain—composed of Blues Project alumnus Andy Kulburg, Syracuse vocalist-extraordinaire and keyboard player Lloyd Baskin, songwriter Peter Rowan ("Panama Red," "Midnight Moonlight," and many others), electric fiddle whiz Richard Green, and others—was one of the first bands to record with producer George Martin after the Beatles breakup. Their second Capitol release, *Marblehead Messenger* (1972), is one of my all-time favorites.

The same goes for Pure Prairie League's self-titled first RCA release (1972). For the first two albums, the driving force in this Cincinnati band was singer-songwriter-guitarist Craig Fuller. His songs, including the follow-up album hit "Amie" (#27, April 1975), were delightful examples of the folk/country/rock fusion so popular at the time. "Harmony Song" still touches me deeply. After the second album, *Bustin' Out,* Fuller resisted the draft, went to jail, did alternative service, and was barred from returning to the group by his former bandmates—their loss.

Folk-rock is very accessible music—then and now. All one needs is an acoustic guitar and an idea. The British invasion tantalized folk artists with the power of rock/pop music and some jumped ship immediately; many others later climbed aboard. This course inevitably steered away from the protest song, so easily sung to folk audiences, to something less controversial. There is the occasional "Ohio" (where Neil Young strongly criticizes Richard Nixon and the Vietnam War), however, most stories and commentaries were more personal and less zealous. The folk-rock genre continues to thrive; dinosaurs like Dylan, Paul Simon, Young, and others now coexist with younger strummers like R.E.M., Tracy Chapman, and others, asking questions and giving answers, while the band plays on.

# 12. Soul Music: R-E-S-P-E-C-T

*[Soul music is] all about feelings. You can't get away from that fact, no matter what you do.*

**Aretha Franklin**

*We're people, we're like the birds and the bees. But we'd rather die on our feet than keep living on our knees.*

**James Brown, "Say It Loud—I'm Black and I'm Proud" (1968)**

*Reflecting and encouraging black pride, soul is an important psychological component of the black struggle. It is a diffuse almost mystical concept and its emphasis on subjective qualities—you have to feel it—encourages emotional commitment to it. . . . Its diffuseness allows all black Americans to identify and associate with it and so with each other.*

**Soul music historian Michael Haralambos**

BLACK POPULAR MUSIC OF the sixties was divided into two very different and distinct kinds of music: soul, a sweaty, raw, and relevant Memphis sound; and Motown, an elegant, danceable, more mainstream Detroit sound. Both drew heavily on gospel, doo-wop, and rhythm and blues, but each reflected different ways to build on that musical foundation. This chapter will chronicle the path taken by Soul music—one that began in the era of rhythm and blues and eventually grew to include the sixties musical style as well as the feeling of African-American ethnic pride.

To understand the musical essence of soul, start with late 1950s rhythm and blues—resplendent in its gospel-generated vocal emotion and four-piece driving rhythm sections. Syncopate the bass lines, make the horns more prominent, and turn up the volume. Chronicle the life experience of 1960s African Americans and you have the story of soul: romance and disillusionment, love and lust, pride, pain, and struggle. Like R&B's prodigal child, soul music emerged early in the sixties, precariously climbed the popular music charts, left an enduring catalog, and began the 1970s by evolving into the funk of the next generation.

Like classic rock and doo-wop, soul was a regional sound. It was born and nurtured in the South. Most of its artists were raised in the South; others migrated north during their childhood, only to return southward later as musicians. A significant proportion of soul hits were recorded in southern locations: the Stax/Volt studios of Memphis, Tennessee, or the Fame or Quinn Ivy studios around Muscle Shoals, Alabama. No wonder that the spark that ignited the genre—fanning the flames of intensity and emotionality—came from the South's revivalist religious tradition.

Eventually soul transcended its original musical meaning and came to describe essential, authentic Blackness (as in, "that cat's got soul"). *Webster's New World Dictionary* defines it as "a sense of racial pride and social and cultural solidarity, often with opposition to white, middle-class practices and values." Few songs from the soul repertoire actually addressed the ongoing civil rights movement; nevertheless, the music was adopted by the Black community as a representation of its struggle for Black pride and racial consciousness. Eventually, whites, in a manner consistent with previous co-optations of Black musical and cultural forms, adopted some cultural trappings of the soul concept for use in mainstream America. Soul handshakes and slang terms like "get down" were in.

This story begins with two artists, Ray Charles and James Brown, whose initial successes came during the R&B era. Although both had numerous hits during the fifties, they continued to evolve musically and claimed even more popular success as soul artists. Along with Sam Cooke, they stood as musical and commercial role models to the younger African-American generation of performers who emerged in the late 1950s and formed the backbone of the soul sound.

Georgia-born Ray Charles Robinson, blinded by glaucoma at age seven, was considered something of a child prodigy while studying music at a Florida school for the blind. Having mastered keyboards, sax, clarinet, and trumpet at fifteen, he struck out on his own to become a professional musician. At seventeen he asked a friend to locate a large city as far away as possible from his Tampa, Florida, base. Charles moved to Seattle, Washington, where he occasionally worked with bandleader Bumps Blackwell and the fifteen-year-old Quincy Jones.

In 1954 Charles—who had dropped his last name so as not to be confused with middleweight boxing champion Sugar Ray Robinson—recorded a major R&B hit, "I Got a Woman," for Atlantic Records. In it he directed his soul big band (piano, bass, drums, two trumpets, and two saxes) and sang in the new gritty vocal style that became a Charles signature. After a string of R&B classics and his big 1959 crossover hit "What'd I Say" (which contains the bridge that taught many white listeners the meaning of call and response), Ray Charles was enticed away from Atlantic by ABC-Paramount by a more lucrative contract.

On his new label he recorded numerous pop hits (including #1s "Georgia on My Mind" and "Hit the Road, Jack") and experimented with a broad range of musical styles. His country albums were critically acclaimed and included the hit song "I Can't Stop Loving You." Working again with Quincy Jones, Charles recorded the album *Genius Plus Soul Equals Jazz*. By the mid-1960s Charles—an educated musician, songwriter, singer, and arranger—had achieved popular success. He was hailed as "the genius of soul."

Whereas Ray Charles found popular commercial acceptance, James Brown, "the godfather of soul," had to settle for preeminence in the African-American community. Brown's voice, band, and performances were legendary. He would exhort the audience with a voice so raw that it seemed his vocal chords would shred on the very next note—at the same time thrilling the crowd with his flamboyant and acrobatic physical moves.

Brown's famous concert closer was built around his early R&B hit, "Please, Please, Please." With the band relentlessly pounding the closing musical figures, and the Famous Flames vocal backup group repeating the phrase "Baby, please

James Brown

don't go," Brown would fall to his knees, pleading into the microphone for his baby to stay. From the wings a man would appear with a plush cape; draping it around Brown's shoulders, he would attempt to lead the sobbing singer offstage. Just as it seemed James was ready to retire from the stage, he would toss aside the cape and with renewed vigor return to the microphone for one last pleading chance.

Repeatedly crying "I, I, I," and other words, Brown wailed as the audience became almost mesmerized by the hypnotic chanting. The man and cape would again appear and Brown would again be led toward the wings, where at the last moment he would toss off the cape and resume his plight. Finally the exhortations would end, with Brown, the band, and the audience emotionally spent. "The Hardest Working Man in Show Business," as Brown billed himself, had led everyone through a nonstop parade of his million-selling R&B and soul hits and ended with "the cape."

During his shows the former boxer moved constantly, sliding across the stage on one foot, twirling 360 degrees, then dropping into a split. His moves were observed and copied by many, including a young Michael Jackson and an awestruck Mick Jagger. Of course, this phenomenal movement would come as no surprise to a Black community raised on the physical dexterity of dancing sensations Bill "Bojangles" Robinson, the Step Brothers, and the Nicholas Brothers. Nor would the raw emotionality of his vocal style, focus on rhythm, and physicality in performing surprise those who had been raised in the pentecostal Baptist Church, where unbridled emotion in the service of the Lord was typical of worship.

These musical and performance characteristics, so deeply ingrained in African-American tradition, were part of what endeared Brown to the Black community. However, the same elements, despite their authentic presentation, probably prevented Brown from having the crossover success that he hoped and worked for. Although soul was "in," some related aspects were just too alien for white culture to assimilate. So Brown had to be content with spectacular R&B and soul chart success, some pop chart action, and a reputation as "Soul Brother #1."

Like most soul artists, Brown was raised in the South, in his case Augusta, Georgia. Also typically, he immersed himself in music early, was recognized as being extremely talented, sang both gospel and R&B, and was doggedly determined to succeed. Brown overcame impoverished beginnings and a stint in reform school, finally choosing music over possible careers in baseball and boxing. By 1955 his group, the Famous Flames, with James on drums and vocals, crashed a Little Richard gig and impressed Richard's road manager. They were brought to Macon, Georgia and eventually signed to King/Federal Records of Cincinnati.

A string of R&B hits followed as Brown expanded and fine-tuned the band—he sometimes carried two drummers because one lacked the stamina to play the entire show. In October 1962 Brown recorded a midnight show at New York's legendary Black theater, the Apollo. The album, *Live at the Apollo*, reached #2 on the pop charts and stayed in the top 40 for thirty-three weeks, alerting pop music circles to a fresh, unique sound. This proved to be his greatest chart success.

Between 1960 and 1970 Brown had thirty songs on the top-40 charts, including his biggest, 1965's "I Got You (I Feel Good)" (which climbed to #3). This celebratory smash opens with the patented James howl, a drum beat, and the exclamation "I feel good!" Brown's musical recipe calls for the obligatory syncopated bass line, straightforward drum pattern, and sparse, choppy rhythm guitar part. This rhythm section is spiced by punctuating blasts from the horn section and topped by a generous serving of the raw, gritty (though somewhat restrained) Brown touting his good feelings.

Although "I Got You" and other singles had some chart success, the popular music scene, flooded by the British invasion and charmed by Motown, was ultimately unwilling to share the mainstream with James Brown. This former shoeshine boy owned a private jet, two hundred suits, a Victorian-style castle, three radio stations, and could always be counted on to sell a million copies of any record to an adoring Black public. In Europe and even Africa James played to tens of thousands. When Black communities erupted after the assassination of the Reverend Martin Luther King Jr., the mayors of Boston and Washington, D.C. asked the godfather of soul to help settle things down.

In the late sixties Brown's releases reflected the growing movement of Black pride and consciousness. Journalist Thulani Davis, reflecting on her youth, writes, "JB was proof that Black people were different. Rhythmically and tonally Blacks had to be from somewhere else."[1] Brown later alienated fans by supporting Republicans Richard Nixon and Ronald Reagan, lost substantial sums as his businesses failed, ran into big trouble with the I.R.S., and finally went to jail. He remained an enigma to most whites, but to many in the Black community he is still Soul Brother #1.

Whereas Brown captivated his audience with raw power, Sam Cooke, another significant role model for aspiring soul musicians, forged his career on the smooth, cool end of the spectrum. He had an extraordinary voice and legendary vocal control. Cooke's choice to leave gospel music and a successful gospel group, the Soul Stirrers, to pursue a popular music career inspired many young singers, including Aretha Franklin and Jackie Wilson, to leave religious music and strike out on their own.

Born in Mississippi, Cook (the "e" was added later) was raised in Chicago, where his father was a minister. By the age of nine he was singing professionally; at thirteen he was already singing in gospel's minor leagues. Cooke was invited to join the Soul Stirrers in 1951 at the age of twenty. Even the early gospel recording of "Jesus Gave Me Water" shows the powerful but lilting tenor voice soaring over multiple notes in his delivery of the first syllable of "Je-sus." By 1956 Sam was not only recognized for his voice and control, but also for the good looks and charisma that attracted a substantial number of young people to the group's concerts. Although gospel was now big business, the financial and pop chart successes of Black rock and roll artists like Little Richard and Fats Domino were a lure to Cooke. His gospel label, Specialty Records, was reluctant to record the secular

Cooke and discarded him along with producer Bumps Blackwell after one pop record.

The tiny Keen Records signed them both and released "You Send Me" in 1957. It climbed to the top of both the R&B and pop charts. The secular Cooke was still cool and smooth but with an added sensuality. Notes still cascaded, as they had during his gospel years, with that familiar woo-oh-oo-oo, all on the same sylla-ble—a multinote, one-syllable technique termed melisma. The public was now able to hear what soul producer and Atlantic Records vice president Jerry Wexler called "the best singer who ever lived."

After more hits for Keen, including "Wonderful World," Sam signed with ma-jor-label RCA. Within months "Chain Gang," containing rhythmic grunts and hammering designed to replicate road gang life, hit #2 (August 1960). Although Cooke's RCA sound contained lush orchestration representative of the era's pop genre, it was the voice that sold. His hits ranged from the traditional "Frankie and Johnny" to the blues of "Little Red Rooster" and the soulful "Bring It on Home to Me," with backup vocals by Lou Rawls. After hearing Dylan's "Blowin' in the Wind" for the first time, Cooke was inspired to write "A Change Is Gonna Come," an attempt to sort out the ongoing civil rights movement. In a situation similar to the release of Otis Redding's "(Sittin' on) The Dock of the Bay," Cooke's forebod-ing tale of "Change" was released as a single soon after his death.

Under the tutelage of musical and business mentor J. W. Alexander, Cooke also learned the importance of self-sufficiency. Rather than sign away the publishing rights to Sam's extensive catalog of songs, they established Kags Music and created SAR Records to produce other artists. This financial independence and control was atypical of the era's Black artists, and it was used as a model by Redding and others who followed.

Cooke's power and financial independence may have led to his untimely death in December 1964. The common story has Cooke driving his Ferrari to a seedy motel and, once inside the room, attempting to rip the dress off his beautiful companion. According to the story, she then absconded with his pants; clothed only in an overcoat, he broke into the night manager's office in search of his com-panion. The manager, a middle-aged woman, shot him three times. To his friends, this story—with Cooke driving a very expensive car to a three-dollar motel and losing control over a woman he had just picked up in a restaurant—was implausi-ble. Instead, industrywide rumor had him being set up and killed by the mob, in-censed at his refusals to their overtures.

By the time of his death, Sam Cooke was a creative artist with unlimited poten-tial as well as a role model for a generation of new artists. He was already a vocal inspiration to singers as disparate as Otis Redding and Smokey Robinson, and his success in popular music inspired the eighteen-year-old Aretha Franklin to seek fame and fortune in secular rather than gospel music. Cooke was a prolific song-writer and was on his way to creating a self-sufficient music business network. He was also interested in producing other artists. Like his friend Malcolm X, who was assassinated three months after Cooke's death, Cooke left just as great fame and accomplishment appeared within grasp.

The person who scaled the artistic heights as the king of soul music was Otis Redding. Raised in Macon, Georgia, Otis sang gospel in his father's church and left school in the tenth grade to help support the family as a singer. In a city that had already spawned Little Richard and James Brown, Redding first built his reputation as an amateur, winning talent contests and sometimes fronting Richard's former band, the Upsetters, with a vocal style reminiscent of the classic rocker.

Otis had already recorded for two small labels when his friend and manager Phil Walden—who booked many of the soul era's artists and went on to form Capricorn Records for the Allman Brothers—persuaded Atlantic Records execu-

Otis Redding

tive.Joe Galkin to take Redding to a recording session in Memphis. At the time, Otis was the vocalist for band leader-guitarist Jimmy Jenkins and his group, the Pinetoppers. Stax Records president Jim Stewart, unimpressed with Jenkins, was convinced to record Redding in the last half-hour of the session. Haltingly, Otis sang the title words, "These . . arms . . . of . . . mine"; not everyone present saw the potential, and it took six months for the record to climb the soul charts, but Redding's career, and the Stax studio sound, began to take off.

Stax Records had been around since the late fifties. In 1960 they had moved their studio into the old Capitol Theater and started to record early soul artists like Rufus Thomas and William Bell. In the summer of 1961 the Mar-Keys, a local white band composed mostly of recent high school graduates, recorded the instrumental "Last Night," which astoundingly climbed to #3 on the pop charts. Mar-Keys guitarist Steve Cropper and bass player Donald "Duck" Dunn joined studio keyboardist Booker T. Jones and drummer Al Jackson Jr. to form Booker T. and the M.G.s. This Stax studio unit (with Lewis Steinberg, Dunn's predecessor) recorded "Green Onions" in 1962, and by September it had also reached #3.

Over the ensuing five years, Booker T. and the M.G.s helped to define the musical essence of soul. Jackson's straightforward, simple drumming provided the solid foundation for the syncopated bass patterns created by Dunn, Cropper's distinctive elemental rhythmic chops and fills, and Booker T.'s prolonged organ chords. The popularity of "Green Onions" in particular, and the Memphis soul sound in general, probably accounted for the resurgence of the organ in popular music during the sixties.

Booker T. and the M.G.s, who became the studio musical foundation for Otis Redding, Wilson Pickett, Sam and Dave, and many other Stax/Volt hitmakers, present an interesting paradox. Soul music became identified with essential Blackness, yet the group at its musical core was integrated, evenly divided between Black members Booker T. and Al Jackson and white members Cropper and Dunn (the original bassist, Lewis Steinberg, who left in 1964, was also Black). Soul's white players (Cropper and Dunn, as well as Chips Moman, Dan Penn, Jimmy Johnson, and others in Muscle Shoals) experienced similar roots to soul's Black artists—raised in the South, immersed in R&B, blues, classic rock, and country music, and itching to play modern, syncopated, emotional music. These whites evidenced an innate feel for the genre.

An even greater paradox lies in the fact that Motown—a music we discuss in Chapter 13—produced for an essentially white market but was devised, written, directed, and performed exclusively by African Americans. Soul music, identified as inherently Black and quite popular in the Black community, was controlled by white-run record companies like Atlantic and Stax and produced and recorded by an integrated crew. As a rule, only the individual soul vocalists were Black.

The fortunes of Otis Redding rose in tandem with those of Stax/Volt Records. Stax had signed a licensing and distribution agreement with independent-label Atlantic Records, guaranteeing nationwide clout and sales without the potential business risks and headaches. Otis continued to record in Memphis with the

M.G.s and finally penetrated the pop charts in 1965 with the classic "I've Been Loving You Too Long." Thirty years later, the purity and depth of his emotion still pierces the cultural clutter of our lives. Here is Redding at his best, the balladeer with his halting, urgent pleas capped by exploding exhortations—an agonizingly authentic emotional roller coaster.

From the critically acclaimed album *Otis Blue* came his classic "Respect," a song that earned Redding some radio airplay at the time, but which is best known through Aretha Franklin's 1967 chart-topping rendition. Whether Otis intended it or not, "Respect" became an anthem of Black consciousness, with the demand for racial recognition being substituted for the song's masculine plea for equality in a relationship. The Redding version features the Memphis Horns, an integrated studio group composed of former Mar-Keys members plus some of the area's best Black players—another signature of the Stax sound. They launch the song with horn bursts of pure driving energy, keeping it up with dynamic blasts throughout.

Redding cut a version of the Rolling Stones hit "Satisfaction" (#31, April 1966), and in the spring of 1967 he headlined the Stax/Volt Revue tour of Europe. For five weeks, Sam and Dave, Eddie Floyd, Arthur Conley, the Mar-Keys, Booker T. and the M.G.s, and Otis crisscrossed the continent, conquering overflow crowds and being astounded themselves at the adulation they received. Upon his return to the United States, Redding appeared at the June 1967 Monterey Pop Festival— like other artists, he played for free. Following hometown darlings the Jefferson Airplane at approximately 1:00 AM Sunday morning, Redding, backed by Booker T. and the M.G.s, brought down the house.

Like many other critically acclaimed but relatively unknown performers at the festival—the Who, Hendrix, and Janis—Otis scored big with both the predominantly white audience and the industry representatives in attendance. Redding played San Francisco's Fillmore, wore out the groves of the Beatles' new *Sgt. Pepper's* album, and, while staying on a houseboat docked at Sausalito, California, wrote "(Sittin' on) The Dock of the Bay." On December 7, 1967, Otis, Steve Cropper, and other friends laid down the basic tracks to this classic. Many who heard it questioned its lightness, its lack of grit; Otis said it would be his first #1. On December 10, 1967, Redding and members of his band, the Bar-Keys, flying in his new twin-engine Beechcraft, crashed in a storm near Madison, Wisconsin. Although most commercial flights had been grounded, Otis, driven by his zeal for success, had vowed not to cancel the band's next concert date. Steve Cropper put the finishing touches on "Dock of the Bay"; three months later it was #1.

Otis was twenty-six years old when he died. Like Sam Cooke, he was a man with musical and commercial vision, an artist with an abundance of talent as well as the motivation and brains to forge his way to the top. Also like Sam Cooke, he never had the chance to get there. Stax survived the accident, although in 1968 the label was sold to conglomerate-bound Paramount Pictures. Some artists began to leave, and Stax later lost its Atlantic connection.

Still, Cropper and other producers continued to turn out hits from the Memphis studio. Between 1966 and 1968, Stax's roster included soul's top duo of

Sam (Moore) and Dave (Prater). Both had deep gospel roots—Sam was actually invited to try out for the Soul Stirrers—and they immediately found themselves in a symbiotic relationship when they met in Miami in 1958. Their apprenticeship with Roulette Records proved inconclusive, but early Atlantic sessions at Stax produced the national soul and pop hit "Hold On, I'm Comin'" (#21, June 1966). This song, which is typical of their sound, has Sam's soaring but gritty tenor providing the counterpoint response to Dave's lower emotive growl as both cruise atop the typical drums/bass/guitar-driven groove.

On the road, the Sam and Dave Revue, part of the Stax/Volt European tour, was hard to top for sheer energy; the men usually finished their shows drenched in sweat. More than once Otis Redding was reported to have scolded his managers for placing him as the headliner, closing the show after Sam and Dave. At their peak they recorded two top-10 hits, "Soul Man" (#2, September 1967)—in which Sam rewards Cropper's guitar fill during the second chorus with "Play it, Steve"—and "I Thank You" (#9, February 1968), written and produced (like most of their hits) by the team of Isaac Hayes and David Porter.

In the late 1960s these prolific songwriters (Hayes and Porter) became part of the core Stax staff group along with the M.G.s. Hayes eventually became a highly touted solo artist, writing the music for Black exploitation films (including a #1 hit with "Theme from Shaft" in October 1971) and receiving critical acclaim for his seminal, soul-rap, extended-jam tour-de-force album, *Hot Buttered Soul* (#8, August 1969). Meanwhile, Sam and Dave's personal relationship deteriorated to the point where the team didn't talk to each other except onstage.

Numerous other artists made the pilgrimage to Memphis to record for Stax or for Atlantic at the Stax studio. Alabama-born Wilson Pickett sang lead for Detroit vocal group the Falcons before signing with Atlantic in 1964. In 1965 Atlantic v.p.-producer Jerry Wexler brought Pickett to Stax and, with the M.G.s rhythm section and Cropper cowriting, started his string of pop chart hits by recording "Midnight Hour" (#21, August 1965). Pickett's aggressive personality radiates from the record. Over the bass pattern foundation, with horn blasts and guitar strums emphasizing the backbeat, Pickett, in his raw, scratchy voice, belts out his missive of macho promises.

"The Wicked" Pickett scored a series of top-40 hits in the next three years, including "Land of a Thousand Dances," "Mustang Sally," "Funky Broadway," and a version of "Hey Jude" that included studio musician Duane Allman on guitar. By 1966 Stax had closed the door on all visiting Atlantic artists—including Pickett and his volatile personality—citing lack of open studio time. Stax executives also apparently resented the minimal compensation and pittance of publicity that the studio gleaned from allowing Atlantic artists to use the Stax sound.

Wexler, aware of the impending lockout, had already scouted the South for another studio with the "soul" sound. In the northeastern Alabama town of Muscle Shoals he found Fame Studios, which was operated by Rick Hall. Wexler also found an experienced soul-oriented house band with proven recording success, including Joe Tex's "Hold on to What You've Got" and soul music's first pop chart

#1, Percy Sledge's "When a Man Loves a Woman." The relationship proved fruitful as Atlantic found another studio with the players and the sound, Fame gained national notoriety, and Pickett recorded more hits.

The next Atlantic artist to arrive in Muscle Shoals was Memphis-born Aretha Franklin, a twenty-five-year-old singer steeped in gospel tradition. Her father, the Reverend C. L. Franklin, migrated from the South and became minister at Detroit's large New Bethel Baptist Church, single father to his five children. Reverend Franklin was known as "the man with the million-dollar voice"; he recorded over seventy albums of the spoken word. Aretha grew up in a household where close family friends like gospel greats Mahalia Jackson, Clara Ward, James Cleveland, and Sam Cooke, and jazz legends Art Tatum and Dinah Washington, visited regularly.

By age six Aretha was being billed by her father as the world's youngest gospel singer; at fourteen she had quit school and was on the road with her father as a gospel soloist. At the urging of Sam Cooke, Aretha moved to New York and signed with John Hammond Sr. at Columbia Records in 1960; he declared her's "the best voice I've heard since Billie Holiday." Over the next six years she labored at Columbia, unable to find a consistently suitable style of music to record. She covered show tunes, ballads, gospel, blues, and pop material, earning her only top-40 success with the Al Jolson classic "Rock-a-Bye Your Baby with a Dixie Melody."

In 1966 Atlantic signed Aretha, and another one of those historical "moments" had arrived. The artist was ready, the studio and musicians had the sound, Atlantic producer Wexler and engineer Tom Dowd provided savvy direction, and the soul genre was firmly established. Soul was ready to crown its queen. On her first song, over the rolling electric piano of Spooner Oldham, Aretha spat out the epithet "You're no good, heartbreaker!" at an imaginary lover—Ted White, her husband and manager at the time, was notoriously abusive. The record, "I Never Loved a Man (The Way I Loved You)" backed by "Do Right Woman," served notice to soul fans and the world that Aretha had arrived. Her next record, cut at Atlantic's New York studios, was one of the finest tunes of the decade—Otis Redding's "Respect" (#1, May 1967).

In the ensuing years Aretha continued her success on both the soul and pop charts. Her gospel heritage—evidenced by explosive, soaring, passionate vocals combined with a forceful piano accompaniment—provided the foundation for her entrancing style. Fans were treated to a string of gold singles (including Don Covay's "Chain of Fools," "Think," "Bridge Over Troubled Water," and "Spanish Harlem") and albums *Lady Soul, Live at the Fillmore West* (containing a duet with Ray Charles), and *Young, Gifted, and Black.* In 1972 she recorded the live gospel album *Amazing Grace* in Los Angeles with choir director James Cleveland. Even into the 1990s, Aretha has conducted periodic forays into the world of popular music, earning additional artistic and popular chart successes.

Numerous soul artists worthy of mention barely brushed the pop charts or remained exclusively on the soul side. Some of the genre's greatest singers were virtually unknown to most white pop music fans. Bobby "Blue" Bland was a pioneer, starting as B. B. King's valet before recording a string of sixties soul hits. Solomon Burke, dubbed "the king of rock and soul" by the Atlantic publicity machine and cited by some as soul's best singer, began his career at age nine as "the wonder boy preacher." Joe Tex actually scored three top-10 pop hits but remained essentially out of the music mainstream. Arthur Alexander, Don Covay, and William Bell released soul classics as well.

When once asked about his successful daughter Aretha, the Reverend C. L. Franklin commented that she never really left the church—a statement that is also appropriate for soul as an entire genre. Soul artists apprenticed in the church, receiving invaluable vocal and instrumental training and a relatively optimistic outlook; little changed in their musical transition to the secular arena. The major musical vehicle shifted from the choir to a rhythm and blues band with a punchy horn section. Songs about the Lord and the hereafter became the here and now of everyday life in Black America—sung with the same vocal intensity.

Although the "core band" rhythm-section instrumentation remained constant during the evolution from R&B to soul (drums, bass, guitar, and keyboard), some interesting musical changes were taking place. Whereas R&B bass parts usually consisted of a "walking," steady quarter-note or eighth-note pulse (reminiscent of the blues), soul bass lines were more melodically and rhythmically complex—highly syncopated parts providing a bouncy alternative to the straight-ahead groove laid down by Al Jackson Jr. and others drumming in a similar style. Aretha's "Respect," Sam and Dave's "Soul Man," and Eddie Floyd's "Knock on Wood" are outstanding examples of this bass line syncopation. In addition, the soul horn section increased in prominence since the days of R&B, adding emphasis to syncopated beats and providing much of the gospel-generated call and response with the vocalist.

*　　　*　　　*

Soul, the music and the concept, affected white and Black America in different ways. Most white Americans heard only the hits and saw only the most commercially successful crossover artists—Aretha, Otis, and a few others. Some white Americans adopted the cultural trappings of soul, including language ("Right on!") and gestures (the raised fist). As a genre, however, soul music could not compete on the popular charts with Motown and the British invasion groups and commercially remained a second-class citizen.

For many people in the African-American community, soul was a unifying force. A large percentage of black radio listeners in urban centers were reached by black stations emphasizing soul music. Black DJs talked about soul and soul music as something that represented the black experience that no one could take away. Eventually both the music and the concept came to symbolize Black pride. Whereas few of the hits that whites heard contained direct or symbolic messages of black pride, the soul charts—especially in the late 1960s and early 1970s—contained numerous songs with references to a heightened positive black self-image.

Many Blacks, including James Brown, adopted the afro, an unprocessed African-American hairstyle reflecting this attitude of personal acceptance.

Soul music helped to create the atmosphere in which Black pride grew. Along with the civil rights movement, rising economic expectations, and the era's growing idealism, soul music reflected and spurred further Black advances. Both white and Black audiences experienced the music as an expression of that subjective quality called emotional authenticity, terming that feeling "soul." Paradoxically, this music was produced by an integrated studio band and by white-owned labels; yet the music was interpreted by listeners in the idealistic sixties as an honest and artistically authentic expression of a Black musical and cultural aesthetic.

In Chapter 13 we turn our attention to Motown, the other Black-generated style of 1960s popular music. Motown's reputation as an assembly-line musical commodity is in direct contrast to the notion of spontaneously generated authentic soul music. However, as the story of Motown unfolds, we shall discover numerous similarities to soul—gospel and R&B roots, vocal virtuosity, innovative song production, a top-notch studio band, and a brilliant "sound"—reframed in a way that made a lot of sense to white record buyers.

# 13· Motown: Hitsville, U.S.A.

*Berry [Gordy] wanted to make crossover music. Crossover at that time meant the white people would buy your records. Berry's concept in starting Motown was to make music with a funky beat and great stories that would be crossover, that would not be blues. And that's what we did.*

**Motown legend Smokey Robinson**

*Baby love, my baby love/ I need you, oh, how I need you/ But all you do is treat me bad/ Break my heart and leave me sad.*

**The Supremes, "Baby Love" (Holland/Dozier/Holland, 1964)**

---

MOTOWN IS THE FLIP SIDE of Soul. It is the North (Detroit) to soul's South. It's the rich doo-wop harmonies to soul's searing lead vocals. It's the suave, bouncy rhythmic feeling to soul's torrid, sweaty beat. And yet the two musics were molded from the same raw materials of gospel and rhythm and blues—R&B's core rhythm section, gospel's vocal dexterity, and the beat-laden music of both.

Motown, unlike soul, was the product of a single record company and guided by a strong, visionary leader, Berry Gordy Jr. Gordy's songwriting and production skills, his organizational and business sense, and his zeal to be a part of the American dream provided the impetus for the formation and growth of the company known as Motown and the Motown sound. Of course, Gordy was only one part of this success story. Since Motown's early years occurred during the lull between classic rock and the British invasion, the time was ripe. And the Motown label tapped the enormous talent of Detroit's Black musical community, helping to polish the rough edges and presenting it in a way that excited white America. The success was so monumental that by 1969 Motown was one of America's top-five record companies.

The preamble to the Motown story is mostly a personal history of the Gordy family's migration to the North, their establishment in Detroit as well-respected small-business owners, and Berry Gordy Jr.'s individual growth. Gordy senior (known as "Pops") came to Detroit in the early 1920s and, by the end of World War II, had fathered seven children, built a construction company and a printing business, and had opened the Booker T. Washington grocery store. The grocery's namesake provided the Gordy family with a guiding philosophy: Blacks could get ahead only through hard work and education. Mrs. Bertha Gordy took college business classes, was secretary-treasurer of an insurance company serving a Black clientele, and was active in the Michigan Democratic Party.

In this atmosphere of self-reliance, Berry Jr. searched for his own calling. He boxed professionally—a five-foot-six bantamweight—did a stint in the army, and, with funds borrowed from the family, opened a jazz record store, 3-D Record Mart, in 1953. After the store folded in 1955, Gordy succumbed to the lucrative lure of the auto industry, fastening upholstery at a Lincoln-Mercury plant. His entry into the music business came as a songwriter, coauthoring "Reet Petite," "Lonely Teardrops" (#7), and "That Is Why" (#13) for former sparring partner Jackie Wilson.

Next, Gordy produced an R&B hit for Marv Johnson ("Come to Me") and wrote and produced the often-copied "Money" for Barrett Strong. The song was leased to Gordy's sister, Gwen, for her Anna label and contained Berry and second wife Raynoma singing the echoing "That's what I want" on the chorus. By 1959 Gordy had solidified his friendship with Miracles songwriter and lead singer William "Smokey" Robinson and had begun to set the pieces of the Motown empire. Two labels—Tamla and later Motown—were created, headquarters and studios were established in the house at 2648 West Grand Boulevard, and the Jobete Music Publishing house was formed. In late 1960 the combination of Smokey and Gordy produced the Miracles hit "Shop Around" (#2), the company's first major popular hit.

The first few years (1960–1963) were a time for building—each piece of the foundation for Motown's success had to be crafted and set in place. The talent had to be discovered and acquired, the creative process (in this case, a musical assembly line) organized, and sound business practices established. The Gordy family played an important role in Motown's development, serving the organization in key positions and providing a model of dedication, experience, as well as nepotism. Sisters Esther and Louyce played key fiscal and organizational roles in the company. Pops and a crew of teenage aspirants, including future Temptation David Ruffin, rebuilt much of the interior of the building. In-law Harvey Fuqua (married to Gwen Gordy), former Moonglow lead singer and indie president, polished acts and worked in record promotion. Marvin Gaye (married to Anna Gordy) worked as a session drummer and piano player before turning to a solo career.

The Motown house band—its version of Stax's Booker T. and the M.G.s—was nicknamed the Funk Brothers. Led by pianist Earl Van Dyke (who succeeded Choker Campbell in 1964), the band included James Jamerson on bass, Benny "Papa Zita" Benjamin on drums, and numerous guitarists, including Robert White. Most had formal musical training, and many played in the burgeoning Detroit jazz scene. Van Dyke paid his dues playing with future jazz luminaries Yusef Latteef and Kenny Burrell, national artists like Dizzy Gillespie, and popular performers Lloyd Price and Aretha Franklin.

The Funk Brothers became the core of the Motown sound. Like soul's Al Jackson Jr., Benjamin established a relatively simple rhythmic foundation on drums and was heralded for his ability to establish a song's "groove" (the rhythmic feeling and pulse). For example, the verse section of "Heatwave," a hit for Martha and the Vandellas, is carried along on the crest of Benjamin's forceful drumming; even with the addition of more syncopated snare beats during the chorus, Benjamin is able to keep the forceful groove intact. This ability to propel a song forward without calling undue attention to the drums was one of Papa Zita's many talents.

James Jamerson was one of the era's most creative bassists, credited by many for extending the boundaries of popular-music bass playing toward a more complex and syncopated direction. His early material (for example, the 1965 Temptations hit "My Girl") evidences that active sound and Jamerson's patented unobtrusive fluidity. Material from 1967, like "I Second That Emotion" (the Miracles) and "I Heard It Through the Grapevine" (Gladys Knight and the Pips), shows Jamerson at his syncopated best.[1] As label musical director Maurice King once pointed out, "I attribute the Motown sound to Jamie Jamerson's busy bass."

While industry regulars scoffed at the notion that a roster of mostly Detroit-bred artists could rise to national prominence, Gordy, who regularly prowled the city's Black musical showcases, began to collect the early members of the Motown family. Joining Marv Johnson and the Miracles was Motown's first successful girl group, the Marvelettes, who scored Motown's first #1 in 1961 with "Please Mr. Postman." They continued their pop success throughout 1962 but lost momentum as the company's attention turned to other artists. This inattention was to haunt many of Motown's early top artists. Some, like Mary Wells, left the label while others (the Marvelettes and the Contours) stayed and languished at the bottom of the roster.

Mary Wells, Motown's first important female vocalist, was guided by Smokey Robinson—who wrote and produced most of her eight pop hits. Singing in traditional Robinsonian dulcet tones, Wells reached her commercial pinnacle with the 1964 hit "My Guy." However, having just scored Motown's third #1, and two top-40 duets with Marvin Gaye, Wells left the label. In a scenario that was often repeated at Motown, the artist (or songwriter) became disillusioned with their share of "the family's" growing wealth and left the fold. In Wells's case she, like most other Motown artists of the time, was on salary and received none of the production, songwriting, or label profits that made only a select few wealthy.

Thus, at her zenith—which also included Motown's first British #1, an English tour, and the royal treatment by the Beatles—Wells could show little substantial monetary remuneration. Offered a reported $500,000, two-year contract by Twentieth Century-Fox Records, she left Motown. After one further hit, she fell from the charts. Perhaps, as Motown would later assert, it was the label assembly line and its quality team players that were important, not the individual stars. Others, like Temptation lead singers David Ruffin and Eddie Kendricks, artist and repertoire stalwarts Mickey Stevenson and Harvey Fuqua, and musical director Maurice King, left for similar reasons. Eventually, a mass exodus would signal Motown's demise.

The one consistent artistic and commercial success throughout this developmental period turned out to be the Miracles and their leader, Smokey Robinson. Staring out as the Matadors in 1954, they added Smokey's high school sweetheart and future wife, Claudette, in 1957; they scored with a Gordy-written and -produced hit, "Got a Job," in 1958. During the sixties the Miracles scored multiple top-40 hits every year, in large measure due to their marvelous built-in songwriter-producer-lead singer, Smokey Robinson.

The group's 1965 hit, "The Tracks of My Tears" (#16), is an example of Robinson's prodigious combined talents and his ability to collaborate with others. Written by Robinson and Miracles Warren Moore and longtime guitarist Marv Tarplin, the introduction has Tarplin chiming out a lilting melody on guitar. Instruments are introduced in layers, first in the loping groove established by the drums, two guitars, bass, and congas, and then by the addition of multiple keyboards, a horn section that includes baritone sax, celeste, strings, and the ever-present tambourine accenting the backbeat. Gliding over this musical mixture is Robinson's airy, urgent lead vocal and choral and unison background counterparts from the Miracles.

The ability to tastefully blend musical ingredients into a coherent, pleasing, and commercially successful sound was a most important talent-craft of the Motown family. In early years Robinson and Motown stuck close to the R&B band-and-horns format (heard on the 1963 hit "You Really Got a Hold on Me"), but by 1965 they were opting for a fuller range of instrumentation, including strings. By this time they also had an eight-track recording machine, more flexible than the old three-track model used in the early years. Part of Motown's true genius was the manner in which it arranged instruments into a distinct "sound." Gordy had long ago recognized that most of his listeners were young and that they heard popular music either in their cars or on transistor radios. He also realized the limitations of these units; car and transistor radios produced lousy, thin sound. Thus, Motown tailored its music to overcome these limitations; certain elements in the music were emphasized while others were pushed to the background.

The three major musical elements Motown brought to the forefront were vocals, drums—usually emphasizing the backbeat on the snare drum—and a syncopated bass line. The vocals showcased the attractive singing voices, harmonies, and lyrics, the drums kept time and provided a forceful backbeat, and the bouncy bass impelled the listener to physical excitement (like dancing). The rest of the instruments were moved to the background, providing more of a cumulative musical effect. Two other contemporary producer-writers were famous for this type of instrumental balance and distribution: Phil Spector (noted for his "Wall of Sound") and Beach Boy Brian Wilson.

The Motown musical formula is in evidence on "The Tracks of My Tears." During the first verse, Robinson's lead vocal, the backbeat (played on the snare, tambourine, and rhythm guitar), and the bass take their places in the forefront of the mix. The effect of this type of arrangement, heard through tinny three-inch speakers, was to emphasize the vocals and various rhythms and deemphasize everything else. For sixties youth, this musical formula worked.

The Motown lyrical style was similarly outstanding. Writers excelled at creating a romantic scenario that listeners could identify with, and Robinson was one of the best at this tactic. His talent as a wordsmith prompted Bob Dylan to characterize him as "one of America's greatest living poets." Robinson's specialty was what writer Nelson George describes as "the understanding and dissection of love's paradoxes."[2] In "The Tracks of My Tears" these paradoxes are delivered in the form of a confession. While the singer appears to be the gregarious life of the party, telling jokes and putting on the face of a clown, he confesses to the listener that it is all a masquerade, hiding his devastation at the loss of a true love. To confirm this disclosure, the listener is told to look beyond the smile to the nearly invisible tracks of the tears the clown has shed—a delightfully inventive and sophisticated lyrical construct.

Throughout the midsixties, Robinson had numerous successes, including "The Way You Do the Things You Do," "My Girl," and "Get Ready" (all by the Temptations); Marvin Gaye's "Ain't That Peculiar" and "I'll Be Doggone"; "Don't Mess with Bill" and "The Hunter Gets Captured by the Game" by the Marvelettes; and almost all of the hits scored by the Miracles. Substantial monetary rewards from a variety of roles at Motown, plus his long-standing friendship with and loyalty to Gordy—aided by his 1962 promotion to label vice-president—kept Robinson at Motown in the wake of the late-1960s defections. After his 1972 final appearance with the Miracles, Robinson embarked on a solo career and earned his first Grammy Award in 1988.

The title of most successful writer-producers during Motown's golden years of the mid-1960s goes to brothers Brian and Eddie Holland and partner Lamont Dozier. Known as Holland/Dozier/Holland (or HDH), they created most of the major hits for the Supremes, Martha Reeves and the Vandellas, and the Four Tops plus numerous others for Marvin Gaye, the Miracles, and Junior Walker. Between 1963 and 1967, HDH wrote and produced forty-six top-40 hits including a dozen #1s. When the team formed in 1962, each member had talent and experience as solo vocalist, writer, and outside producer. Eddie Holland specialized in words and working with lead singers, Brian focused mostly on the melodies, and Lamont Dozier covered both in addition to directing the backup vocalists. Brian Holland and Lamont Dozier are generally credited with in-studio production work.

Because of this division of labor, the team fit well with Motown's assembly-line approach to song construction and production. This step-by-step approach—similar to pop music's Tin Pan Alley/Brill Building methods—resembled the auto industry's assembly line. First, the need for a song was established. (For example, a particular group might need a follow-up to their recent hit.) In the case of the Supremes or the Four Tops, HDH would be assigned to write and produce the next song. In the case of a new artist or one without specific writers, Gordy or A&R chief Mickey Stevenson might assign the task to a writer or to two competing writers. Once the song was finished, or an already completed song assigned to a group or individual performer, the recording process would begin. The studio band, generally the Funk Brothers, would be called in to record the rhythm tracks; the singer(s) were then brought in to record vocals, followed by the extra instruments such as strings, horns, and percussion. Finally, the song was mixed down into a final product and an acetate or test pressing was ready for label scrutiny.

The Motown process contained an innovative step that the label called "quality control." A staffer would listen to the finished product in an attempt to determine whether the person in the street would like the record. One early quality-control staffer was future songwriting-production great Norman Whitfield; at the time, he was a quiet, talented teenager hanging around the studio. The acetate would finally reach a weekly meeting where Gordy, label sales and A&R executives, quality-control personnel, and others would vote on all potential releases. The record went to the manufacturing plant only after a positive vote. Although the creative forces, writers, and producers were given substantial artistic freedom, the decision to release a record was concentrated in the hands of a few. Thus, the public heard only what people at the top felt were the best results of Motown's assembly line. This entire process accounted for Motown's incredible release-to-hit ratio. Approximately 65 percent of all label releases reached the Hot 100 charts; no other major label touched even 15 percent.

Holland/Dozier/Holland's Motown successes started with Martha and the Vandellas. Leader Martha Reeves, who was laboring as a Motown secretary while awaiting her chance to record, started singing in a Detroit church and later with her vocal group, the Delphis. After singing backup on some early Marvin Gaye hits, the group changed its name to Martha and the Vandellas and HDH wrote them a hit for the summer of 1964 called "Heatwave" (#4). Although still early in their creative career, HDH exhibited a keen understanding of the pop formula. The musical elements were arranged to emphasize the backbeat (on snare and "clap") and Reeves's emotive vocals. The song also contains a "hook"—a catchy, repeated lyrical and/or musical element designed to remain with the listener.

In "Heatwave" the musical hook, played by baritone sax and kick drum, was on the first and anticipated third beats of the four-beat measure. A lyrical hook was also in evidence, the title word being repeated over and over. HDH and Gordy knew the value of repetition and familiarity. Assisting people to enjoy and remember their songs by the use of hooks was a vital ingredient in the Motown formula. As if to prove this point, the Vandellas follow-up to "Heatwave" a few months later had the same rhythmic musical hook (this time emphasized by the piano, guitar, and kick-drum), and a lyrical hook also consisting of two syllables and describing a natural phenomena (in this case "Quicksand," #8).

The biggest hit by Martha and the Vandellas was "Dancing in the Street" (#2), written by A&R director Mickey Stevenson and Marvin Gaye for release in the summer of 1964. The group disbanded in 1971, not having had a hit since 1967, and Martha Reeves left the label the next year. Like other early Motown performers, the Vandellas took a seat near the back of the bus around 1964, as Gordy and HDH geared up to promote their newest female group, the Supremes.

Florence Ballard, Mary Wilson, Barbara Martin, and Diane Ross (who changed her name to Diana) were teenagers from Detroit's Brewster-Douglass housing projects when they formed a group called the Primettes—the Temptations were billing themselves as the Primes at the time—and hung out at the Grand Boulevard headquarters hoping for their big break. Although Gordy had told them to come back after they had finished high school, the Primettes were signed to Motown in early 1961. Initially, the group split lead vocal chores; and though both Ballard and Wilson had stronger voices, Ross's unique, nasal sensuality attracted key Motown personnel, including Berry Gordy, Dozier, and Brian Holland. Ross's aggressive personality—some would later characterize her as manipulative and pushy—and penchant for hard work earned her the position of lead vocalist.

After numerous earlier releases and a minor hit in late 1963, HDH handed the Supremes "Where Did Our Love Go," the first of five straight #1s. The July 1964 hit cemented a group-writer relationship that would produce sixteen hits, including ten #1s, before 1968. In "Where Did Our Love Go" HDH establish a forceful quarter-note "clap" pulse reinforced by the bass to carry Ross's delicate voice. During the first two verses, between Ross and the backup singers, the word "baby" is repeated nineteen times. No doubt, many a commuter left their cars that summer humming "baby, baby." It is no coincidence that the first actual word sung three months later in their follow-up #1 hit was the "baby" in "Baby Love." The follow-up, as well as many future hits, including "Stop in the Name of Love" and "Reflections," also contained the emphasized quarter-note pulse, which was probably used to compensate for the lack of lead-vocal forcefulness.

There were a multitude of reasons for the success of the Supremes. The ladies had talent, and Ross's unique voice and doe-eyed charisma were infectious. HDH wrote and produced catchy, danceable songs admirably interpreted by the studio musicians. However, a transformation had to take place in order to make this all work; three Black women from the projects had to appear as princesses, acceptable to white American sensibilities. This is where the Motown finishing school, singing lessons, and dance sessions came in. All the major acts, especially the women, were schooled in how to talk, eat, walk, use correct deportment, dress, and carry on charming but uninformative relations with the press. The matron of one of Detroit's better-known finishing schools was persuaded to close her doors and come to work for Motown. Dancemaster Cholly Atkins was persuaded to relocate and choreograph label acts. It was said that Motown acts were being groomed to appear in two places: Buckingham Palace and the White House.

The combination of Diana Ross's coquettish demeanor, bright smile, and airy voice, the mid-tempo soap-opera dramas crafted by HDH, and the best promotional campaign Motown could mount (including Berry Gordy's personal efforts), helped to create the label's most successful group. Their string of HDH #1s included "You Can't Hurry Love," "You Keep Me Hanging On," and "The Happening." The group traveled with the Motortown Revues, a label package show in the early 1960s that toured the States and Europe but became too big and moved on to the country's most prestigious venues such as New York's Copacabana and some of the Vegas showcase palaces.

Events during 1967 eventually proved to be disastrous for the group. That July, Gordy dismissed Flo Ballard from the group. The original leader and the group's most powerful singer, Ballard had been pushed into the background to allow for the emergence of Ross. Whereas Mary Wilson could rationalize Ross's aggressiveness and ego-driven zeal as her being "just Diane," Florence became increasingly frustrated and depressed at her secondary status. Without warning Ballard was out and Cindy Birdsong, who had already been thoroughly rehearsed, became a Supreme.

Next, Holland/Dozier/Holland sued Motown for back-royalties and left the label. Even Hitsville's top team came to view Gordy's accumulation of wealth with resentment; they felt they deserved a more representative share. HDH later collected a substantial sum, and their absence was felt immediately. Morale dropped as the Supremes and the Four Tops searched for another winning writing/production team. The Tops never found one, and the Supremes, after 1968's "Love Child," had to wait until Ross announced her departure for their final #1, the absurdly titled "Someday We'll Be Together." The group carried on into the late 1970s with Mary Wilson as the only original member. In 1977 she sued Motown, citing the $200–300 weekly salary she had been receiving during the glory years and asking for an equitable settlement. Diana Ross was successful as a pop music personality and received wide acclaim as Billie Holiday in the Gordy-directed movie *Lady Sings the Blues*.

The Four Tops lacked the momentum to maintain their success after HDH's departure. These Detroit natives had been singing together since 1954 (originally as the Four Aims) and had recorded with a variety of labels, including Chess and Columbia, before signing with Motown in 1964. Paired with HDH, they hit big with "Baby, I Need Your Lovin'" (#11) in 1964 before their first #1, "I Can't Help Myself (Sugar Pie, Honey Bunch)" (spring of 1965). On "Sugar Pie" the HDH formula worked well. The rhythmic accents abound as tambourine and guitar cover the backbeat, the snare pulses on quarter-notes, and the bass and another guitar press forward on a circular syncopated pattern. Levi Stubbs's dynamic, slightly gritty lead vocal rides over the groove, echoed by a typical HDH unison response by the rest of the group.[3]

In an anecdote illustrative of Gordy's business acumen, Motown received word that Columbia Records, in an attempt to capitalize on the first #1 by the Four Tops, would flood the market with previous Four Tops products. The legend has HDH summoned to headquarters, ordered to beat the other label to the punch. Ostensibly, they wrote the follow-up on Monday, recorded the rhythm section Tuesday morning and vocalists that night, put sweeteners (strings, horns, and so on) on Wednesday, and mixed it that same day. The disc was in the stores the following Monday. Recorded in the same key, using a similar circular bass pattern and quarter-note snare, and featuring unison background vocals, the follow-up was aptly named "It's the Same Old Song" and rose to #5 on the charts. The Four

Tops were moderately successful, scoring four more top-10 hits (including the highly dramatic "Reach Out I'll Be There" and "Standing in the Shadows of Love") before leaving Motown for ABC/Dunhill in 1972.

With a career dating back to 1960, the Temptations, Motown's most critically acclaimed and commercially successful male group, stayed on with the label. Not only did they achieve outstanding chart success (twenty-eight top-40 hits between 1964 and 1972 including four #1s), but their live performances were legendary—composed of equal amounts of high energy and beautifully choreographed synchronized fancy steppin'. Whereas the Supremes and the Four Tops relied on HDH, the Temps' early mentor was Smokey Robinson, who wrote and produced most of their pre-1967 hits. Like the Four Tops, the Temps came to the label via the Detroit doo-wop circuit, singing in groups with names like the Distants, Elegants, Questions, and Primes. The Primes changed their name to the Temptations at Gordy's suggestion. By 1962 the lineup had solidified to include tenors Eddie Kendricks and David Ruffin, baritones Otis and Paul Williams (no relation), and bass Melvin Franklin.

Their first pop hit, the Robinson-penned "The Way You Do the Things You Do," featured the Smokey-like high tenor vocals of Eddie Kendricks, cleverly list-

The Temptations

ing the romantic attributes of his lover. It is interesting to note that the handclaps reinforcing the backbeat on record were actually Motown's legendary studio two-by-fours being hit together. By 1965 David Ruffin—with his gritty, intense vocal style—had emerged as the lead singer, fronting Robinson's follow-up to Wells's hit "My Guy" with the group's first #1, "My Girl." This classic contains one of Motown's most memorable musical moments as Ruffin's "my girl" is echoed by Paul Williams on the three of the scale, followed by a harmonized "my girl" by the rest of the group.

Starting in 1966, one of Motown's most important but least-known writer-producers, Norman Whitfield, replaced Robinson as the Temptations' mentor. Over the next six years, he wrote, mostly with Barrett Strong, numerous top-10 hits for the Temptations, including: "Beauty Is Only Skin Deep," "I Wish It Would Rain," "Cloud Nine," "I Can't Get Next to You," "Ball of Confusion," and "Papa Was a Rollin' Stone." In 1968 Ruffin left for a solo career, replaced by another fine vocalist, former Contour Dennis Edwards, and in 1971 Kendricks departed.

The change in personnel was paralleled by a shift in Whitfield and Strong's songwriting vision. Beginning with "Cloud Nine," the songs turned from a focus on romance toward first-person accounts of the physical and emotional struggles of Black urban existence. In both lyrical content and musical production, these were seminal works. When "Cloud Nine" was released in late 1968, Motown music had yet to reflect the profound political and social changes being experienced by the Black community. "Cloud Nine"—through its lyrics and music—recounts the experience of smoking "consciousness-altering drugs," much in the same way the Jefferson Airplane did one year before with "White Rabbit."

"Cloud Nine" broke Motown's lyrical formula taboos, at the same time loosening musical boundaries. No longer restricted to a romance-oriented permutation, the song describes the hardships of living in lower-class Black America, accompanied by the strains of wah-wah guitar, strong quarter-note snare-driven pulse, and funk-like syncopated bass. Using influences from Jimi Hendrix and Sly Stone, Whitfield shaped a sound that would have an impact on many early 1970s Black musicians—including Isaac Hayes, Curtis Mayfield, and the Philadelphia team of Kenny Gamble and Leon Huff. In a move that paralleled popular music trends, Whitfield extended playing length; the short version of "Papa Was a Rollin' Stone" was six minutes, the album cut nearly twelve.

Of Whitfield's many commercial successes during that era, two are worthy of special note: "I Heard It Through the Grapevine" (1967) and "War" (1970). Whitfield cowrote (with Strong) and produced both hit versions of "Grapevine," the original for Gladys Knight and the Pips (#2, 1967) and Marvin Gaye's follow-up (#1, 1968). Knight and the Pips had come to Motown in 1965 with the reputation as an extraordinarily dynamic and polished stage act—they had been singing together since 1956 and their steps were choreographed by dancer Cholly Atkins. Knight had been considered something of a child prodigy since her appearance at age seven on TV's "Ted Mack Amateur Hour." "Grapevine" was their first major hit, and Knight's explosive, gospel-style lead vocals served notice that Motown had a new outstanding vocalist on its roster. Unfortunately, with Motown's attention turned toward Diana Ross's pending solo career, insufficient attention was lavished on the group and they left the label in 1973. "War," with a prefunk rhythmic groove and Edwin Starr's raw-voiced pentecostal pleadings, expressed exasperation at the senselessness of the current armed conflict in both the ghetto and Vietnam—"War . . . what is it good for . . . absolutely nothing."

Unlike the Pips, Marvin Gaye had been at Motown since the early days. Having grown up in Washington, D.C., as the son of an authoritarian pentecostal minister, Gaye—born Gay, he added the "e" for homophobic reasons—was raised singing in the church. He turned to secular doo-wop vocalizing as a rebellious response to a physically and psychologically abusive home environment. His group, the Marquis, cut an unsuccessful Bo Diddley-produced record before doo-wop star Harvey Fuqua tabbed them to become the new Moonglows. Fuqua became Gaye's mentor and benevolent father figure, and when he moved to Detroit to form his own label, Marvin came with him. By 1962 Gaye had worked as a backup drummer and piano player, recorded his first album *The Soulful Moods of Marvin Gaye*, scored his first R&B hit with "Stubborn Kinda Fellow," and married Berry's sister Anna Gordy.

In the sixties Gaye recorded seventeen hits for a variety of producers. These included "Ain't That Peculiar" (#8, 1965) with Smokey, "How Sweet It Is to Be Loved by You" (#6, 1965) written and produced by HDH, "Ain't Nothin' Like the Real Thing" (#8, 1968) written and produced by Valerie Simpson and Nicholas Ashford, and Whitfield and Strong's "Grapevine." One major reason for this success was Gaye's vocal dexterity, ranging from a Nat Cole-like smoothness to a Ray Charles-inspired raw forcefulness. Gaye also exhibited a suave demeanor, sensuality, and charisma onstage that attracted more than his share of female admirers.

Female fans were especially thrilled when, beginning in 1964, Gaye released a series of duets with some of Motown's leading ladies. Gaye had top-20 hits with Mary Wells and Kim Weston, but his most praised work was with Tammi Terrell, a former feature soloist with James Brown's Mr. Dynamite Review. Gaye's apparently platonic adoration for Terrell translated into ultimate romance on vinyl; the duo released three albums and had seven pop hits between 1967 and 1969. Tragically, Tammi collapsed in Marvin's arms onstage in the summer of 1967. She never fully recovered, and after numerous operations she died from the effects of a brain tumor.[4]

It was nearly two years before Gaye sufficiently recovered his composure to perform at Marvin Gaye Day in Washington, D.C., in May 1972. However, in the studio, the ever-reluctant Gaye was recording his magnum opus, the label's best-selling album of the era, *What's Goin' On*. The sensitive, troubled Gaye found what he called "a path of the heart." Like Whitfield and other African-American writers of the time, Gaye chose to explore the Black urban experience. Gaye weaves tales about personal and political war and peace ("What's Goin' On" and "What's Happenin' Brother"), the environment ("Mercy Mercy Me"), drugs ("Flyin' High"), and life in the ghetto ("Inner City Blues").

Historically, Motown rarely gave an artist control over a major project, so this album represented a 180-degree shift in production—no artist, other than Smokey, wrote, produced, and arranged so much original material. Motown was reluctant to release *What's Goin' On;* Gaye threatened to stop recording altogether if they didn't. It went to #1. This artist-control precedent was later demanded and won by Stevie Wonder and Michael Jackson.

Gaye's ambivalent feelings about life complicated what was largely a successful musical career at Motown. He was tormented by his relationship with his father, by the legacy of a strict religious upbringing conflicting with the real life that contained sins of music and the flesh, and his ability to meet the day-to-day demands of music and the road. His escape led him to psychoactive drugs—Gaye claimed to have smoked marijuana for twenty-five years and snorted cocaine since the early sixties—relocation in Europe, and frequent contemplation of suicide. On the day before his forty-fifth birthday, Marvin Gaye was shot to death in his bedroom by his father.

Another artist who worked within the Motown system only to struggle free in the early seventies was Stevie Wonder. Signed to a contract at age eleven, Little Stevie Wonder (changed by Gordy from Steveland Morris) was all of thirteen when he released Motown's second #1 hit, "Fingertips Part II" (1963). Although blind from birth, Wonder had, by his teen years, become an accomplished harmonica, piano, bongo, and trap-drum player. In addition, he wrote or cowrote most of his sixteen hits of the 1960s. During Wonder's teen years, a time that is not always kind to a boy's voice as he reaches puberty, his church-trained, high-tenor voice mellowed gradually—lowering slightly for the 1965 hit "Uptight" and even further for the critically acclaimed, bass-driven "I Was Made to Love Her" (#2, 1967).

Throughout the sixties Wonder labored in the Motown factory, where the company maintained control over all aspects of production. Wonder cowrote the material and Clarence Paul or Hank Crosby produced most of the hits. In the late 1960s the two albums, *My Cherie Amour* and *Signed, Sealed and Delivered,* produced four top-10 singles including both title tracks. Then, in 1971, Stevie Wonder—the "Little" had long since been dropped—turned twenty-one and became an instant millionaire from royalties Motown held in trust. Wonder decided to leave the factory. He moved to New York, formed a production company (Taurus, like its owner) and a publishing company (Black Bull), hired attorney Jonathan Vigoda to field the substantial record company contract offers, and set out in search of his liberated musical self.

The quest led him to the keyboard synthesizer. Inspired by the work of the two-musician group the Expanding Headband (Malcolm Cecil and Robert Margouleff), Wonder sequestered the three of them in the late Jimi Hendrix's Electric Ladyland Studio for a year's worth of experimentation. A quarter of a million dollars later over three hundred songs had germinated; some of them appeared on his next four pioneering albums, *Music of My Mind* (1972), *Talking Book* (1972), *Innervisions* (1973), and *Fulfillingness First Finale* (1974).

Stevie Wonder

These four albums, plus the 1976 classic *Songs in the Key of Life*, established Wonder as the most important Black popular musician of the era. Not only did he have chart success (*Songs in the Key of Life* was the #1 album for fourteen weeks), but his overall compositional brilliance, musical talent and craftsmanship, and in-spirational lyrics were critically acclaimed during this period. In addition, Wonder's vision of spiritual enlightenment and peaceful coexistence shone as a popular music beacon during and after the dark days of the prolonged Vietnam War and Watergate.

The late 1960s and early 1970s also gave rise to Motown's first family from Gary, Indiana: the Jackson 5. The group was initially brought to Motown's atten-tion by Gladys Knight, whose recommendations were ignored. The Jackson kids were already a polished group, guided by the aggressive and experienced "Papa" Joe Jackson—a former guitarist for a Detroit group called the Falcons—when they signed to the label and left for Los Angeles to record and undergo more Motown fine-tuning.

The racial unrest in Detroit and concentration of music industry power in L.A. had convinced Gordy that a move to the West Coast was necessary. Beginning to move in 1969 (final consolidation came in 1972), Gordy spent increasing amounts of time and recording-budget money on the West Coast. During this period many Funk Brothers, songwriters, and administrators left the label and/or stayed in Detroit. With the key writers gone or busy, Gordy took a more active role in launching the Jackson 5's career, joining with three staff writers (designated "the Corporation") to write and produce many of their early hits. To promote the band, Motown had their diva, Diana Ross, give them a jump start—she claimed to have discovered them, their first album was titled *Diana Ross Presents the Jackson 5,* and they were featured on her 1970 network-TV special.

Their early success rate was phenomenal; their first four hits, including "I Want You Back" and "ABC," were all #1s. All eyes were focused on eleven-year-old lead singer Michael, a prodigious child performer in the tradition of Frankie Lymon and Little Stevie Wonder. His choreographed steps—Michael spent hours studying the moves of James Brown—vocal fluidity, and stage presence evidenced a talent and self-assurance far beyond his years. Their recording successes were enhanced by a second-generation Motown house band punching out the well-crafted, driving musical sound. In 1971 Michael initiated a parallel solo career, scoring four top-20 hits in 1972.

Jackson's solo career languished in the mid-1970s until the release in 1979 of *Off the Wall (#3),* which was followed in 1982 by the blockbuster *Thriller.* Jackson had obviously found a musical and lyrical formula that appealed to a broader-than-normal pop-audience age group. *Thriller* stayed at #1 for thirty-seven weeks, sold more than 40 million copies—making it the best-selling album in history—and produced six top-20 singles. The former child prodigy, Michael Jackson, who had been in the music business for over fifteen years, reached the top at age twenty-four. However, Motown couldn't afford his success. Epic Records (a Columbia Records subsidiary) won the bidding war for Michael and the Jacksons back in 1976, and the company reaped the rewards.

By the early 1970s the Motown roster had lost an appreciable number of its former stars—the glitter and camaraderie of its golden days were fading fast. There are numerous reasons for this decline. Beginning with his announced intention to move in 1969, Gordy spent more of his time and focused much of his attention on the West Coast. The bipolar ship began to drift under its absentee captain. Numerous personnel had chosen, because of family or monetary reasons, to leave the label or not to relocate to Los Angeles with the final contingent in 1972.

The great accumulation of wealth by the chosen few and the relative pittances gathered by the many led to the defection of key players. Already, Holland/Dozier/Holland, songwriter-producer Harvey Fuqua, and the team of

Ashford and Simpson had left. By the early seventies the Four Tops, Gladys Knight and the Pips, Temptation lead vocalist David Ruffin, the Isley Brothers, Martha Reeves and the Vandellas, Mary Wells, and others departed. In the early days artists had signed contracts for small salaries and royalties, reflecting the reality of a small company working together as a family to get to the top. When Motown's success exceeded even their wildest expectations, and money came pouring into the label's coffers, the artists were still on salary, Motown songwriters were still signed to Gordy's Jobete Publishing Company, and artist performances were booked through Gordy's ITM Agency. In the end the factory owner got rich and the workers got steady employment.

Nevertheless, for that golden era between 1964 and 1971, Motown's version of bouncy Black romance took on all comers and beat them on the charts. They became America's teenage soundtrack and everybody's dance track. With Gordy's musical and entrepreneurial genius as the basis for the sound, a successful formula was developed to best represent Black musical roots and to best utilize the technology of the era. The lyrics were crafted to appeal to a broad cross-section of young white America. And, for a time, Motown was on top. But popular tastes changed, key personnel left, and the label was forced to relinquish its popular music crown.

# 14· The San Francisco Sound: People in Motion

*More important than just the music is the whole attitude, the dance thing, the whole fact that there are lots of people getting together. . . . We never grew up where there were things like that. It was pretty isolated. And now suddenly there are large groups of people getting together.*

*Jerry Garcia, of the Grateful Dead*

*One particular element I enjoyed was the breaking of shackles—the intellectual shackles represented by the mentality of the 50's, sexual shackles that had been in place forever . . . anything proscribed by the establishment—everything from Chairman Mao to drugs to acupuncture to Eldridge Cleaver—was looked into with relish.*

*Paul Kantner, of the Jefferson Airplane*

*It used to be that when people came out to hear music it was like they were going to the temple.*

*Rock impresario Bill Graham*

*Sometimes the lights all shining on me, other times I can barely see/ Lately it occurs to me, what a long strange trip it's been.*

*"Truckin'" by the Grateful Dead (1970)*

T HE YEAR WAS 1965. The British invasion was underway. Bob Dylan was rising to national prominence with his first popular hit, "Like a Rolling Stone," and his disciples were spreading folk-oriented rock with a message throughout the land. Soul artists had begun to hit their stride and Motown's golden era was in full flower. Out in San Francisco, a group of musicians, supported and inspired by a growing counterculture community, was giving birth to a music style destined to become one of American rock's most creative and culturally exotic.

Between 1965 and 1970, waves of Bay Area bands were formed, brewed their eclectic blend of folk-rock and revivalist blues, and achieved some level of national prominence. This chapter will focus upon six of the era's most popular bands—the Jefferson Airplane, Big Brother and the Holding Company (featuring Janis Joplin), Country Joe and the Fish, the Grateful Dead, and two later arrivals, Creedence Clearwater Revival and Santana—and the cultural milieu in which their music was created. The region's vibrant music scene produced many more groups than space permits us to chronicle; some are even worthy of mention if only for strikingly unique names like A Cid Symphony, Frumious Bandersnatch, the Cleanliness and Godliness Skiffle Band, and one of my favorites, Black Shit Puppy Farm.

San Francisco-area rock was composed of a variety of musical and lyrical ingredients. Some of it reflected the current musical trends, such as the two-guitar ensemble and two-plus-four rhythmic emphasis of classic rock and early Beatles music; lyrics critical of traditional societal values and behavior; and an emotive, earnest vocal style reflective of the ongoing folk-rock boom. However, there were also significant musical and cultural departures from contemporary popular styles, seen in the distorted, extended guitar improvisations, which paralleled those of the emerging sixties blues revival and took on more major-scale melodic character than their blues counterparts; the lyrics emanating from Bay Area groups, which were more likely to contain references to altered consciousness and counterculture concerns; and Bay Area musicians themselves, who challenged the commonly held music-industry notion of elite star-versus-commoner relationship with the audience.

One reason this challenge took place was that Bay Area artists closely identified with the San Francisco/Berkeley counterculture communities. Even though the Beatles and Stones lived in London, they did so in mansions, isolated from the hoi polloi; many American rock artists did the same. However, a large number of San Francisco's musicians resided in communal living situations in the city's Haight-Ashbury neighborhood, drawing their support and cultural and political attitudes from their immediate environment. Members of the Dead lived at 710 Ashbury, Big Brother resided and practiced at 1090 Page, and the Airplane established their headquarters at the 2400 Fulton mansion. Immersing themselves in the counterculture, they grew their hair long, adopted appropriate modes of dress, played music, and took psychoactive drugs.

During this era the ingestion of psychoactive drugs by the counterculture community, including its musicians, was the rule rather than the exception. Smoking marijuana and taking other drugs was as common as drinking coffee, considered both a search for enlightenment and escape from oppressive elements of "straight" society. Community members believed that recreational drug use enhanced both the individual's quality of life and his artistic creativity. Users made a strong distinction between psychoactive drugs (marijuana, hashish, LSD, mescaline, mushrooms, and the like), which they believed would produce this positive result, and alcohol, methamphetamines or "speed," barbiturates, and heroin, which produced aggressive hostility or numbness.

Due to the close proximity to San Francisco and Berkeley's alternative culture community, the musicians' artistic output strongly reflected the community's escape from the straight world and its idealistic search for a different set of values and existence. This quest manifested itself in many ways, including music that tested existing boundaries and lyrics and were highly critical of mainstream society. Artists produced an inordinately large proportion of what James Carey would term "newer-value" songs.[1] These critical songs covered a spectrum of topics. Some, such as the Jefferson Airplane's "Somebody to Love," dealt with the common topic of romance, adding a touch of societal focus and alienation. Others, such as the Grateful Dead's "Dark Star," explored more metaphysical or esoteric topics, whereas Country Joe and the Fish's "I Feel Like I'm Fixin' to Die Rag" and Creedence Clearwater Revival's "Fortunate Son" proffered political commentary on contemporary subjects such as the Vietnam War.

Just as the objective conditions in Liverpool spawned the Beatles and the Mersey Beat, San Francisco's history as a pioneer boomtown contributed to the new sound's development. Ever since the 1849 gold rush, the "City" had earned a reputation for "anything goes." The Barbary Coast neighborhood of the late nineteenth century was notorious; gambling, prostitution, and gangsterism flourished. Under the philosophy that each neighborhood should be left to its own devices, San Francisco would later allow the topless bars of North Beach and the culturally radical Haight-Ashbury of the sixties to exist. San Francisco became a last frontier for eccentrics.

In the fifties some viewed San Francisco as a haven for creative intellects, with the beatniks or "beats" as the most recent wave. These artistic, counterculture bohemians sought to create an alternative to the rigid, conservative, Cold War–dominated lifestyle of the fifties. They challenged the old order, seeking answers by studying existentialist and Eastern philosophies, writing poetry, listening to jazz and folk music, adopting a try-anything sexual philosophy, and expanding consciousness through the use of psychoactive drugs (in this case, mostly marijuana). From the cultural heights of their Columbus Avenue coffeehouses, it was the beats who identified their sixties counterculture counterparts as only a little "hip," thus a "hippie."

San Francisco also had a tradition of political activism, which added a spark to the alternative community and its music. Elements of the Bay Area's trade union movement, led by the Longshoreman's Union and its head, Harry Bridges, involved themselves in political and social issues. (They would later take a stand against the Vietnam War by refusing to load ships bound for the conflict.) In 1960 a broad political coalition mounted a campaign to bar the House Un-American Activities Committee from holding its McCarthy-style hearings in San Francisco. When demonstrators were brutalized in front of the nation's TV cameras on the city hall steps, the public outcry contributed to the committee's final demise.

In 1964 the University of California at Berkeley (across San Francisco Bay) closed the campus to controversial leftist, student-invited speakers. Students reacted to this abrogation of their academic liberties by forming the free-speech movement and by holding massive demonstrations and sit-ins on campus. This confrontational student activism set the tone for midsixties Bay Area political and cultural activities and was a bellwether for student movements nationwide.

The existence of numerous older ballrooms, able to be rented for reasonable sums, made San Francisco unique. The process of urban renewal—an architectural genocide against America inner cities—that took place across the country missed many of the area's old dance palaces. The midsixties San Francisco music scene adopted these dance halls for their performances. Rather than an audience viewing the musician-elite from distant fixed seating, it became an active participant, a swarm of throbbing, psychedelic, whirling dervishes. Band members expressed the feeling that the audience and artists were part of one large organism, one in which the musician head wagged the dancing tail.

Thus, the conditions under which this San Francisco-based music emerged and flourished included the legacy of a free-spirited, anything-goes attitude, previous successful counterculture communities, a history where political activism played an integral role, and a number of ballroom venues where the symbiotic musician/audience relationship could be born and nurtured. It was within this historical context that a young San Francisco native named Marty Balin (having changed his name from Martyn Buchwald) opened a club called the Matrix in the spring of 1965. He then set about forming a "great" folk-rock group to become the house band.

For his first recruit, Balin tabbed local folkie-cum-rocker Paul Kantner, who had gone to school in nearby San Jose, managed a club, and happened to be carrying a banjo and guitar when they met. Lead guitarist Jorma Kaukonen, a widely traveled Washington, D.C.-based son of a diplomat, had been an acoustic blues aficionado in the Bay Area for a few years before being asked to join. Kaukonen enticed his D.C. buddy, bassist Jack Casady, to the coast and Balin rounded out the rhythm section when he spied Skip Spence and said "there's our drummer." When Spence replied that he was a guitarist, Balin sent him home to practice drums. Folk vocalist Signe Anderson completed the lineup that adopted its name from a friend's dog, Blind Thomas Jefferson Airplane.

The Jefferson Airplane (or "Airplane" for short)—a group of mostly middle-class, ex-folknik, rock and roll converts—debuted at the Matrix in August 1965. Meanwhile, the ballroom scene was being born. A group of friends called the Family Dog rented the Longshoreman's Hall near Fisherman's Wharf, contracted with the region's budding talent, and dubbed the October 16, 1965, event A Tribute to Dr. Strange. Posters were colored in with magic marker, advertising the Jefferson Airplane, the Marbles, the Great Society (featuring vocalist Grace Slick), and area music pioneers the Charlatans. *San Francisco Chronicle* jazz and popular music journalist Ralph J. Gleason, an early scene supporter, described the night: "Long lines of dancers snaked through the crowd holding hands. Free form improvisation ('self expression') was everywhere. The clothes were a blast. Like a giant costume party. . . . It was a gorgeous sight."

The Jefferson Airplane

Within the next three weeks, the Family Dog threw two more parties: A Tribute to Sparkle Plenty, with the Lovin' Spoonful and the Charlatans; and A Tribute to Ming the Merciless (an evil character from the 1930s sci-fi serial *Flash Gordon*) featuring Frank Zappa's Mothers of Invention, the Charlatans, and emcee Howard Hesseman. In December a guerrilla theater group known as the San Francisco Mime Troupe and its business manager, Bill Graham, rented an old second-story ballroom called the Fillmore (in a Black neighborhood of the same name) for a benefit dance/concert. They booked six bands, including the Airplane, the Great Society, and a new group on the scene known as the Warlocks (soon to change their name to the Grateful Dead). Signs inside the hall proclaimed "LOVE" and "NO BOOZE," and the packed house got "high with a little help from their friends."

In December 1965 the Airplane became the first of the new groups to land a major-label contract, signing with RCA Records. Their first album, *Jefferson Airplane Takes Off*, was released the next August and featured Balin's yearning tenor vocals and folk-style guitar strumming. Its generally vague musicianship and looseness were typical of the era's early sound but belied some band members' classical training (Kaukonen, Casady, and future drummer Spencer Dryden). The band was going through other changes as well. Anderson, with a newborn baby, returned to her native Oregon and drummer Spence left the band, strapped on his guitar, and helped to form the group Moby Grape. Their replacements were experienced jazz and rock drummer Dryden and vocalist Grace Slick, lured away from Great Society.

By the first weekend of January 1966 the ballroom dance/concert had achieved institutional status. At the Longshoreman's Hall, top-40 radio station KYA presented a dance with the Vejtables; at the California Hall, the Family Dog hosted the Airplane and the Charlatans; and at the Fillmore, author and LSD-advocate Ken Kesey held his Acid Test with the Warlocks. The ballrooms—the Fillmore, Avalon (used mostly by the Family Dog), Winterland (a converted ice rink), Carousel (renamed the Fillmore West by Graham), the California Hall, and others—became the musical meeting places.

A few weeks after the Acid Test, Kesey and his psychedelic sidekicks put on a three-day event at the Longshoreman's Hall called the Trips Festival. A multimedia circus featuring strobe lights, slides, bands, theater, and Native American tipis, it was billed as an LSD simulation without the drug. (Out in the crowd, someone distributed free samples of acid-domo Augustus Owsley Stanley III's latest batch of still-legal LSD.) Referring to the developing avant-garde culture, Kesey proclaimed, "It's a need to find a new way to look at the world, an attempt to locate a better reality, now that the old reality is riddled with radioactive poison."[2]

The Trips Festival was part of the ongoing odyssey so magnificently captured in Tom Wolfe's book, *The Electric Kool-Aid Acid Test*. Kesey, a prize-winning author—and participant in early Stanford University LSD research—had assembled a crew of creative, eccentric, LSD-addled Merry Pranksters, and they were all involved in a life-cum-bus ride, with the destination being only "further." To them, you were either on the bus or off the bus. Soon after the Trips Festival, Kesey the guru became Kesey the outlaw, retiring to a Mexican beach to avoid serving time for numerous marijuana-related offenses. Although Kesey was out of circulation for a while, the beat went on.

A small group of community graphic artists (Wes Wilson, Alton Kelly, Stanley "Mouse" Miller, Victor Morocco, Rick Griffin, and others) were hired to create posters to advertise the ballroom shows. The concert posters were brightly colored (to be spotted from a distance and attract attention), extraordinarily detailed, highly stylized, and, at times, difficult to read. Potential music patrons, many of whom were in chemically altered states, were known to have stared for hours at a poster in an attempt to decipher its layered meaning. In the early 1970s, as Bay Area ballrooms closed and the demand for posters fell off, the use of posters had spread to other parts of the country. Contemporary critics now view the San Francisco's sixties-era poster art as some of America's finest.

Another nonmusical innovation adopted by the San Francisco scene was the psychedelic light show. Using a constantly changing mixture of slides, film (anything from cartoons to film of last week's show), flashing strobe lights, and colored pigments floating on oil (transmitted by overhead projectors), the light shows filled ballroom walls, stage screens, audiences, and other surfaces with an intense, shifting, pulsating spectrum of images and color. Like the posters, light shows also illuminated music in other areas.

Throughout 1966 numerous counterculture businesses grew alongside the music scene. Much of this activity took place in and around the Haight-Ashbury community, named for the intersection of two central streets. "Hip" merchants opened stores to service the community's physical and spiritual needs. The Psychedelic Shop carried occult books, incense, Indian paisley fabrics, smoking paraphernalia, dance/concert tickets, and myriad other items. Clothing stores and boutiques like Mnadsidika, In Gear, and the Blushing Peony flourished along with the I/Thou coffee shop. Newly arrived residents and tourists could also find nearly any commodity they desired on sidewalks clogged with vendors hawking their wares. Locals could also be heard offering acid, speed, and lids (bags of marijuana).

Support systems were organized to assist the burgeoning population. Settled residents, who had found ways to make ends meet, were now being joined by many younger transients and runaways who were more apt to hit up passersby for spare change in order to exist. A local newspaper, the *Oracle*, offered philosophical discourse, debates on community issues, and event information. The Diggers, a group named for seventeenth-century English radical altruists, were performance artists whose political involvement in the community included collecting food from a variety of sources, cooking it, and offering it free every day on a park strip running through the neighborhood called the Panhandle. In 1967 a free medical clinic opened its doors.

In response to LSD's criminalization in October 1966, writers from the *Oracle* printed a manifesto called "A Prophesy of a Declaration of Independence." In it the authors declared: "When in the flow of human events it becomes necessary for people to cease to recognize the obsolete social patterns which had isolated man from his consciousness. . . . We hold these experiences to be self-evident, that all is equal, that the creation endows us with certain inalienable rights, that among these are: the freedom of the body, the pursuit of joy, and the expansion of consciousness, and that to secure these rights, we the citizens of the earth declare our love and compassion for all conflicting hate-carrying men and women of the world."[3]

Local bands attracted large followings as the vibrant ballroom scene produced at least two major dance/concerts per weekend. The Warlocks, on a name-change mission, found themselves staring into a dictionary at the words "grateful dead." The phrase, from old Irish and Scottish folk ballads, described those deceased who were required to return to earth and perform a good deed before being allowed to rest in peace—and thus, become the eternally grateful dead. The name change, stimulating live performances, constant work, and a big record contract in late 1966 elevated them to second in popularity only behind the Airplane.

Of the popular groups, the Grateful Dead were the most visible in their search for enlightenment and democracy (both within the band and the greater community). Band members believed that LSD enhanced their creativity. Lead guitarist Jerry Garcia (nicknamed Captain Trips) once described LSD's effect: "It was like another release, yet another opening. The first one was a hip teacher when I was in the third grade; and the next one was marijuana; and the next one was music; and the next one was LSD. It was like a series of continually opening doors." In order to be consistent with the counterculture philosophy of egalitarianism, the

The Grateful Dead

band refused to designate or publicly promote one member over another, even though it was obvious to their fans that Garcia, who wrote and sang a majority of their early originals, was an intelligent and astute spokesman.

This notion of equality also translated into the way they treated their audiences. Since everyone was family, the audience deserved the best; for the Dead, the best translated into a lengthy show full of improvisational inspiration. Three-hour concerts were not unusual, and the list of songs changed nightly. With each gig the band delved into uncharted territory, forging musical transitions between songs and long improvisational jams in search of the undefinable. That elusive spontaneity, or "magic," traditionally was an objective of jazz players, and it defined the Dead's final destination. On many good nights and the occasional great one, the group and the audience celebrated a musical and spiritual communion. Because positive results depended on the ability of each band member to listen carefully and communicate with others, sometimes personal overload or technical problems produced erratic, uneven performances. However, unlike most bands, the Dead went for "it" every night.

Their unusually broad range of musical interests and backgrounds endowed the band with a certain creative flexibility. Garcia began by playing Chuck Berry songs on electric guitar, shifted to the banjo and bluegrass music, then to acoustic guitar and folk and jug-band music. Drummer Bill Kreutzmann and rhythm guitarist Bob Weir cut their teeth mostly on rock and roll. Harmonica and keyboard player Ron "Pigpen" McKernan came from a blues and R&B background; his father was a well-known Bay Area blues disc jockey. Phil Lesh had studied avant-garde classical composition and played trumpet in the Oakland Symphony before accepting Garcia's offer to join the fledgling crew and take up the bass. In January 1967 the Dead traveled to a three-track L.A. studio to record their first album. The result, although it contains some interesting versions of their cover repertoire, only reinforced the notion that they were best experienced live.

Another of the ballroom bands, Big Brother and the Holding Company, had also been around since the Trips Festival. They practiced in the basement at 1090 Page and performed an eclectic array of music, ranging from Stones covers to jazz-inspired avant-garde noodling. Family Dog head Chet Helms suggested they get a female singer and recommended his old friend, Janis Joplin. She had visited San Francisco once before in the early sixties. She had strummed folk and the blues with area notables, lost herself in drugs and the frantic pace, and fled back to Texas in one last attempt at a life of conformity.

Joplin grew up in the refinery city of Port Arthur, Texas, and had enrolled as a part-time student at the University of Texas in Austin. Janis was a rebel, an out-spoken hard drinker with a colorful vocabulary, and her brazen style belied a sub-stantial insecurity and need for love and acceptance. Joplin returned to San Francisco in June 1966, full of songs but apprehensive about her ability to stay healthy. Within a week Big Brother and the Holding Company were performing with the gutsy new lead singer.

People weren't indifferent about Joplin's singing; they either loved her voice or couldn't stand it. Coarse sandpaper is how one might describe it. Joplin's fans, concerned that she was destroying her vocal chords with that raw, screaming de-livery—she eventually did develop nodes—urged the singer to save her voice. However, Janis continued and she became one of the era's best white blues singers. Onstage she raged, cried, and cajoled, often with her trademark bottle of Southern Comfort dangling from one hand. After hearing her, B. B. King was driven to comment, "Janis sings the blues as hard as any Black person. It's about the war between the sexes." Big Brother hit the local ballroom circuit, found them-selves broke in Chicago, and signed with tiny Mainstream Records. Their loose and amateurish first album, recorded in Chicago and Los Angeles, wasn't released for almost a year, after their successful appearance at the Monterey Pop Festival.

Throughout 1967 the national media flooded the country with stories about the Haight-Ashbury community and the upcoming Summer of Love. This notori-ety proved fatal to an already burdened neighborhood. However, the same media attention also thrust San Francisco rock groups into the national spotlight. Over the course of the year, record companies converged on the area, signing nearly every band that could tune their instruments (and some that couldn't). Just as Haight-Ashbury's streets became inundated with new immigrants, Bay Area mu-sicians set out on a mission to spread the tie-dyed gospel.

Nineteen sixty-seven began with one of the counterculture community's fond-est moments, the Gathering of Tribes. On January 14, an unseasonably warm Saturday afternoon, 20,000 people gathered at Golden Gate Park's polo grounds to celebrate the ongoing union of love and activism in their community. It was called a Human Be-In, and the grounds were consecrated in an early-morning Hindu religious ceremony by poets Allen Ginsberg and Gary Snyder. Onstage, a parade of speakers, a meditating Buddhist priest, the Dead, Big Brother, the Airplane, Quicksilver Messenger Service, and others entertained an audience that writer Gleason described as being costumed in a "wild polyglot mixture of Mod, Paladin, Ringling Brothers, Cochise, and Hell's Angels' formal."[4] "And so it ended, the first of the great gatherings. No fights. No drunks, no troubles. Two policemen on horseback and 20,000 people. The perfect sunshine, the beautiful birds in the air, the parachutist descending as the Grateful Dead ended a song."[5]

Bay Area residents were becoming increasingly frustrated at their inability to hear the new underground music on the radio. The only rock/pop radio in the nation was top-40 AM stations, featuring a format of hit singles spun over and over and introduced by fast-talking disc jockeys. No album cuts or songs from lesser known groups like the Who penetrated tightly controlled top-40 playlists. Since most early San Francisco music from 1965 to 1967 didn't even dent the singles charts, they were absent from the airwaves. FM radio programming included classical music or a simulcast of a sister station's AM signal and had little commercial importance.

The situation took an important turn in February 1967 when guitarist Larry Miller was hired for the all-night midnight-to-6 AM shift on the predominantly foreign-language FM station KMPX. Miller programmed an eclectic mix of music, ranging from local artists to album cuts, from acoustic folk to Dylan, the Beatles, the Stones, and the Byrds. In April former KYA favorite "Big Daddy" Tom Donahue—a 300-pound top-40 dropout who sometimes dressed in overalls and sported a long beard—started programming the 8 PM-to-midnight slot on KMPX, playing a more rock-oriented array of music. Donahue was a major music-business figure in the area who had promoted concerts by the Rolling Stones and Beach Boys, owned a record company, and managed numerous bands. With the addition of Donahue's former top-40 cohort, Bobby Mitchell, KMPX proved to be a flagship station for the progressive rock radio format that would become so popular in the early 1970s and lead the FM band to dominance over AM.

The one vehicle that brought the San Francisco music scene to national attention via AM radio airplay was the Airplane's second album, *Surrealistic Pillow* (#3), released in February 1967. Recorded in thirteen days in Los Angeles, the record included two songs that Grace Slick had brought with her from the Great Society, "Somebody to Love" (#5) and "White Rabbit" (#8). The tunes reached the hit charts and top-40 radio in midyear; both featured Slick's potent, tremulous, yearning vocal style and lyrics that were critical of society. Over a musical bed of quarter-note snare, a bounding Casady bass line, and Kantner's folk-like strums, "Somebody to Love" asked the listener When "truth" was found to be unbelievable, wasn't it time to find somebody to love?

Slick described "White Rabbit" as her combination of Ravel's "Bolero" and Lewis Carroll's *Alice in Wonderland* story "Through the Looking Glass." The band's counterculture appearance obscures a well-constructed arrangement of a complex group of musical and lyrical ingredients. The band creates the Spanish dance setting (the bolero) with syncopated bass and drums and Middle East-sounding guitar. Slick begins her allegorical tale singing softly, "One pill makes you larger, and one pill makes you small./ And the ones that mother gives you, don't do anything at all."

The song works on many levels. One can interpret it as a children's parable; radio stations used this rationale in giving it airplay. On another level, it is highly critical of authority figures, including mother and "men on the chessboard" who direct society without "logic" or vision. Slick's answer to this misguided authority is to "feed your head," a reference to drug-induced enlightenment and/or counterculture pursuits. On the musical level, the listener is taken along on an acid trip as the song's volume and intensity, quite low at aural ingestion, rush toward a crescendo finish.

The region's cultural activities finally spilled over into the national media. *Life* magazine ran a story in 1966 on the horrors of LSD; later that year *Newsweek* trumpeted "the San Francisco Sound is the newest adventure in rock 'n' roll. It's a raw, unpolished, freewheeling, vital and compelling sound."[6] In June 1967 *Time* magazine added, "The San Francisco Sound encompasses everything from bluegrass to Indian ragas, from Bach to jug band music—often within the framework of a single song. . . . The sound is also the scene. With its roots in the LSDisneyland of the Haight-Ashbury district, the music is a reflection of the defiant new bohemians." By April 1967 the Haight had become a tourist attraction and Gray Line bus tours added a "Hippie Hop Tour," billing it as "the only foreign tour within the continental limits of the United States."[7]

Haight merchants proclaimed the coming months the Summer of Love, a phrase that spread like wildfire throughout the press. In June the strains of "San Francisco (Be Sure to Wear Flowers in Your Hair)," written by John Phillips of the Mamas and the Papas and sung by pal Scott McKenzie, drifted dreamily from the nation's radios. Some of the "people in motion" who were described in the song were the Jefferson Airplane, who had recorded two "psychedelic" radio commercials advertising Levi's-brand jeans. All of this national publicity intensified the already existing problem of community overload, exacerbated by the generally young and indigent nature of recent arrivals.

As the Haight braced for the flood and local merchants oiled up cash registers, musicians planned the nation's first rock festival, the Monterey International Pop Festival. Organized by a combination of artists and industry executives—Papa John Phillips and Ode Records president Lou Adler were the major players—the three-day event presented an intelligently chosen roster of high-quality acts ranging from stars to relative unknowns. The crowd far exceeded original estimates of 50,000 and numbered nearly 200,000 concert-goers resplendent in Flower Power finery.

Although held at the Monterey County fairgrounds, located between San Francisco and Los Angeles, the concert was weighted heavily in favor of the Bay Area. The Friday evening show (June 16) featured the Animals with Eric Burdon (who would have a hit the next month with "[Warm] San Francisco Nights"), Simon and Garfunkel, and Johnny Rivers. Saturday afternoon offered an acid-tinged blues lineup, including Canned Heat, Paul Butterfield, and San Franciscans Big Brother (with Janis), Country Joe, Steve Miller, and Quicksilver Messenger Service. That night soulsters Booker T. and the M.G.s and Otis Redding shared the bill with Moby Grape and the Jefferson Airplane. Sunday afternoon's spiritual brunch offered Indian sitar master Ravi Shankar.

Sunday evening's finale was extraordinary: New York's Blues Project, a Big Brother repeat (D. A. Pennebaker's film crew had ignored the first set of this virtual unknown, who had to be rescheduled for filming), the Byrds, the Who, the Dead, and Jimi Hendrix. Of these performers only the Byrds were commercially sellable, the rest being relatively unknown in the United States. The industry executives in attendance pounced. Big Brother eventually signed with Columbia records and Bob Dylan's manager, Albert Grossman. Otis Redding's career moved into the fast lane and the Who, whose explosive set stunned the laid-back Sunday audience, went on a seven-week tour with Herman's Hermits. Hendrix, who burned his guitar in an attempt to top the Who, earned the touring plum. In a monumental mismatch Jimi was booked as the opening act for top-40 giants the Monkees.

Sunday June 18—just a little over two weeks after the release of *Sgt. Pepper's*—was Monterey board member Paul McCartney's twenty-fifth birthday; he admitted to the press that he had taken LSD four times in the past year. McCartney explained that it had made him "a better, more honest, more tolerant member of society, brought closer to God."[8] World leaders who tried LSD would be ready to "banish war, poverty and famine." These sentiments were quite similar to those expressed regularly by the local music community.

Haight-Ashbury and the musical community were headed in two different directions. The Summer of Love had overloaded the institutional resources of the community, and longtime residents began leaving for other cities or for a few acres of Mother Earth. Many band members moved to Marin County, north of the City. Recent immigrants appeared to favor escape rather than the creative enlightenment of the old-timers. Heroin and methamphetamines began to replace psychedelics as drugs of choice for some newcomers.

The Haight's crime rate soared, in part because of this taste for heroin and speed and in part because the indigent high school dropouts who had replaced the more upwardly mobile college dropouts of recent years found it increasingly difficult to survive. On October 6, 1967, people carrying a coffin paraded down Haight Street in a ceremony symbolizing the death of the hippie. However, the community didn't vanish overnight, and Haight-style counterculture enclaves continued to spring up in cities all over the United States. Not far behind was Madison Avenue, which used counterculture symbols and artifacts in its advertisements.

San Francisco music continued its expansion beyond regional boundaries. FM radio was catching on in other cities and San Francisco artists were getting radio airplay. Many Bay Area groups had albums on the top-100 album charts. In November 1967 Ralph J. Gleason and Jann Wenner, a former Cal-Berkeley entertainment writer, published a magazine based in San Francisco designed to appeal to the rock music fan. *Rolling Stone* carried a blend of artist and industry news, concert and record reviews, and in-depth articles and interviews. Rock/pop was becoming institutionalized, and in recognizing that fact *Rolling Stone* reached the top and began a publishing empire.

Bay Area groups continued the process of musical maturation, creative innovation, and increased commercial success. During this period the local environment became even more politically charged than before. By 1969 over 500,000 American troops were fighting in Vietnam, and Country Joe's lyrics about war casualties returning home in boxes were reality. Soldiers left and returned to the Bay Area. Gun-toting self-defense forces were organizing in Oakland's Black communities to defend themselves from police brutality. And Berkeley officials ordered a tear-gassing of citizens who demonstrated on a small plot of land (People's Park) the city planned to pave for a parking lot.

Many of the local groups reflected this additional turmoil in their music. The Jefferson Airplane released the long-awaited *After Bathing at Baxter's* (#17) in December 1967; the record was delayed, in part because the group felt the need to return to the studio after hearing the studio magic on *Sgt. Pepper's*. The Airplane soared in 1969 with their *Volunteers* release, which contains some of the most forthright and aggressive antiestablishment lyrics in mainstream rock/pop history. On the cut "We Should Be Together," the Airplane call on society to unite in overturning the "dangerous, dirty, and dumb" policies of the establishment. Calling themselves outlaws in the eyes of the enemy (state), the singers resolve to replace America's private property priority with one that favors people. They yell at the establishment, "Up against the wall, motherfucker," calling to the unified audience to tear down the wall.

From this creative peak, the band began to slowly disintegrate in the early seventies. Dryden quit. Balin faded out as fewer of his compositions ended up on vinyl. Kaukonen and Casady, who had formed an eclectic blues duo called Hot Tuna on the side, quit to pursue the endeavor full-time. Slick and Kantner manufactured a baby and a solo project titled *Blows Against the Empire* (which followed a science-fiction theme) using the name Jefferson Starship. The band was forced to use "Jefferson Starship" on their mid-1970s tour behind Balin's #3 composition "Miracles"—a manager owned the name Airplane—and changed simply to "the Starship" in the eighties as Kantner left with the "Jefferson."

Like the Airplane, Berkeley-based Country Joe and the Fish also combined political commentary and counterculture lifestyle. Joe McDonald, who came from a leftist southern California family, migrated to the Bay Area in search of the beat lifestyle. Although he had plenty of creativity, cultural activism, political dedication, and the appropriate quantity of drug-related reckless abandon, major commercial success eluded Country Joe. He is noted for two long-lasting artistic contributions. In 1965 he recorded a jug band-style tune called "I Feel Like I'm Fixin' to Die Rag," a satirical blast at the carnage of the Vietnam War—"one, two, three, what are you fightin' for"—that became an antiwar anthem.

McDonald also composed the famous F-I-S-H cheer, the best-known version of which can be seen on the *Woodstock* film. He calls to the audience—"Gimme an F!" "Fffffff!"—following with U, C, and K—not exactly spelling at its best, but a joy for antiestablishment audiences nonetheless. Early in his career, Country Joe had signed to folk-oriented Vanguard Records (whose roster featured Joan Baez and the Weavers) and released five albums, including *Electric Music for the Mind and Body* (#39, September 1967) and *Together* (#23, July 1968). Country Joe and the Fish were a good draw at major venues, had records that sold moderately well, and were participants in the era's cultural and political events.

Their lack of monetary success, which frustrated an artist who felt the equal of the area's big guns, can be ascribed to a number of reasons. Country Joe's breadth—the ability to be both politically active and acid-focused—proved confusing to one-issue audiences. In spending more time pursuing political causes, donating time and money, the band had less time to devote to promoting its career. By living their ideals they partly sacrificed their careers. The Fish also found that Vanguard Records was unable to compete in promotion and sales with majors like RCA and Warner Bros. Nevertheless, Country Joe, with and without the Fish, continued his creative pursuits into the eighties.

Creedence Clearwater Revival (CCR) was another band from the wrong side of the bay and was criticized for a proclivity to produce three-minute AM hits. To many Bay Area critics, Creedence was an East Bay top-40 band who wrote AM-oriented ditties that contained none of the counterculture experimentation that characterized the "authentic" San Francisco sound. They were late (their first hit came in 1968) and straight. In hindsight, however, this criticism is somewhat shortsighted; CCR was, of course, affected by the surrounding societal turbulence, and their songs do reflect, at least lyrically, some of the same issues as those of their psychedelic neighbors.

John Fogerty was the dominant creative force in CCR. John was playing with junior high school buddies Stu Cook (bass) and Doug Clifford (drums) in 1959 when they were joined by John's older brother Tom. Known then as the Blue Velvets, the group signed to Berkeley-based Fantasy Records, released numerous teen-oriented singles, and had the name the Golliwogs foisted upon them by a label executive. In 1968, having reverted to a name of their choice, CCR released their self-titled first album, which included covers of Dale Hawkins's "Suzie Q" (Parts I [#11] and II), and Screamin' Jay Hawkins's "I Put a Spell on You." Throughout the rest of its relatively short career, the band scored multiple top-40 hits from each successive album. In 1969 CCR released six million-selling singles and two million-selling albums.

CCR's most famous release, "Proud Mary" (#2, February 1969) is one of the era's most-played and also most-derided songs. Its charm lies in the basic Creedence formula. Over a simple, steady rhythmic groove, characterized by a strong two-plus-four snare, John drawls a folk parable about leaving the city for

Creedence Clearwater Revival

the simple welcoming life among America's common folk. Here was classic rock rhythm and instrumentation, gritty soul-tinged vocals, folk-rock strums and lead solo, and slightly antiestablishment tales about ordinary citizens. For critics steeped in counterculture music, this tight, three-minute AM hit that lacked any real experimental or improvisational musical qualities represented straight society. Thus, CCR took most of America by storm while being castigated by its local music community.

Between 1969 and 1971 CCR scored a dozen top-40 singles; all five albums were in the top 10 (including two #1s, *Green River* and *Cosmo's Factory*). Most originals such as "Green River," "Lodi," and "Down on the Corner" followed the classic rock/folk story formula. However, Fogerty also expressed strong antiestablishment sentiments with songs like "Fortunate Son," in which he derides the privileged (politically, monetarily, and militarily) who grow rich and powerful at the expense of the common person. CCR was also known to improvise occasionally, releasing an eleven-minute version of "I Heard It Through the Grapevine" and an extended "Suzie Q."

In 1971 Tom Fogerty left the band, happy to be out of John's shadow. One year later the band disintegrated as Cook and Clifford demanded equal space on the albums and John (who had written, sung, played lead guitar on, and directed nearly all the efforts) wondered, Why fix something that wasn't broken? The members, some of whom released solo efforts, were devastated to learn that millions of dollars in royalties had been invested by Fantasy Records in the Castle Bank of the Bahamas, a front for the U.S. Central Intelligence Agency. When the bank folded, the money disappeared. After many troubled years, John returned to the limelight in 1985 with his #1 album, *Centerfield*.

History treats CCR with more kindness than did their contemporary critics. The idealistic, change-oriented Bay Area music community equated the band's commercial success with lack of artistic integrity. Given some historical perspective, it is easier to judge CCR's formula and appeal on its own merits. There is a certain charm in the band's ability to combine beat-driven, classic rock-rooted music, a soul-styled vocal authenticity, and stories with which working-class America can identify. This recipe was liberally spiced with musically rebellious elements (beat and vocal style) and occasional antiestablishment lyrics. It has aged well as one form of original, stylistically integrated music.

Another San Francisco band that combined an unusual sound with a late arrival on the scene was Santana. Named for Mexican-born leader Carlos Santana, this band featured his guitar virtuosity and multirhythmic percussion stylings drawn from his Latin American heritage. In 1966, at age nineteen, he formed the Santana Blues Band, shortened a few years later to simply Santana. A revolving lineup, which originally included keyboardist Gregg Rolie, later was joined by drummer Mike Shrieve, percussionists Mike Carabello and Costa Rican star Jose Chepito Areas, and, in 1971, guitarist Neal Schon. In 1973 Rolie and Schon formed their own group, Journey.

Whereas most Bay Area audiences focused on a band and/or its material, Santana listeners were drawn to Carlos's guitar playing. Key to Santana's playing was the blues philosophy that "it can all be said in one note." His guitar style emphasized a crisp, edgy, sustained note as the basic medium of exchange. Like the best urban blues guitarists, Santana made his guitar cry in a series of fluid but not crowded passages. His cover of "Black Magic Woman" (#4, November 1970, written by Peter Green of early Fleetwood Mac) provides an excellent example of this type of playing. The band's version of "Oye Como Va" (#13, March 1971) evidences this guitar work combined with the exciting Latin percussion feeling of Tito Puente's salsa original.

Within a short time frame, Santana signed with Columbia Records, appeared at Woodstock—his torrid "Soul Sacrifice" is one of the film's highlights—and released a self-titled album that went to #4 (September 1969). His next two albums, *Abraxis* and *Santana III,* topped the charts. Santana soon became a disciple of the guru Sri Chinmoy, took the name Devadip, and moved in more eclectic and jazz fusion directions. His artistry, commercial success, and longtime management by Bill Graham allowed Santana to become a global ambassador of American rock/pop.

At the same time that these new groups were emerging, old bands were learning new tricks. Although the Grateful Dead had gained a legendarily devoted following and had numerous releases on a major label, they lacked substantial record sales. The Dead found it difficult to capture that live magic on the studio albums, had no hit (or even underground singles), and consequently were absent from the nation's airwaves. They moved a step closer in 1969 with *Live Dead,* a two-record set that featured lengthy compositions, esoteric lyrics, long improvisational jams, and musical segues between numbers. A high level of musicianship is exhibited in the difficult song "The Eleven" in eleven/eight time; the song segues into to the four/four time, R&B-style classic "Turn on Your Love Light."

Under pressure from sagging record sales and strongly influenced by Crosby, Stills, and Nash and the Band, who were friends, the Dead turned to writing shorter songs consisting of parables and historical vignettes. The new music emphasized acoustic folk and country-rooted instrumentation (Garcia also played the banjo and pedal-steel guitar), more focus and precision on lead and harmonies vocals, and Lesh-led, creatively accented rhythms. From their 1970 sessions came the band's two most critically acclaimed albums, *Workingman's Dead* (#27, July 1970) and *American Beauty* (#30, December 1970).

These efforts brought the Dead more in line with mainstream rock/pop music—spotlighting the lyrics of silent partner Robert Hunter without losing the band's uniqueness. Classics like "Casey Jones" (with the chorus line, "Drivin' that train, high on cocaine"), "Truckin'" (the on-the-road anthem that went to the top of the charts in Turlock, California), and "Ripple" (the Zen-like ballad with a perfect seventeen-syllable Haiku chorus) became FM favorites. This new music was the key to expanding the Dead's extended audience-family. Both records went gold (with sales of over 500,000 units), cuts received radio airplay, and the band appeared at major music festivals, spreading the San Francisco gospel.

As one of the few groups to enter the seventies intact, the Grateful Dead continued their role as innovators. Known primarily as musical, psychedelic, and audience-relationship pioneers, their visionary work in sound amplification technology has often been overlooked. Whereas most groups were abysmally ignorant of sound reproduction technology and how crude they could sound in concert, the Dead concluded that a sound system was analogous to a foreign language translator—and that their concert sound was only as good as their translator. This led them to form their own research-and-development firm called Alembic and to construct "the System," a three-story, twenty-five-ton sound system placed on scaffolding behind the band onstage. Generally acclaimed as the world's best, this system delivered virtually distortion-free sound to the audience.

In the ensuing years the Grateful Dead found a median point between the raw, energetic, improvisationally oriented early material and the more structured vocally oriented folktales of the early 1970s. Their live three-record *Europe '72* (with surreptitiously dubbed studio vocals) and two releases on Grateful Dead Records, *Wake of the Flood* (#18, November 1973) and *Mars Hotel* (#16, July 1974), are marvelous examples of this fusion. After twenty years of album releases they scored their first platinum effort in 1987 with *In the Dark* (#6) and their first top-10 single, the aptly titled "Touch of Gray" (#9). Midway through the 1990s the band's concerts were still over three hours long, featuring different songs from their vast repertoire each night. They still reached for the magic that kept their audiences, which ranged in age from fifteen to fifty, filling the halls every night. To many the Dead were the only contemporary musical performers who symbolized the idealism, purity, and integrity of the sixties. On August 9, 1995, Jerry Garcia died of cardiac arrest, and the congregation—Garcia once likened the Dead's concerts to a spiritual and religious communion—lost a guru and music master.

Like the Dead, Janis Joplin's career underwent massive changes in the late 1960s. Following the Monterey Pop Festival, Big Brother, now advertised as Janis Joplin and Big Brother and the Holding Company, saw their fortunes soar. From March through June 1968 they were in Hollywood, recording their Columbia Records debut *Cheap Thrills* (the record company had vetoed the original album cover, which showed the band naked in bed, and the original title, *Sex, Drugs, and Cheap Thrills*). That fall the album raced to #1 as the country adopted a new rock queen. On *Cheap Thrills* Joplin sings concert mainstays like Big Mama Thornton's R&B classic "Ball and Chain" and Gershwin's "Summertime" from *Porgy and Bess*. The concert stopper, "Piece of My Heart," is a good example of how Joplin, the blues screamer, melds with the powerful, unpolished band; Peter Albin's throbbing bass and Sam Andrew's edgy, distorted lead guitar complement Joplin's raw dynamism.

At the time, however, Janis was the target of a campaign of whisper and innuendo: "They [Big Brother] aren't any good, you're the star, Janis." Big Brother received some limp reviews, and even manager Albert Grossman favored a change. In December Janis played her last concert with Big Brother and her first with the Kosmic Blues Band, a unit that retained Andrews on guitar, adding new bass, drums, keyboard, guitar, and a full horn section. This group appeared at Woodstock and disbanded in January 1970, to be replaced in April with Joplin's last band, the Full Tilt Boogie Band. Kosmic Blues had power and improved musicianship but lacked interpersonal harmony; Full Tilt, retaining some players, worked as a unit and exhibited both power and finesse. Finally Janis had a band she could call her own.

One time Joplin had bragged that despite her huge thirst for alcohol she had never missed a concert; the same could be said of her heroin habit, though she couldn't brag about that. Nineteen seventy was perilous: there were the highs of an impending marriage, a concert tour by train across Canada with the Grateful Dead, Delaney and Bonnie Bramlett and friends, and the recording of a new album. There were also emotional lows, renewed heroin use (after months of being clean), and a growing reputation for inciting audiences. To this last accusation Joplin countered, "My music ain't supposed to make you want to riot! My music is supposed to make you want to fuck!"[9]

Joplin took some heat for acting like a rock and roll star instead of a woman. Her bravado, crass language, and ability to match the band in sexual promiscuity was seen by many as coarse and unladylike. Women weren't supposed to drink and screw like men. In the end Janis couldn't maintain her challenge to the male-dominated industry. On the night of October 3, 1970, Janis returned to her hotel after an album session and a few drinks. Once upstairs she injected herself with heroin, returned to the lobby for a pack of cigarettes, went back to her room, and then died. The coroner's verdict was a mixture of heroin and alcohol—another case of self-annihilation in rock and roll's fast lane.

The sound of most San Francisco bands had faded by the early seventies. Of the early groups we have chronicled in these pages, only the Grateful Dead survived and flourished. Other Bay Area favorites such as Quicksilver Messenger Service, Moby Grape, and the Sons of Champlin also stumbled turning the decade. The vibrant, visionary, counterculture community was also dissolving—and along with it the major local support system and impetus for musical growth and change. Commercially successful bands moved to the outlying areas, bought fancy cars, and focused their concerns on fighting for a larger piece of the recording-industry pie. Those who could compete in the marketplace, like promoter and manager Bill Graham, did quite well. Even though he closed both Fillmores (East and West) in 1971, he continued his reputation as the nation's best concert promoter. Bill Graham died in a helicopter crash on October 25, 1991.

✹    ✹    ✹

It is difficult to separate the impact of San Francisco music from the impacts of the counterculture values it transmitted. Few bands of the seventies chose to adopt the sound of the Airplane, the Dead, Big Brother, or the Fish; interestingly, some elements were revived in the eighties. Culturally transmitted values of integrity and humanitarian idealism were subsequently overcome by other goals, the selfishness and greed of ensuing decades. The seventies began the Me Generation, and song lyrics soon turned away from societal criticism toward the less politically threatening: sex, drugs, and rock and roll. Meanwhile, the San Francisco sound faded in volume as the seventies began.

Chapter 15 will focus on rock's major electric-guitar soloists. They emerged during the blues revival of the midsixties when, for the first time, the improvised guitar solo took centerstage. The cast of players includes Eric Clapton, Jimi Hendrix, and many others: the Guitar Kings.

# 15· The Guitar Kings:
## And I Gave Her the Gun

*I copied most of my runs from B. B. [King] or Albert King or Freddie King. There's no reason why they [other guitarists] should listen to me when they can listen to the masters, you know, the source.*

**Eric Clapton, in an interview with journalist Fred Stucky**

*Lots of young people now feel they're not getting a fair deal, so they revert to something loud or harsh, almost verging on violence. . . . It's more than music. It's like a church, like a foundation for the lost or potentially lost.*

**Jimi Hendrix, as quoted in Hopkins's The Jimi Hendrix Story**

SWINGING LONDON IN THE MIDSIXTIES was a creative epicenter for the rock music explosion. Future legends like the Beatles, the Stones, and the Who patronized the many local clubs in a never-ending party and musical quest. In 1966 two London-based guitarists and their newly formed trios emerged from the scene with an innovative musical blend—a guitar-centered style that fused elements of the blues with the culturally acquired conceptual distortion of the experimental sixties. Eric Clapton, a blues aficionado and former guitarist with the British R&B band the Yardbirds, formed the group Cream; Jimi Hendrix, an American without substantial success as a soul guitarist, was enticed to England to form the Jimi Hendrix Experience.

For the first time in rock music's evolution, audiences were attracted primarily by an instrumentalist playing a series of improvised solos rather than by a group, singer, or repertoire of songs. The previous generations of classic rock and the early 1960s had their guitarists—Chuck Berry, Scotty Moore, Buddy Holly, Duane Eddy, and others—but at no time did the instrument or the instrumentalist achieve such monumental status as it did during the Guitar King era.

## A Short Digression

The guitar has existed since 1200 B.C. The first mass-produced, unamplified, steel-stringed models, the direct predecessor of today's electric guitar, were made by a Kalamazoo, Michigan, shoe clerk by the name of Orville Gibson in the 1870s.

They had an arched top, patterned after the violin; by 1894 Gibson had sufficient interest in his products to form the Gibson Company. German immigrant C. F. Martin opened his guitar factory in Nazareth, Pennsylvania, and started to build steel-stringed guitars in the early 1900s. By the 1920s steel-stringed acoustic guitars were used in blues, folk, country, and popular music.

The first artists to envision the guitar as a lead instrument were early jazz musicians. During the 1920s jazz rhythm sections underwent a process of evolution; the guitar replaced the banjo as the strummed rhythm-keeper. Within ten years guitarists—emulating the brass and reeds—began to play single-string improvisational solos. Eddie Lang, who made numerous recordings with jazz violinist Joe Venuti and other era greats between 1923 and his death in 1933, is considered the first major jazz guitarist. Another pioneer, Belgian gypsy Django Reinhardt, moved to Paris and formed the Quintet of the Hot Club of Paris. Reinhardt, in spite of two paralyzed digits on his left hand, traded brilliant solos with classically trained jazz violinist Stephane Grappelli. ·

The increased popularity of the guitar, as well as the need to be heard over the expanding big band ensembles, necessitated its amplification. In 1924 instrument engineer Lloyd Loar designed the first known guitar pickups; when mounted on top of the guitar's body, just underneath the strings, pickups translate sound frequencies created by vibrating strings into electronic impulses. These impulses moved through a connecting cable to an external amplifier, where the impulses were enhanced and transmitted to a speaker. Loar's devices went unheralded, but ten years later, guitar manufacturers like Gibson, Rickenbacker, and National began to serve the jazz market with guitars fitted with pickups. These were the first electric guitars.

Eddie Durham, a jazz guitarist and trombonist, debuted the electric guitar solo on record with his Kansas City Five in 1938. But two other early guitarists, Charlie Christian and Aaron "T-Bone" Walker, played even more prominent roles in the development of electric guitar as a solo instrument. Both men came from the Southwest and actually played together in 1934 in Fort Worth, Texas. Christian ascended from playing the streets of Oklahoma City to recording as a member of Benny Goodman's famous small ensembles between 1939 and 1941. He was considered a brilliant and tactile melodic innovator and riff-maker, approaching the guitar solo in a manner stylistically similar to the era's horn players. His playing evidenced a mellifluous fluidity, rich tone with a touch of distortion, and the ability to either solo or play rhythm. Christian left the Goodman lineup due to poor health. He died of tuberculosis in 1942 at the age of twenty-six.

T-Bone Walker began his career in the same geographic region—he was six years older than Christian—but he remained more firmly rooted in the blues. Walker accompanied blues vocalist Ma Rainey and was a "lead boy" for the famous blues guitarist and singer Blind Lemon Jefferson. Walker moved to Los Angeles in 1935 and played electric on disc for the first time with Les Hite's band in 1939. In 1947 T-Bone recorded his blues classic "Stormy Monday," with its atypical harmonic complexity and a single-string solo that prompted B. B. King to once comment, "It drove me crazy. I could never believe a sound could be that pretty on an instrument." Numerous blues artists have credited Walker as a primary model, and even Chuck Berry's pioneering rock style is more than vaguely reminiscent of Walker's (listen to T-Bone's 1950 version of "Strollin' with the Blues" to hear the bent notes, repetition, and choke so prominent in Berry's playing). Walker was also a master showman and played the guitar behind his back and suggestively between his legs decades before Jimi Hendrix.

Concurrent with the development and evolution of electric-guitar playing styles were changes in the instrument itself. Early jazz players favored a hollow-bodied arch-top guitar with one pickup that delivered a rich bell-like tone—the result of pickup placement and of the design's large resonating body and air cavity inside. Both Christian and Walker played the popular hollow-body Gibson model ES-150, although Walker switched to other guitars in later years. In post–World War II America, urban blues players used not only a variety of hollow-body guitars but also the thinner, multipickup models called semi–solid-body guitars. Because they contained less interior air space and resonating wood surface, these guitars provided a crisper, punchier sound. B. B. King's famous guitar, which he affectionately named "Lucille," is a semi–solid-body Gibson ES-335.

Wisconsin-born Les Paul (originally Leslie Polfuss) is credited with designing the third body style, the solid-body guitar. Paul sought to solve the problem of feedback (instantaneous buildup of specific frequencies) and the short sustain (prolonged single notes) that plagued players using a hollow-body guitar. He determined that due to the high density, a solid piece of wood could solve both problems. Paul experimented with a railroad tie, finding that "you could go out and eat and come back and the note would still be sounding." In 1941 he built his "Log" at Epiphone's New York guitar factory from a four-by-four length of wood, two wings fastened on to make it feel like a guitar, and two pickups. This was the prototype solid-body guitar, a design that has come to dominate rock/pop music for the past three decades.

Paul was not only an innovative craftsman, he was also an electronics wizard and a talented player. In 1929 at age thirteen he designed some guitar-pickup prototypes. In the late 1930s he pioneered a method of multiple input recording, which allowed him to dub numerous vocal and instrumental parts separately onto tape and mix them together into one final product. This process, later termed multitrack recording, defied the contemporary logic, which stated that all material had to be recorded in one place and at one time. In 1951 he and his wife, Mary Ford, started their series of million-selling records with songs such as #1 hits "How High the Moon" and "Vaya Con Dios" featuring multitracked instruments and vocals and expert guitar work.

The solid-body guitar was finally mass-produced in the late 1940s. Early in the decade Les Paul had moved to California, continuing to work on the solid-body and eventually attempting to interest the Gibson Company. Meanwhile, his two neighbors, Paul Bigsby (inventor of the Bigsby tailpiece) and Leo Fender (who founded Fender Electrical Instrument Company in 1947), were also working on the same concept. Bigsby built a custom solid-body for country star Merle Travis in 1947; Fender manufactured their Broadcaster model a year later (renamed the Telecaster in 1950).

In the early 1950s and within the space of one year, the world's two most prestigious electric-guitar manufacturers issued what would become rock music's two most popular guitar models. In 1952 Gibson's new top management relented and issued the first Gibson Les Paul-model solid-body guitar, featuring numerous Paul-designed innovations. In the ensuing years a variety of Les Paul models have been issued, including the Custom, Junior, and Standard (or SG). In 1953 Leo Fender responded with his triple-pickup solid-body Fender Stratocaster, a model widely used today and one that has remained essentially unchanged since its arrival on the music scene.

Classic rock guitarists, who were strongly rooted in the blues and country traditions, gave solid-body guitars mixed reviews. Elvis's guitarist, Scotty Moore, and Carl Perkins continued to use hollow-bodies; Eddie Cochran and Chuck Berry played semi–solid-bodies. Buddy Holly became the first major rock artist to favor the thin, twangy sound of the Stratocaster. James Burton—who played the solo on the Dale Hawkins 1957 hit "Susie Q" at age fifteen and joined Ricky Nelson's band a few years later—used a Telecaster. Frankie Beecher—a former jazz guitarist with Benny Goodman—switched to a Gibson Les Paul while in Bill Haley's band.

As the electric guitar physically evolved, so did the nature of the instrumental solo. Jazz guitarists tended to fully explore the melody and harmonic structure of a song using a multitude of notes and arpeggiated and strummed chords. Blues players, on the other hand, generally followed the axiom that it could all be said in one note. Thus, urban blues guitarists concentrated on the feeling and emotion generated by bent notes, choking, slides, and repetition rather than the speed and harmonic exploration of jazz. Country pickers relied on crisp, quick runs (or phrases) derived from bluegrass and groups like the Delmore Brothers, combined with the innovative fingerpicking styles of Merle Travis and Chet Atkins, with a dash of blues thrown in for flavor.

Each of the major fifties guitarists mixed styles in order to create their individual sound. Berry took repetition and bend from blues to go along with speed and slides from country. Scotty Moore adapted bend from blues plus slides and fingerpicking from country; all three are evident in his solo on Elvis's first record, "That's All Right (Mama)" (1954), from the Sun Sessions. Beecher borrowed heavily from jazz while also leaning on the blues. And Holly displayed his country roots with slides and strummed solos, using limited, blues-derived single-string work.

## Back to the Future

It is from this historical context that Clapton and Hendrix emerged in the early 1960s. Each drew from a variety of sources to find early artistic and commercial success—Clapton initially as a blues revivalist and Hendrix as a soul and R&B session man—and each finally played solid-body guitars, the Gibson Les Paul (Clapton) and Fender Stratocaster (Hendrix) during their peak years. Eric Clapton was the first of the two to achieve commercial notoriety. Born out of wedlock and raised by his grandparents in suburban London, Clapton, like many other British rock musicians, gravitated toward art school. At thirteen he was given his first guitar—an acoustic—and immersed himself in the music of blues masters like Robert Johnson and Big Bill Broonzy. Also introduced to players like B. B. King, Freddie King, Albert King (no relation), and Chuck Berry, Clapton spent much of his spare time practicing in his room. He would later claim that the pain derived from his childhood was transformed into creative energy and applied to music—a dynamic that is common to the careers of Lennon, McCartney, Hendrix, and many others.

Clapton, apparently more interested in his music than in a career in commercial art and stained glass, was dismissed from Kingston College of Art. He soon joined the Roosters, one of the minor acts on the budding English R&B scene. Rooster bassist Tom McGuiness, reflecting on their naiveté and idealism, comments on those days: "The idea of there being a real commercial market for what we were doing just didn't strike us. . . . We were doing it because we loved playing rhythm and blues."[1] "It used to be," states longtime Clapton associate and Rooster pianist Ben Palmer, "We would get enough money for a brown ale and a packet of crisps and we'd walk home."

Nine months later, in October 1963, Clapton took a step up. He joined the Yardbirds, a band with a regular gig at the Crawdaddy Club (replacing the fast-rising Rolling Stones) and a real manager named Georgio Gomelsky. Although still considered an R&B band, there were strong feelings within the band, supported by Gomelsky, to climb aboard the pop-oriented British invasion gravy train. This led to the wide disparity in Yardbird sounds, ranging from the gritty, bluesish Howlin' Wolf cover "Smokestack Lightning" to a bouncy "Good Morning Little School Girl" (featuring a Clapton slide-guitar solo) to the 1966 pre-psychedelic hit "Shapes of Things."

This stylistic schizophrenia is most obvious on their biggest hit, "For Your Love" (#6, June 1965). The verse section quickly introduces the listener to a harpsichord, bongo drums, Ringo-signature two-plus-and-four snare hits, and a bouncy paean to love. The chorus feels like an up-tempo Chuck Berry tune due to the eighth-note rhythm-guitar pulse. Clapton, who was still immersed in the Black music aesthetic, found the pop direction repulsive and his relationship with leader Paul Samwell-Smith untenable; he quit just before "For Your Love" became the band's first major hit. Studio guitarist Jimmy Page was offered the job and declined but recommended Jeff Beck. One year later Page joined the Yardbirds on bass, switching to guitar three months later to join Beck in a two-guitar lineup.

Meanwhile, Clapton pursued his blues dream, accepting John Mayall's invitation to join the Bluesbreakers. Clapton had honed his already considerable skills as a blues-rooted guitarist during a nearly year-long string of one-nighters. As a Yardbird Clapton had been nicknamed Slowhand, a tongue-in-cheek accolade by manager Gomelsky to Clapton's picking dexterity. During his term with Mayall, Clapton's reputation as a guitarist reached new heights. Graffiti appeared in London underground stations proclaiming "Clapton Is God"; at performances, audience members were known to shout "Give God a solo!"

This adulation, and its concurrent media hype, were heady stuff for a twenty-one-year-old guitarist with all of three years' experience. In a mixture of vanity and wisdom, Clapton proclaimed, "I'm not interested in guitar sound technique, but in people and what you can do to them via music. I'm very conceited and I think I have a power—and my guitar is the medium for expressing that power. I don't need people to tell me how good I am, I've worked that out by myself. . . . My guitar is the medium to make contact with myself. It's very, very lonely. That is blues."[2] Clapton felt he was the best white blues guitarist around.

Like Alexis Korner's Blues Incorporated, the Bluesbreakers lineup was a continuously shifting mélange of high-quality players. During Clapton's tenure the rhythm section consisted of drummer Hughie Flint and bassist John McVie (who later cofounded Fleetwood Mac). On occasion, when McVie's intemperance flared, bassist Jack Bruce (from the Graham Bond Organization and Manfred Mann) was invited to fill in. The Clapton-era Bluesbreakers released a self-titled album (their cover of Freddie King's "Hideaway" shows Clapton at his bluesy best) just in time for Eric to leave the band in a renewed quest for blues nirvana.

England's blues and R&B community included the perpetual all-star jams inherent to vibrant music scenes. Thus Clapton jammed with Graham Bond drummer Ginger Baker. Baker suggested they form a band. Clapton insisted they include bassist Bruce, and Cream was born in July 1966. Interestingly, Baker—once leader of the Graham Bond Organization—had fired Jack Bruce, citing musical and personal differences. Bruce had refused to be fired and an onstage brawl ensued, ending as both crashed into Baker's drum kit. In forming Cream Clapton had chosen to sandwich himself between two people who loathed one another but who were making an effort to overlook differences. Bruce claims, "Because of the very pain of our relationship, we were the hottest rhythm section I've ever played in."

On the surface Cream—a name chosen because they intended to rise to the top—had ample talent and a simple goal: they would become a blues trio. Baker, a Londoner of Irish decent, was schooled on trumpet as well as drums and played with a number of England's top jazz bands before joining the rock scene. Bruce, from Glasgow, Scotland, studied cello and attended the Royal Scottish Academy of Music, in addition taking up the acoustic and electric basses. Clapton, who Stevie Winwood claims wasn't a particularly good technician and was limited by his lack of technique from performing jazz, was nevertheless in peak form as a blues-derived guitarist.

But the trio hadn't factored in the "moment." Because Clapton initially viewed Cream as a blues band, he felt their future would be in the home of the blues, the United States. When they reached America they found audiences filled with counterculture fans favoring long improvisational jams. "I think it was pure accident," reflects Clapton. "It stunned us and we leaped in and took advantage of it. When we saw that in America they actually wanted us to play a number for a whole hour—one number—we just stretched it."[3] The audience was ready for a change, and this trio of instrumental rock virtuosos took up the challenge. To Bruce, "It was like jazz playing in a rock setting."[4]

Cream

The introduction of Bruce's original material all but sealed the fate of Cream being a blues trio. Bruce became the lead vocalist and front man; Clapton's guitar playing attracted most audience attention. Although initially consumed by the hype surrounding this superstar unit, the band settled down and let their music speak for itself. Clapton was being pushed by the musicianship of Bruce and Baker to extend himself beyond his blues-derived boundaries, and it was working. At the time, he commented, "I don't really think I represent the blues anymore. I have more of that in me and my music than anything else, but I don't really play the blues anymore."[5] Clapton's fusion of blues and his musical representation of the era's cultural climate thrilled audiences.

Cream released four albums during their two-year existence. Given the climate and the improvisational nature of their live performances, it is not surprising that the albums fared much better in the United States than did their single releases. However, rather than albums of loosely organized lengthy compositions—one live *Wheels of Fire* version of "Spoonful" does run 16:44—each release contains a mixture of material, including rambling jams and concise but driving love songs.

*Fresh Cream*, the group's first LP release, scored well on the English charts (#6, December 1966) but not in the United States (#39). The single, "I Feel Free," was similarly successful in England and featured Bruce's Winwoodian, raw, emotive vocals, atypical harmonies, and Clapton's Les Paul guitar, driven to a distortion that would soon come to dominate the era. In April 1967 Cream traveled to the United States for the first time, playing in New York with the Who and others on

Murray the K's Easter show. They received attention from the underground press, who were especially impressed with Clapton's guitar playing.

Their performance format solidified during two weeks of gigs at the Fillmore in San Francisco, where promoter Bill Graham gave them the green light to play their improvised material until the sun rose. This spontaneity created a love affair between the psychoactively oriented Bay Area audience and the band. Clapton felt that San Francisco audiences "were the best anywhere. They're so obviously critical. Every move you make. Every note you play is being noticed, devoured, accepted or rejected."[6] The dawning of the Summer of Love found Cream confident that at least a certain segment of American music fans would rally to their sound.

The release of *Disraeli Gears* (#4, November 1967) flooded the American market with quality Cream material, including their most popular song, "Sunshine of Your Love" (#5, July 1968). Most of Cream's essential ingredients are present on this classic: the forceful riff, in this case the famous ten-note phrase, played by both bass and guitar; Bruce's powerful vocals expounding protestations of love; and Clapton's distorted, edgy, improvised guitar solo. In this case Clapton adds a bit of humor to his solo, beginning with the first two musical lines of the 1930s pop hit "Blue Moon." The solo evidences the pioneering fusion of bends, note sustain, and finger vibrato from the blues with a distorted tone setting and infusion of speed and extra notes that would characterize the guitar playing of the late 1960s. As a bonus, Clapton, the ever-shy vocalist, alternates every two verse lines with Bruce.

Other outstanding cuts on *Disraeli Gears* include the bouncy "Strange Brew," with atypically airy, doubled, almost falsetto voices and overdubbed guitar; "Tales of Brave Ulysses," a Clapton-conceived flower-power tribute to Homer's *Odyssey,* containing a wah-wah guitar solo reminiscent of Hendrix (but without the speedy brilliance); and "SWLABR," a pop tune with blues riff and doubled guitar solo. The album cemented Cream's place in the American rock scene and garnered mainstream press accolades.

The follow-up, *Wheels of Fire* (#1, July 1968), contains one studio record and one recorded live at the Fillmore and reflects the group's improvisation-versus-studio dichotomy. Cream creates a masterpiece with their version of the Robert Johnson classic, "Crossroads," in which the group shines as a blues-inspired, improvisational unit. Clapton generates heat with his fast, biting, staccato runs and dexterous work up the neck; Bruce instrumentally spans the other two, playing in rhythmic concert with Baker and his driving, beat-filled style while providing a tight, syncopated harmonic foundation for Clapton's guitar work. A formidable example of their in-studio mastery is "White Room" (#6, October 1968), a song about a lover's disenchantment and that features an inventive arrangement and wah-wah guitar fills.

Cream had established their position as the first rock band to succeed as a result primarily of their instrumental abilities. However, the fabric of the group, never very strong to begin with, was chronically torn by the enmity between Bruce and Baker. After two years Clapton had neither the emotional constitution nor stamina to mediate any longer. Clapton was also exhausted by the pressure of living up to his deified status each time he appeared—especially with Hendrix on the scene—and was distraught by a *Rolling Stone* review that called him "the master of the cliché." Clapton abdicated and Cream held their farewell concerts at London's Royal Albert Hall in November 1968.

Cream left a substantial legacy for seventies rockers. Although Cream was not the first popular power trio—the Who, with the powerhouse rhythm section of Moon and Entwistle and "no-lead" guitarist Townshend, created the formula—they refined the format and designed its most popular application. Their recipe called for a blues-rooted guitarist with sufficient talent and charisma to thrill an audience; a powerful, emotive vocalist; and a bass player and drummer capable of creating both a strong rhythmic and harmonic foundation while adding exciting dynamic accents. The Cream legacy is seen in Led Zeppelin and that band's many progeny.

Before Cream's birth Clapton and Stevie Winwood had discussed playing together; after its demise Eric sought out the veteran from the Spencer Davis Group and Traffic. Clapton, who wanted to include a keyboard in his next group, felt inclined toward more melodic music and still didn't want to be the frontman. The multitalented Winwood fit the bill. Bass player and violinist Rick Gretch was seduced away from the group known as the Family and, at the strong urging of Winwood and against Clapton's better judgment, Baker was invited to play drums. The group's name, Blind Faith, reflected the reality of the situation. Clapton, after the pressure of Cream, wanted out of the hype and to be accepted as just a guitar player appreciated for his art. He envisioned the band traveling around England, arriving unannounced at small pubs and halls, blowing audiences out of their seats.

The band lasted less than a year, the dream much less. They recorded one self-titled album, debuted in front of 150,000 fans at London's Hyde Park in June 1969, and booked a six-week American tour for arena-sized venues. The album reached #1 and the band earned lots of money. However, the specter of Cream, in the person of Baker and persistent audience demands for Cream material and long jams, depressed Clapton. Lacking the fortitude to mold the situation, he sat back and let it happen: "It's easier to be led than to lead. . . . I felt very insecure sometimes inside Blind Faith, and that was my own hang-up that had to be cured in its own time."[7] Despite a delightful album, an all-star lineup, and competent representation by longtime manager Robert Stigwood, Clapton left the band in January 1970.

What followed was a solo career—and a struggle within the young man's soul. The insecure, pained, faceless guitarist who wanted to hide nameless in a rock and roll band was pitted against the once-confident master instrumentalist, loved by his fans and deserving of solo success. There followed a self-titled album, recorded with the help of vocalists Delaney and Bonnie Bramlett, Leon Russell, Stephen Stills, and friends. There was a second solo effort recorded at Miami's Criteria Studios with Bobby Whitlock (keyboards), Carl Radle (bass), and Jim Gordon (drums), and a special friend. In an attempt to even further distance himself from his own legacy, Clapton called the group Derek and the Dominos.

The classic album that emerged from those sessions, *Layla and Other Assorted Love Songs* (#16, November 1970), is one of those underground gems that people were bound to include in their record collections. (*Cheap Thrills* by Big Brother and Janis, *Crosby, Stills, and Nash,* and *The Band* are three others that come to mind.) The title cut, "Layla" (#10), was an aching, up-tempo blues song about Clapton's unrequited love for Patti Harrison (good friend George's wife), who eventually left Harrison and moved in with Clapton, marrying him in 1979. The song features the inspired slide-guitar work of then studio musician Duane Allman (the original Allman Brothers had formed in 1968). The guitar midsection contains overdubbed, swirling Clapton guitar figures and Allman's slide soaring through the upper reaches. Drummer Jim Gordon's epilogue on piano adds a fitting, melancholy close to the song.

The *Layla* album was Clapton blues circa 1970—full of anguish and some tenderness. "Bell Bottom Blues," "Why Does Love Have to Be So Sad," traditional blues number "Keys to the Highway," and Hendrix cover "Little Wing" are but a few of the quality numbers. Clapton already had one foot out of the band by the time it toured late in the year. Within the space of a few months, Hendrix died, as did Clapton's step-grandfather (the man who had raised him), and the pain of Patti's absence became unbearable. Clapton fell into a heroin-fueled numbness that lasted nearly three years. With his patrician girlfriend, Alice Ormsby-Gore, Clapton sat in his mansion snorting heroin and diddling on his guitar. He emerged to play in public on two occasions—the first being at Harrison's Concert for Bangladesh, on August 1, 1971. Although not a particularly close friend, Pete Townshend, in an attempt to arouse Clapton from his stupor, organized a premature welcome-back concert at London's Rainbow Theatre in January 1973. The all-star band included Townshend, Faces veteran Ron Wood, Clapton on guitar, Gretch on bass, Winwood on keyboards, Jim Capaldi on drums, and Ree Bop on percussion. Clapton arrived backstage one minute before showtime, and although the concert was an artistic success and Clapton played well, it would be another year before he sought treatment. Acupuncture eased the addictive cravings, and work as a day laborer helped heal the body. Clapton traded in his heroin addiction for alcoholism.

In the spring of 1974 Eric returned to Criteria Studios with bassist Carl Radle, Radle's Oklahoma pals Jamie Oldaker (drums) and Dick Sims (keyboards), guitarist George Terry, and vocalist Yvonne Elliman. They recorded *461 Ocean Boulevard,* which was named for the Florida residence where the musicians stayed, in two and a half weeks. This was Clapton's third solo album, and he had at last become comfortable with his role as group leader and lead guitarist. No longer would he have to shoot it out for the title of top guitar-gunslinger (no doubt Clapton still lived with the image of Hendrix, who once came to a Cream gig, asked to sit in, and blew everybody off the stage). Faster, more technically proficient players were on the scene; all Eric Clapton had to do was play like himself.

On *461 Ocean Boulevard* Clapton also found a formula for commercial success and made his peace. The songs range in length from 2:51 to 4:57 and cover a spectrum of styles, from adaptations of Robert Johnson's blues ("Steady Rollin' Man"), Johnny Otis's R&B ("Willie and the Hand Jive"), and Clapton originals.

The album also contained a cover of a 1973 Bob Marley reggae tune, "I Shot the Sheriff," which climbed to #1 (along with the album) in the summer of 1974. The formula developed on this album has continued to provide Clapton with a string of hit singles and discs into the nineties. Clapton still does well that which he did best: play blues-based guitar with feeling.

❋ ❋ ❋

Jimi Hendrix also began his career listening to blues records in his room and he never forgot those roots. Although his quasi-blues music differs a great deal from Clapton's, in one way they are the same. Both loved the blues and never lost the ability to transmit the depth and emotionality of the blues to the audience. But unlike Clapton, Hendrix expanded guitar playing beyond a fusion of stylistic elements, past the borders of notated music into the realm of sounds. In creating this sound spectrum he was also forced to master the evolving "effects" technology of the time. In creating sound by controlling the guitar and its effects technology, Hendrix had no peer. In some ways—more than two decades after his untimely death—he has yet to be equaled.

As with Clapton, Hendrix's blues were an expression of personal pain. He was born Johnny Allen Hendrix in Seattle, Washington, on November 27, 1942, while his father was in the army; he was shuffled from relatives to friends of relatives to foster homes. His mother was wild and consumptive, leaving the family for the final time when Jimi was ten. His father, Al, returned from the war, but it was many years before he could earn enough as a gardener to establish a home for Jimi and younger brother Leon. Jimi found solace in music, his father's jazz and R&B record collection, and his first guitar, an acoustic that he acquired when he was fourteen.

Al Hendrix had been a dedicated tap dancer before the war; his son became a rock music fanatic. At fifteen he joined the Rocking Kings, playing hits of the day, including Richie Valens's "La Bamba," the Everly Brothers tune "Cathy's Clown," Eddie Cochran's "Summertime Blues," and the Coasters hit "Yakety Yak." For over two years Jimi played contemporary popular music up and down Washington's Interstate-5 corridor, going as far north as Vancouver, Canada. His musical interests were varied and included classic rockers Berry, Presley, and Holly and modern blues players Muddy Waters, Elmore James, and B. B. King.

Hendrix also became involved in petty crimes in the Seattle ghetto (midnight clothing sales, for instance). In all probability he entered the army to avoid a jail sentence for his second joy-riding offense. By January 1962 he was training at Fort Bragg, North Carolina, as a Screaming Eagle, a 101st Airborne paratrooper, and eventually completed twenty-five jumps before breaking an ankle and mustering out on a medical discharge. The paratrooper who had taken his electric guitar to bed decided to become a professional musician. Along with his army buddy, classically trained bass player Billy Cox, Hendrix and friends got work in nearby Nashville, Tennessee, clubs. There he met a young white guitarist from Memphis,

Steve Cropper. Their plans to record an album together were scrapped when Cropper's group, Booker T. and the M.G.s, scored a national hit with "Green Onions."

For the next four years Jimi Hendrix paid his dues. He worked as a rhythm guitarist with many of the era's great soul artists, then as a hired lead player, and finally as leader of his own small unsuccessful ensemble. During this period Hendrix marshaled his considerable repertoire of songs, created his phenomenal catalog of guitar riffs and solo styles, and developed his own version of the Black performance dynamic called "the show." Living mostly out of a suitcase, Jimi worked behind and recorded with Little Richard intermittently from the spring of 1963 into 1965. He also played with the Isley Brothers, Solomon Burke, Wilson Pickett, Jackie Wilson, and others. There was no better school for an aspiring musician-showman.

By 1965 Hendrix had settled in New York City, straddling the Black music scene of Harlem and the counterculture folk and rock worlds of Greenwich Village. He caught on with the band lead by tenor sax great King Curtis, sharing guitar chores with another young Black guitarist named Cornell Dupree. Soul artist Curtis Knight also provided some regular local club work. However, enamored of Dylan's lyricism and antiauthoritarian sentiments and the downtown community's acceptance of eccentric artists, Hendrix gravitated toward the Village. Jimi also found the counterculture's psychoactive drug scene attractive, smoking marijuana regularly and experimenting with LSD.

Many times the door to success is found in strange places. For Jimi it materialized during his appearance as Jimmy James and the Blue Flames at one of the Village's marginal clubs, the Cafe Wha? In walked white acoustic blues artist John Hammond Jr.—the son of Dylan mentor John Hammond—who, upon hearing Hendrix play the blues, recruited him for future Village dates. As Hammond's lead guitarist Hendrix soon impressed British rock royalty, as members of the Rolling Stones and the Animals came to view the new guitar wonder.

Mike Bloomfield, Butterfield Blues Band guitarist and Dylan studio pal, also stopped in to catch one of his gigs. He recalls, "[At the time] I was the hot shot guitarist on the block. . . . Hendrix knew who I was and that day, in front of my eyes, he burned me to death. I didn't even get my guitar out. H-bombs were going off, guided missiles were flying—the surf—waves. . . . He was getting every sound I was ever to hear him get right there in the room with a Stratocaster, a Twin [Fender Twin guitar amplifier], a Maestro Fuzztone [fuzz-producing special effects foot pedal] and that was all—he was doing it mainly through extreme volume. He just got right up in my face with that axe, and I didn't even want to pick up a guitar for the next year." Obviously, this unknown had something extraordinary to offer.[8]

Animals manager and former bassist Chas Chandler came to see Hendrix back at the Cafe Wha?, stating categorically that Jimi was wasting his time in the United States. Come to England, he said, and we'll make you a star. After assuring Hendrix that he could introduce him to Eric Clapton and attempting to disentangle him from the myriad contracts he had signed over the years, Chandler and

Hendrix stepped through the door to success in September 1966. Hendrix entered the tumultuous Swinging London of the midsixties, with its vibrant, ever-changing music scene. He was introduced to Paul and Ringo, Pete Townshend, Clapton, and John Mayall. He asked to sit in with Cream and, as Clapton describes it, "He did his whole routine. . . . It was incredible."

Chandler and Hendrix envisioned a power trio lineup, figuring no one could keep up with Jimi on guitar. Enlisted on bass was twenty-one-year-old former art student Noel Redding, who had auditioned for the lead guitarist slot with the Animals. Drummer John "Mitch" Mitchell had been performing professionally since his stint on BBC radio at thirteen; a TV series at sixteen followed, as did the role of the Artful Dodger in the original London stage production of *Oliver*. The roster was finalized on October 12, 1966; the Jimi Hendrix Experience played its first gig three days later, opening for France's own Elvis, Johnny Hallyday, at the prestigious Olympia Theatre in Paris.

For the initial release Hendrix and Chandler chose "Hey Joe," a minor top-40 tune (#31, June 1966) by a one-hit American group called the Leaves. The Experience version was a modified blues containing an emotive, talking vocal style by Hendrix (complete with vocal fills such as "dig," "yeah," and the famous "I gave her the gun!"), falsetto, droning background vocals, a short, rather simple guitar solo (containing a profusion of bent notes and vibrato but lacking the dissonant noise qualities of later works), Hendrix's typical chorded guitar fills, and the second guitar found on most studio cuts. The biggest and most pleasant surprise was the quality and dominance of the drums in the mix. Mitchell, rather than Hendrix, embroidered the song with creative and dynamically effective one- and two-measure fills.

"Hey Joe" reached #6 on the English charts in January 1967, and the Experience's appearance on TV's "Top of the Pops"—where Hendrix exposed England to the "show"—generated media descriptions such as the "Wild Man of Pop" and the even more racist "Wild Man from Borneo." Indeed, Hendrix's live performances were wild, as one account describes it: "Falling suddenly to his knees like James Brown during 'Please, Please' and lip-synching a scream as his Stratocaster emits an orgasmic howl. Then moving the guitar across his body, standing straight up from his haunches panning the instrument before him like a machine gun cock emitting staccato bursts; humping his ax as it rumbles into low-pitched feedback, and then letting it all out as he falls back to his knees and then over backward."[9]

The first album, *Are You Experienced* (#2 U.K.), released in May 1967, was kept from the top of the charts only by the extraordinary *Sgt. Pepper's*. It exhibits Hendrix's full range of talent and accomplishment; the years of paying dues and establishing an instrumental foundation were paying off. Numerous outstanding cuts fill the album, each one revealing a different facet of Hendrix's volatile musical and psychological personalities.

"Purple Haze" (#3 U.K.), a musical reference to psychoactive drugs that was written in his dressing room, featured Hendrix both as hard-driving riff-maker and as celestial traveler. Mitchell's introductory snare-driven quarter-note pulse explodes as Hendrix bangs out two highly distorted introductory riffs—these initial measures have become a signature for hard rock and roll music. For three verses Jimi sing-speaks about being transported into a higher but disorienting state of consciousness, punctuating the intervening instrumental passages with licentious oohs and aahs. The song fades, as a seemingly endless sustained note rings, an inventive mechanical technique that Hendrix was able to duplicate live by repeated picking.

"The Wind Cries Mary" (#6 U.K.), the third single released from the album, presents the gentle Hendrix, the Dylanesque balladeer. To a melodically pleasing soundtrack featuring hammer-on chorded fills, abstract and obscure lyrics tumble forth, framed by the titular reference "And the wind cries Mary." Some fans cite "The Wind Cries Mary," "Little Wing," and other ballads as their consistently favorite Hendrix material. "Third Stone from the Sun" is a surreal romp introduced by a delightful melody played on the guitar in octaves reminiscent of jazz guitarist Wes Montgomery. This song (the title is a reference to the solar system's third planet) introduces the listener to a broad collage of the master's guitar-generated sounds—swirling winds, atmospheric static, screams, roars, and much more—that astounded his audiences and was one factor that distinguished him from other players.

On "Foxey Lady" the erotic Hendrix emerges—just one more of his many personalities. Jimi's performance style lacked sexual subtlety. His guitar, played between his legs T-Bone Walker-style, symbolized a phallus and he'd often simulate sex with his guitar against the stack of amplifiers during live performances. The title cut with musical references to the Beatles hit "Strawberry Fields," with the sustained note, military-snare cadence, backwards tapes, and musical reprise.

The Hendrix revealed on *Are You Experienced* was brash and innovative. Certainly no one approached his mastery of the guitar and its sounds, nor had anyone displayed such a variety of intense and forceful musical personalities, from the pounding hard rocker to the ethereal space pilot to the erotic lover. For those who listened (and, as Reprise Records executive Stan Cornyn commented, "Hendrix was an acquired taste") new musical and emotional directions were being revealed. The junior high and high school generation, buffeted by the turbulent sixties, were crying for more, and as their older siblings continued to embrace the Beatles and friends, many younger fans were attracted by Hendrix's forceful, explosive sound.

America's first exposure to Jimi Hendrix as guitar king came at the Monterey Pop Festival. Festival board member Paul McCartney had strongly recommended Jimi, releasing him from a previous commitment to travel with the Beatles on the filming of the Magical Mystery Tour. Cognizant of Hendrix's power, festival planners scheduled him to perform next to last on Sunday night, after the Who and the Dead and before the closing act, the Mamas and the Papas. Dressed in his colorful Carnaby Street finery (Jimi normally wore boldly colored and frilly shirts, embroidered jackets and vests, scarves, headbands, and jewelry as his costume) Hendrix jammed a six-song set.[10]

On Dylan's "Like a Rolling Stone" Hendrix once again demonstrated his unique ability to sound like a lead and rhythm guitar, proffering strums and tasty hammer-on fills seemingly simultaneously. His set-closer, a cover of the Troggs hit "Wild Thing," began with a rambling "stoned" rap about his previous night's love-making and a cryptic reference to sacrifice. Launching into his combined British and American national anthems, Hendrix blasted feedback bursts of fireworks along with speedy, indistinguishable melodic passages. The finale sounded much the same, but suddenly Hendrix placed his guitar on the ground, soaked the body with lighter fluid, and while he kneeled onstage set his axe on fire. Finished with this ritual sacrifice, the guitar moaning from feedback, Jimi finished the job by smashing it on the stage (echoes of Townshend) and exited to tumultuous applause.

Critical response to this performance was mixed. The *Los Angeles Times* observed, "When Jimi left the stage, he had graduated from rumor to legend."[11] But Robert Christgau in New York's *Village Voice* called Hendrix "an Uncle Tom, a caricature, a modern incarnation of long-dead Negro minstrelry."[12] Promoters, however, were not ambivalent and hustled to offer concert dates. Jimi appeared with the Airplane at the Fillmore. Clubs in New York and Los Angeles scrambled for bookings. Peter Tork of the Monkees and Dick Clark wanted the Experience to open for top-40 idols the Monkees. They actually started a tour but it proved to be a mismatch—the Monkees' teenybopper audience couldn't handle Hendrix's raunchy, hard-driven rock. *Are You Experienced* was released in the United States—rising to #5—but received mixed critical reviews. Jon Landau in *Rolling Stone* noted the poor quality of songs and their inherent violence, yet he cited Jimi as a great guitarist and arranger.

The next eighteen months found Hendrix in perpetual motion. He released two albums, *Axis: Bold as Love* (#3, February 1968) and *Electric Ladyland* (#1, November 1968), and toured constantly in England, Europe, and the United States. When Jimi wasn't recording or performing he was out on the town or sequestered in one of the many apartments or hotel rooms he had set up with special girlfriends around New York. Hendrix spent up to $5,000 per week recording at the Record Plant in midtown Manhattan. Jimi also frequented the Scene, a trendy nightspot a few blocks away from the studio. On any given evening Hendrix might sit in with club headliners or jam after hours till dawn. His musical cohorts at the Scene included an amazing assortment of players: bluesmen Johnny Winter, Muddy Waters, Buddy Guy, and James Cotton, Led Zeppelin, Fleetwood Mac, Eric Clapton, Jeff Beck, and Rick Derringer.

Hendrix's later studio output was prolific and generally well received. *Axis: Bold as Love* opened with a simulated radio interview between imaginary station ESP disc jockey (manager Chas Chandler) and a man from outer space (Hendrix). Feedback effects simulating spaceships lifting off and other intergalactic sounds punctuate the first two minutes. The album's panoply of songs include "Spanish Castle Magic," a riff-driven tune with a blues-rooted harmonic structure and minimalistic bluesy solo, and "Little Wing," the winsome ballad to sometimes-companion Devon Wilson, featuring crystalline percussion and other ethereal effects, along with a demonstration of controlled whammy-bar detuning, evidencing Hendrix's great control of the instrument. "If 6 Was 9" features a broad range of feedback effects sprinkled around a laissez-faire, let-me-live-my-life-the-way-I-want-to political rap—Hendrix's political outlook didn't include the notion of collective action found in the era's counterculture movements. For the cut's final passages Hendrix replicates a crazed pan blaring his wooden pipes.

*Electric Ladyland* garnered even more acclaim at the time. It was Hendrix's only #1 yet still proved too hard and raunchy for a major segment of the rock audience. Like *Axis: Bold as Love*, it was uneven, containing brilliant and innovative guitar music and compositions of multilevel meaning alongside seemingly directionless, improvised fuzz. *New York Times* reviewer Robert Palmer saw it as one of those albums that contained messages "to be savored and probed for hidden meanings and listened to again and again."[13] To Richard Goldstein of the *Village Voice,* you came away "feeling that it's overlong, indiscriminate, and needlessly jammed." Beyond that, however, "for sheer texture, this [was] an uncanny piece of sound collage."[14] Hendrix brought in big guns Stevie Winwood, Al Kooper, Buddy Miles, and Airplane bassist Jack Casady to spice up the work. Excellent cuts included "Voodoo Chile (Slight Return)," exhibiting a mature guitarist going through his blues-rooted paces, and "All Along the Watchtower," a Dylan cover as forceful and brilliant as the original.

By the end of 1968 Jimi was at his peak. *Rolling Stone* critic Jon Landau called *Electric Ladyland* "the only two-record set of the year that made it in my book. [Hendrix] is the authoritative lead guitarist, the coolest showman, an excellent songwriter, and a constantly improving vocalist. Of touring performers on the scene today, Hendrix is tops and 1968 was his year."[15] *Rolling Stone* declared, "For creativity, electricity and balls above and beyond the call of duty, he has won for himself the *Rolling Stone* Performer of the Year award."[16]

There were, however, stormier days on the horizon. Disputes continued among critics and fans over Hendrix's alleged abandonment of his Black roots in favor of a white counterculture musical aesthetic. Cuts on both *Axis: Bold as Love* and *Electric Ladyland* fueled the arguments. Some pointed to blues-rooted chord structure and stylistic elements, call and response, and emotive vocals as an example of attention to tradition. Others pointed to his distorted guitar feedback explosions and obscure stream-of-consciousness lyrics as evidence of drug-induced, bohemian-oriented content with a white pop audience focus.

Blues guitarist Bloomfield would come to Hendrix's defense, calling him "the Blackest guitarist I ever heard. His music was deeply rooted in pre-blues, the oldest musical forms like field hollers and gospel melodies. From what I can garner, there was no form of Black music that he hadn't listened to or studied . . . and they poured out in his playing."[17] Yet when he sat in with Chicago blues great Howlin' Wolf at the Scene, Wolf "put him down" bad. Blues guitarist Johnny Winter was struck by the paradox and commented, "Jimi really loved the blues, the real thing though isn't what he wanted to play. . . . The Wolf couldn't understand that Jimi's style of blues was legitimate too. He just felt like his own blues were the blues, and didn't accept anybody else's with feedback and fuzz and everything."[18] When Hendrix jammed with Muddy Waters, they were both thrilled.

Nineteen sixty-nine was a year of turmoil for Hendrix. Former army buddy and bassist Billy Cox joined the Experience that summer, replacing Redding on bass. Tired of being away from England and exasperated with Hendrix's leadership and the necessity of subjugating his ego to the guitar master, Redding left the group. Mitchell parted at the same time but returned within the month and remained with Jimi throughout most of his career. Jimi was spending quite a bit of money, and although the success of his records and concert appearances earned him top dollar, unfavorable contracts with management and some shady dealings by another manager, Mike Jeffries, left Hendrix barely solvent. He poured a quarter of a million dollars of advance royalties into his dream studio, Electric Ladyland, but construction delays and poor planning postponed its completion until March 1970.

Yet there were some artistic successes in this year's roller coaster ride. Jimi's management negotiated top dollar and closing-act status for Hendrix at Woodstock. Unfortunately, his legendary version of "Star Spangled Banner," captured so beautifully in the Woodstock film, was played before only 40,000 tired, mud-caked survivors of the festival on Monday morning. The closing-act demand had inadvertently caused Hendrix to miss the opportunity to play to the 500,000-person audience that attended during the previous three days of the lovefest. That May Hendrix had been arrested at Toronto's airport and charged with possession of heroin; customs officials had found a glass jar containing four glassine packets of heroin on top of Jimi's clean underwear. In December Hendrix was found not guilty—the jury believed the string of witnesses testifying that fans and bed partners sometimes slipped presents into the star's luggage. Anyone familiar with Hendrix would have known about his loathing for that particular drug.

New Year's Eve 1969 brought the reunion of Jimi and old friend Buddy Miles. Since meeting on the soul circuit when Miles was a sixteen-year-old drummer for Wilson Pickett, the two had jammed together often. Miles had joined guitarist Mike Bloomfield in soul powerhouse Electric Flag and then formed the Buddy Miles Express. Partially in response to calls from Black activists for Hendrix to play with Black artists, for two nights—December 31, 1969 and January 1, 1970—Hendrix, Cox, and Miles were the Band of Gypsys.

The concerts produced a self-titled live album, including the 12:38 gem "Machine Gun." In a contemporary gesture Hendrix dedicated the song to all the troops fighting in Harlem, Chicago, and Vietnam. "Machine Gun" is the best single exhibition available on a major-label release of Jimi's multifaceted approach to guitar. Present are the repetition, the tearing bends, and the gritty sustain of the blues along with an ever-changing kaleidoscope of feedback-driven riffs and sounds. The lyrics of "Machine Gun" tackle a war he describes as being conducted against Blacks and Vietnamese by the "evil man." To Hendrix, "They force us [Black soldiers] to kill you and you to kill me even though we're only families apart."

In addition to the superlative playing on some of the *Band of Gypsys* cuts, 1970 found Jimi planning efforts with numerous jazz artists, including an album with jazz luminary Gil Evans. His life, however, was still plagued by business and personal problems. Management fired Cox and Miles and manipulated an Experience reunion for early 1970. Jimi needed the money and hadn't the stamina nor temperament to resist. He sought refuge in alcohol and drugs. Cox returned for a series of shows in Europe but was slipped a dose of LSD and unwittingly reduced to a zombie state. Hendrix canceled two Dutch shows and slumped back to London.

Jimi was staying with a British girlfriend, Monica Danemann. One night the couple ate a late dinner, drank some wine, and retired at dawn. Later that morning, September 18, 1970, Monica went out for some cigarettes. She returned to find Hendrix unconscious and in respiratory distress. An ambulance arrived and the attendants, assuring Danemann that Jimi would be all right, took him away. He was dead on arrival at the hospital. The coroner's inquest ascertained that Hendrix had died "as a result of an inhalation of vomit due to barbiturate poisoning." Hendrix had taken nine of Danemann's Vesperax sleeping tablets, probably unaware that the European dosage was considerably more potent than the American equivalent. When his stomach rejected the drug, his numbed gag reflex could not prevent fluids from entering the lungs.[19]

Hendrix biographer David Henderson contends that the ambulance attendants mistakenly secured Hendrix seated rather than in the normal position (lying on his side). Thus when Hendrix aspirated, his head thrust back, his windpipe was closed and the fluids filled his lungs.[20] The body was flown to Seattle, where family and musical friends, including Redding, Mitchell, Buddy Miles, and John Hammond Jr., attended the funeral. Some writers focused on Jimi's drug-plagued life and early demise. Others called Hendrix "a genius Black musician . . . and composer of brilliantly dramatic power."[21]

His greatness and legacy are not easy to characterize. He was closer to the cutting edge than the mainstream. In comparison to most music of the time, his sound was hard-edged, brash, and abrasive. But these qualities were a conscious effort on Hendrix's part: "We try to make our music so loose and hard-hitting, so that it hits your soul hard enough to make it open. It's like shock therapy."[22] The hard-driving rock music of Led Zeppelin and its seventies progeny is, in part, a reflection of this Hendrix shock-therapy aesthetic. Other elements—like Hendrix's sloppy speak-sing vocal style or his obscure, stream-of-consciousness lyricism—appealed to few musicians and thus had little or no impact.

Hendrix's most important contribution to rock music was in his willingness and ability to redefine the boundaries of rock and roll guitar. He did this as a technician (his ability to master the instrument) and as an artist. As an artist Hendrix conceptualized the musical expansion and as a technician he replicated the vision. One of Hendrix's most important innovations was the notion that guitar music should not necessarily be limited to transcribable pitch; notated music is only one kind of sound. Other sounds can and should be reproduced on the guitar. As he set about to create this kaleidoscope of sound, Jimi drew from many sources. Some ideas, like the machine gun and the rushing wind, even came from his experiences in the army.

Hendrix the technician determined that these sounds could be best achieved through the manipulation of feedback—the overload of a sound reproduction system by the instantaneous surge of produced amplified frequencies. Hendrix found that by playing on the edge of feedback, and controlling how and when specific frequencies would feed back, he could reproduce his collage of sounds. This took constant practice and a thorough understanding of the primitive technology of the time. Contrary to popular belief, Hendrix did not play without effects devices but rather used a number of enhancements to bring his sound to the edge.

Hendrix was a regular customer at Manny's, the famous New York musical instrument superstore. "Any kind of new toy or sound effect he bought immediately. Whenever he walked in, he was good for $1,500–2,000," claims Manny's son, Henry Goldrich. "Jimi used to buy three or four guitars every other week."[23] His guitar of choice was the Fender Stratocaster (known as "the Strat"). However, he played numerous others over the course of his career. Although Hendrix was left-handed, he preferred a right-handed Strat turned around and restrung. This enabled him easy access to the volume and tone controls—now situated above instead of below the strings—important components of his feedback-generation system.

Hendrix usually used a Vox wah-wah foot pedal (which produced a narrowing "wah" sound when depressed), a Fuzz Face (which distorted the sound), and a Univox Univibe (which simulated the phasing produced by a rotating Leslie organ speaker). In addition to this arsenal of effects technology, Hendrix manipulated the guitar with what observers have called enormous hands. This enabled him to span large portions of the neck while utilizing the guitar controls. In fact, Hendrix could produce feedback on two or three strings while playing lead on others. Constantly playing close to feedback, he would tap the back of the neck with his hands, bump it with his hip, or fiddle with the pickup toggle switch, pushing the guitar over the screaming edge.

His enormous hands, the Stratocaster guitar, various sound-manipulation devices, a stack of high-powered Marshall amplifiers, an innate talent to reproduce anything he heard, and his own brilliant imagination helped Hendrix become, as Bloomfield once put it, "the man that took electric music and defined it. He turned sounds from devices like wah-wahs into music. They weren't gimmicks when he used them. In fact, they were beyond music, they were in the realm of pure sound and music combined."[24] His guitar legacy is not that so many others copied his style—even twenty years later there are still things contemporary guitarists cannot reproduce—but that they, too, liberated themselves from the boundaries of pitch in an attempt to take advantage of the possibilities opened by use of feedback. Unfortunately, subsequent guitarists also aped his speed and voluminous use of notes without understanding that these elements were anchored by Hendrix's innate feeling for the blues.

Hendrix epitomized the quiet man who, as a performer, explodes on stage. In front of an audience, it was all show—an erotic, high-energy, colorfully costumed jester parading his bag of tricks before an adoring white audience. Behind the musical mask, however, he was a closely guarded and private man who had few, if any, confidants. Survivors find ways of eluding or outgrowing their haunting pain; those, like Hendrix, who try to numb or escape it rarely make it. Although Jimi's death was most likely a tragic accident, his inability to deal with the lifelong pressures and pain left him only one step from the edge.

*　　　*　　　*

Other lead guitarists emerged in the late sixties, though none approach the status or influence of Clapton, Hendrix, and Led Zeppelin's Jimmy Page (whose work will be explored in the next chapter). The closest in talent and compositional skill was Jeff Beck, who unfortunately had difficulty in maintaining the social relationships and making the compromises necessary to function in the commercial marketplace. Nevertheless, Beck released two solo albums after leaving the Yardbirds, *Beck-Ola* (#15, September 1968) and *Truth* (#15, August 1969), which showcased his imaginative use of controlled feedback and various modal feelings and featured cuts with vocalist Rod Stewart and bassist Ron Wood. Other players who garnered further acclaim in the seventies included Steve Howe (of Yes), Leslie West (Mountain), Robin Trower (Procol Harum), Alvin Lee (Ten Years After), and Joe Walsh (James Gang).

Between 1966 and 1970 Eric Clapton and Jimi Hendrix played their finest, most imaginative, and most important music. They helped to focus some popular-music attention on the exploits of electric guitarists. Their beat-driven, blues-derived music of the sixties became the foundation for the sex, drugs, and hard rock of the seventies—a time when social commentary was out and the pursuit of pleasure was in. Youth, trained by Madison Avenue to strive for instant gratification, demanded more input. They turned the volume up a few decibels in an attempt to anesthetize themselves against the increasingly problematic aspects of society. Chapter 16 thus focuses on rock/pop of the seventies and the band that led this parade: Led Zeppelin.

# 16· The Seventies: Dazed and Confused

*The essential ingredient for any successful rock group is energy—the ability to give out energy, to receive energy from the audience, and to give it back to the audience. A rock concert is in fact a rite involving the evocation and transmission of energy.*

**Author William S. Burroughs**

*[Led Zeppelin's] success may be attributable at least in part to the accelerating popularity among the teenage rock and roll audience of barbiturates and amphetamines, drugs that render their users most responsive to crushing volume and ferocious histrionics of the sort that Zeppelin has dealt exclusively.*

**From a review in the Los Angeles Times**

*The way I see it, rock and roll is folk music. Street music. It isn't taught in school. It has to be picked up.*

**Led Zeppelin guitarist Jimmy Page, from a 1975 interview in Rolling Stone**

*We just get out there and rock. If your amp blows or your guitar packs it in, smash it up and pick up another one. And that's how it always was with us. We can't even stop and tune up. Those kids are all wound up. A second or two is too much for them. They've gotta have it.*

**AC/DC guitarist Angus Young**

---

B Y THE END OF 1971 MOST of the melodious creativity that characterized the golden era of rock/pop music had dissipated. Regional styles such as soul, Motown, and the San Francisco sound were in decline as artists succumbed to the fast lane, groups disbanded, and stylistic changes took hold. The first British invasion had run its course—the Beatles had disbanded, the Stones had scaled the heights and were resting up for the moment, and the Who were between projects.

Pioneering guitar kings Clapton and Hendrix had relinquished their thrones, Clapton to heroin and Hendrix to the grim reaper. Yet the music of the late 1960s didn't disappear like its classic rock counterparts. Rock veterans like Paul McCartney and John Lennon, Motown's Stevie Wonder, Marvin Gaye, and Michael Jackson, the Rolling Stones, and Paul Simon continued to score commercial successes.

## Digression: The Changing Landscape

Pop/rock's musical evolution during the late 1960s and 1970s occurred at a time when the music industry expanded rapidly in size and power. Record sales, which had topped $1 billion for the first time in 1967, reached $2 billion in 1973 and $4 billion in 1978. Record and tape sales revenues also surpassed other types of entertainment earnings, including sports and movies. Pop music had finally entered the realm of Big Business, and the consequences were formidable. With profits soaring and growth levels approaching 25 percent annually, record-label subsidiaries came under closer scrutiny by corporate bosses. Lawyers and accountants replaced old-time music aficionados like Atlantic's Ahmet Ertegun and Elektra's Jac Holzman as the final arbiters of major-label decisionmaking.

In addition, because of the monstrous profits to be earned, music-industry giants began to swallow smaller companies as the trend toward corporate consolidation increased. By 1973 Warner Bros./Reprise, Elektra/Asylum, Atlantic/Atco (combined, given the acronym WEA) and other related subsidiaries were united under the corporate umbrella of the Kinney Corporation, a company that began in funeral homes and parking lots. Industry giant Columbia Records was only one cog in the CBS conglomerate that owned the CBS TV network, Hertz Rent-a-Car, Banquet Foods, and much more. By 1973 the top six record corporations were selling approximately 66 percent of all the Hot-100 singles and albums. By 1980 this figure, in part because of further consolidation by the record industry, had reached 82 percent.

The audience, seen merely as a segment of product consumers to be wooed by this increasingly powerful industry, was also changing. The second wave of the baby boom was about to hit puberty, ready for the latest teen-focused top-of-the-pops. What had essentially been a single teenaged rock audience of the fifties, and then a larger-yet-diverse audience brought together by the Fab Four in the sixties, was beginning the process of fragmentation. Age, class, race, education, and gender became natural dividing lines; these began determining the kids' interest in and identification with the many different evolving rock styles.

The rock audience of the late 1960s was now encompassing much of the American under-thirty population. It was no longer the exclusive province of the very young or the disenchanted; rock was part of mainstream culture. In the seventies the older and middle-class audience segments continued to purchase music by artists that wrote meaningful lyrics and accentuated melody and harmony—characteristics they enjoyed during the sixties. Their younger brothers and sisters and working-class cousins were usually more attracted to the evolving music, which contained a stronger beat, loud distorted guitars, and simple, sexually oriented, escapist sentiments.

All this—industry consolidation and audience expansion—occurred in the context of a society exhausted by past and ongoing struggles over human rights issues (at home and abroad). In 1970 the U.S. government and military still had nearly 500,000 troops committed in Vietnam. Yet a majority of Americans opposed the war, with many taking their cause to the streets in the form of protests and marches in acts of civil disobedience. Minorities were also engaged in an ongoing struggle to obtain economic, social, and political equality. The counterculture movement had also spread beyond regional centers to the country's high schools.

By middecade the war had been lost and Republican President Richard Nixon—who was elected in 1972 by dint of criminal activity and a reign of terror against legal dissent—had resigned his office in disgrace in the wake of the Watergate break-in scandal.

## And Now Back to Our Story

The early 1970s became a time of contradiction. On the one hand there was the institutionalization of the counterculture's dress, appearance, drug experimentation, and language. On the other there were efforts by government and big business to reverse the recent era's political and cultural openness and expressiveness. Into this confusing milieu burst the bombastic, hard rock-rooted stream of popular music. Led Zeppelin was at the front of the charge, followed by a roster of attentive disciples. Together they constituted the third rock music explosion, which caught the attention of the era's adolescents—solidifying a trend begun by the Who, Cream, and Hendrix. "Sex, drugs, and rock and roll!" became the rallying cry, and the pursuit of pleasure and money became the ultimate goal. Now art-rock (rock with artistic pretense) and singer-songwriter pop/rock joined heavy metal (as the hardest rock has come to be called) and dinosaur rock as the seventies lumbered on.

In its early days Led Zeppelin was unsure of its direction, much like the era in which it was born (the late 1960s). Personnel had been hired by guitarist Jimmy Page and manager Peter Grant originally as roster replacements for the Yardbirds. A lengthy process of attrition, including the departure of guitarist Jeff Beck in November 1966, left Page in control. Brought on board in order to honor Scandinavian concert commitments as the New Yardbirds, the replacement players—bassist John Paul Jones, vocalist Robert Plant, and drummer John Bonham—were astounded by the magic they experienced during their first rehearsal. They decided to continue, although as Page describes, "When Robert and I first got together we realized we could go in two possible directions—heavy blues, or an Incredible String Band trip."

The players represented two levels of experience: the older, studio-wise Londoners (Page and Jones) and the teenage provincial greenhorns (Plant and Bonham). Jimmy Page (born January 9, 1944) was an only child, a self-described loner whose outlet and first love was the guitar. His first, an acoustic that he acquired at age fourteen, was replaced by an electric so that he could more easily reproduce the bent-note solos of classic rockers James Burton and Scotty Moore. Page also delved into the works of blues artists B. B. King and Elmore James, and at seventeen he landed his first important gig with Neil Christian and the Crusaders—a lineup that also included superlative guitarist Albert Lee and, later, future Deep Purple wizard Richie Blackmore.

Physical frailty, a condition that would continue to plague Page throughout his career, forced him off the road. Like many of his contemporaries he enrolled in art school, but two years later he was lured into the recording scene by engineer and friend Glyn Johns. Between 1963 and 1966 Page was in constant demand as a studio guitarist, a favorite of top producers Shel Talmy, Mickie Most, and Andrew Oldham. He played on numerous hit records, including the Who's "I Can't Explain," the Kinks hit "You Really Got Me," Them's "Gloria," and even Tom Jones's pop classic, "It's Not Unusual." Page, content with the abundance of studio work, turned down an offer to replace Eric Clapton in the Yardbirds in 1965, recommending instead childhood buddy Jeff Beck.

By June 1966 Page succumbed to the temptations of the road, first joining the Yardbirds on bass and then, months later, sharing lead-guitar duties with Beck. The band was a strange amalgam of brilliance and contradiction. Page, with his wealth of studio experience, new musical ideas, and fresh enthusiasm, buoyed up the rest, who were becoming tired of the rock and roll treadmill. Although initially enthused at the prospect of playing harmony lead solos with Beck, Page found the other guitarist "an inconsistent player, in that when he's on, he's probably the best there is, but at the time, and for a period afterwards, he had no respect whatsoever for audiences."[1] Beck, pleading illness, failed to show for yet another concert and was sacked.

The last original Yardbirds (Keith Relf and Jim McCarty) left in July 1968. Page, who had previously been close to forming a band with session keyboard player Nicky Hopkins, drummer Keith Moon, and bassist John Paul Jones, now invited Jones to join the Yardbirds. Born John Baldwin on January 3, 1946, Jones entered the group with musical training, session work on bass and keyboard—he and Page had worked together on numerous records, including Donovan's "Hurdy Gurdy Man"—and experience in arranging numbers. Page initially wanted singer Terry Reid and drummer B. J. Wilson (who later played with Procol Harum), but neither was available. Instead he went to Birmingham to scope out nineteen-year-old Hobbstweedle vocalist Robert Plant. Plant, criticized by some local musicians for his stage posturing and lack of singing ability, apparently impressed Page, who later recalled, "It unnerved me just to listen. It still does, like a primeval wail."[2]

Plant was invited to London, developed an immediate rapport with Page, and eventually convinced his old Band of Joy crony, drummer John "Bonzo" Bonham, to join them. In describing their initial session together, Plant recounts, "I've never been so turned on in my life. Although we were all steeped in blues and R&B, we found out in the first hour and a half that we had our own identity."[3] The new identity required a new name. After rejecting the Whoopie Cushion and the Mad Dogs, the group settled on Led Zeppelin—derived from a pronouncement by the Who's John Entwistle and Keith Moon that the projected band would go over like a lead balloon.

Led Zeppelin's future commercial success was based, in part, on their version of the "team." This included the musicians, the studio-production skills of Page, the songwriting consistency of Page and Plant, and aggressive, competent management. Their business leadership came in the form of a 250-pound former professional wrestler, former Yardbirds manager Peter Grant. An astute businessman and promoter, Grant also successfully employed verbal and physical intimidation to get what he wanted. The band was shepherded on the tour by road manager Richie Cole, whose job has been described as mother hen, field pimp, and hit man.

Grant, Page, and the three relative unknowns secured an astronomical $200,000 advance and a commensurate royalty rate from Atlantic Records. Company executives correctly surmised that audience interest in hard rock labelmates Cream, Iron Butterfly, and Vanilla Fudge would translate into even stronger support for Zeppelin. By 1973 Zeppelin accounted for 10 percent of Atlantic's record sales.

Led Zeppelin's self-titled first album was recorded straight away, during a three-week period just after their return from the final Yardbirds tour. The album, with favorites like "Dazed and Confused" (an uncredited rewrite of the Jake Holmes original) and the guitar vehicle "Communication Breakdown," is mostly an unrefined catalog of the band's basic elements and a preview of things to come. Guitarist Page, an acknowledged studio master and stylistic innovator, lays the foundation for metal guitar with speeded-up riffs based on repetition and pull-offs (listen to "Communication Breakdown" and "Good Times Bad Times"). He also exhibits competence as a blues player—mimicking B. B. King's style on "I Can't Quit You Baby" and screams and bent notes on "You Shook Me"—but lacks the emotional veracity of era counterparts Clapton ("Crossroads") and Hendrix ("Red House"). Page's interest in acoustic players such as Bert Jansch and John Renbourn translates into a unique versatility for the hard rock/heavy metal genre. Thus listeners could relax to cuts like "Black Mountain Side," which featured fingerpicking on the acoustic guitar. This ability to produce material with a wide dynamic range—from soft to stentorian—was also telescoped into one song, "Babe I'm Gonna Leave You" and was later used most successfully on their all-time classic, "Stairway to Heaven."

The surprise to most listeners was Robert Plant's unique voice and singing style. Here was a man who sounded as though he was singing one octave above his natural range in a way that would shred his vocal chords at any moment—a Janis Joplin in drag, so to speak. However, this seemingly unnatural act worked in the context of the newborn lineup. Plant's repertoire of screams, moans, wails, and lascivious groans generated the excitement mandated by the material itself. It was also a perfect call-and-response foil for Page's catalog of guitar sounds (listen to "Dazed and Confused" for the wah-wah, bowed guitar, octaves, and other improvised sounds matched by Plant's variety of moans). Bassist Jones provided a literate harmonic foundation to the music, and Bonham just plodded along, pounding out the basics with his enormous drumsticks. His elementary style reversed the trend toward flashy, technique-oriented drumming, popularized by hard rock predecessors Mitchell, Baker, and Moon.

The band left England around Christmas 1968 for the first of six U.S. tours over the next year and a half. Work at home was scarce, but in America they were enthusiastically received by young fans while opening for Detroit's MC5 and Vanilla Fudge; they positively tore down both Fillmores, a supporting act first at the West, then blowing Iron Butterfly off the stage at the East. That first album, released in January 1969, went to #10 and "Dazed and Confused" and "Communication Breakdown" received FM airplay.

This popularity—on the radio and live—flew in the face of scathing reviews by the rock press, a paradox that would continue to haunt them into the midseventies. *Rolling Stone*'s John Mendelsohn called the album self-indulgent and restricted. Calling Page an "extraordinarily proficient blues guitarist and explorer of his instrument's electronic capabilities," Mendelsohn also described him as "a very limited producer and a writer of weak, unimaginative songs." Plant wasn't spared either: "He may be as foppish as Rod Stewart [at the time, lead singer for Beck's solo efforts], but he's nowhere near so exciting, especially in the higher registers."

It was easy to forget the bad reviews with legendary alcohol- and drug-fueled sexual escapades that took place on the American tours. Mainly through the efforts of road manager Cole, women and drugs were made available for the band, anytime, anywhere. On the second U.S. tour *Life* magazine assigned reporter Ellen Sander to cover the band-on-the-road angle, providing the group an opportunity to score positive national press. Sander called Zeppelin one of the finest British bands on tour, adding that "no matter how miserably the group failed to keep their behavior up to a basic human level, they played well almost every night of the tour."[4] In what would prove over time to become typical Zeppelin conduct, some band and crew members took a liking to animalistic behavior. Entering the Fillmore East dressing room to congratulate the band on its final tour date, Sander was physically assaulted: "Two members of the group attacked me, shrieking and grabbing at my clothes, totally over the edge. . . . Bonzo came at me first, and then there were a couple more. After that I didn't see much. All of a sudden there were all these hands on me, and all these big guys. My clothes were half torn off; they were in a frenzy. I was absolutely terrified that I was going to be raped and [I was] really angry."[5] Sander refused to complete an article, concluding in a later account, "If you walk inside the cages of the zoo, you get to see the animals close-up, stroke the captive pelts, and mingle with the energy behind the mystique. You also get to smell the shit firsthand."[6]

Their next album, *Led Zeppelin II* (#1, November 1969), hit the charts in 1969, the same year as its predecessor. Written and rehearsed on the road, it was recorded in studios in England and across the United States. The album's center-piece, and the group's most successful single release of all time, "Whole Lotta Love" (#4, December 1969), was recorded in L.A. and the mixing process for the album took two days in London. It epitomizes the Zeppelin formula: a driving, sexually oriented rocker featuring the carnal-screamer Plant and guitar-innovator Page. In this tune Page's guitar ranges from edgy, Clapton-like blues—Page had switched to a Gibson Les Paul from the 1958 Telecaster given to him by Jeff Beck—to the swirling sound pastiche reminiscent of Hendrix. The song is also full of not-so-subtle sexual double entendre, no doubt a delight to Zeppelin's largely adolescent male audience. During the chaotic guitar midsection, for exam-ple, Plant improvises concurrent orgasmic wails. A bit later he boasts, "Gonna give you every inch of my love."

Other material on the album is inconsistent. On "The Lemon Song" and "Heartbreaker" Page the studio-wise perfectionist surprisingly stumbles during the solos, reaching for riffs and speed beyond his grasp. "Moby Dick," a concert favorite, features the mandatory hard rock drum solo, characterized by Bonham's bare-handed improvisation and Baker-like double kickdrum rolls. Bonzo made no pretense about being a flashy or expert technician, stating "I'm a simple, straight-ahead drummer and I don't try to be anything better than I am."[7]

The disturbing audience/critic paradox continued. The group increased in popularity, playing high-energy sets to sold-out houses while being panned as primordial headbangers by most critics. Reviewers accused the band of taking credit for old blues songs, noting, for example, the similarity between "Whole Lotta Love" and Willie Dixon's "You Need Love." Writing a piece in the dialect of the proverbial raving and wasted teenage Zeppelin fan, *Rolling Stone* reviewer Mendelsohn implied that their music was best listened to in a narcotic trance in-duced by Romilar cough syrup, Novocain, strong Vietnamese marijuana, and mescaline. Zeppelin, who initially had respect for *Rolling Stone*, were now dis-traught and hostile—all the way to the bank.

Meanwhile, on tour the band foisted gratuitous violence on people and objects around them. At a Danish art gallery reception, Page goaded Bonham into de-stroying some paintings, which Grant was then forced to purchase. A free-for-all between Bonzo, Cole, and reporters then erupted. In Vancouver the road crew spotted a microphone pointing from the audience toward the band. The band was tired of competing with bootlegs (unauthorized recordings of live performances); its roadies dragged the offender backstage, where Cole smashed his equipment. The man turned out to be a Canadian government official recording concert vol-ume levels. A frustrated Bonzo destroyed the dressing room to the tune of $1,500.

At times Zeppelin management and band members acted like infantile gang-sters, taking whatever they wanted. At the 1970 Bath Festival a band called the Flock ran later than scheduled, so Grant and the road crew commandeered the stage and halted the show by shutting off the electricity. Grant and Cole backed up these antics with their fists. When concert officials in the French city of Nantes were slow opening a backstage gate, Grant crashed it with a Mercedes-Benz. Bonham's distaste for the culinary offerings then turned into a rampage that destroyed the three dressing-room trailers. Back at the hotel, Plant couldn't find milk for his tea so he unleashed the road crew; the toll included destroyed furniture, flooded floors, and ruined plumbing.

Off the road Page pursued his avid interest in magic and the occult. In 1970 he purchased Boleskine House, the former residence of mystic Aleister Crowley located on the shores of Loch Ness in Scotland. Crowley, an occultist and philosopher who believed that real magic was hidden in a person's will, spent his life writing poetry, climbing mountains, living openly with multiple women, and reveling in opium, cocaine, and heroin. Besides acquiring Boleskine House—its history included a beheading and a church congregation once trapped by a fire—Page collected Crowley manuscripts, books, and memorabilia.

Page's eccentricities weren't limited to his leisure time. As Stephen Davis describes in his Zeppelin biography, *Hammer of the Gods,* Page also exhibited some bizarre behavior on the road: "Jimmy spent days in his suite with the shades drawn and the candles lit. He gave several interviews sitting before a coffee table covered with numerous switchblades and ratchet knives. . . . With an armed guard sitting outside his door, Jimmy had the isolation of a monk. He spent days and nights wide awake, holding his guitar and, as he told a reporter, 'Waiting for something to come through.'"[8] This behavior appears to reflect Page's mystical leanings, although when queried in 1975 he refused to discuss his beliefs or involvement in the occult. In fact, Page refused to align the music with any of the artistic or sociopolitical movements of the times. "I feel that some so-called progressive groups have gone too far with their personalized intellectualism of beat music. Our music is essentially emotional like the old rock stars of the past. . . . We are not going to make any political or moral statements. Our music is simply us."[9]

Page's simplistic interpretation of rock music history does not account for the variety of meanings intended by songwriters or interpretations by audiences of previous rock generations. Many of the classic rock masters of the fifties, and early members of the British invasion, intended to write and/or record antiauthoritarian, rebellious music. Songs like Berry's "Almost Grown" and "Roll Over Beethoven," Haley's "Rock Around the Clock," and many of the sexually daring numbers by Jerry Lee Lewis and Little Richard are inherently provocative, impelling some of the era's teens to exhibit prohibited behavior. In his inability to see the consequences of this early, "simply emotional" music, Page cannot accept that Zeppelin's audiences may have also ascribed political or moral meaning to the band's music. Simply because they did not make explicit political statements does not mean that certain values and meaning aren't given the music by their listeners.

The rapid rise, enormous success, and increasingly bizarre behavior caused Led Zeppelin to pause in the spring of 1970. "It was a time to step back," Plant once revealed, "take stock and not get lost in it all. Zeppelin was starting to get very big and we wanted the rest of our journey to take a very level course."[10] Plant took Page to a childhood haunt, Bron-Y-Aur (the Golden Beast), a cottage without electricity in the remote Welsh countryside. Enamored with the Crosby, Stills, and Nash sound and the work of California folkie Joni Mitchell, they spent evenings strumming acoustic guitars and sipping hot cider. Days found the duo wandering through the hills composing a very different Zeppelin sound.

*Led Zeppelin III*, released in fall 1970, reflected their Welsh sojourn; in addition to the normal rock fare it contained an album side dominated by acoustic instruments. The band was proud of this musical diversity, although critics and the record buying public were not as convinced. The critics decried blues rip-offs, weak rock material, and pale imitations of California folk-rock. Although it reached #1 (October 1970), sales fell off rapidly. The band was again stung by the criticism and became even further alienated from the press.

The electric side of *Led Zeppelin III* begins with the hit single "Immigrant Song," a tale of Viking invaders filled with the mythic lore that would become an integral part of Zeppelin's lyrical landscape—proving that they were not simply debauched headbangers after all. "Since I've Been Loving You" was the finest blues-flavored cut to date. Page opens with a simple but elegant guitar introduction and later a convincing blues/early metal solo that showcases biting blues notes and fluid repetitive riffs. Riding above a relatively complex blues-rooted harmonic structure and rich texture added by Jones's organ, Plant wails the blues with phrasing and tone similar to Janis Joplin at her best.

Although they obviously shared an affinity for folk music that came through on the acoustic-flavored side, they dabbled with only limited vision and competence. Page's long-held interest in acoustic-guitar fingerpicking gave him a basic proficiency in the form, but not the inflated level of accomplishment cited by supporters in their praise of the band's alleged versatility. One need only listen to British pickers like Jansch and Renbourn and Americans Leo Kottke, John Fahey, and Merle Travis for an inspiring level of accomplishment. In contrast, Zeppelin mostly mangles the folk form. On "Gallows Pole" Page tastefully adds mandolin, but his banjo playing is so poor as to be distracting—Page generously describes his banjo picking as a "cross between Pete Seeger, Earl Scruggs, and total incompetence." The song breaks down completely as Bonham's thudding drums lead the chase to its conclusion. "Bron-Y-Aur Stomp" fares somewhat better, a knee-stomping romp combining the stylistic attributes of Kottke and country music outlaw Waylon Jennings.

British rock fans offset the hostile media reviews by crowning Led Zeppelin England's most popular group in the September 1970 *Melody Maker* public opinion poll—the first time in eight years the Beatles hadn't won. The band was also able to take solace in their extraordinary commercial success; on tour they played to sell-out crowds in increasingly larger venues, and their record sales were reportedly three times that of the Rolling Stones. The writers soon returned to Bron-Y-Aur, hoping to compose a song to replace "Dazed and Confused" as a show-stopper.

Page and Plant succeeded far beyond their expectations with "Stairway to Heaven." Artistically, Page thought "Stairway to Heaven" crystallized the essence of the band. "It had everything there and showed the band at its best . . . as a band, as a unit. . . . It was a milestone for us. Every musician wants to do something of lasting quality, something which will hold up for a long time, and I guess we did it with 'Stairway.'"[11] Although the band refused to release it as a single, "Stairway to Heaven" became one of the most requested songs on FM album-oriented rock (AOR) radio. Radio programmers called it the most popular song of the decade.

Page and Plant divided the song into two dynamic levels (much like the Who's "Behind Blue Eyes"). It began softly with Page's acoustic guitar introduction and a long section of verses building in intensity until it erupted, three-quarters of the way through, into a full rocker. After the guitar solo, which is filled with Page's repertoire of edgy blues riffs and premetal pull-off figures—he used the Telecaster for the first time in years—the song returned to a tasteful a cappella refrain. The obscure lyrics, sung with the voice of a yearning balladeer, reflected Plant's interest in British and Celtic folklore and followed the quest of a mythical golden lady for her "stairway to heaven" or spiritual nirvana.

Although constantly touring, the band was nevertheless able to write and record the rest of an album's worth of material by the spring of 1971, mixing by fall. The quality of this effort (which is untitled) reflects more time taken for studio assembly; the riff-masters are also hard at work crafting recognizable hooks and phrases for rockers such as "Black Dog" and guitar and synthesizer orchestration for "Four Sticks." The fast-paced "Rock and Roll" is pure Berry, plus some, with an eighth-note rhythmic pulse on keyboard and an assortment of guitar licks. "Going to California" is Page and Plant's idealized longing for the southern California Topanga Canyon dream life and is a homage to one of Page's idols, singer-songwriter Joni Mitchell. With this album the acoustic material, particularly "Stairway to Heaven" and "Going to California," begins to make sense—the songs are more carefully crafted, offering a better integration of music, subject matter, and voice than on previous material.

Serious controversy developed between the band and Atlantic Records over the album cover. Zeppelin insisted that there be no identifying marks on the outside cover or inside the jacket. At the top of the liner sleeve appeared four symbols, each band member choosing one. To find the band name or songs listed one had to look on the label itself. Tired of media condemnation, Page decided to symbolically let the music speak for itself and won out the dispute with Atlantic. (In fact, the label had little leverage, as Page refused to turn over the master tapes.) The album became known by many names: *Untitled, The Runes, Led Zeppelin IV,* and *Zoso* (for Page's symbol).

During the years 1972 to 1975 Led Zeppelin owned the road. Their tours continued to set attendance and dollar records, due in part to the visionary tactics of

Peter Grant. For the 1972 tour Zeppelin decided to offer local promoters 10 percent of the gross instead of the more typical 40 or 50 percent. The band rented the stadium venues, created the promotional plan, and hired local promoters to carry it out. The risk paid off. Touring at the same time as the Rolling Stones, Zeppelin played to larger crowds; still, the Stones garnered all the positive press. For the 1973 American tour, when *Houses of the Holy* was released, Zeppelin hired a new publicist and a sound and light company called Showco; the light show, which utilized balls, revolving reflectors, smoke bombs, and cannons, was considered top-notch. They closed their American concerts with classic rock and rockabilly tunes such as Holly's "Peggy Sue," Ricky Nelson's "Hello Mary Lou," and Elvis gems "That's All Right (Mama)" and "Heartbreak Hotel."

On the 1973 tour in Tampa, Florida, Zeppelin broke the Beatles' eight-year-old attendance record for a single headliner, drawing 56,000 fans (a thousand more than the Beatles drew to Shea Stadium in 1965). They also outgrossed the Fab Four by $8,000, taking in $309,000 for the one show. Although Zeppelin had the comfort of touring the country in their luxurious charter funjet, named the Starship, by the time they reached New York and the last three shows at Madison Square Garden they were totally exhausted. These are the concerts captured on the film *The Song Remains the Same* and the original soundtrack album released in 1976.

The 1975 tour was even larger. Touring behind the double-album *Physical Graffiti*, the band crisscrossed the United States to even more gigantic crowds. In New York they attracted writer William S. Burroughs, a kindred spirit and occultist who once likened Zeppelin's music to Moroccan trance music of the Jajaika tribe. But music was not the only source of trances on the 1975 tour, as Page and certain other bandmates reportedly added heroin to their lifestyles, a habit that would increase and eventually cause real problems on subsequent tours.

In August 1975 Plant and his family suffered an automobile accident in Greece; his wife, Maureen, almost died. Bonham's periods of violent insanity, brought on by heavy drinking and drug abuse, caused publicist Danny Goldberg to comment, "Bonzo was a large adult with the emotions of a six-year-old child, and an artistic license to indulge in any sort of infantile or destructive behavior that amused him."[12] On September 24, 1980, Bonham consumed forty measures of vodka over a seventeen-hour period to celebrate Zeppelin's pending American tour. His death the next morning was similar to Hendrix's; Bonham vomited, aspirated, and never woke up. Zeppelin, unlike the Who without Keith Moon, did not survive Bonham's death.

However, their fusion of hard rock, mutated blues, and the hedonistic-sexist bent of the seventies created the musical foundation for subsequent hard rock and heavy metal stylings. "Led Zeppelin was widely perceived as a group of bombastic showboaters with a heavy beat and pseudo-profound lyrics," wrote critic Ken Tucker in 1986, "but, it is now clear that the band changed the landscape against which rock is played. And so the basic formula for heavy metal was codi-

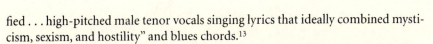

fied . . . high-pitched male tenor vocals singing lyrics that ideally combined mysticism, sexism, and hostility" and blues chords.[13]

Page's solo-guitar style, use of effects, and studio layering also frame the genre. Hard rock of the sixties (Cream, Hendrix, Iron Butterfly, Vanilla Fudge, and others) provided Page with the impetus to create a guitar-based Zeppelin and mold an instrumental solo style fusing blues ideas with Hendrix's sonic orientation. Page created an inventive mixture of these elements and speedy repetitive pull-off–based riffs. Page generally abandoned the long improvisational guitar solos in favor of more concentrated, efficient efforts—possibly a result of Page's studio-based early years—and favored speed and repeated riffs over the emotionality of the blues. Unfortunately, the application of this trend has lead to two decades of guitarists who generally lack an education in, and emotional understanding of, the blues and who substitute speed and technique for taste and simplicity.

Another shift from previous hard rock styles was Bonham's drumming. Though he adapted some elements from Moon, Baker, and Mitchell—such as the drum solo and double-kick fills—Bonham veered away from their flashy, technique-oriented style and toward a more simplistic, pounding timekeeping. Most metal drummers followed suit. Contrary to Page's protestations, the group did maintain some affinity for, and take elements from, relevant sixties styles. The pretentious lyrics swathed in Celtic lore and mysticism reflected the previous decade's folksy ramblings of groups like Pentangle and Fairport Convention. The healthy dose of anger and hostility is in part attributable to the onstage ravings of the Who, MC5, the Stooges, and others.

Zeppelin contemporaries added weight to the heavy metal formula. Americans Blue Cheer (San Francisco), Blue Öyster Cult (New York), and British bands like Black Sabbath (with lead singer Ozzy Osbourne) and Deep Purple were in the game early and covered the volume spectrum, from loud to thunderous. They proffered macho rock for male teens and garnered negative critical reviews similar to Zeppelin's—and also laughed all the way to the bank. By the midseventies the Zeppelin formula dominated the hard end of the rock/pop spectrum.

Some critics incorrectly accused hard rock/heavy metal bands of sounding the same; however, the stylistic differences were mostly in how much as opposed to what. The formula called for at least one lead-guitar wizard; a lead singer able to emote in the higher registers (and look good in tight pants); a forceful but not too flashy drummer; and a bassist who was often the best musician in the group and a decent harmony vocalist. Lyrics usually expressed adolescent anguish about situations involving the unholy trinity—sex, drugs, and rock and roll—plus a healthy dose of antiauthoritarian, rebellious sentiment (often transmitted during live performances).

Alice Cooper (a band name adopted by lead singer Vince Furnier) was known for its provocative theatricality. Among other things Furnier generally donned a boa snake for a boa wrap. Kiss took theater a little farther, wearing greasepaint makeup and platform shoes and spitting fire and blood, as smoke and firebombs exploded around them. Singer Ozzy Osbourne, whose post-Black Sabbath band employed noted guitar wizard Randy Rhoads (who was killed in a crash at age twenty-five) took it one step farther, using images of animal mutilation to advance his career.

Some bands softened musical elements of the hard rock/heavy metal formula on their way to substantial mainstream success. Zeppelin buddies Bad Company scored major success, as did New Hampshire's Aerosmith (with Jagger look-alike frontman Stephen Tyler), Boston's Boston (guitarist-composer-electronics wizard Tom Scholz layered sounds in his basement studio), Chicago's Styx, San Francisco's Journey (with Santana veterans Rolie and Schon), and Englishmen/New Yorkers Foreigner. Seattle's Heart featured two sisters, Nancy and Ann Wilson, more acoustic guitar, lyrical sensitivity, and less onstage posturing. The Canadian power trio Rush, whose mysticism took more of a sci-fi bent, was known for carefully crafted studio productions.

These bands, plus many others that go unmentioned, made up the Zeppelin-rooted hard rock/heavy metal end of the seventies commercial rock/pop spectrum. As this genre evolved it tended to get even harder and faster, with lyrics emphasizing escapist/rebellious/sexist content in an attempt to deal with an increasingly violent, troubled life-experience and the fading of the American dream. However, this was only one segment of the popular music audience and only one route along the rock/pop landscape. There were teenage women and a large group of post-adolescents reaching their thirties who wanted and expected music containing different lyrical and musical values, such as songs emphasizing melody, harmony, and more intricate rhythms and lyrics with less braggadocio and more substance.

These elements had their roots in the music of the Beatles, Dylan, folk-rock, and the San Francisco sound that encouraged experimentation and a focus on society. Some was still available from the musical dinosaurs who roamed the landscape, putting out product at regular intervals. However, the conservative political environment, conservative music-industry policies and radio programming, and artist self-censorship—the common practice of artists writing solely for commercial success or to please labels—combined to reduce creative experimentation or expression of controversial ideas. Musical creativity focused on the studio and the utilization of its rapidly developing technology; the voices of political and cultural dissent faded to a whisper.

Art-rock and progressive-rock became common terms to describe British bands like Pink Floyd, Yes, King Crimson, and Genesis, who created lush, well-orchestrated music while expounding on the world through lyrics. More often than not, allegorical tales were woven with strange and sometimes menacing fairy-tale characters. Art-rock was structurally complex when compared to blues-rooted hard rock contemporaries, and it featured a sound collage of keyboards, synthesizers, and studio-layered instruments.

Pink Floyd, who began as the darlings of the London psychedelic underground, shifted gears when leader Syd Barrett lost touch with reality and was replaced by guitarist David Gilmour. Floyd created two major lengthy works, the 1973 song-cycle *The Dark Side of the Moon*, which remained on the top-200 LP charts for fifteen years, and the two-record, Roger Waters-conceived epic *The Wall*. Live performances of *The Wall* featured the construction and destruction of a gigantic brick wall during the show. Yes produced lushly orchestrated works with a revolving lineup that included guitarist Steve Howe, keyboardist Rick Wakeman, and drummer Bill Bruford. King Crimson relied on the considerable talents of guitarist Robert Fripp. Peter Gabriel began Genesis in 1967 with Mike Rutherford on bass and guitar and Tony Banks on keyboards; Phil Collins joined on drums in 1970 and, after Gabriel departed in 1975, emerged as the driving force.

Other popular artists of the period attained the large sound without the artistic pretensions. Elton John (born Reginald Dwight) played piano in Long John Baldry's R&B band before meeting lyricist Bernie Taupin, who was working as a pop songwriter; he cut his first album, *Empty Sky*, in 1969. Beginning with the 1972 *Honky Chateau* (with singles "Rocket Man" and "Honky Cat"), Elton John scored six straight #1 albums, decorating live shows with increasingly outlandish costumes and sets. Vocalist Linda Ronstadt, with the assistance of producers John Boylan and Peter Asher, molded a career interpreting a variety of classic rock, folk, country, Motown, and contemporary material.

Fleetwood Mac began in 1967 as a blues revival group led by former Mayall guitarist Peter Green. The band was named for the rhythm section of drummer Mick Fleetwood and bassist John McVie—known for a distinctive, elementary, yet forceful rhythmic style. After many personnel shifts, only Fleetwood, McVie, and McVie's wife, Christine (who had been performing as Christine Perfect in her own band Chicken Shack), were left. Having moved to Los Angeles, they auditioned and hired singer-songwriters Lindsay Buckingham and Stevie Nicks and recorded the gem *Fleetwood Mac* (#1, August 1975). Their follow-up, *Rumours* (#1, February 1977), was recorded as relationships between the McVies and Buckingham and Nicks fell apart, but it nevertheless sold 15 million copies worldwide, stayed at #1 for thirty-one weeks, and was on the American charts for over 130 weeks.

Bands fusing large combos and horn sections also maintained some popularity through the era. Chicago, who released their first album as Chicago Transit Authority, was the most successful, scoring five #1 releases in a row (*Chicago V* through *IX*) in the midseventies. Blood, Sweat, and Tears and the more funky Oakland-based Tower of Power (boasting the studio-monster horn section known as the Tower of Power) were also well received.

By the late 1970s certain important economic and artistic trends were affecting the way music was created and sold. Record-industry consolidation was continuing at a steady pace; fewer labels, owned by larger corporations, were selling a greater percentage of the product. The ramifications of this trend were enormous. Since rock music radio programming was also highly concentrated in the hands of a few major consultants, and because smaller markets took their cues from the larger ones, AOR radio-station playlists were becoming shorter and shorter and more tightly controlled. These facts conspired to make it very difficult for musicians, other than those signed to the top labels, to become popular nationwide.

At the same time, major labels were in the process of pruning their rosters of the acts that could not guarantee significant future profits—a consequence of lawyer and accountant leadership and bottom-line thinking. The strategy of the major labels thus consisted of signing proven dinosaurs to lengthy contracts, with the rationale that these artists could be safely relied upon to sell each release. Should new artists or musical styles be needed, they could turn to the industry's farm system, the independent labels. The indies provided a place for new talent to be discovered and nurtured. This was a shift for the majors, who would previously sign and release ten new or unknown acts themselves, hoping that one would succeed and cover the losses of marketing the rest. Now, they only signed what they believed to be sure things. The ramifications of this philosophy were considerable.

Record labels and radio programmers took fewer chances on unknown talent, relying on known quantities to generate profits. The newer artists they did sign tended to sound a lot like other profitable acts, thus shrinking the aural and lyrical landscape. When listeners became bored with the same old music and infuriated at record prices that had jumped two dollars in nearly as many years, they began to react. The burgeoning cassette technology (which allowed for home taping), coupled with other economic variables plus the loss of interest on the part of certain (generally older) segments of the listening public, caused a fall in product sales in the late 1970s. The number of units sold dropped for the first time in 1979 and didn't reach the 1978 peak again until 1988. Dollar figures for gross sales took until 1984 to surpass the 1978 levels—an event that would have taken longer had it not been for the introduction of the costly compact disc (CD).

This tightly controlled, economically oriented, financially conservative environment provided the context for the fourth rock and roll explosion. Against a backdrop of lush, studio focused, rock/pop music, with lyrics lacking significant societal commentary, there erupted a raw, primal, reactive form called punk rock. Its in-your-face mentality, primitive musicality, and relevant lyrics eventually forced popular culture, rock/pop music, and the industry to sit up and take notice. The story of punk and its effect on popular music is the subject of our next chapter.

# 17· Punk Rock: Buzzsaw Bravado and Shock Politics

*We took the rock sound into a psychotic world and narrowed it down into a straight line of energy. In a era of progressive rock, with its complexities and counterpoints, we had a perspective of non-musicality and intelligence that took over from musicianship.*

**Tommy Ramone, drummer for the Ramones, quoted in Dave Laing's** One Chord Wonders

*God save the Queen*
*She ain't no human being*
*There is no future in England's dreaming.*

**"God Save the Queen," the Sex Pistols (1977)**

*Their clothes were elaborately contrived to make the wearer appear as terrifyingly repugnant as possible, alluding to anything that would induce immediate outrage in the eye of the beholder. . . . Hair shorn close to the skull and dyed any color so long as it didn't look natural, spiked up with Vaseline; noses, ears, cheeks, lips, and other extremities pierced with a plethora of safety pins, chains and dangling insignia; ripped and torn jumble sale shirts, strangled with a thin tie and mangled with predictable graffiti of song titles, perversions or Social Observations; black leather wrist bands and dog collars studded with silver spikes sometimes with leashes attached.*

**A 1977 description of punk rock fans at London's punk venue, The Roxy, by Julie Burchill and Tony Parsons in** The Boy Looked at Johnny

---

THE SUMMER OF 1976 WAS A HOT ONE in London. The British economy was struggling as unemployment climbed and violence exploded in the ghettos. Into this turbulent environment swaggered the early punk rock bands, led by the Sex Pistols, trashing British sensibilities with gobs of musical distortion, shocking appearance, and spewed invective. By the time the Pistols had disintegrated less than two years later, numerous others had joined in the fun that would change the face of rock/pop music forever. The mainstream acts would eventually adopt many elements from punk music, including lyrics, stance, and style. In so doing they rejuvenated the music industry's sagging fortunes. The subsequent amalgam, which became known as new wave, would be a popular mainstay of the eighties.

Punk was a heterogeneous style, comprising a complex mélange of ingredients and orientations, spread across a spectrum of artists. The music was generally driven by a frantic, eighth-note pulse carried by the entire ensemble. Words were spewed forth by vocalists unconstrained by previous notions of pitch or melody. The majority of lyrics reflected feelings toward a disintegrating and corrupt society and the plight of subcultural compatriots. The music and lyrics were imbedded in a confrontational stance that reflected varying degrees of righteous anger, performance technique, avant-garde artistic exploration of shock value, and intent to bypass the usual music-production institutions.

The punks' music, lyrical worldview, stance, and style (clothes and behavior)—the elements of rock/pop's fourth major explosion—had roots on both sides of the Atlantic. Groups on the fringes of sixties American rock/pop contributed heavily. Michigan rockers the Stooges played with such an unabashed enthusiasm and minimalist musical orientation that selections from their early recordings sound remarkably like seventies punk. Lead singer Iggy Pop's (James Osterburg) behavior was self-destructive and shocking. He was sometimes so stoned and intoxicated while onstage that he stumbled about ranting and raving, threw up on the audience, and fell off the stage. Detroit-based MC5 exhibited a combative, cultural-activist stance and monotonous driving lead vocals by Rob Tyner that were also reflected in punk.

New York's Velvet Underground provided their own shocking contrast to the prevailing pop-rock sensibilities of the day. Under the watchful eye of artist Andy Warhol, the band—touring as a part of his Exploding Plastic Inevitable mixed media show and playing at his East Village Electric Circus venue—turned out their otherworldly version of the sixties. Rather than follow the trend toward studio-derived, complex musicality, the Underground, as they became known, viewed less as better. Lead vocalist Lou Reed (born Louis Firbank) crooned his stories in a limited vocal range and inexact attack, a pioneer of punk's vocal drone. The strummed guitars and rhythm section emphasized sparsity and intensity over harmony and musical accomplishment. John Cale, a former Eastman music student, added tension with suspended notes and eclectic avant-garde solos on viola.

The Underground's appeal—they had a small but avid following—was also derived from Reed's chronicles of the underside of East Village life in the sixties.

Absent were the flower children and euphoria of psychoactive enlightenment, replaced by personal narratives of heroin addiction, ghetto drug connections, and sexual perversity. These shocking explorations of self-destructive behavior tested society's cultural sensibilities; they also didn't have much of an impact on the rock/pop mainstream. However, Reed (along with Iggy Pop) was taken under David Bowie's wing, had a hit album, *Transformer*, and a hit single about sexual experimentation, "Walk on the Wild Side" (#16, March 1973). The Underground and Reed were important punk forebears, creating musical, topical, and stylistic foundations upon which subsequent artists, and eventually the punk genre, stood.

The New York Dolls adopted the lack of musical pretension and group intensity and added transvestite costuming, glamour makeup, Jagger-like stage posing by lead singer David Johansen, and stage-lurching by guitarist Johnny Thunders. Their no-frills repertoire included "Pills" and "Trash" and they were popular in the burgeoning lower Manhattan New York club scene (CBGB's, for example) of the midseventies. There, they demonstrated an I-couldn't-care-less attitude. Punk's direct musical antecedents, the Ramones, were four leather-jacketed high school dropouts from Forest Hills, Queens. They redefined music as a sparse, intense, three-minute buzzsaw blast dominated by eighth-note unanimity from strummed, distorted guitar, bass, and drums. This became the musical basis for the Sex Pistols. (The Ramones reportedly played thirty-three songs in a single one-hour performance.) Like Lou Reed, the Ramones adopted stage names (Joey, Johnny, Richie—replaced by Dee Dee—and Tommy)—all ending with the surname Ramone.

Briton David Bowie (born David Jones) was one of punk's most influential ancestors. Bowie, whose schooling and training included art, theater, mime, and music, was a master at creating stories and characters that both symbolized and became reality. Bowie's incarnation as Ziggy Stardust in *The Rise and Fall of Ziggy Stardust and the Spiders From Mars* (1972) embodied the struggle to succeed in the music business and society. The man who had appeared in a dress on the cover of a previous album was transformed into a cosmic traveler. Bowie's expressions of alienation worked at two different, sometimes competing, levels; his costumed personae were sometimes symbolic, shocking statements while his feelings were taken as a realistic expression of alienation. This duality of pretense and reality side-by-side also came to exist in punk.[1]

There are two major explanations for the emergence and in-your-face nature of punk music in midseventies England. They are contrasting but do not have to be seen as exclusive; combining them provides a plausible rationale for the birth of punk. One theory cites the deteriorating British economy as punk's major impetus. Under this scenario, a growing underclass of disaffected youth was created by the lack of economic and educational opportunities in Britain. Jobs paying living wages were unavailable, and the schools with class-based entrance systems forced many working-class youths into a dead-end education. These increasingly disillusioned youth faced a future of subsistence living within the British welfare system (the dole). The youth saw it as no future, and so they struck back. It is possible to view the music, the reactive lyrics, and the antiauthoritarian nature of their stance as reflective of these conditions.

Another interpretation of punk music places much of the impetus, especially for the style and stance, on the art-school origins of punk mentors and rock band members. Simon Frith and Howard Horne argue that numerous band members attended art school—the Pistol's Glen Matlock, the Clash's Joe Strummer, Paul Simonon, and Mick Jones, punkette Siouxsie Sue, and Adam Ant, to name just a few. In addition, many important managers (like the Pistols' Malcolm McLaren) and other genre businessmen brought their art-school backgrounds to the mix. Art-school dialogue about shock value, performance as art, situationist theories of subversion, and fashion were manifested in punk rock. What artists wore, the material they performed, how they performed and what they said through lyrics, and audience communication during shows were the function of aesthetic considerations. To them, "Punk rock was the ultimate art school music movement."

Both arguments are mirrored in the events that brought about the rise of punk in midseventies Britain. Against the background of the studio-centered pop-rock that dominated the charts—Elton John, Led Zeppelin, Chicago, Abba, and others—a small but enthusiastic group of "pub rock" bands belted out R&B and classic rock covers along with some originals. For them, pop-rock's stadium-sized concert extravaganzas had lost touch with the music and its meaning. Thus these disaffected rockers returned to the intimate sweaty pubs where it all began in the early sixties. These bands were also critical of music-industry giants and the way they conducted business. Pub rock's success prompted the establishment of small record labels that initially distributed records through a network of oldies specialty shops. Dave Laing credits pub rock with creating viable venues and the alternative network of labels and distribution used by transition punk rockers. Some band members, such as Joe Strummer of the 101ers, simply stepped over the line from pub to punk.

Sex was a shop where the era's musicians could find the latest fashions; it was an underground mecca run by music impresario Malcolm McLaren and clothes designer Vivienne Westwood. The store's name was controversial, its designer clothing shocking—walking billboards intended to outrage society's elders and goad them into states of apoplexy and sputtering pomposity. Anatomically correct figures on t-shirts were to be worn with appropriate leather and bondage pants joined at the knees. But Sex was more than a store, it was also a scene. Regular customers and employees were musicians and future players. McLaren, who had managed the New York Dolls for a brief period of time before their breakup, encouraged a bunch of former skinheads to form a band they called the Swankers.

Swanker bassist Glen Matlock, drummer Paul Cook, guitarist Steve Jones, and mentor McLaren were looking for a lead singer when John Lydon showed up at the store. Burchill and Parsons relay a marvelous description of the scene: "Mal licked lascivious lips when he clocked the lad's sadistically mutilated Pink Floyd t-shirt with the words I HATE scribbled in a biro trembling with furious loathing above the Dodo's moniker. John was not a pretty sight; when Mother Nature was handing out the good looks he'd been at the back of the queue, and by the time he'd got to the counter all She had left was meningitis, weak eyes, teeth held together by steel rods, stunted growth and a permanent sinus. He also boasted to having the pick of the piles, which he claimed dangled down his inside legs and required frequent pruning with a razor blade."[2] The Swankers invited Lydon to join and formed the Sex Pistols in the summer of 1975. Their first gig was at St. Martin's College of Art that November.

Nineteen seventy-six saw the rise of punk rock, with the Sex Pistols as the most visible proponent. Bands were formed by former pub rockers and assorted street youth, who saw the opportunity for expression despite minimal musical proficiency. The Damned, with members Rat Scabies and Captain Sensible, released punk's first album and were known to shed clothing during their performances. The Clash formed that July and appeared with the Pistols at the 100 Club's summer punk festival. The Buzzcocks, the Vibrators, Generation X (with lead singer Billy Idol), Siouxsie and the Banshees, and the Slits all formed and had some success that year.

As quickly as venues opened for this new underground sound, fights would erupt at gigs, and the bands (even including the Pistols) would be banished. Bands were in the process of developing new modes of communicating with their audiences and also breaking down the audience/musician barrier. In a solution that was true to punk's aggressive stance and shock value, band members sometimes incited the crowd, which responded with flying bodies, cans, and gobbers (spit). Typical of this behavior was Johnny Rotten's epithet to an April 1976 audience: "Bet you don't hate us as much as we hate you!"[3] If punk artists sought to shock and incite their audience, as well as straight society, the ability to get an aggressive response out of the audience was a measure of potency, effectiveness, and bonding.

Other responses to the music and stage exhortations came in the form of dance, or what Robert Christgau called "airborne playfight."[4] With working-class macho ethos, audience members launched themselves onto the dance floor, stopping every four to five minutes for a thirty-second punch-out with fellow punkers. Others practiced the pogo, a dance introduced by Rotten's mate John Beverly (soon to change his name to Sid Vicious) at a Manchester Free Trade Hall gig in July 1976. Dancers resembled a mass of sweaty pogo sticks, bouncing and bashing one another with sinister delight. In this turbulent world of epithet and physicality, band and audience cemented their relationship as members of the same community. Interestingly, this was similar to that of sixties San Francisco bands, but the medium was aggressive and angry as opposed to philosophical and warm.

Alternative industry institutions sprang up alongside the growing musical genre. Record labels were developed to record and promote punk bands. Chiswick and Stiff, with their origins in pub rock, signed punk acts; Step Forward, Fast Product, Factory, Beggars Banquet, Rough Trade, and multitudes of others formed and followed suit. Some continued the pub rock practice of independent distribution, bypassing the majors and the economics of big-business sales and promotions. Others signed distribution contracts with industry giants EMI, WEA, and CBS. Local scene promoters also published fan magazines (called fanzines), covering what the band Desperate Bicycles termed Xerox music.[5] These fanzines—sporting names like *Sniffin' Glue* (by fanzine pioneer Mark P.), *Hangin' Around, Jolt, White Riot,* and *These Things*—became the most observant and sympathetic commentators on the punk scene.

By the end of 1976 the Sex Pistols had signed a record contract with England's largest label, EMI, and recorded and released their first single, "Anarchy in the UK." The notion of playing in the corporate-rock ballpark was anathema to the punk players and caused all sorts of emotional and economic turmoil. The situation became such that the industry felt it was possible, in fact necessary, to commodify artists whose personal and performance dynamic included shocking and overtly aggressive behavior, language, and dress. The majors didn't necessarily like the music, however they knew it would sell.

The situation came to a head in three months. "Anarchy in the UK" contained the outfit's typical blast at tradition and authority. Rotten growled lyrics designed to put fear and loathing in the hearts of upstanding citizens. They contained buzzwords like "anti-Christ," "anarchy," and "destroy" and visions of spike-haired, self-mutilated, booted punks roaming the urban landscape bent on destruction. The music was not simplistic three-chord or one-chord idiocy, as journalists painted it. Although the verses contained the basic I-IV-V (plus ii and iii passing chords), the instrumental solos were played over the basic plus II, iii, and biv chords.

The rumor that the Sex Pistols didn't record many of their songs themselves is bolstered by this music. Although I have no authoritative information, Paul Cook's lack of drumming experience is not reflected in the drummer's precise timekeeping and fills. The guitar and bass are played with similar precision. It is possible that Matlock, who had previous experience on his instrument, was responsible for the surprisingly melodic bass part.

"Anarchy in the UK" sold 50,000 copies and reached the top 40. The print media and television had fewer vested interests in promoting punk rock than did the record industry. Mainstream newspapers were most likely to use terms such as crazed, pathological, rancid, and savage to describe the music and its players. On December 1, 1976, the Pistols were interviewed live on the British news magazine show "Today." Host Bill Grundy's not-so-subtle attempts to incite the Pistols finally paid off; he urged Steve Jones to "say something outrageous." Jones responded, "You dirty bastard," Grundy exhorted "Go on, again," and Jones threw out, "You dirty fucker" and "You fucking rotter."[6] The next day's headline stories contained the U.K. press screaming with outrage over the Pistols' behavior. An upcoming U.K. concert tour, with the Clash scheduled to open, shrunk from nineteen to three dates. EMI chairman Sir John Read apologized, but pressure from a variety of sources, including other label artists, allowed EMI to drop the Pistols from its roster. The band received 30,000 pounds in compensation.

March 1977 was a busy month for the Pistols: Rotten's mate, the barely musical Sid Vicious, was recruited to play bass, and the McCartney-lovin' Glen Matlock was out. The Pistols also signed to A&M Records, but three days later they were dropped, receiving 75,000 pounds in compensation. Thus in the space of three months the band had accrued approximately US$250,000 for being kicked off two record labels. Not bad for a group of malcontents.

Virgin Records became the third label to sign the band. They released "God Save the Queen" in May 1977. The negative publicity surrounding punk and the Pistols had caused the band to be banned from performing at most venues. (They would tour later in the year billed as the Spots.) "God Save the Queen" caused further problems. Its release was coordinated with Queen Elizabeth II's Silver Jubilee, a celebration of her twenty-five-year reign as England's beloved monarch. However the lyrics on the new release mocked the Queen and labeled her regime as mindless and fascist, and they were considered under the circumstances to have gone far beyond the boundaries of good taste. The Sex Pistols had entered the zone of sacrilege. The tune was banned from most radio playlists and was unavailable at major record stores. Yet "God Save the Queen" sold 2 million copies and was listed, signified in the racks by a blank piece of paper, at #2 on record store charts.

"God Save the Queen" contains more than early rock's three-chord structure. Its verse includes a minor ii and iii over and above the basic I-IV-V chords, and the repetitive blues-based guitar solo is played over a vi, II, V progression. While not the techno-pop harmonic structure of material from art-rock bands like Pink Floyd, Yes, and Genesis, this song and those appearing on the subsequent album, *Never Mind the Bullocks, Here's the Sex Pistols,* are harmonically more complex than most blues and classic rock.

The fact that their songs contain some harmonic complexity (a chord pattern containing more than blues basics), is only one indication that punk rock was not written and played by musical illiterates. Tom Carson wrote of the Ramones that they "define the music in its purest terms: which was both primitive and revisionist."[7] This is only partially true of the Sex Pistols on record. Their musicianship is a cut above that of the Ramones. Their playing is relatively precise and under control (the stop and fill on "God Save the Queen" and the cleanliness of the rhythm section on "Anarchy in the UK" are good examples). As Dave Laing points out, the guitarist had mastered the effects of distortion, reverb, and delay to play gritty, distorted guitar under control. On record, even the guitarist's buzzsaw drone is deft at times. The bass lines, especially on earlier material, defy the tonic-note throb, displaying more melodic passages.

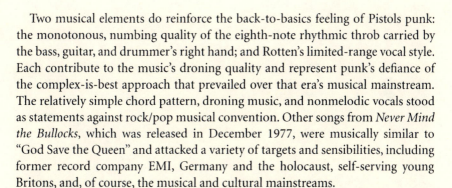

Two musical elements do reinforce the back-to-basics feeling of Pistols punk: the monotonous, numbing quality of the eighth-note rhythmic throb carried by the bass, guitar, and drummer's right hand; and Rotten's limited-range vocal style. Each contribute to the music's droning quality and represent punk's defiance of the complex-is-best approach that prevailed over that era's musical mainstream. The relatively simple chord pattern, droning music, and nonmelodic vocals stood as statements against rock/pop musical convention. Other songs from *Never Mind the Bullocks*, which was released in December 1977, were musically similar to "God Save the Queen" and attacked a variety of targets and sensibilities, including former record company EMI, Germany and the holocaust, self-serving young Britons, and, of course, the musical and cultural mainstreams.

In time, the Sex Pistols themselves became targets of punk's violent attitude against the establishment. Rotten was slashed by razor-wielding attackers; Cook was beaten with iron bars as he emerged from the tube (subway). By now their performing options were limited, the band had lost its most proficient song-writer in Matlock, and Vicious was feeding a healthy heroin habit (courtesy of his American girlfriend, Nancy Spungen). Under these circumstances they careened through a January 1978 U.S. tour. After their January 14 date at Winterland in San Francisco, Rotten left, Vicious overdosed, and Jones and Cook, following McLaren's instructions, flew to Rio to record with Great Train Robber Ronald Biggs. Johnny Rotten would later revert to his given name, John Lydon, and front a new band, called Public Image Ltd. (PiL). After attempting to make it solo, Vicious was charged with brutally murdering Spungen in their room at New York's Chelsea Hotel in October 1978 (see the 1989 movie *Sid and Nancy*). The next February he died of the effects of a heroin overdose. Steve Jones maintained a musical career as a studio guitarist; Paul Cook faded from the scene.

The Sex Pistols were the seminal punk group, shock rockers assaulting the strictures and conventions of mainstream society. For them it was fun and games. Other bands and artists traveled similar paths, diverging from the Pistols model at certain junctures to produce their own punk parables. The Clash functioned as an alter ego for the Pistols. Inspired by the Pistols, the Clash were also personally reckless and abusive, but as a group they were more artistically thoughtful, politically insightful, and musically creative. The Clash even endured commercial success, fought and won music industry battles, and found life after punk.

The Clash began in July 1976 after pub rocker Joe Strummer saw the Pistols and prevailed upon former London SS members Mick Jones (guitar) and Paul Simonon (bass) to form a new band. Drummer Terry Chimes (later replaced by Topper Headon) rounded out the band. The Clash signed with manager Bernie Rhodes, a former McLaren assistant. They opened a number of shows for the Pistols and were signed to CBS Records in January 1977 for 100,000 pounds as the

The Clash

majors rushed to find punk acts. By spring the Clash's first single, "White Riot" (#38), and first album, *The Clash* (#12), were on the British charts.

There was something about the Clash, at least on record, that transcended the line drawn by the Pistols. Without abandoning punk's simplicity and aggressiveness, the Clash displayed more musical literacy. Their ensemble of two guitars gave the songs more texture, Simonon abandoned the eighth-note, tonic drone for more bouncy, syncopated, melodic bass parts, and Chimes used more cymbals and fills to color his drumming. As instrumentalists they were better and their musical choices were more interesting—the little touches like the harp and Cropper-like soul-guitar fills on "Garageland" and claps and stops on "Remote Control" are indicative of this approach.

The Clash also had an interest in reggae, the Jamaican import favored by Britain's West Indian working class. The band recorded with famed reggae producer Scratch Perry ("Complete Control"), recorded his song "Police and Thieves," and also added reggae rhythmic elements to other tunes. Laing asserts that punk's fascination with reggae ran deeper than the music. Reggae's Rastafarians were seen as an alienated, oppressed community who had successfully been able to channel their rage into a music that combined the very personal with the political. They were its living essence with no compromise—harassed by the police, forced to live in untenable conditions, yet markedly proud and visible in their dreadlocks (long uncut hair) and camouflage clothing.

Some punk bands admired reggae from afar, adopting a symbolic stance or even some musical elements; others, like the Clash, went further and became actively involved in Britain's racial politics. With skinheads and British Nazis (under the banner of the National Front) conducting forays into minority communities, the Clash and others (X-Ray Spex and Sham 69 being two) participated in concerts sponsored by Rock Against Racism (RAR) and the Anti-Nazi League. Paradoxically, punk's anti-anything stance attracted young supporters of the rightist organizations; some punk groups didn't care but others rejected this audience.

Basic differences surfaced between punk's two major proponents. Whereas the Pistols stayed within a limited musical framework, the Clash were consciously assimilating influences from external styles and rapidly expanding their musical boundaries. The Clash, through lyrics and social deeds, chose to present their criticism of imperialism, racism, and an abusive economic system in concrete personal and political terms, as opposed to the unconscious, undirected rage of the Pistols' shocking stories and situations. The Pistols were content to strike out and expose; the Clash wanted to have some impact on their audience.

To a chorus of claims that they had sold out punk, the Clash released their third album in January 1980. Chosen in 1989 as the #1 album of the eighties by *Rolling Stone* magazine, *London Calling* contains more breadth in music and topics than previous works; as punk's audience was diminishing, the Clash was expanding beyond punk's limiting borders. A number of styles grace this double-album release: swing ("Jimmy Jazz"), Berry-style classic rock ("Brand New Cadillac"), Bo Diddley beat ("Hateful"), reggae-influenced rock ("Guns of Brixton" and "Revolution Rock"), and even a Springsteen-like song ("The Card Cheat," with familiar keyboards, sax, and lyric meter). Most songs contain social and political commentary, including the especially poignant "Spanish Bombs" (about Spain's Civil War and contemporary struggles); the "Guns of Brixton" (asking "When the police kick in the door, will you die with your hands on your head or a gun in your hand?"); and the potential nuclear hell and ice-age holocaust of the title cut.

The Clash toured the United States, and their opening acts reflected some of their music's influences: Sam and Dave, Screamin' Jay Hawkins, Bo Diddley, former Dolls singer David Johansen, and American punks the Cramps. In a practical application of their politics, the Clash negotiated with CBS (even giving up some of their own royalties) to keep the price of the two-record set just above the single-disc price. The band returned to the United States later in 1980, where at Electric Ladyland Studio they recorded the three-disc successor, called *Sandinista* (named to celebrate the recent success of the leftist revolution in Nicaragua). Although both previous albums broke the top 40, their 1982 effort, *Combat Rock* (#7, June 1982), and the single release, "Rock the Casbah" (#8), propelled the Clash into the American mainstream. Within a few years, however, the strains within proved too severe and, after accusations of selling out were hurled among band members, the group disintegrated.

The vast artistic territory between the Pistols and the Clash was populated by a colorful collection of punk rockers. Some went down with the ship before 1980, clinging loyally to the true stuff; others made the transition, along with the Clash, into new wave. Punk was clearly reactive, to popular music and the music industry, to the economic and cultural status quo, and even to members of the punk community itself. Punk's intention was to disrupt the everyday life of the established order in an attempt to expose society's oppressive nature. The resulting actions—shocking, rude, and obscene behavior, confrontational dressing, minimalist music, and attacking lyrics—produced a ripple effect, first inside the music world and then moving outward.

However, punk music was too offensive and unpredictable to join the stagnating rock/pop world. Still, when punk's musical and lyrical elements were co-opted into the mainstream, there occurred a rejuvenation of popular music. These were the new wave musicians, a repugnant media term coined to signify an undefinably broad spectrum of music (much like the term "alternative" is used in the nineties). New wavers reproduced some of punk's minimalist musical feelings, including an eighth-note rhythm but without the rigidity, the droning vocal style, and the absence of harmony and improvised solo. Many new wave lyrics adopted punk's critical attitude toward society but without the shock element. It also borrowed punk's penchant for unconventional dress and quirky stage movement.

Talking Heads

The first wave of this punk-pop synthesis included English artists Elvis Costello and the Attractions, the Police, the Jam, punk survivor Billy Idol, Joe Jackson, the Pretenders (with American Chrissie Hynde), UB40, and integrated (or two-tone) bands such as Madness, the Specials, and the English Beat. In the United States punk had appealed to a white, suburban drop-out aesthetic, but it did not achieve the commercial success garnered in England. American punk-pop synthesists included Talking Heads, Blondie, the B-52s, the Motels, Pere Ubu, and the hardcore Dead Kennedys. Each of these bands in one way or another adapted punk's music, worldview, dress, and performance style. Thus an era that began with a new, controversial, underground form exploding upon the public consciousness, ended a few years later as more palatable elements were molded and co-opted for use in the rock/pop mainstream.

This new pop-punk had similar rejuvenating properties for the music industry in the late 1970s and early 1980s, much as classic rock and the British invasion did in earlier eras. Initially rejected for radio airplay and major-label promotion, new wave's freshness (in the face of the tired rock/pop formula), rebelliousness, and critical outlook caught the attention of increasingly disenchanted rock/pop music fans. Its sartorial potential for new looks and images wasn't lost on industries connected with popular culture and the teen market. Finally, the punk fire, visible in subsequent styles of rock/pop, gave a sense of power and community to millions of youth who, despite the assurances of the power players in the industrialized world, felt lost in a life out of control.

# 18· The Eighties:
## The Revolution Will Be Televised

*They're closing down the textile mill across the railroad tracks/ Foreman says these jobs are going boys and they ain't coming back to your hometown.*

**Bruce Springsteen, "My Hometown" (1984)**

*Popular culture is important because that is where most people get their "entertainment" and information; it is where they find dominant definitions of themselves as well as alternatives, options to try on for size.*

**Robert Walser, in his book on heavy metal music, Running with the Devil**

*Rap is Black America's CNN.*

**Public Enemy's Chuck D**

---

THE ROCK/POP LANDSCAPE IN THE EIGHTIES was filled with a number of different styles that were arranged and formatting neatly on radio dials across the country. Rock dinosaurs like the Rolling Stones, Led Zeppelin, Paul McCartney, the Doobie Brothers, and Rod Stewart were still significant players on album-oriented rock (AOR) radio, the dominant rock format for youthful American listeners. In addition to Led Zeppelin, AOR also sported middle-of-the-road hard rockers like Foreigner, Journey, Styx, Rush, and Bob Seeger and his Silver Bullet Band. Pop-rockers like Neil Diamond, Linda Ronstadt, Diana Ross, and Olivia Newton-John populated the softer adult contemporary (A/C) stations that appealed more to women and an older pop-rock clientele.

Punk-influenced new music (the so-called "new wave") was just budding on radio, however; within a few years it would proliferate and cover the media. The key ingredient in new wave's success was the linkage of music and video, a dynamic that was institutionalized with the birth of MTV (Music Television) on August 1, 1981. At a time of Reagan administration deregulation and declining record sales, the Warner Bros. conglomerate, in partnership with American Express, took a chance. They created a twenty-four-hour television channel, beaming to a target audience of twelve- to thirty-four-year-olds music videos much the same way that radio broadcast songs.

On a studio set in New York, actors playing the role of VJs (as opposed to DJs), dressed in the latest clothing, walking the walk and talking the talk. As writer Cathy Schwichtenberg points out, these VJs, following a rigid musical format but playing to the audience on a set designed to look casually thrown together, attempted to reproduce visually the music and feel of AOR radio. During the early years MTV lost money, in part due to cable's lack of penetration into major urban centers (entire boroughs of New York City and the city of Los Angeles were not yet wired for cable). However, after years in the red and a continued refinement of the format, MTV was able to succeed in a way that would change popular music.

Videos or films of musical events had been around almost as long as movies. Short movies depicting songs existed in the twenties and thirties and there was an experiment with video jukeboxes during the big band era. In 1967 the Beatles helped pioneer the music video with a promotional film for their double #1, "Strawberry Fields"/"Penny Lane." The former featured disappearing band members prancing about an old upright piano in the countryside; the latter depicted the band parading on horseback past a shopping district pictured as Penny Lane.

In MTV's early years it was the more eclectic artists who were most likely to produce videos. Thus, MTV introduced numerous new wave selections to its viewing public. However, radio viewed MTV as a threat and did its best to denigrate the new format. Yet when Men at Work scored two #1 singles without significant radio airplay, MTV pointed out that the band's videos were in heavy rotation on the channel. Exposure on MTV sold records, influenced buying habits, and provided exposure for unknown artists. Beginning in 1984 MTV charged record companies for broadcasting videos (until that time it had been free).

What may have initially been the impulse by musicians to expand artistic expression to the visual dimension was, by middecade, recognized as an important way for record companies to promote product. Major labels viewed music videos essentially as TV commercials, designed to sell merchandise. Writer Simon Frith points out that in using videos the labels were also trying to help create, by emphasizing a particular visual image or identity, new audiences for their artists. Also by middecade numerous media analysts were exploring the impact of the new marriage between rock music and video. Music videos capitalized on what Frith asserts were contemporary rock music values of brash individualism, impatience, youthful rebellion, and sensual delight. Lynch identified effective cinematic techniques such as dissolves, split screens, superimpositions, backlighting, and intercutting among others. In other words, music video equals "Miami Vice" equals movies.

Many critics felt that music videos reinforced negative trends already occurring in society. Kids already sat passively in front of a box, waiting for the "answer." This supported President Reagan's penchant for simplistic explanations and solutions for society's growing problems. Some also felt that when song became video, the consequence was to lose the music; story, image, and style took precedence. In addition, others cited the issues of authenticity and lip synching. The practice of lip synching (pantomiming words to hit songs) was the practice on Dick Clark's

"American Bandstand" for decades. Music videos required artists to lip synch their songs. For some, this practice merely confirmed John Lennon's pronouncement in "Strawberry Fields" that "nothing is real." The Milli Vanilli scandal didn't help matters. (It was revealed that this male duo not only didn't sing on their record, but used a tape of their voices during live concerts.) Though it was not uncommon in the eighties for performers to "double" their voices electronically in concert (or, as in the case of the vocal group the Nylons, use additional voices on tape), lip synching a "live" show stretched artistic credibility.

In its early years MTV had a democratizing or pluralistic impact on the music industry. It introduced new and less mainstream artists to mainstream audiences. By the mideighties, however, MTV was acting much more like a radio station in business and formatting practices. Majors soon realized the promotional and popular value of videos and began to contract with professional cinematographers and television directors for important artists. New videos contained more sophisticated, professional production and cost significantly more to create. Airtime was now a coveted vehicle and eclectic, low-budget videos by less mainstream artists now had stiff competition. Which video would advertisers prefer to pay for—a new one from Michael Jackson, Madonna, or Prince or one from an unknown new wave band without radio exposure? Which one would generate a larger audience? The business of rock triumphed and noncommercial music was once more relegated to the sidelines.

Charges of racism were also leveled against MTV in its early years as African-American artists received little or no airplay. Very few Black performers were successful on the AOR rock charts. When Michael Jackson hit big in 1982 (and "Billie Jean" and "Beat It" dominated the *Billboard* charts in 1983), MTV was able to point to Jackson's videos in rebuttal. It wasn't until the significant crossover success of rap in the late 1980s that MTV viewers were regularly exposed to Black music. "Yo! MTV Raps" went on the air in 1989 and became the channel's most popular show.

Clearly MTV and the many other music-video channels (such as VH-1) have succeeded, also broadcasting in Europe and Asia. The video format has had an extraordinary impact on the promotion and sale of product. Recognizing the success and impact of music television, major labels have begun to release artist videos for sale. In 1988 no music video sales category existed in the annual Record Industry Association of America (RIAA) sales report. Six years later the 1994 report showed that 11.2 million music videos were sold for $213 million (an average price of $21 per video). We are now into our second MTV generation. Instead of doing homework to radio these kids sit in front of the television, plugged into the audio-visual excitement of MTV.

In another business decision of the early 1980s by Sony, Philips, and other market controllers, a decision that Frith contends saved the U.S. music industry, the public was introduced to the compact disc. For about $12 to $15 consumers could buy the cleanest most precise sound available. Thus, at a time when multinational conglomerates had acquired the major record labels, consumers would now buy the hardware (amplifier and CD player) and software (disc) from one company (Sony/Columbia Records, for example). The strategy was to convince consumers that the CD was so superior in quality to vinyl records and tapes that it was imperative they replace their entire record collections with CDs. It was a clever move, as the greater profit margin of the CD ($12 per unit as compared to $6 for records and tapes) garnered windfall profits for the record industry. In 1982 the sale of 53 million CDs generated nearly the same amount of money as 125 million albums.

By 1983 the record-selling slump was over. Total product revenue on sales of CDs, cassettes, vinyl, and videos has nearly tripled between 1984 and 1994, from $4.37 billion to $12.06 billion. In 1994 nearly twice the number of CDs were sold (662 million) as cassettes (345 million), and the sales of CDs continue to increase as cassette sales decline. Vinyl LPs are nearly extinct (1.9 million total sales for 1994) but will never die; they continue to be manufactured as specialty items and are still a viable medium of exchange in some parts of the world.

❈ ❈ ❈

During the eighties popular music increased its dialogue around issues of political, economic, and social justice. In fact, artists and concert promoters chose to link those causes with major concert events in order to publicize issues, raise funds, involve more artists, and help promote the business of rock music. These "mega-events"—Live Aid, Farm Aid, and the Amnesty International human rights tours were the biggest—hoped to redirect some focus from sex, drugs, and rock and roll toward a discussion of social responsibility.

Scholars disagree on the cumulative impact of these and other events. Some felt that they served to co-opt the oppositional intentions of the artist and audience for industry gain while providing a social safety valve to fans wishing to express dissatisfaction. Others, like Dave Marsh, believe that it enhanced "the reawakening of a section of the rock audience to its own social potential and a quantum leap in the public awareness of the horrifying problems of poverty, hunger, homelessness and racism"[1]

The mega-events of the 1980s reflected the structure and format of the golden era concerts—the Monterey Pop Festival, Woodstock, and Watkins Glen—lineups of big-name stars at highly publicized events. The Concert for Bangladesh, organized in 1971 by former Beatle George Harrison at New York's Madison Square Garden, was a prototype that raised nearly $250,000 with performances by Ringo Starr, Bob Dylan, Eric Clapton, Leon Russell, and other friends. In the late 1970s anti-Nazi and antiracist groups in England staged a series of concerts called Rock Against Racism featuring the Clash, Aswad, Elvis Costello, X-Ray Spex, and Steel Pulse.

Live Aid, an event organized by Boomtown Rats frontman Bob Geldoff, raised $67 million for starving Africans. On July 13, 1985, concerts were held simultaneously in London, Philadelphia, and Sydney, linked electronically and broadcast to

1.5 billion people in a hundred countries. Entertainers included Paul McCartney, the Who, and David Bowie at England's Wembley Stadium and Eric Clapton, Mick Jagger, Tina Turner, Madonna, and the Led Zeppelin survivors at Philadelphia's Veteran's Stadium. Phil Collins hopped a supersonic Concorde and played both shows.

Live Aid was a catalyst, and it was closely followed by Farm Aid in September 1985, an effort by Willie Nelson and John (Cougar) Mellencamp to publicize the plight of the family farm. In October 1985 Artists United Against Apartheid (AUAA) released the album *Sun City*, organized by "Little Steven" Van Zandt, Bruce Springsteen's former guitarist. AUAA members Springsteen, Peter Gabriel, Bob Dylan, Bonnie Raitt, Miles Davis, and others challenged all musicians to confront the political system in South Africa and also to uphold a performance ban by not playing Sun City—"I ain't gonna play Sun City!" was their rallying cry.

Similarly, in June 1988 another musical and political challenge was issued to the South African government: free Nelson Mandela from prison. London's Wembley Stadium was host to Nelson Mandela's seventieth birthday party, an eleven-hour event broadcast to 600 million people in sixty countries. The broad range of performers included Whitney Houston—who agreed to perform only if it wasn't billed as a political event—Stevie Wonder, Dire Straits, Sting, UB40, Salt-n-Pepa, Phil Collins, and the Eurythmics. Again the message was unambiguous: free Mandela and change the system. Commenting on popular music's potential to promote social change, Mandela stated, "Your message can reach quarters not

Live Aid

necessarily interested in politics, so that the message can go further than we politicians can push it."[2]

In the fall of 1988 Amnesty International, the international organization working worldwide to free political prisoners, organized its Human Rights Now! Tour. Bruce Springsteen, Peter Gabriel, Sting, and Tracy Chapman made up a core of touring musicians who added local performers at each stop. They played six U.S. cities and then twenty other shows in places like London, India, Zimbabwe, the Ivory Coast, Costa Rica, Argentina, and Brazil. Springsteen commented, "I think Amnesty makes the world a less oppressive, less brutal place to live, and I want to help Amnesty do its job."[3] In the fall of 1990 artists including Sinead O'Connor, k.d. lang, David Byrne, and Annie Lennox released *Red, Hot and Blue,* a tribute to Cole Porter with proceeds going to benefit AIDS research.

From 1985 to 1990 the mega-events promoted progressive issues and causes. These actions raised funds and told audiences that some stars were not afraid to take public stands on political and social issues. One might ask, How much consciousness-raising and political activity did these actions generate from audience members? For one thing, Amnesty International gained 200,000 new members after the tours and, following a large letter-writing campaign, three of the six political prisoners that had been targeted were released. Other organizations also felt an upsurge of interest and activity. Thus artist involvement did make a difference: It exposed fans to important issues, prodding them to think and act. At the same time, however, it is also apparent that the music industry, though always careful to promote its liberal image, makes decisions based on the bottom line, a status quo favorable to huge multinational corporations maintaining increasing control over the sale of popular culture. Political controversy is dangerous to this kind of control and does not sell records like other topics such as sex and (safe) rebellion. For example, when Rupert Murdoch's FOX-TV network broadcast its five-hour version of the eleven-hour Mandela Birthday Celebration to the United States, the political introductions to songs by Peter Gabriel, Jackson Browne, and Little Steven—as well as most of the African musical performances—were cut. Thus, the American public viewed a concert devoid of much of its more forceful political content.

\*     \*     \*

One of the most politically active major rock/pop artists of the seventies and eighties was Bruce Springsteen. The son of a bus driver and hailing from Freehold, near the New Jersey shore, his songs—depicting young people as they struggled in the small-town decay of the American dream—resonated throughout the land. Having paid his dues as a guitarist and singer in rock bands, Springsteen walked into the office of John Hammond Sr.—the man who had brought Billie Holliday, Miles Davis, Aretha Franklin, and Dylan to Columbia Records—and, strumming an acoustic guitar, sang his American parables. The Boss's two 1973 albums, *Greetings from Asbury Park, N.J.* and *The Wild, the*

*Innocent and the E Street Shuffle,* display a Dylanesque stream of lyrical stories. Many were driven by what would become the ultimate rock and roll band—the E Street Band: drums, bass, two guitars, two keyboards, and the R&B flavoring of Clarence Clemons on tenor sax. In 1974 *Rolling Stone* editor Jon Landau pronounced to the world this now-famous prediction: "I saw rock and roll's future and its name is Bruce Springsteen."

With the release of his classic *Born to Run* in 1975, Springsteen's stories of yearning, escape, and reflection reached the musical mainstream. In concert the E Street Band would power through an emotional three-hour journey, led by the nonstop Springsteen. The man who listened to Buddy Holly every night before he went on and paid his dues playing Jimi Hendrix covers in the sixties was viewed as a grandson of the earlier genre, delivering authentic rock and roll to the next generation of disciples. *Born to Run* went to #3 and the Boss appeared on the cover of both *Time* and *Newsweek.* A contractual wrangle with his former manager kept Springsteen out of the limelight for three years, however his 1980 #1 *The River* and the acoustic *Nebraska* sold well.

In the summer of 1984, when Springsteen was popular but not quite a superstar, he released *Born in the U.S.A.,* complete with American flag imagery on the cover. It went to #1 for seven weeks, stayed on the top-40 album charts for nearly two years, and produced seven top-10 singles, including "Dancing in the Dark," "Glory Days," and the poignant "My Hometown." The title cut, "Born in the U.S.A.," describes the story of dead-end working-class life in America. The singer's brother goes to Vietnam, marries there, and is killed, and the singer, a veteran who comes home and can't get a job, wails the agonized and cynical "Born in the U.S.A." refrain. President Reagan once cited the song during a self-serving appeal to voters, and Springsteen was forced to rebut Reagan from the stage. He backed up his actions by donating money from concert proceeds to local food banks, veterans groups, the homeless, and activist trade-union groups. Springsteen continues into the nineties with only a few releases, some political activity, and a focus on his family.

❋ ❋ ❋

Michael Jackson's solo career spanned the same twenty years as the Boss's; his live shows were also important to his popular success. In Jackson's case, however, it was his use of a video representation of live performance, dance, and story, that cemented his place as one of the megastars of the eighties. While still a member of the Jackson 5, Michael began to record solo albums, beginning with *Got to Be There* in 1972. A child star of extraordinary talent and charisma in the Frankie Lymon/Stevie Wonder tradition, Michael had performed since age five and had his first #1 hit at eleven. His solo career was unextraordinary until he began working with producer and arranger Quincy Jones; the team released *Off the Wall* (#3, September 1979) and *Thriller* (#1, December 1982), the biggest-selling album in history at over 40 million copies.

*Thriller* was the perfect package for the rock/pop mainstream: a talented song-writer and storyteller; a sufficiently accomplished and innovative dancer who created a dance style combining images of hip-hop, Broadway, and disco (including the moonwalk); beat-driven music; a combination of up-tempo dance songs and ballads; and guest appearances by contemporary stars Paul McCartney ("The Girl Is Mine") and Eddie Van Halen (guitar solo on "Beat It"). Jackson's use of video as a promotional tool, his conceptualization of short stories, and his focus on quality (he hired director John Landis for the "Thriller" video and shot all three videos in 35mm film) helped to solidify this album as one of the defining popular music moments of the eighties.

The quest to top an artistic and commercial success like *Thriller* usually ends in frustration and disillusionment for the artist. There is no place higher to go, especially when megastardom is achieved at age twenty-four. Two solid releases (*Bad* and *Dangerous*) followed, but the interest in Jackson in the nineties ran more toward personal history than musical accomplishment. Questions about plastic surgeries that changed his negroid features to caucasian; his man-child persona (living on an estate called Neverland surrounded by animals), and his marriage to Elvis's only child, Lisa Marie, persisted. It is difficult to say whether Michael Jackson's music will endure. It is clear, however, that Michael Jackson was the driving force behind many of the most important popular culture moments of the eighties.

\*　　　\*　　　\*

Madonna was another artist who ascended to megastardom during this period. Unlike Jackson, Madonna's popularity reflected less her particular synthesis of disco, funk, and hip-hop than how she challenged the mainstream on issues of race, gender, sexual activity, sexual orientation, and power. Like Jackson, Madonna understood the power of creative music video to promote both product and artist. And through the creative and intelligent use of video, radio, television, magazines, movies, and books, Madonna presented the world with such a spectrum of images that she was able to appeal to different audiences.

Madonna Louise Ciccone was born in 1958, grew up in suburban Detroit, and found her way briefly to the University of Michigan to study dance. After additional study and employment as a dancer, she immersed herself in the dance club scene of New York and released her self-titled first album in 1983. Along with her next two releases, *Like a Virgin* (#1, December 1984) and *True Blue* (#1, July 1986), also rose Madonna the artist and cultural commentator. The singles and videos from these albums offered the opportunity for the public to experience a series of contradictions. Madonna appears in *Like a Virgin* in a white bridal gown, but her movements are sexual. Who is she, a virgin or a whore? Was she Marilyn Monroe? Was her concert attire that of a slut or the redefinition of fashion and sexual power?

Madonna

"Papa Don't Preach" also presented audiences with contested moral terrain. The singer tells her father she is pregnant by her boyfriend; she is determined to keep the baby but asks the father's blessing. At the same time, Madonna achieved critical acclaim in her first major movie role as a bohemian character afloat in Lower Manhattan in *Desperately Seeking Susan* (1985). Ever the cultural antagonist, Madonna's video for the 1989 title cut from *Like a Prayer* took on the issues of religion, race, and eroticism as a white woman in love with a Black saint-man. In the 1990 video "Justify My Love," Madonna and her boyfriend, Tony Ward, acted out sexual fantasies, including heterosexual sex, bisexuality, and bondage. While moral critics screamed for crucifixion, Madonna signed a services contract with Time-Warner for a reported $60 million.

*     *     *

At the same time the pop megastars topped the charts, heavy metal's fourth generation was born. Together, hard rock/metal styles achieved sufficient commercial success to lay claim to being the most popular rock genre of the decade. This guitar-based power rock—the first generation was the Who, Cream, and Hendrix, the second generation Led Zeppelin—developed a third style called heavy metal in the late seventies. Though initially a cult style, metal matured and broadened its appeal in the eighties. By 1989 *Rolling Stone* magazine had announced that heavy metal was in the mainstream of rock and roll.

Back in the 1970s the audience for early metal was most often young, white, alienated, working-class male teens, who embraced a music that offered an identity and image of power, intensity, spectacle, and danger. Some observers have maintained that the difference between a Boston-Foreigner fan (hard rock) and an Iron Maiden-Judas Priest fan (heavy metal) is that the former had a life and lived with the music, whereas the latter didn't have a life and lived for the music. By the mideighties the audience for heavy metal had expanded to include preteens, those in their late twenties, and some from the middle class.

The early metal ensemble consisted of drums, bass, and one or two guitars. In the mideighties bands like Van Halen added keyboard and synthesizer, broadening both their sound and appeal. The earlier rhythm section best reflected the Zeppelin model—solid, simple, and at times lumbering. Later on, responding to punk and classical influences, rhythm players cranked it up a couple notches in speed, thus requiring better technique. Though the guitarist shared the spotlight with the vocalist, the guitar solo remained the musical highlight. It evidenced roots in both the blues, using bent notes and repetition, and also the classical tradition, with classical music guitar technique, song structure, and arpeggiated chords and phrases. The lead vocalist drew some moves and energy from earlier hard rock performers but also adopted shock stance from punk and dress and entertainment from glam (an early-1970s rock style dominated by the so-called glitter bands, such as the New York Dolls).

Heavy metal evolved in England and the United States simultaneously. England's Black Sabbath, with lead singer Ozzy Osbourne's wails and growls, provided an early image of death, demons, and the occult. Osbourne left to go solo in 1978, importing American guitar wizard Randy Rhoads from Quiet Riot and employing various gruesome actions as a part of his stage show. Noted for images of animal mutilation during shows, legend has it that Osbourne had to undergo painful rabies shots when he bit the head off a bat thrown from the audience. Rhoads died in a plane crash in 1982.

Judas Priest added a second guitar to its lineup in the midseventies, speeded up the songs, and became known for its biker look and leather theatricality. Iron Maiden, named for a medieval instrument of torture, continued the themes of gloom and doom along with images of the anti-Christ, as on their *Number of the Beast* album (1982). Def Leppard paid close attention to studio details and used keyboards and special effects to move closer to the musical mainstream and increased commercial success.

In the United States, Van Halen released its self-titled first album in 1978—produced by Kiss's Gene Simmons—and by the mideighties had a #1 single, "Jump" (1985), and #1 album, *5150* (1986). David Lee Roth flaunted his showmanship and ego as frontman, but it was Eddie Van Halen, the guitarist and composer, who drove the band. Eddie reinvented metal-guitar virtuosity, using superior dexterity, speed, and a two-hand hammer/harmonic technique on the fretboard that challenged and awed all other contemporaries. With "Eruption," the second cut on the first Van Halen album, Eddie served notice of his arrival. Robert Walser maintains that Van Halen's classical music training as a pianist and violinist and his study of music theory were instrumental to this success. The education and advanced technique was reflected in the facility, fluidity, and musicianship that Eddie demonstrated as composer and guitarist. (He even quotes violin etudes in the "Eruption" solo.)

Los Angeles was also the base for other American bands, like Mötley Crüe, Quiet Riot, and later Guns 'n' Roses, whose 1987 release, *Appetite for Destruction,* was hailed as a blend of old hard rock boogie and the deep emotionality of the blues. Lead singer Axl Rose drew praise from fans for his performance style, nihilistic authenticity, and vocal wail. At the same time, however, he was criticized for lyrics and remarks that put down gays, women, African-Americans, and immigrants.

Another strain of metal, which derived some of its power and pace from punk, is speed metal—a style considered by metal purists to be more authentic. Metallica, speed metal's most successful proponent, combines outstanding guitar work with fast and synchronized ensemble playing. In her description of "Master of Puppets," the title cut from their 1986 album, writer Katherine Charlton notes that this is far from a simplistic form, with changes in meter, tempo, accent, and the use of arpeggio patterns—all coordinated at a speed of over 200 beats per minute.

Swedish-born Yngwie Malmsteen is another metal guitarist acknowledged as a stylistic pioneer. Malmsteen studied classical guitar and piano as a youth and was especially dazzled by the music of violin virtuoso Nicolo Paganini. Crediting Bach and Paganini on his albums, Malmsteen developed a style based on technique, speed, and precision. Like Eddie Van Halen and Randy Rhoads, Malmsteen doesn't just quote from classical music, he integrates his training and attitude with that musical form. Listen to a young Yngwie playing the instrumental "Evil Eye" on Alcatraz's 1984 live album, *Live Sentence*.

Many mainstream critics describe heavy metal music as unidimensional, artistically impoverished, vacant, and deviant. Though the level of musicianship varies in any style, it is clear that some metal musicians and composers are among the most accomplished of any rock/pop genre. In addition, some critics don't understand audience attraction to heavy metal music, painting it as a style imposed upon youth by artists and the music industry. These critics posit that if they could only censor it or, even better, make it disappear, the problems of teens would go away.

Scholar Robert Walser addresses some of those criticisms by placing the music in its historical context: "The context . . . is the United States during the 1970s and 1980s, a period that saw a series of damaging economic crises, unprecedented corruptions of political leadership, erosion of public confidence in governmental and corporate benevolence, cruel retrenchment of social programs along with policies that favored the wealthy, and tempestuous contestations of social institutions and representations, involving formations that were thought to be stable, such as gender roles and family."[4] With society's social and economic institutions, including family relationships and the educational system, faltering and the number of family-sustaining jobs disappearing, it was natural for a style of popular music to reflect the disillusionment, fear, and powerlessness that accompanied those conditions. Male teens look for identities of power, and early metal was male and powerful. There are still bands that appeal to that particular segment of the population, and with the broadening of stylistic characteristics such as increased tempo, less morbid lyrics, and stunning guitar virtuosity combined with existent performance theatricality and driving beat, hard rock/heavy metal maintains a place in the nineties mainstream.

*        *        *

Rap is another style that began as the soundtrack of a marginal musical community and has come to greatly influence the American musical mainstream. Rap lyrically reflects roots in the African, African-American, and Caribbean cultural traditions of "playing the dozens," "signifying," the griot tradition of reporting and praise, and also "toasting" and "dub" from Jamaican sound-system DJs. These expressive forms contributed boasting, praise, mockery, and storytelling to the genre. Musically, rap derived from jazz improvisations and avant-garde musical essentialism, social commentary of the blues and rhythm and blues, and the syncopated soul and funk sounds of James Brown and others from the seventies.

These influences combined during the mid-1970s in New York's South Bronx, with its neighborhoods dominated by crumbling housing and its lack of economic opportunity for citizens. Rising from this environment of urban decay was the multiethnic culture called hip-hop, a phenomenon that created a source of identity and group affiliation in "crews"—such as DJ Afrika Bambaataa's Zulu Nation—and acted as an alternative to gang warfare. This hip-hop culture spawned dress styles, break dancing, graffiti, and rap music.

Initially modeling themselves after the Jamaican mobile sound-system DJs, early rap DJs would play at indoor dance clubs or tap into power from a city lamppost and set up an outdoors dance. DJ Kool Herc, a Jamaican living in New York, is credited with numerous innovations that led to rap. With his monster speakers (named Herculords), Herc extended the instrumental breaks from selections to such an extent that dancers would seize the time to demonstrate their latest steps. As Tricia Rose describes in her outstanding book on rap, these "breakdancers" would take ten to thirty seconds to show off their latest acrobatic steps and pantomime moves. The DJs soon began inviting the dancers to the local dance clubs where the DJs worked. DJ Kool Herc would sometimes recite rhymes along with these breaks.

Grand Master Flash was another South Bronx DJ and pioneer who is credited with popularizing scratching, and thus the use of the turntable as an instrument. He would manually turn a record back and forth under the needle, causing a scratching sound to provide rhythmic accents and syncopation. Flash, after attaching a microphone to his system, invited friends Melle Mel and Cowboy to rap along with him. As rappers began to display lyrical and rhythmic talent they became entertainers along with, and then eventually superseded, the dancers. Rap crews like Grand Master Flash and the Furious Five were formed alongside the already existing dance and graffiti crews.

A small New Jersey label, Sugar Hill Records, capitalized on this new sound, releasing "Rapper's Delight" in 1979. Over a disco track lifted from the group Chic, the Sugar Hill Gang introduced rap to the musical mainstream. In spite of criticism from the 'hood that the record's rap was plastic, it eventually sold over 10 million copies worldwide and made the top-40 charts at #36. In 1982 Grand Master Flash and the Furious Five released "The Message," a song chronicling the hardships of life in the neighborhood. Jon Schecter, in the liner notes to the 1992 Rhino release *Street Jams,* calls it an "epic poem of the urban landscape." In the refrain, in response to the litany of struggles, the rapper decries, "It's like a jungle sometimes, makes me wonder, how I keep from goin' under."

Rap musicians had a steady stream of releases on independent labels like Tommy Boy, Profile, and Def Jam through the mideighties. In 1986 Run-DMC, three Queens rappers, had a #4 hit with their remake of the Aerosmith song "Walk This Way."[5] Critics cited the unique use of rock music samples, including some of the original guitar and vocals, but Tricia Rose notes that rappers had been appropriating a variety of musics in their genre for years.[6] From this point in time, with the tremendous media exposure of Run-DMC, rap entered mainstream consciousness. A white New York group, the Beastie Boys, followed the next year with "(You Gotta) Fight for the Right (to Party)" (#7, January 1987). The same year, Queens rapper L. L. Cool J (for Ladies Love Cool James) had the first of his five top-40 hits, "I Need Love."

Rap artists emerged from other African-American communities. Gangsta rap was a new subgenre with commentaries on urban life in Los Angeles, gangs in the community, ordinary citizens in danger, and a police force viewed as perpetrators of violence. Ice T was its first popular voice and had a hit album, *Power*, in 1988. On his 1992 album *Body Count* the cut "Cop Killer" contained the lyric "dust off" some cops and his record company, under public pressure, removed the song from subsequent releases.

N.W.A. (Niggas With Attitudes) profiled struggles in the L.A. ghetto of Compton much the same way Grand Master Flash had done for the Bronx earlier in the decade. Their 1989 release, *Straight Outta Compton* (#37, April 1989), was described as "graphic, lurid streetscapes" and included the single, "F—k the Police." Set as a courtroom trial of the police, the cut charged that the police "think they have authority to kill the minority" and "thinkin' every nigga sellin' narcotic." A "gangsta" was a tough talking, streetwise, expletive-hurling Black man, and the album earned N.W.A. a warning from the F.B.I. Like white working-class youth finding power in the heavy metal identity, it is easy to see how disenfranchised Black youth could concur with these macho expressions of power and bravado. It is also clear that rap's characterization of American society as oppressive and unfriendly found support across broad segments of the African-American community.

Back on the East Coast, Public Enemy released its second album, *It Takes a Nation of Millions to Hold Us Back,* in 1988. Evident were not only the illuminating Black power sermons of "Bring the Noise," "Party for Your Right to Fight," and "Prophets of Rage," but also the brilliant collage of samples, sounds, and beats driving the message. This musical maturing of the rap style manifests itself in a more sophisticated use of samples to layer multitimbral, rhythmic elements behind Malcolm X speeches and guitar solos by Living Color's Vernon Reid. Public Enemy continues its tradition of strident commentary on the hypocrisy and injustices of American society into the nineties.

At the same time, Queen Latifah emerged as one of the few women to accept the rapper challenge. Up to this point a considerable segment of the rap genre contained sexist sentiment, describing women as objects for sexual gratification and physical domination. On her 1989 album, *All Hail the Queen* (which included KRS-One as a producer), the cut "Ladies First" proclaimed, "A woman can bear you, break you, take you / Now it's time to rhyme, can you relate to."

Public Enemy

2 Live Crew typified the kind of objectification Latifah fought. In all likelihood they would have remained only a southeastern regional success if a Broward County, Florida judge had not cited as obscene the sexually explicit lyrics found on the album *As Nasty as They Wanna Be*. A censorship battle ensued that garnered national attention and increased record sales. In 1990 rapper M. C. Hammer—his music is termed by some as rap lite—sold 15 million copies of *Please Hammer Don't Hurt 'Em*, thanks in part to his dance-oriented, high-energy shows.

Rap is, historically, one of many African-American styles that initially became popular as a regional effort and was sold by independent labels before breaking into the musical mainstream—rhythm and blues and soul followed similar paths. And, like these other styles, rap was a synthesis combining numerous musical and lyrical roots to produce a broad, heterogeneous form—there is no such thing as rap but many different kinds and styles. Music ranged from the most elemental sampled or produced beats to the most complex multirhythmic layering, from few melodic or harmonic elements to rich melodies and chords. The topical spectrum is just as broad, and includes personal stories of romance and relationship, sophisticated political analyses, calls for action, sexually explicit fantasies, and violent rage and terror.

Rap has had a significant impact on American popular music, not because we find other musicians emulating the style, but because it expresses a clear and direct relationship between popular music and the struggles involved in an increasingly problematic everyday life. In addition, its strident tone has called upon Americans to again consider the continuing struggles of the African-American community. As Tricia Rose explains, "African-American musicians find a way to unnerve and simultaneously revitalize American culture."[7] In our next and final chapter, we will reflect on our lengthy journey across the landscape of rock/pop music and make some sense of trends and issues over the last thirty years.

# 19· It's Only Rock and Roll but I Like It

*One of the most important and oldest strands in the world's music is body-based straightforward message music. It is found in every culture in many guises.*

**Historian and composer Tom Manoff, in** Music: A Living Language

*[Rock] lyrics embody a set of beliefs about the self and larger society. They celebrate autonomy both in personal relationships and the larger community.*

**Sociologist James T. Carey**

*Don't interpret me. My songs don't have any meaning. They're just words.*

**Bob Dylan**

W E HAVE NOW COMPLETED OUR socio-musical odyssey through the first three decades of rock and roll. As we traversed the landscape we experienced many people and their creative works and also explored the many factors that have contributed to the production and reception of this popular music. With each chapter we visited important artists, their neighbors, and even some folks across the tracks. We stuck to the major highways, regrettably missing some of the outlying musical communities worthy of visit. We hope you enjoyed the continuity of our journey, the way in which the people and their surroundings impacted the next stop along the road. We hope you took some good pictures.

The function of this final chapter is to identify the major elements of our journey and to make some sense out of them. To this end we will divide the information into the categories outlined in the Rock Window: music, lyrics, performance/style, music industry, and technology. It is impossible to analyze rock and roll music, as some have, as though a single style of music existed. One must always wonder which rock is being talked about: Elvis's "Hound Dog" (1956), the Beatles' "A Day in the Life" (1967), the Sex Pistols' "God Save the Queen" (1977), or Public Enemy's "Fight the Power" (1990). There is no single rock and roll, but rather a spectrum of interrelated musical, lyrical, cultural, economic, and technological elements in a perpetual state of transition.

## Music

The music of rock and roll began, as we saw in Chapter 3, with the evolution of classic rock, which draws from the root styles of rhythm and blues, blues, country, and rockabilly. The instrumental configuration of the bands reflected this: Little Richard and Fats Domino kept the R&B band (blues core-band rhythm section of drums, bass, guitar, and piano, plus saxes); the Everly Brothers retained a country string band; the rest fell somewhere between. Berry, Elvis, and Lewis used the basic core and embellished it at times with a second guitar. Although the core ensemble provided the basic foundation for rock's first era, surprisingly it was Holly's two-guitar/bass/drums format that had the most impact on the British invasion groups, which became part of rock's second generation.

Like the Beatles, most major British invasion bands of the early 1960s adopted the Holly arrangement: the Stones threw in a lead singer, and the Who dropped the second guitar. For the musically unrefined rockers, this guitar-centered formula was easier than having to master the piano. This "essential" rock band would remain a major ensemble configuration during rock's first quarter-century—Creedence Clearwater Revival, the Byrds, Big Brother with Janis Joplin, Aerosmith, and Kiss all used it successfully. Others, such as the Grateful Dead, the Animals, and the Allman Brothers—all with some roots in the blues—followed the lead of the classic-era majority and added a keyboard.

The third principal ensemble configuration, the power trio, was introduced by the Who in 1964. This format was adopted by Cream and Hendrix in 1966 and by Led Zeppelin in 1968. In some cases the three musicians were supplemented by a lead singer (the Who and Zeppelin being the most successful). This ensemble produced a blues-rooted hard rock that became the basis for a breed of seventies rockers that included the James Gang, ZZ Top, Van Halen, and Bad Company.

The Beatles chose 1965—the three basic ensemble formats had already been well established—to explore the instrumental boundaries of rock-based popular music (releasing *Help* and *Rubber Soul*). The teen idols and girl groups were already using lush orchestration, however this reflected their pop music orientation rather than rock/pop music experimentation. The Beatles blazed the trail, using a string quartet, sitar, piccolo trumpet, a forty-one-piece mini-orchestra, and studio-produced sounds of backward instruments and tape loops made of random calliope snippets. This expansion of the ensemble boundaries provided an impetus for other groups to explore new territory.

Not only did musical experimentation include innovative use of instruments, it also included exploration of evolving studio technology. By the late 1960s eight-track and sixteen-track recording (including the complex mixdown process), and effects devices such as echo, delay, distortion, and phasing units, added an entirely new dimension of sound manipulation to the artistic process. Artists learned to play the studio much the same as an instrument. In addition, the synthesizer appeared in early seventies rock—promoted by pioneers like Roxy Music's Brian

Eno, Pete Townshend, and Stevie Wonder—expanding the musical parameters even further.

Thus, ensemble expansion proceeded along two paths: the borrowing and use of instrumentation from other musical styles and the application of newly developed technology. A cyclical return to trio format—the Who in the sixties and punk in the seventies—allowed for a periodic simplification of ensemble and instrument function before striking out in more complex and, at times, innovative directions.

The boundaries of vocal style among rock's first three decades expanded very little in comparison to those of the rock ensemble. For rock's first fifteen years vocal styles essentially emulated those that existed in 1955. Viewed on a continuum of emotionality, they ranged from a high of the gospel/R&B stylings of Little Richard, James Brown, and Aretha Franklin through the moderately emotive, relatively clearly articulated vocals of Buddy Holly, the Beatles, folk-rock artists, and some San Franciscans. Between the two are vocalists and styles ranging from Elvis and Chuck Berry to the Stones, CCR, Motown, and Heart. Inherent in these styles was also a commitment to a relatively accurate reproduction of pitch and harmony.

The two major stylistic digressions from this continuum were Robert Plant's unique high-register stentorian wails and the thrusts of Sex Pistol Johnny Rotten and the punk singers who followed. Both of these styles existed at the emotional end of the continuum. Plant's blues-rooted soaring, though lacking the vocal sophistication of the church-trained soul shouters, nevertheless was a unique method of transmitting emotion and intensity. Punk singers also ranked high in uniqueness and emotionality, but their deliberately abrasive and nonmusical qualities set them apart from the mainstream. (Interestingly, these are the same qualities that distinguished a young Bob Dylan from the folk mainstream and drew the ire of many listeners.)

During the classic rock era the vast majority of songs contained instrumental solos. The solos were distributed among three instruments: the tenor saxophone, electric guitar, and piano. By the end of the fifties guitar solos dominated the genre and sax solos had all but disappeared. In the sixties the sax solo resurfaced (in soul music), the guitar established its supremacy, and the piano continued its fade from the spotlight. By decade's end the frequency of solos in rock/pop remained relatively unchanged. However, stylistically the guitar solo had increased in length, compositional and tonal complexity, and importance. Audiences were known to attend performances and purchase records by bands such as Cream and the Experience simply to hear extended, improvisational guitar solos.

Following this creative, improvisational burst, the number of bands and type of styles that used guitar solos stabilized—mostly hard rock/heavy metal and some San Francisco and folk-rock dinosaurs. Even with the addition of the synthesizer to the rock ensemble, the proportion of styles utilizing improvised solos and the almost singular focus on the guitar as a solo instrument didn't change. However, the punk explosion's reaction to contemporary form nearly eliminated the number and length of guitar solos outside the hard rock/heavy metal genres.

Guitar solos in the classic rock era began with a synthesis of blues and country elements. Chuck Berry's innovative fusion had the greatest impact as many sixties guitarists, including George Harrison, Eric Clapton, and Keith Richards, cited Berry as a major stylistic influence. Other guitarists, such as Scotty Moore, Roland Janes, Carl Perkins, Eddie Cochran, Frankie Beecher, and James Burton, were also classic rock era stylistic innovators. The Beatles and Stones continued the verse-length solo tradition until the late sixties, when they drastically reduced the number of solos in their music.

At the same time, however, the guitar kings created their extended improvisational solos, which could last up to twenty minutes. Guitar-oriented bands of the late 1960s and early 1970s filled their concerts and recordings with improvised solos. During the later 1970s, groups that maintained the extended solo tradition generally reduced their frequency to only two or three per concert. With the evolution of heavy metal, guitarists became technically more proficient, adopting virtuosi stylistic elements and practice techniques from the classical music tradition.

Classical music and early popular music supporters have consistently derided rock and roll for its simple chord pattern (or harmonic structure). Early rock/pop material closely followed the three-chord, blues-rooted, I-IV-V progression. With the British invasion, however, songs became more complex. The Beatles' first American hit, "I Want to Hold Your Hand," contained not only the I, IV, and V chords but also bVII, ii, iii, and vi chords. During the next two decades rockers adopted a more complex harmonic structure. Even sixties blues-revival material (like Cream's "Sunshine of Your Love") and the Black musical forms of soul and Motown stretched their harmonic boundaries beyond standard three- and four-chord structures. There were the elementary "Where Did Our Love Go" (the Supremes) and "When a Man Loves a Woman" (Percy Sledge), as well as the more complex "My Girl" (the Temptations) and "Respect" (Otis Redding). Although jazz had more of an influence on rock in the seventies—note the popularity of Steely Dan and the crossover success of George Benson—and more exotic chords such as ninths and thirteenths appeared in rock, the overall harmonic environment did not become appreciably more sophisticated than before.

The one constant among the changing musical variables was the "beat" (backbeat or emphasis on the second and fourth beats in the measure). With roots from gospel through R&B to classic rock, the backbeat (played most often on the snare drum), provided the counterpoint ROLL to the top-of-the-measure ROCK of the bass and other instruments. It was this beat that excited teenage bodies to move uncontrollably and threaten the moral sensibilities of parents. Each successive rock music genre incorporated the beat as an integral musical component. When the range of instrumentation narrowed in rap, the beat assumed a position of musical preeminence.

As society addressed emergent issues and the pace of life quickened in the sixties, accented pulses other than the beat found their way into the musical mix. The Rolling Stones and other blues-derived groups were known to emphasize the denser quarter-note pulse ("Let's Spend the Night Together," for example), causing bodily excitement on twice as many beats as before. Soul and Motown styles stressed more complex syncopated patterns on bass as well as the beat on the drums. The seventies witnessed a further acceleration of the musical pace, with the frantic eighth-note emphasis of punk on drums, bass, and guitar.

Thus, rock/pop music began with a beat-driven, vocally emotive, harmonically simple classic rock genre and added and subtracted, over three decades, instruments, vocal styles, improvisational solo formats, and chords. The size of bands grew, the music got louder and more forceful (with an assist from advances in sound amplification and reproduction technology), and the emphasized pulse got faster. Societal and musical elements—including the reintroduction of previous styles and material—were continually fused with existing genres to produce new syntheses. The more things changed, the more they remained the same; the music of late-1970s artist Elvis Costello and the Attractions contains many similarities to that of 1957 Chuck Berry.

## Lyrics

Rock music lyrics have always generated controversy. Critics have ascribed a cause-and-effect relationship, charging that lyrics incite America's youth to rebel against their parents and society. They have also argued that rock/pop lyrics have undermined the moral fiber of Western civilization with their sexually crude, politically radical, and, more recently, violent content. Rock music supporters have applauded the genre's rebellious and its sometimes politically inflammatory lyrics, crediting them with causing cultural, political, and even "revolutionary" change.

Both of these viewpoints fail to account for a number of important variables. First, finding meaning in a popular music song is not as simple as interpreting lyrics—if you can understand them in the first place. As we discussed in Chapter 1, words carry different meanings for different people; a Washington politician and an African-American teen from the South Bronx probably hear and create different meanings from the same rap song. The music, lyrics, stance, performance, indeed the whole hip-hop culture help each listener to create her own construction of meaning—dependent always upon their knowledge and understanding of the song. Second, it is difficult, if not impossible, to prove that a cause-and-effect relationship exists between rock music lyrics and group or individual behaviors. Popular music is a reflection of the society and culture from which it emanates.

It would also be useful to keep in mind James Carey's categories of older- or newer-value lyrics: older values are acceptance of conventional values, morality, and relationships; newer values are criticism of conventional roles and/or society.[1] By considering rock lyrics in light of the larger societal context, we can begin to make some judgment as to whether rock lyrics—as produced by the artist and interpreted by the reader—are as rebellious and inflammatory as one side or the other would have them be.

The dominant topic in rock music lyrics has always been romance. This is evident whether one looks at the current charts or reads the many studies examining the lyrics of rock hits. Most songs of the classic rock era were about romance. Elvis, Fats Domino, and Buddy Holly sang almost exclusively about clean teen infatuation. The songs of Little Richard and Jerry Lee contained some references to sex with shakin', ballin', and rock and rollin'. The Everly Brothers produced some of the mushiest, dance-for-romance ballads of the era. Depending upon your source, between 67 percent (Friedlander, 1987) and 83 percent (Horton, 1955) of that era's hits were about romance.

Chuck Berry, Bill Haley, and the Everlys recorded songs about rock music itself and the struggles of adolescent existence. These were the songs that were most likely to contain newer-value lyrics—Berry sang that school was a drag, Haley challenged everybody to rock, rock, rock. Criticism of society in fifties lyrics was indirect, subtle, and made no mention of a direct assault on the prevailing conservative values. Only 15 percent of the era's top-40 hits could be interpreted as containing newer-value lyrics. This figure is somewhat misleading, however, because many rebellious elements were found outside the lyrics, in the music and performance. Thus, only when experienced as a part of the music/lyric/performance package does a song reach its rebellious potential.

By the midsixties the times and lyrics were a changin'. A substantial percentage of the top hits (60 percent to 70 percent) were still about romantic relationships, but now the discussion included topics like physical attraction and premarital sex previously considered off limits. In addition, a gigantic body of music was being created—on albums, by groups not geared to three-minute hits—that was absent from top-40 rock radio and didn't appear on the charts. A smaller percentage of this "underground" music also sang about romance, but many of these songs reflected on contemporary societal issues. This material and these artists would eventually appear on the more eclectic FM progressive-rock radio format of the late 1960s and early 1970s.

Between 1964 and 1966, with the British invasion, Motown groups, and a variety of folk rockers and pop balladeers dominating the charts with romance gained and lost, some of the same groups were turning their artistic attention toward less conformist topics. Lennon traveled the cosmic world of "Tomorrow Never Knows," McCartney examined all the lonely people in "Eleanor Rigby," the Kinks satirized "A Well-Respected Man," and the Lovin' Spoonful spent a hot time in "Summer in the City"—each song in some way critical of the prevailing mores yet bereft of inflammatory rhetoric.

Nineteen sixty-seven was a watershed year. Lyrics covering the Vietnam War, the search for a new humanistic morality, and the fight for minority rights emerged in the day's rock/pop music. Era giants like the Beatles proclaimed "All You Need Is Love" and examined the generation gap in "She's Leaving Home"; unknown Janis Ian's "Society's Child" told a poignant tale of a stifled integrated romance; Country Joe McDonald shouted his antiwar anthem, "I Feel Like I'm Fixin' to Die Rag"; and Buffalo Springfield's "For What It's Worth" told us, in any case, to beware of the men in blue. Whispers were being joined by cries as rock/pop music critical of contemporary society became available nationwide. One could escape in a variety of ways: The Stones castigated the "straight" prescription-drug abuse in "Mother's Little Helper," Velvet Underground chronicled the ultimate in "Heroin," Jefferson Airplane followed the "White Rabbit" through the looking glass and down the hole, and the Beatles sailed with "Lucy in the Sky with Diamonds."

During the next four years (1968–1971), numerous rock/pop top-40 and FM hits contained controversial discourse on political, philosophical, and cultural issues. Most of these songs were critical of prevailing conditions but rarely called for specific action or political solutions. In 1968 Woody Guthrie's son Arlo recorded the eighteen-minute antidraft classic, "Alice's Restaurant," which indeed called for massive civil disobedience to the draft; the Rascals also released their #1 hit, "People Got to Be Free." Even the Rolling Stones got into the act, celebrating the working class in "Salt of the Earth." The era's philosophy of social responsibility was expressed in Spanky and Our Gang's "Give a Damn" (about your fellow man).

The Vietnam War played a prominent role in these "relevant" releases. CCR sang about privilege and the draft in "Fortunate Son"; Neil Young, shaken by the 1970 Kent State massacre, wrote "Ohio"; Edwin Starr decried the folly of "War"; and Cat Stevens exhorted the audience to climb on the "Peace Train." Racism became the target in Neil Young's "Southern Man" and Marvin Gaye's "Inner City Blues"; even Elvis was moved to describe the plight of life "In the Ghetto." The topic of marijuana escape and/or enlightenment was aired in "Don't Bogart Me," the Fraternity of Man classic on the *Easy Rider* movie soundtrack; "Henry" and "Panama Red" from New Riders of the Purple Sage; "One Toke Over the Line" from Brewer and Shipley; and "Seeds and Stems" by Commander Cody and His Lost Planet Airmen.

Other topics of concern were urban renewal (Joni Mitchell's "Big Yellow Taxi" and Cat Stevens's "Where Do the Children Play"), mental illness and suicide (James Taylor's "Fire and Rain"), and society's outcasts (Jerry Jeff Walker's "Mr. Bojangles" and the Allman Brothers' "Midnight Rider"). The common person was pictured at the mercy of powerful economic and governmental interests. Some rockers felt unwilling to get involved (the Who's "Won't Get Fooled Again" and the Rolling Stones hit "Street Fighting Man"). A limited number of songs called for individual or collective action for political change. Examples range from the nebulous "Get Together" (the Youngbloods), to the pro-education "Teach Your Children" (CSNY), the more activist "Peace Train" (Cat Stevens), the rhetorical "Power to the People" (Lennon), and the Jefferson Airplane's call to arms "We Should Be Together."

This cross-section of era favorites represents the moderate-sized portion of songs that commented directly on contemporary issues. Other material also generated thought or controversy, dealing with such commonplace topics as romance and relationships. (Carey's 1966 survey concluded that nearly 70 percent of 176 hits surveyed were newer-value songs.) More songs spoke directly of extramarital and premarital relationships as the sexual revolution began to be reflected in the charts. The Who sung about masturbation in "Pictures of Lilly," and Lou Reed exposed us to alternative lifestyles with his "Walk on the Wild Side" in 1973. Many songs dealt with dissatisfaction and striking out on one's own.

As political activity directed at ending the war dissipated, elements of the counter-culture were co-opted by the mainstream; the government vendetta against left and liberal activism took its toll—although the women's movement would soon emerge and generate significant heat—and popular music lyrics turned away from direct commentary on political and cultural topics. A focus on the individual, one's role in society, relationships, and happiness replaced criticism of the status quo. Individual acts of rebellion replaced analytical thinking and collective consciousness.

One reason for this turn away from serious societal concerns toward relation-ships, sex, and escape was that a new generation of late-baby boom teenage rock lis-teners—a younger and more easily manipulated cohort—had arrived on the scene. The leading edge of this group entered junior high school in the late 1960s and es-pecially enjoyed listening to Jimi Hendrix, Led Zeppelin, and their hard rock con-temporaries. These listeners, and the audience of mostly male siblings that followed, were comfortable with the narrower spectrum of youthful concerns (in much the same manner as the teen classic rock audience had been). The rebellious content in this new music lacked the societal focus and political sophistication of its immedi-ate predecessors. Rebellion was transmitted through provocative subjects like sex, escape, and aggression and the music and performance styles reinforced this sedi-tious content. Newer-value songs reacted to conventional sexuality, parental au-thority, and proscribed lifestyles rather than political and countercultural concerns.

The discussion of romance more frequently included the topics of casual sex and romantic sex between unmarried persons; at the same time, American society was becoming more permissive. But political and social commentary didn't cease entirely: Stevie Wonder recorded "Living for the City," Three Dog Night covered "Black and White" (about racial integration), Helen Reddy's "I Am Woman" was a forceful paean to feminism, and even the Eagles recorded "I Wish You Peace." However, mid-1970s album giants Elton John, John Denver, the Eagles, Fleetwood Mac, and Kiss, and singles stars Rod Stewart, K. C. and the Sunshine Band, Diana Ross, and the Bee Gees, released less controversial fare.

Suddenly, from the depths of the British pub scene, the abrasive, reactive rantings of the Sex Pistols, the Clash, and their punk rock mates exploded forth from the un-derground. Outrageously outfitted English youths screamed culturally and politi-cally controversial lyrics to a buzzsaw background of simplistic, distorted rock. Although punk never became a commercially viable genre, its focus on society and its discontent became one of its most co-opted elements. Johnny Rotten spewed a ni-hilistic vision of the British "fascist state" self-destructing. The Clash targeted record companies, war, racism, television, and sexual hypocrisy. The new wave that followed adopted some of punk's criticism of contemporary society. Talking Heads envisioned urban existence as underground warfare ("Life During Wartime"), Devo ridiculed modern techno-life, and Elvis Costello slammed media-manufactured passivity.

Once again, music began reflecting values, and the attitudes of one subcultural grouping (punk) became sufficiently powerful to have an impact on mainstream rock/pop music, and thus on popular culture. This had occurred in the sixties with the San Francisco sound (counterculture), and folk (political activism), and in the seventies with reggae (Rastafarianism). In each case the music helped to re-focus mainstream pop on societal issues.

In the eighties, metal lyrics covered the spectrum of male-centered topics and rap reawakened popular music lyrics with societal criticism. More than any other music we have discussed, rap lyrics reflect the oppressed feelings and experiences of the poor African-American urban resident. Highly stylized expressions of de-sire and rage abound.

The history of rock/pop lyrics is one of a transmission of implicit and explicit messages, stories, and symbols of rebellion, social change, and romance. During each major era, the definition of what constitutes the status quo (the prevailing morality), and therefore what constitutes rebellion or reaction, changes with the cultural and historical conditions. The classic rock era was characterized by con-servative, Cold War–dominated politics and stringent moral and sexual codes. Therefore, lyrics that even suggested sexual activity, uncontrolled movement to the music, and a challenge to authority were by their very nature a threat to pre-vailing attitudes. On its face this constituted rebellious behavior. In another era lyrics of this nature might be considered part of a normal dialogue—thus the im-portance of viewing lyrics in historical context.

Each succeeding era expressed its defiance in its own culturally specific man-ner. Ten years later subjects not even whispered about in the fifties—psychoactive drugs, revolt, revolution, and a gay lifestyle—were part of the rock/pop dialogue. Rebellious behavior and calls for social change permeated the lyrical landscape along with the old standbys of sex and romance. The next decade experienced shocking songs about riots, the holocaust, and sexual bondage. In rock/pop's first three decades the range of topics continued to expand as former controversies be-came less shocking and new confrontations took their place.

## Performance

---

*In the late 1940s, youth was not even considered a significant category. In the 1980s, it has become the symbol of (post-) modernity, of the present, of the now, presided over by the "brats" of the fashion, music, video-clip, and cin-ema world.*

### Ian Chambers

*I got my band playing "When the Saints Go Marching In." I sent them out among the audience, up one aisle and down the other. . . . I climbed onto the piano and threw my shoes and diamond ring to the people crowding around*

*with their hands in the air. . . . I really had no intention of throwing my six-
hundred-dollar cape to the crowd, but I was pretending to do it, and teasing
them by swinging it around my head, when someone grabbed a corner. . . . I
only just managed to avoid being dragged off the piano.*

**Little Richard**

*The subcultural stylistic ensembles—those emphatic combinations of dress,
dance, argot, music, etc.—bear approximately the same relation to the more
conventional formulae ("normal" suits and ties, casual wear, twin sets, etc.) that
the advertising image bears to the less consciously constructed news photograph.*

**Researcher Dick Hebdige**

---

The rock musician's "costume" and stage movements communicate to the audience information about the artist's identity and the messages the artist wishes to
convey. Most attempts to "look like" or "perform like" are deliberate—they are
choices based on economic, cultural, and creative factors. This summary of performance factors will focus on two areas: stage mobility, especially the presence of
sexual mimicry in the artist's movements; and the degree to which the performer's stage apparel reflects the prevailing "straight" dress of the era. By review-
ing these factors, we will gain a clearer picture of whether and how artist's performance styles contribute to the rebellious nature of rock/pop music.

Most classic-era performers wore suits and ties; some even wore tuxedos. The occasional rebel, like a rockabilly Elvis, mixed and unmatched his separates: red pants, a
pink shirt and socks, and a lime-colored jacket, for example. For some artists—Elvis,
Jerry Lee, Little Richard, and to a lesser extent Chuck Berry—stage mobility and bodily movements were interpreted as statements of rebellion and dangerous sexuality.

Elvis mimicked the licentious movements of Black performers: he swiveled his
rear end, straddled the microphone, fell to his knees, and lifted his upper lip in
that famous sneer. The real stage activists, those whose songs contained the greatest amount of sexual innuendo, were Jerry Lee Lewis and Little Richard. Both assaulted the piano and used it as a platform upon which to perform. Lewis would
stand atop his instrument, yelling "Shake it baby, shake it!" Richard was known to
fling parts of his costumes into the audience. This behavior, although mild by today's standards, was outrageous and sexually provocative for the time.

The three major British invasion groups covered the spectrum of stage mobility and sexuality. The Beatles stood firmly near the immobile end of the spectrum, bouncing on their heels and giving their heads an occasional shake, exhibiting little in the way of prohibited movement. This inactivity—a symbolic

conformity—was reinforced by their collarless Pierre Cardin suits and ties. The Rolling Stones stood somewhere toward the middle of the spectrum. Mick, the most mobile, took to parading across the stage, borrowing his moves from the era's Black performers. At the far end of the spectrum, the Who will never be surpassed for shocking, raw, frantic stage energy. The Who demolished guitars, amplifiers, drums, and microphones during their early performances and on occasion even set explosive charges to give their set a dramatic send-off. Dressed as mod outcasts, the band epitomized the defiant rebel—"Hope I die before I get old!"

The early Beatles generated very little sexual heat; they were cute, clean, and cuddly. More hair, paisley costumes, and the search for love and meaning didn't change their asexual manners. And though Roger Daltrey bared his chest, the rest of the Who didn't follow suit. The Stones were nearly as bland. However, Jagger's salacious, undulating, androgynous frontman persona (a copy of Little Richard) set the tone for white performance sexuality of the sixties. The Stones were the bad boys because Mick acted the part.

Of the Black artists, Motown's acts, though extremely mobile, emphasized the classy and suave, whereas soul singers sweated, dropped to their knees, and pleaded for mercy. Neither overtly appealed to prurient interests, although soul gave the audience a taste of sex. Motown artists were opulently and elegantly costumed; their soul counterparts wore stylish suits. San Francisco rockers, some blues revivalists, and many seventies pop-rockers like Fleetwood Mac and Ronstadt were relatively immobile and exhibited little stage sexuality. Hard rockers of the seventies leaped from the tops of amplifiers and strutted across the stage, posing periodically in a Jagger-derived macho posture.

The late 1960s saw theatricality creep into rock staging. San Francisco artists created colorful consciousness-raising environments with mind-bending light shows; Bowie countered with offbeat messages from out-of-this-world characters. Seventies Stones sets included a giant phallus. Pink Floyd flew a giant inflated pig and even constructed a huge wall onstage. Smoke bombs, flash pots, and other explosive instruments regularly populated hard rock shows. The animal kingdom was even brought onstage to shock the audience (Alice Cooper with the snake). Kiss wore layers of greasepaint and spouted flames.

Shock value progressed to self-mutilation as punk artists safety-pinned their noses and chests. Some punk bands engaged in physical combat with their audiences. Not content to just bare parts of their anatomy Jim Morrison-style or fling themselves off the stage like Iggy Pop, punkers waded into the slamdancing pit in the ultimate expression of teen angst and shared struggle.

Each stage posture—or absence thereof—communicated symbolic messages about the artists, their values, and the audience they intended to reach. Most information transmitted in this manner spoke to the issues of conformity/rebellion and cultural identification. The sexual nature of Little Richard's disrobings and Jagger's undulations represented an explicit challenge to society's prohibition of overt sexual behavior. Little about the Beatles' stage performance reinforced rebellious content of their music or lyrics. The aggressive stage stance of the Who, metalists, and punks told their public "We're not gonna take it!"

Finally, rock/pop music over time has become stylistically fragmented, and audiences have come to identify favorites as much by appearance as by other qualities. Teens adopt an artist who looks like and acts like others accepted by their circle of friends. New bands, then, appropriate the "look" of particular subcultural groups or other musicians, hoping to establish a shared identity. Even back in 1964 the Who adopted mod dress, in part for these reasons. Thus, each era contains those artists whose stage appearance and movements are predominantly acts of defiance; for other artists they may be acts of cultural conformity. Each falls somewhere on the continuum between content and style.

## Music Industry

In 1954, before the dawning of the rock era, the top eight record companies sold 85 percent of charted records. In 1973 the top eight record companies sold 82.9 percent of charted records and tapes. In 1980, on the year-ending *Billboard* charts, the top eight companies sold 88 percent of the top 100 albums; in 1994 the figure was 86 percent. This concentration of power is extraordinary and its ramifications are widespread. The nearly absolute control of an industry by a small group of companies directly affects the ability of rock/pop audiences to determine the nature, direction, and cost of their favorite music.

The industry would argue that it is simply providing a commodity to consumers and that the industry's amazing growth proves it has responded to the evolution of audience tastes. There are several hidden problems with that argument. First, profit and loss is the industry's most important consideration. Second, the major multinational corporations that control the industry are politically conservative and would prefer to homogenize the music and neutralize any culturally or politically controversial content. Third, the radio industry and the record industry are in a symbiotic relationship and driven by similar interests. Finally, the first three problems work against musical and cultural pluralism in rock/pop music and society.

It has never been the goal or function of the record industry to provide the public with a full sampling of the music generated by cultural and musical communities worldwide. Instead, the major labels have pursued financial gain through the purchase (from the artists) and sale (to the public) of a variety of popular music styles. This contract between artist and industry entitles the company to manufacture and promote popular music product for which they receive the bulk of the profit. At certain times artists have been in positions of negotiating strength relative to record companies—during a seller's market, to use a real estate term. But generally the record industry has been able to pick and choose the acts it is interested in producing (the buyer's market).

We have seen the ebb and flow of industry power through rock/pop's brief history. The majors controlled a significant portion of popular music before R&B

and classic rock burst onto the scene. The majors chose to sign Elvis and Haley and wait out the rock music fad. They were wrong and paid for it by losing a sizable percentage of the popular music market to the large independent record labels such as Chess, Sun, and Imperial. Radio, reeling from its battle with the new upstart, television, found itself an unwilling ally of classic rock. In American urban centers, rock/pop music established itself as radio's most popular broadcast format—a situation that remains unchanged more than three decades later.

At the time of the second rock explosion, in the midsixties, the majors didn't make the same mistake again. With the success of the Beatles (signed by EMI kidsister subsidiary Parlophone) and Motown (a Detroit ghetto indie), it became obvious that popular music was again in an explosive state. The majors again had a choice of owning the manufacturing rights or sitting on the sidelines. This time the majors, plus the film-industry majors (such as MGM, United Artists, and Capitol) became active players, signing multitudes of unknown artists to contracts, releasing records, and watching gross receipts nearly double in only four years. Columbia Records hired Clive Davis as its president and became an active player. Warner Bros. began a transformation that would turn it into the conglomerate WEA, the largest record company in the United States. Some record companies—who were formerly called indies and initially traded in music outside the rock/pop mainstream—became successful enough to compete with the big boys (like Atlantic, the largest R&B label, and Elektra, a label that emphasized folk). They were eventually absorbed into the small family of majors.

Unlike the first rock era, large record companies of the sixties, recognizing the profitability of the new music explosion, became bidders in the artist marketplace. Label executives and A&R staff sported beards and mustaches, socialized, and even took drugs with their acts. At the same time, top-40 hit radio found itself under attack by a new FM progressive-rock format that offered listeners a wide, eclectic range of album-oriented programming. All of these trends had the effect of making a wider variety of music available to the listening public. This included major-label production of controversial groups like MC5 and Velvet Underground. Between 1964 and the end of the decade, at the same time artists were expanding the boundaries of rock/pop music, the majors, taking a page from the indie book, signed a broader stylistic range of artists. As long as the product offered no serious threat to the economic status quo, label leaders led the charge and reaped record profits.[2]

By the early seventies changes in the music industry had the effect of reversing the stylistic expansion of rock/pop music. Consolidation became the industry norm as smaller companies merged, were gobbled up by the majors, or went bankrupt. The giants grew even larger, and the top eight manufactured and released over 80 percent of all hit records. However, corporate decisions were no longer being made at the label level by men with A&R experience and an ear in the streets. They were being now made almost solely on the basis of profit-and-loss statements. The new label leaders, conservative lawyers and accountants, dictated a cautious course of action: Sign the big sellers to costly multiyear contracts, trim the rosters of all the marginal acts, and only sign new acts if you put them through a rigorous screening process and were reasonably sure they would be profitable.

At the same time, radio was going through a similar change. Stations, which had initially been owned at a local level, were purchased by multistation owners who had their attention focused squarely on the balance sheet. In addition, the mid-1970s became the years of programming consultants—people who for a fee would send you a playlist based on their success in other similar markets. A few consultants dominated rock/pop radio programming. To them, taking chances on broadcasting unproven music was almost sure financial suicide.

By the late seventies consolidation by an entrenched industry oligopoly had produced a narrowing range of commercially viable pop-rock, which was exposed to the public by a radio industry with similarly constricting playlists. But in 1979 the record industry experienced an unexpected event. Their gross sales in dollars fell 11 percent in the United States; this sent a shudder through the industry. The result of consolidation and myopic adherence to profit-and-loss statements (as opposed to artistically driven factors) had led to boring stylistic conformity. In addition, there were a number of other factors. As Simon Frith points out, fewer teens were coming of age, and they had less money to spend on leisure activities.[3] In addition, the money they did spend was beginning to flow toward newer technologies offered in video. It wasn't until 1988 that unit record/tape/CD sales reached the 1978 peak.

Given this historical context, it is necessary to ask what impact this record-industry oligopoly has on the public's ability to purchase music of choice or listen to it on radio. The answer depends, in part, upon where you live. Most large urban areas are sufficiently culturally heterogeneous to have record stores that sell nearly any genre of music, as well as radio stations (mostly publicly owned or college-operated) that broadcast most any style. However, if your city or town doesn't have an alternative radio station or record store, chances are slim that you will be exposed to an intelligent variety of nonmainstream rock/pop-based styles. The current structure of the music industry, with its multinational corporation dominance, doesn't support pluralistic popular music with easy national access for regional or international acts.

The concentration of power presents a perplexing picture. As we've made clear earlier, the top six companies, their subsidiaries, and licensing partners produce or distribute over 80 percent of all hit discs (the term album has become an anachronism). Rock/pop radio stations have strict programming guidelines that limit playlists to hit or former hit records; they are still afraid to take chances and possibly lose rating points, which translate into advertising revenue. Thus, if an artist wants to earn a decent wage playing original rock/pop material, she must break into this closed, star-oriented system dominated by the superlabels and their willing radio partners. These labels are gatekeepers to national success and therefore exert an inordinate amount of control over the artist's access to the system and the public's access to the artist.

The record/radio industry is one piece in the complex set of factors that determine the nature of a specific era's rock/pop music. As of this writing, control has moved even one step further from the regional level of control that was experienced during the classic rock era. The world's largest record company, Columbia Records, is owned by Sony Corporation of Japan; WEA International has bought three European record companies; RCA is owned by the West German Bertelsmann group; A&M, Mercury, and RSO are controlled by Philips's Polygram; Matsushita owns MCA; and EMI-Thorn, an English-French conglomerate, owns Capitol. Only one of the big six is owned by an American corporation. Corporate decisions about the nature of rock and roll are now made even farther from the streets and neighborhoods.

Thus the individual's ability to influence rock/pop music is becoming even more problematic as control moves increasingly into the international corporate arena. However, the music industry is caught between a desire to increase its profit levels and its need to discover new raw materials to exploit. And it is at the regional and local levels that these raw materials are found, shaped, and influenced. Regional musical movements can impact the international scene. Classic rock, soul, Liverpool "beat" music, the San Francisco sound, reggae, punk, and rap were all generated from the provinces and forced their way onto the international stage. Thus, supporting and strengthening community and regional musics is one important way to counteract industry tastes and work toward the goal of musical pluralism.

Simon Frith would also contend that periodic technological innovations have had the effect of enhancing public access to rock/pop music and countering corporate control. The evolving cassette technology is a good example. At first, prerecorded cassettes offered the public mobility; one could travel and listen to music of choice. Using blank cassettes for home taping allowed an entirely new range of possibilities. Listeners recorded entire albums from radio broadcasts until pressure from the record industry stopped radio stations from broadcasting albums. Friends purchased a single copy of a record, copied it on a blank cassette, and passed it to others. Often the record ended up in used record stores—another by-product of cassette technology—to be recycled. This process of taping reduced the product cost, increased consumer control over the material consumed, and enabled the increasingly mobile listener (in car or via portable player) to have her music of choice on hand.

Another technological trend that has led to increased consumer control over rock/pop material is the proliferation of affordable multitrack recording machines using cassette technology. For a reasonable price artists can purchase a four-track home studio, record original material, and duplicate copies for sale. Regional music can become self-supporting—and therefore self-sustaining—through this process. It gives regional artists an ability to bypass radio and record-industry gatekeepers and move directly into audience homes.

An even greater change in the economics of popular music is already at hand. Record labels and their corporate sponsors are recognizing that revenues from secondary sources have overtaken revenues from sales of the individual product. Licensing the use of a record by the publishing arm of a conglomerate for commercials, airplay, in-flight programs, artist use, or other applications has produced substantial income. In addition, the future for the sale of individual product to consumers is not bright, as fiber-optic lines and satellite dishes promise to deliver a variety of services to the home (so-called multimedia, including unlimited music selection, radio stations, movies, and television; banking; grocery shopping; and other services). Songs could be delivered directly to you via video catalog shopping. In a situation similar to the change from sheet music to records in the mid-twentieth century, popular music technology and the music industry of the twenty-first century will find new ways to do business.

## It's Only Rock and Roll

Although it's only rock and roll, it can't be ignored. It means something, touches each listener's soul in some way. No matter how one uses the music—the ultimate escape, soothe the pain, liberate the spirit, contemplate life, have fun, make passionate love—it remains an integral part of our lifescripts. Somewhere, there is a bit of rock/pop music that represents the aspirations and feelings of us all.

For those of you whose rock/pop experiences are mostly memories, I hope this journey has allowed you to again experience the landscape, to know it better and feel the music more deeply. Even today there exists a bountiful supply of music you may not be aware of throughout the world—in Africa, Europe, Central and South America, and Asia—and it awaits your attention. You don't have to stop looking. For those whose youthful enthusiasm is for today's rock/pop music scene, don't forget that Paul McCartney was in a band before Wings. Without knowing this history, we all run the risk of not understanding the present.

I hope you have enjoyed the journey and that you seek out some of the music that tantalized you during the trip. As Pete Seeger once said, Take it easy, but take it.

# Appendix A: Some Artists
# Who Fell Through the Cracks

There are numerous important contributors to the development of rock/pop music whose stories fell outside our historical narrative. In the following pages we chronicle a few of the many who deserve mention.

## JACKIE WILSON

Jackie Wilson was one of the most talented rock/pop vocalists, with a career spanning three decades. Yet commercial success and recognition commensurate with Wilson's talent and skill eluded the singer. A native of Detroit, Michigan, he sang gospel music, was a welterweight golden gloves boxing champion, and had recorded "Danny Boy" for Dizzy Gillespie's Dee Gee label by the age of seventeen. When Clyde McPhatter left the gospel-turned-R&B group Billy Ward and His Dominoes to later form the Drifters, Wilson was chosen to take his place as lead vocalist.

Three years later Wilson left to pursue a solo career, signed with Brunswick Records (the same Decca subsidiary that signed Buddy Holly), and recorded "Reet Petite," "To Be Loved" (#22, April 1958), and "Lonely Teardrops" (#7, December 1958)—all of which were cowritten by Berry Gordy Jr. Wilson chose to stay with Brunswick rather than go with the fledgling Motown label. He had twelve top-40 hits during 1960–1961, but fate and the lack of label and management clout prevented his rise to the top during the soul era. In a temporary setback, Wilson was shot by a frustrated female admirer in 1961. By the midsixties Wilson had made the stylistic transition to soul and the pop charts with "Whispers" (#11, November 1966) and the classic "(Your Love Keeps Lifting Me) Higher and Higher" (#6, September 1967).

During live shows this charismatic, handsome, sexy performer went through a series of physically demanding moves—matched only by other former athletes like James Brown—twirling, dropping to his knees, and even wading out into an adoring audience. As a singer, Wilson, with his gospel and R&B background, displayed a soaring tenor virtuosity similar to stars like Clyde McPhatter and Sam Cooke. Relegated to oldies shows in the seventies, Wilson suffered a heart attack onstage in Cherry Hill, New Jersey in September 1975. The comatose Wilson never fully recovered and died on January 21, 1984.

## ROY ORBISON

Initially, the Texas-born Orbison resembled the second-generation classic rockers. Raised on country, bluegrass, and popular music, the young Orbison came from a musical family and started playing guitar at age six. Like Holly, Orbison performed through high school, with the Wink (Texas) Westerners, entertaining at local functions until he enrolled at North Texas State University in Denton. His college group, the Teen-Kings, recorded "Ooby Dooby" at Norman Petty's studio in Clovis, New Mexico (where Holly recorded most of his early hits). Sun Records liked Orbison's demo, so he went to Memphis and rerecorded "Ooby Dooby," which broke into the top 100.

Not really comfortable with the Sun rockabilly sound—the Sun roster included Jerry Lee Lewis, Johnny Cash, and Carl Perkins, among others—Orbison left for Nashville to make a living as a songwriter for one of the area's giants, Acuff-Rose Publishing. "Claudette," written for his wife, was recorded as the B side of the Everly Brothers hit "Dreams" and went to #30. In Orbison's second attempt at a singing career, he signed with RCA, entered the studio with Presley/Everlys producer Chet Atkins, but was still unsuccessful.

Not until he signed with indie Monument Records (the classic rock era had faded by then) did Orbison's softer but heartfelt sound mature and find acceptance. From 1960 through 1964 he scored seventeen top-40 hits, including "Only the Lonely" (#2, June 1960), "Running Scared" (#1, April 1961), "Crying" (#2, August 1961), and "Pretty Woman" (#1, September 1964). The formula called for rich, supple, tenor crooning, in both regular voice and soaring falsetto, and emotional tributes to mostly absent lovers. Although an accomplished guitarist, Orbison chose to surround his voice with studio orchestration and background vocals. During the calm before the British invasion, Orbison provided a unique alternative to the teen idols.

Orbison was also quite popular in England, where he headlined shows that included the Beatles. He continued to have English hits into the seventies. In 1966, just as he scored his last top-40 hit in the United States, his wife was killed in a motorbike accident. Two years later during a tour in England, Orbison learned that his two eldest sons had burned to death at home in Nashville. In 1978 he underwent open-heart surgery. Just as his career was taking off again—including his 1987 induction into the Rock and Roll Hall of Fame and a hit song as a member of the Traveling Wilburys (the illustrious crew of Orbison, Bob Dylan, George Harrison, Tom Petty, and ELO's Jeff Lynne)—Orbison died of a heart attack suffered while visiting his mother.

## THE ANIMALS

We mention the Animals not only because of their talent and commercial success, but because they also represent the numerous blues-rooted groups to emerge from the English countryside during the sixties British blues revival. Although best known for their Black-sounding lead vocalist, Eric Burdon, the band began in Newcastle-on-Tyne as a traditional jazz band in 1961. Burdon joined as vocalist and helped shift the focus toward blues, R&B, and classic rock material. On the strength of their regional popularity, their quality of cover material, and the success of the British invasion, producer Mickie Most found them a contract with the giant EMI label.

In 1964 the Animals recorded two covers of American rural blues tunes Burdon had heard on Bob Dylan's first album. "Baby Let Me Take You Home" achieved moderate success in England (#21), but "House of the Rising Sun" (#1, August 1964) took both Britain and the United States by storm. Played at a dirge-like pace, the song centered on the arpeggiated hook on keyboard as Burdon wailed his gritty tale of self-destruction. It was a hard song to duplicate, but the musicianship of the band (especially keyboardist Alan Price) and Burdon's authentic lead vocals helped the band to maintain popularity. They turned to contemporary material and recorded the raucous "We Gotta Get Out of This Place" and "It's My Life" before Price left. With a new lineup Burdon appeared at the Monterey Pop Festival and turned countercultural with "[Warm] San Francisco Nights" and "Sky Pilot," both hits in the late sixties.

## THE KINKS

The Kinks were unique. Musically they were minimalists, resisting the first-generation British invasion trend toward the use of orchestral instrumentation, increasingly complex arrangements, and a studio-based sound. Instead, they proffered simple strummed rhythm guitar, Ray Davies's flat lead vocal, classic rock-style bass and drums, and an occasional James Burton/Scotty Moore-type guitar solo. Lyrically they began in the boy/girl British invasion groove but quickly expanded their horizons with composer Ray Davies writing numerous parables about, and parodies of, English life. Because of their artistic focus on England, the Kinks had less of an impact on the United States market than many of their contemporaries.

Their first two hits, "You Really Got Me" (#7, October 1964) and "All Day and All of the Night" (#7, January 1965), were sparse representations of a "Louie Louie" mentality. They featured percussive distorted rhythm-guitar strokes (guitarist Dave Davies sliced the speaker cones with a razor blade to get the sound), Dave's classic rock lead solo, and Ray's urgent, nonmelodic lead vocals. (Jimmy Page admitted in a 1973 interview that, contrary to popular rumor, Dave Davies played lead guitar on their records.) One reason for the Kinks' seventies postpunk revival was the raw, driving, distorted, nontechnical nature of these early hits.

By late 1965, however, Ray Davies's attention had turned to societal rather than personal relationships and he developed a lighter musical sound without the power chords and blared vocals. His "Well Respected Man" (#13, January 1966) satirized the proper but hypocritical lifestyle of straight British society. The music remained anchored in the Beatles-rooted first British invasion. Their 1966 hit "Dedicated Follower of Fashion" satirized the pleasure-seeking, trend-conscious London Mods, musically invoking the English music hall with the one-and-three bass pattern (mimicking a tuba) and a call and response. Davies's "Sunny Afternoon" (#14, August 1966) found the singer having lost a partner and material possession but garnering solace in a sunny afternoon. It was a "good-time tune" with a strong resemblance to the Lovin' Spoonful.

The Kinks managed these hits even though they were unable to tour in the United States due to an intemperate incident that involved a musician's union representative. The band was banned from union-sanctioned gigs. Members also regularly engaged in intraband bouts. Lacking a Brian Epstein, or even the commercial common sense of a Mick Jagger, the Kinks were unable and unmotivated to rectify the situation until 1969. They continued to write well-received songs (like the wistful, working-class ballad "Waterloo Sunset") and tour throughout the rest of the world.

Like the Who, the Kinks turned to thematic projects of connected songs in the late sixties, and this garnered them increased critical acclaim. (In another parallel to the Who, Ray, like Pete Townshend, was the dominant composer.) *The Kinks Are the Village Green Preservation Society* introduced the listener to a "quaint" village in the English countryside, its inhabitants, and their daily pursuits. *Arthur (or the Decline and Fall of the British Empire)*, originally composed for the soundtrack to a TV movie production, followed. Davies again focused on and was able to capture the essence of the life of the citizenry. This project's songs encompassed subjects ranging from the aspirations of working-class Britons to sexual mores in Victorian England. Later projects helped the band regain their popularity in America and retain it in England. The song about a transvestite, "Lola" (#9, September 1970), became part of *Lola Versus Powerman and the Moneygoround*. *Muswell Hillbillies* reflected life in the working-class London district (Muswell Hill) of their youth.

Had they enjoyed stronger management and record-company support, the Kinks may have garnered the acclaim and financial rewards of their contemporaries. However, their laissez-faire attitude let them drift, yet it also guided them to their particular brand of creativity. They exhibited an unusually wide range of autobiographical, political, and social commentary on British life. Their unpretentious music, a simple, guitar-based, rhythmically unadulterated sound, was alluring and played a stark contrast to the increasingly studio-based rock/pop of the late sixties. They also engaged in self-destructive behavior (involving violence and substance abuse). They exhibited an uncanny resemblance to the next decade's punk dynamic.

## VAN MORRISON

When he had it together, Van Morrison was one of the golden era's most talented singer-songwriters. He began in northern Ireland as the vocalist for the R&B-revival band Them. The group wrote and recorded the classic "Gloria." Eventually Morrison left the band, migrated to the United States, and released a series of critically acclaimed albums in the late 1960s and early 1970s. His 1969 *Astral Weeks*, a synthesis of the celestial and the emotional, didn't chart, yet it was named Album of the Year by *Rolling Stone* magazine. Later hits included albums and title cuts from *Moondance* (#29, May 1970), *Tupelo Honey* (#27, November 1971), and *St. Dominic's Preview* (#15, September 1972). At his best Morrison combined his passion for Black-rooted American music with an intense search for some basic truths.

## STEVE WINWOOD AND TRAFFIC

Steve Winwood is another supremely talented artist who possesses, among other things, one of white rock/pop's finest and unique voices. A teen prodigy, Winwood joined Birmingham England's R&B/blues revival outfit the Spencer Davis Group in 1964 at age sixteen. Before leaving in 1967 to form Traffic, Winwood wrote, sang, and played organ on "Gimme Some Lovin'." With lyricist-drummer Jim Capaldi, winds player Chris Wood, and the intermittent contributions of guitarist-writer Dave Mason, Winwood crafted Traffic—the thinking person's rock/pop band. They relied on the musicianship of Winwood and company to weave a textured tapestry of interesting melodies, rhythms, and instrumentation over which Winwood's distinctive voice soared. Songs with the eclectic titles of "Paper Sun" (nicely integrating sitar), "Shanghai Noodle Factory," and "Empty Pages" are good examples of Traffic hitting its stride. The band experienced several personnel changes and survived into the midseventies. In the eighties Winwood returned for a successful solo career, however it's the Traffic of "Please, Mr. Fantasy" and "John Barleycorn Must Die" that has withstood the test of time.

## FRANK ZAPPA

The late Frank Zappa was an extraordinarily talented rock/pop composer who was equally comfortable playing rock and roll guitar, scoring an album titled *Jazz From Hell* (for which he won a 1987 Grammy Award), or conducting the London Symphony Orchestra playing one of his original compositions. Zappa treated his moderate-sized but dedicated audience to a stream of eclectic rock/pop music for three decades, offering social and political satire. His album titles alone were worth the price of admission: *Freak Out* (1966), *We're Only in it for the Money* (1968), *Uncle Meat* (1969), and *Weasels Ripped My Flesh* (1970), just to name a few. Zappa is also to be commended for not abandoning his intellect and principles in the pursuit of status and monetary reward. This is evidenced by his appearances in Washington, D.C. to testify before the Parents' Music Resource Council (PMRC).[1]

## PAUL SIMON

Paul Simon was one of the most consistent, high-quality songcrafters of the sixties and seventies, creating two generations of musically and lyrically sophisticated folk-rooted pop-rock music. A native New Yorker, his career began with partner Art Garfunkel (as the duo Tom and Jerry) with "Hey Schoolgirl" (#49 in 1957). His early efforts reflected a combination of classic rock and Brill Building pop stylings. For a few years Simon worked in the bustling New York pop music scene pushing his songs—he worked with a young Carole King (then Klein)—embarking on a solo career, and enrolling in law school. Struck by the nascent folk scene of the early sixties, Simon turned toward material accompanied by acoustic guitar about self-awareness, relationships, and the changing cultural climate.

In 1964 Simon and Garfunkel reunited and, performing under their real surnames, signed to Columbia records with Dylan producer Tom Wilson. Their initial album, *Wednesday Morning, 3 AM* sold poorly, but Wilson took one of the cuts, "The Sounds of Silence," and added drums, bass, and electric guitar. (The additional instrumentation is not quite synchronized with its acoustic predecessor; the electric rhythm guitar closely resembles the circular crosspicking style of CBS labelmates the Byrds.) It went to #1 on the charts and the stunned Simon returned from solo dates in England to tour with Garfunkel. For the next five years the duo continued their popularity with a series of Simon-penned songs combining Garfunkel's ethereal tenor voice, Simon's strummed acoustic guitar, and a variety of instrumental shadings. Simon's songs captured a personalized odyssey through the alienating and fast-changing society of the sixties.

Simon and Garfunkel contributed five tracks to the movie soundtrack to *The Graduate,* including the Grammy-winning cut "Mrs. Robinson." After approximately 800 hours in the studio, exacerbating already strained relations, they released the album *Bridge Over Troubled Water* and scored with the title cut (#1, February 1970); this effort garnered six Grammy Awards, including single, album, and song of the year. They then dissolved the team, Garfunkel to concentrate on moviemaking and Simon on moving into the solo spotlight. They would reunite periodically over the next ten years.

As a solo artist, Simon's vision of the world matured and expanded. He remained searching and skeptical, often glancing at life with a sardonic smile. His musical frontiers expanded, offering his listeners the unique fusion of folk-rooted strumming and a variety of international musical flavors. This brilliant recipe surfaced immediately on the album *Paul Simon* (#4, February 1972) with "Mother and Child Reunion" (recorded with reggae musicians), "Duncan" (which included Latin American instruments like the pan pipes and charengo), and "Me and Julio Down by the School Yard" (featuring Brazilian percussionist Airto Moreira). His follow-up album, *There Goes Rhymin' Simon,* continued to mix genres. "Loves Me Like a Rock" featured the gospel virtuosity of the Dixie Hummingbirds and their famous lead vocalist, the Reverend Claude Jeter. "Something so Right" ventured into the jazz realm with time-signature changes and some well-known sidemen.

The 1975 release *Still Crazy After All These Years* continued the jazz and gospel trend (employing fusion session players like drummer Steve Gadd and saxman Phil Woods) and reflects the turmoil caused by conflict between a stable family relationship and life on the road as a musician. In 1980 Simon appeared in the movie *One Trick Pony,* the delightful semiautobiographical portrait of an artist torn between family responsibility and the road, artistic compromise and creative integrity. Simon continued his international approach with *Graceland* (#3,

September 1986), inspired by South African Black music and featuring groups such as Ladysmith Black Mambazo, Stimela, the Boyoyo Boys, and bassist Baghitti Kumhalo and drummer Isaac Mtshali. His use of South African musicians generated substantial controversy (in the light of the UN boycott of the South African government's apartheid policies). It also once again showed Simon's extraordinary ability to combine very personal insights and tales of alienation with some of the best musical genres the world has to offer.

# Appendix B: The Rock Window—
# One Way to Listen and Understand

The Rock Window is a tool designed to help the listener seek, identify, organize, and analyze the elements contained in rock/pop music. The process involves listening to the song and collecting aural information, collecting written information, and organizing both into five major topic areas: Music, Lyrics, Artist History, Societal Context, and Stance. This method allows the listener to analyze and make some sense about the nature and context of song and artist and provides a format for comparing music.

Imagine if you were trying to compare one song from the 1950s and another from the 1980s. What information would you collect from each one in order to make a viable comparison? The Rock Window will help you compare similar aspects of each song in the music, lyrics, artist's life, and artist's public actions.

The following is an example of how the Rock Window is applied; let's use Chuck Berry's 1958 hit "Johnny B. Goode" as our sample song. Remember that the answers listed, especially in the music and lyrics sections, are subjective in nature. Therefore they are not the only "correct" answers, but they are the most defensible.

I. MUSIC

*a) Ensemble*
What instruments are present in the selection?
*Drums, bass, two electric guitars, piano.*

*b) Rhythmic Emphasis*
What is the dominant beat? This answer comes in two parts: (1) what is the beat? and (2) what instrument carries this beat? Choices for the first part consist of either half-, quarter-, or eighth-note pulses or a syncopated beat. Generally, the dominant beat will be carried by an instrument in the rhythm section; thus the choices will often be drums, bass, guitar, or piano.
*Half-note pulse by drums (two and four on the snare), quarter-note pulse by the bass and eighth-note pulse by the rhythm guitar are all acceptable answers.*

*c) Vocal Style*
What is (1) the level of emotionality and (2) the articulation? (3) What are two adjectives that you would use to subjectively describe the vocal style? In order to quantify (1) and (2) use the following scales: Emotion—1 = Pat Boone singing

"Love Letters in the Sand" (#1, 1957); 10 = Robert Plant's banshee-like screams during "Dazed and Confused"; in the second, the slur quotient depends on how well you understand the lyrics—think of it as the number of marbles lodged in the mouth—where 0 = totally understandable and 3 = totally slurred and garbled, much like Big Joe Turner's third verse in "Shake, Rattle and Roll."

*Emotionality level at a seven; articulation is .5; adjectives suggested are shouting, playful, and urgent.*

### d) Instrumental Solo

Is there an instrumental solo and if so, what instrument is playing it and what is its most important stylistic root? A solo is defined as: (1) the absence of sung lyrics, (2) an instrumentalist plays an improvised melody, and (3) for at least a verse in length.

*Guitar solo from the blues. Indicators are bent notes and repetition.*

### e) Harmonic Structure

What chords are present in the song?

*Chords are I, IV, and V.*

## II. LYRICS

### a) Story

Summarize the major lyrical theme or themes in the song. Use these topical classifications as a way of beginning your organization of the material: (1) romantic love, (2) sexuality, (3) alienation, (4) justice and injustice, (5) introspection/the person, (6) personal narrative or story, and (7) other. Use at least three sentences of lyrics from the song to clarify your thematic choices.

*Johnny B. Goode is a personal narrative about a young, impoverished "country boy," a talented guitarist, who is encouraged to pursue a dream of musical fame.*

### b) Message

Do you find there is an underlying message of cultural and/or political importance contained in the lyrics? If so, describe the message. If not, answer no.

*While aspirations of artistic and/or economic success are not culturally or politically unique for the middle 1950s, it is important to note that Berry's original lyrics contained the words "colored boy" in the place of "country boy." Berry consciously changed words because of his awareness that existent racism would make it more difficult for this song to be commercially successful were the hero an African American. Thus, this song could be construed, in its original form, as an exploration of Black aspirations.*

## III. ARTIST HISTORY

*a) Youth and Personal Characteristics*
What two things about the artist's youth or early career are most important in helping to understand the work? Why?

*1) Berry was a talented musician who had some early training on piano, saxophone, and guitar, as well as in voice and choral singing. This helped him to achieve later success as an instrumentalist and enabled Berry to supplant Johnny Johnson as leader of his early quartet.*

*2) As an African-American living in a border state, Berry was in the position to bear the full burden of American racism. His arrest as a teenager for robbery—he was a passenger in a stolen car and was present at a hold-up—and subsequent ten-year sentence, of which he served three years, gave him plenty of ammunition to use in chronicling paradoxes of teen life that might parallel the Black experience.*

*b) Musical Roots*
What two musical styles or artists were the most important influences on this artist? What evidence substantiates this?

*1) Urban blues—Berry's innovative synthesis of guitar styles begins with the blues. Bending notes, choke, and repetition are cornerstones of his playing and are evidenced in both the guitar introduction and instrumental solo of "Johnny B. Goode." Berry cites T-Bone Walker and Carl Hogan (Louis Jordan) as major influences.*

*2) Popular music—Both lyrically and vocally, Berry consciously reflects popular music of his youth. He cites Frank Sinatra and Nat "King" Cole as his favorite singers and his well-articulated vocal style evidences this. Berry tells us that his lyrics were carefully crafted in a painstaking process of creation and they closely represent the complexity, form, and humor of the works of Tin Pan Alley tunesmiths such as Porter and Gershwin (see "Too Much Monkey Business" and "Roll Over Beethoven" for examples).*

*c) Career Landmarks*
What three events do you believe are the most important landmarks of this artist's career? Why?

*1) Chuck Berry journeyed to Chicago with a friend, and while making the rounds of some South Side blues clubs, he garnered enough courage to approach Muddy Waters for advice on recording his songs. Waters, who was the king of the Chess Records blues roster, said "Go see Leonard Chess." Berry met with Chess, played a tape of some material and had a recording session scheduled for his fast-paced "hillbilly" tune "Ida Red" for May 21, 1955, in Chicago. Berry's first record, now titled "Maybellene," became a top-5 hit on the pop charts that August.*

*2) Within the space of ten months, Berry placed his three important teen anthems on the popular charts, "School Days" (April 1957), "Rock and Roll Music" (November 1957), and "Sweet Little Sixteen" (February 1958). Each chronicles an important segment of teen life and its concomitant generational struggles. "School Days" follows the difficult and boring student existence to day's end in the soda shop or "juke joint." The final refrain begins with, "Hail, hail rock and roll, deliver me from the days of old." "Rock and Roll Music" celebrates the music itself, its various components and kinesthetic impulses to dance derived from the famed "backbeat." Finally, "Sweet Little Sixteen" delivers the paradox of every father's little girl begging mommy to convince daddy that it's okay just to have fun at the dance while at the same time denoting the potential pitfalls of rocking and rolling in tight dresses, lipstick, and a case of the "grown-up blues." In these three selections, Berry was the magnificent rock-poet and chronicler.*

*3) Chuck Berry was prosecuted twice in 1960 on charges stemming from alleged sexual misconduct. In the first instance he was charged with a violation of the Mann Act, a federal statute designed to curtail racketeering and prostitution. He was charged with bringing Janice Escalante—an Apache-Mexican woman he added to his entourage in El Paso, Texas and gave a job to in his nightclub—to St. Louis for the purpose of engaging in prostitution. The first guilty verdict was vacated due to the racism evidenced by the prosecutor and the judge. In May 1960 he was charged with another offense of having sex with Joan Bates, a married white woman aged eighteen. On the stand Bates admitted to having sex and loving Berry. He was acquitted of any crime. Berry was retried for the first offense, found guilty, and served time in a federal penitentiary from 1961 to the fall of 1963. Although the classic rock era was coming to an end, Berry, with his songwriting talent and artist charisma, may have had a chance of transcending the musical eras between the fifties and the British invasion. These prosecutions sealed his fate and essentially ended his creative career.*

## IV. SOCIETAL CONTEXT

### a) Cultural and Political Forces

Describe two important cultural and/or political movements of the era and how they relate to the music of this artist.

*1) The mid-1950s were a time when racism remained a potent political and cultural force. Discrimination due to race was still legal in many states, lynching still occurred in the South, as did the persecution (and occasional assassination) of leaders of the growing civil rights movement. On a macro level, an artist as talented as a writer, guitarist, and performer and as handsome as Chuck Berry could still only achieve a limited level of commercial success. The world would await a lesser talent like Elvis Presley to be crowned the "King of Rock and Roll." On the micro level, the racially motivated prosecution of Berry by St. Louis authorities essentially destroyed Berry's career by forcing him to spend nearly two years defending himself (during which time he lost a significant amount of resources, including his successful club).*

*2) As Berry's career began, he was able to capitalize on a changing popular music marketplace formed at the confluence of forces. The adolescent lifestyle had been in-*

*stitutionalized in postwar America, and with a rapidly growing economy, evidenced by a burgeoning suburbia, a teen economic cohort was born. Products, including rock and roll records, were offered to teens, who had an increasing amount of disposable income. At the same time, television had challenged radio for media dominance and was winning. Radio's prospects were dim when markets for rhythm and blues, country, and rock and roll records provided a unique entertainment format that could again deliver listeners to advertisers. Radio recovered because of artists like Berry.*

### b) Music Industry
Is this music being produced by the music industry mainstream (the majors), by alternative means (indies), or a combination of both? Explain.

*Berry recorded for the Chess label based in Chicago; it was run by rock and roll visionaries Leonard and Phil Chess. With its subsidiary, Checker, it challenged, along with Atlantic (New York), King (Cincinnati), Sun (Memphis), Imperial and Specialty (Los Angeles), and others, the dominance that the majors enjoyed in the popular music marketplace. By 1958 the indies had twice as many hits on the top-100 charts as did the majors.*

## V. STANCE

### a) Live Performance
What image does the artist present during live performances through dress and actions?

*Berry's dress was typical of the day's rock and rollers. Onstage he was costumed in fancy suits, or jackets and slacks, and bow ties. His hair was well coifed—slicked back—and he sported a pencil-thin mustache. Berry's stage presence was fairly active and included his famous duck-walk. (Rock mythology has Berry developing his most famous bit after he appeared at an important multiday gig with only one pair of pants. In order to hide his pant creases, he bent over, guitar in front of thighs, and shuffled across the stage.) Berry also swung his guitar back and forth while singing his songs at the mic.*

### b) Public Positions
Does the artist take public positions on political and/or cultural issues?

*Though never noted for taking public stances on issues, Berry—once described as open and easygoing—has been characterized as uncommunicative, terse, and even morose ever since his incarceration in 1961.*

# Notes

## CHAPTER 1

1. For a more detailed explanation of the Rock Window and its application, see Paul Friedlander, "A Characteristics Profile of Eight Classic Rock and Roll Artists, 1954–1959: As Measured by the 'Rock Window,'" December, 1987, Dissertation Abstracts Volume 49A, p. 652.

2. A hit song or album is defined as one that attained at least #40 on either the *Billboard* Hot-100 singles charts or top-200 album charts. The weekly *Billboard* magazine popular music charts, although not above criticism, are considered to be the most accurate gauges of commercial success. All chart quotations are taken from Joel Whitburn's *Billboard* books, *The Billboard Book of Top 40 Hits* (New York: Billboard Publications), and *The Billboard Book of Top 40 Albums* (New York: Billboard Publications).

## CHAPTER 2

1. Don J. Hibbard, with Carol Kaleialoha, *The Role of Rock* (Englewood Cliffs, N.J.: Prentice-Hall, 1983), p. 13.

2. Cousin Brucie Morrow and Laura Baudo, *Cousin Brucie: My Life in Rock and Roll Radio* (New York: Beech Tree Books, 1987), p. 59.

## CHAPTER 3

1. Jerry Hopkins, *The Rock Story* (New York: Signet Books, 1970), p. 31.

2. Charles White, *The Life and Times of Little Richard* (New York: Pocket Books, 1984), pp. 47–48.

3. Arnold Shaw, *The Rockin' '50s: The Decade That Transformed the Pop Music Scene* (New York: Hawthorne Books, 1974), p. 139.

4. Ibid., p. 143.

5. Charlie Gillett, *The Sound of the City* (New York: Dell Publishing, 1972), p. 34.

6. Decca executive and Haley producer Milt Gabler had suggested that part of the success of "Rock Around the Clock" was due to the fact that it was a rewrite of an old blues tune, "My Daddy Rocks Me with a Steady Roll." He claimed that the words rock and roll came straight from the lyrics of that song.

7. From a 1969 interview with Greil Marcus. See *The Rolling Stone Interviews: 1967–1980* (New York: Paperback Library, 1981), p. 175.

8. Ibid.

9. White, *The Life and Times of Little Richard*, p. 47.

10. Gillett, *The Sound of the City*, p. 37.

11. From a 1969 interview with David Dalton. See *The Rolling Stone Interviews: 1967–1980*, p. 366.

## CHAPTER 4

1. Peter Guralnick, *Lost Highway: Journeys and Arrivals of American Musicians* (Boston: David R. Godine, 1979), p. 120.

2. Peter Guralnick, *Feel Like Going Home: Portraits in Blues and Rock 'n' Roll* (New York: Outerbridge and Dienstfrey, 1971), p. 140.

3. Guralnick, *Lost Highway,* pp. 100–101.

4. Jerry Hopkins, *Elvis: A Biography* (New York: Warner Paperback Library, 1972), p. 135.

5. Guralnick, *Lost Highway,* p. 120.

6. Alfred Wertheimer, *Elvis '56* (New York: Collier Books, 1979), p. 26.

7. Red West, Sonny West, and Dave Hebler, with Steve Dunleavy, *Elvis: What Happened?* (New York: Ballantine Books, 1977), pp. 188–189.

8. Arnold Shaw, *The Rockin' '50s: The Decade That Transformed the Pop Music Scene* (New York: Hawthorne Books, Inc., 1974), p. 191.

9. Guralnick, *Feel Like Going Home,* p. 147.

10. J. W. Brown tinkered with technology. Experimenting with electric instruments, he was one of the era's first major bass players to adopt the Fender electric bass for use in the studio and on the road.

11. John Goldrosen, *The Buddy Holly Story* (New York: Quick Fox, 1975), p. 61.

12. Holly had hits under two different names, the Crickets and Buddy Holly. Although not exactly typical, it is not unique. Black vocal groups sometimes recorded up-tempo music under one name and ballads under another. Holly also had a more compelling reason to exclude his name from "That'll Be the Day." Brunswick Records rushed to sign Holly immediately after hearing the song. However, Holly was still under contract to Decca (ironically Brunswick's parent company) who, had they known, could have prevented Holly from signing with Brunswick. Even worse, they might have released their terrible, inferior version of the song that languished somewhere in their vaults. Holly chose to hide as a member of the Crickets; thus the record was released under the group's name. Once the Decca contract expired, Holly nevertheless decided to maintain the Black vocal group tradition—most fast songs were released by the Crickets and the ballads by Buddy Holly.

13. Goldrosen, *The Buddy Holly Story,* p. 91.

14. See Goldrosen's *The Buddy Holly Story* for a marvelous description of the 1957 tour.

15. Goldrosen, *The Buddy Holly Story,* back cover.

16. Bruce Pollack, *In Their Own Words* (New York: Collier Books, 1975), pp. 139–140.

17. Terence J. O'Grady, *The Beatles* (Boston: Twayne Publishers, 1983), p. 11.

18. From a 1972 interview with Patrick Salvo. See *The Rolling Stone Interviews: 1967–1980* (New York: Rolling Stone Press, 1981), p. 233.

## CHAPTER 6

1. Cousin Brucie Morrow and Laura Baudo, *Cousin Brucie: My Life in Rock and Roll Radio* (New York: Beech Tree Books, 1987), p. 74.

2. Alan Betrock, *Girl Groups: The Story of a Sound* (New York: Delilah Books, 1982), p. 106.

3. Steven Gaines, *Heroes and Villains: The True Story of the Beach Boys* (New York: New American Library, 1986), p. 79.

4. Ibid., p. 108.

## CHAPTER 7

1. Nicholas Schaffner, *The Beatles Forever* (New York: McGraw-Hill, 1978), p. 22.

2. *See The Rolling Stone Interviews: 1967–1980* (New York: Rolling Stone Press, 1981), p. 142.

3. Schaffner, *The Beatles Forever*, p. 59.

4. Terence J. O'Grady, *The Beatles* (Boston: Twayne Publishers, 1983), p. 109.

5. Barry G. Golson, ed., *The Playboy Interviews with John Lennon and Yoko Ono* (New York: Playboy Press, 1981), p. 149.

6. Ray Coleman, *Lennon* (New York: McGraw-Hill, 1984), pp. 261–262.

7. See interview with Jann Wenner, in *The Rolling Stone Interviews*, p. 140.

8. *Rolling Stone*, vol. 5, XII, p. 47.

9. *The Playboy Interviews*, p. 166.

10. Beatles friend Jimi Hendrix was recruited to join the tour, but his extraordinary success at the Monterey Pop Festival in June led to a series of important concert dates, and he was released from his commitment.

11. Peter McCabe and Robert Schonfeld, *Apple to the Core: The Unmaking of the Beatles* (New York: Pocket Books, 1974), p. 94.

12. *The Playboy Interviews*, p. 160.

13. McCabe and Schonfeld, *Apple to the Core*, p. 113.

14. Ibid., p. 142.

15. Ibid., p. 134.

16. Ibid., p. 179.

## CHAPTER 8

1. Philip Norman, *Symphony for the Devil: The Rolling Stones Story* (New York: Linden Press/Simon and Schuster, 1984), p. 41.

2. From a 1971 interview with Jeff Greenfield. See *The Rolling Stone Interviews: 1967–1980* (New York: Rolling Stone Press, 1981), p. 159.

3. Ibid., p. 159.

4. Ibid., p. 160.

5. Nicholas Schaffner, *The British Invasion: From the First Wave to the New Wave* (New York: McGraw-Hill, 1982), p. 59.

6. Ibid., p. 68.

7. From an interview with Mikal Gilmore, *Rolling Stone*, issue no. 512, p. 34.

8. From the *Rolling Stone* interview with Jeff Greenfield. See *The Rolling Stone Interviews*, p. 170.

9. Ibid., p. 168.

10. Ibid., p. 166.

11. Stanley Booth, *The True Adventures of the Rolling Stones* (New York: Vintage Books, 1985), p. 248.

12. Chet Flippo, *On the Road with the Rolling Stones* (Garden City, New York: Dolphin Books, 1985), p. 37.

13. From the *Rolling Stone* interview with Mikal Gilmore, p. 32.

14. From the *Rolling Stone* interview with Jeff Greenfield, p. 171.

15. Tony Sanchez, *Up and Down with the Rolling Stones* (New York: New American Library, 1979).

16. Booth, *True Adventures*, p. 156.

17. Ibid., p. 156.

18. Ibid., p. 374.

19. Ibid., p. 339.

20. Ibid., p. 394.

21. Norman, *Symphony for the Devil*, p. 337.

22. From the *Rolling Stone* interview with Mikal Gilmore, p. 35.

## CHAPTER 9

1. Dave Marsh, *Before I Get Old: The Story of the Who* (New York: St. Martin's Press, 1983), p. 80.

2. Richard Barnes, *The Who: Maximum R & B* (New York: St. Martin's Press, 1982), p. 41.

3. From an interview with Jann Wenner. See *The Rolling Stone Interviews: 1967–1980* (New York: Rolling Stone Press, 1981), p. 34.

4. Marsh, *Before I Get Old*, p. 126.

5. From a 1987 interview with David Fricke. See *The Rolling Stone Interviews: The 1980s* (New York: St. Martin's Press/Rolling Stone Press, 1989).

6. From an interview with J. Cott, *The Rolling Stone Interviews, vol. 2* (New York: Rolling Stone Press, 1973), p. 41.

7. Ibid., p. 45.

8. From the 1987 interview with David Fricke.

9. From an interview with J. Cott, p. 53.

10. Ibid., p. 49.

11. From the 1987 interview with David Fricke.

12. Ibid.

13. Ibid.

## CHAPTER 10

1. Anthony Scaduto, *Bob Dylan* (New York: Signet Books, 1973), p. 69.

2. Robbie Woliver, *Bringing It All Back Home* (New York: Pantheon, 1986), p. 67.

3. Ibid., p. 73.

4. From a 1969 interview with Jann Wenner. See *The Rolling Stone Interviews: The 1980s* (New York: Rolling Stone Press, 1981), p. 83.

5. Roseburg is a city of 20,000 located in western Oregon. It is sufficiently removed from major markets to be served during the day by only radio stations located within the area. In the 1960s Roseburg had only one top-40 radio station playing rock music. "Roseburg status" postulates that if a song reached the playlist on a top-40 station in a market so removed as Roseburg, Oregon, it was most probably available to all listeners nationwide.

6. Paul Gambaccini, *Critics' Choice: The Top 100 Rock 'n' Roll Albums of All Time* (New York: Harmony Books, 1987), p. 8.

7. Alan Rinzler, *Bob Dylan: The Illustrated Record* (New York: Harmony Books, 1978), p. 63.

8. Ibid., p. 68.

## CHAPTER 12

1. Peter Guralnik, *Sweet Soul Music: Rhythm and Blues and the Southern Dream of Freedom* (New York: Harper and Row, 1986), p. 243.

## CHAPTER 13

1. Since the band recorded rhythm-section parts—usually consisting of the drums, bass, keyboard, and guitar—to numerous songs during the course of a working day, it was often difficult to recall, years later, who actually recorded on which songs. Some controversy has arisen over who played on what songs. New York session drummer Bernard Purdie claims to have rerecorded numerous drum parts for Motown over the course of the

1960s. Los Angeles bassist Carol Kaye was also known to have recorded for the label during this era. Nevertheless, it is clear that the Funk Brothers were innovative, high-quality players and played on the vast majority of Motown hits.

2. Nelson George, *Where Did Our Love Go?* (New York: St. Martin's Press, 1985), p. 67.

3. Though Motown groups are known for background harmony, the HDH formula often called for background vocalists to sing in unison (for example, "Sugar Pie" and "Where Did Our Love Go").

4. Gaye contends that Terrell was so ill during the last album, *Easy* (1969), that writer/producer Valerie Simpson, copying Terrell's style, sang on the hits "What You Gave Me" and "The Onion Song."

## CHAPTER 14

1. See *American Journal of Sociology* 74 (May 1969), pp. 720–731.

2. Ralph J. Gleason, *The Jefferson Airplane and the San Francisco Sound* (New York: Ballantine Books, 1969), p. 17.

3. Charles Perry, *The Haight-Ashbury: A History* (New York: Vintage Books, 1985), p. 96.

4. Gleason, *The Jefferson Airplane and the San Francisco Sound*, p. 41.

5. Ibid., p. 43.

6. Gene Sculatti and David Seay, *San Francisco Nights: The Psychedelic Music Trip, 1965–1968* (New York: St. Martin's Press, 1985), p. 99.

7. Ibid., p. 99.

8. Perry, *The Haight-Ashbury*, p. 208.

9. Myra Friedman, *Buried Alive: The Biography of Janis Joplin* (New York: Bantam Books, 1974), p. 319.

## CHAPTER 15

1. John Pidgeon, *Eric Clapton* (Suffolk: Panther, 1976), p. 19.

2. Ibid., p. 55.

3. From an interview with John Hutchinson in *Musician* magazine.

4. Ray Coleman, *Clapton!* (New York: Warner Books, 1985), pp. 58–59.

5. Pidgeon, *Eric Clapton*, p. 69.

6. From a 1968 interview with Jann Wenner. See *The Rolling Stone Interviews: 1967–1980* (New York: Rolling Stone Press, 1981), p. 26.

7. Coleman, *Clapton!*, p. 89.

8. See Anthony DeCurtis et al., *The Rolling Stone Illustrated History of Rock & Roll* (New York: Random House, 1992), pp. 411–412.

9. David Henderson, *'Scuse Me While I Kiss the Sky: The Life of Jimi Hendrix* (New York: Bantam Books, 1981), p. 114.

10. The four final songs, "Like a Rolling Stone," "Rock Me Baby," "Can You See Me," and "Wild Thing," are available as one side of *Historic Performances Recorded at the Monterey International Pop Festival, Otis Redding/Jimi Hendrix* (Reprise Records).

11. Jerry Hopkins, *Hit and Run: The Jimi Hendrix Story* (New York: Perigee Books, 1983), p. 118.

12. Ibid., p. 119.

13. Ibid., p. 180.

14. Ibid., p. 182.

15. Ibid., p. 191.

16. Ibid.

17. *Guitar Player Magazine,* Jimi Hendrix special edition.

18. Ibid.

19. Henderson, *'Scuse Me While I Kiss the Sky,* pp. 359–365.

20. Ibid., p. 365.

21. Hopkins, *Hit and Run,* p. 304.

22. Ibid., p. 170.

23. *Guitar Player,* special Hendrix edition.

24. Ibid.


## CHAPTER 16

1. From a 1977 interview with Steve Rosen. See *Rock Guitarists: Volume II* (New York: Guitar Player Books, 1978), p. 151.

2. Stephen Davis, *Hammer of the Gods: The Led Zeppelin Saga* (New York: Ballantine Books, 1986), p. 51.

3. Ibid., p. 56.

4. Ibid., p. 81.

5. Ibid., p. 87.

6. Ibid., p. 88.

7. Ibid., p. 155.

8. Ibid., p. 242.

9. Ibid., p. 104.

10. From a 1975 interview with Cameron Crowe. See *The Rolling Stone Interviews: 1967–1980* (New York: Rolling Stone Press, 1981), p. 318.

11. Ibid.

12. Davis, *Hammer of the Gods,* p. 259.

13. Ed Ward et al., *Rock of Ages: The Rolling Stone History of Rock and Roll* (New York: Rolling Stone Press/Summit Books, 1986), p. 485.


## CHAPTER 17

1. In *One Chord Wonders* (Philadelphia: Open University Press, 1985), Dave Laing raises this and other important theoretical issues about the nature of punk music and its roots.

2. Julie Burchill and Tony Parsons, *The Boy Looked at Johnny: The Obituary of Rock and Roll* (Boston: Faber and Faber, 1987), p. 18.

3. Laing, *One Chord Wonders,* p. 83.

4. Ibid., p. 90.

5. Ibid., p. 17.

6. Ibid., p. 36.

7. Ibid., p. 59.


## CHAPTER 18

1. Neal Ullestad, *Diverse Rock Rebellions Subvert Mass Media Hegemony,* in Reebee Garofalo, ed., *Rockin' the Boat: Mass Music and Mass Movements* (Boston: South End Press, 1992), p. 46. A good place to begin reading up on this issue is Reebee Garofalo's own chapter *Rockin' the Boat.*

2. Garofalo, *Rockin' the Boat,* p. 65.

3. Ibid., p. 50.

4. Robert Walser, *Running with the Devil: Power, Gender, and Madness in Heavy Metal Music* (Hanover, N.H.: Wesleyan University Press, 1993), p. xvii.

5. "MC" is a hip-hop term for "mic controller."

6. See Tricia Rose, *Black Noise: Rap Music and Black Culture in Contemporary America* (Hanover, N.H.: Wesleyan University Press, 1994).

7. Ibid., p. 188.

## CHAPTER 19

1. Carey defines older-value lyrics as those that enjoin explicitly or implicitly the acceptance of conventional values—for example, romantic notions about boy-girl relationships, fatalistic acceptance of the demands placed on one by the larger community, or expressed anxiety over social change. He defines newer-value lyrics as those concerned with maximizing one's freedom in personal relationships and freeing oneself from social constraints. They advocate or imply a more autonomous relationship between the sexes and/or criticize conventional society because of its misplaced values.

2. The 1960s music industry was considered by some observers to be politically liberal, thus the rationale that newer-value lyrics—antiwar issues, the search for justice, and enlightenment messages—fell on sympathetic ears. Though this may have been true at the label level, the corporate ownership at CBS or at movie studios evidenced little support of the era's counterculture.

3. James Lull, ed., *Popular Music and Communication* (Newbury Park, Calif.: Sage, 1992), p. 70.

## APPENDIX A

1. In the late 1980s Tipper Gore, wife of then U.S. Senator Albert Gore, was a leader in the PMRC's attempts to have rock/pop music lyrics rated and have the "appropriate" ones labeled as violent, obscene, and so on. Frank Zappa testified in Washington, D.C. against such a system, citing censorship and other civil liberties concerns.

# Discography

*Compiled by John Etheredge*

This discography is designed to guide the casual fan or beginning listener to a good "starting place" for each artist listed. The discography is heavily weighted in favor of "Best of" or "Greatest Hits" packages. When it is not obvious from the title that a given release is a "best of" collection, I have noted that fact. In recent years record companies have found that reissues can be quite profitable because of the limited production expenses involved. In other words, it's cheaper to go to the vaults and reissue previously recorded tracks than it is to record, produce, promote, and release new material. The record companies have also found that there's a huge "second-sale" market among listeners who are buying compact discs to replace vinyl LPs that they already own. These economic facts have led to the release of some fairly extensive multi-CD packages. These collections, generally known as "boxed sets," usually contain from three to five CDs, but in some cases the complete works of an artist have been made available in boxed sets of up to ten discs or even more. These I've generally not included here, recognizing that their purchase price gives them appeal only to the most ardent fan. I've tried to list only smaller and less-expensive packages.

As of this writing, CDs outsell cassettes by a margin of about two to one. However, since some listeners prefer cassettes, I have tried to list material that is currently in print and easily available on both CD and cassette. In cases where releases are not available in both formats, I have noted this and tried to list alternate choices.

Releases are regularly deleted from record-company catalogs, and new releases hit the shelves every week. This discography is accurate as of February 1995. Beware rerecording! Many artists of the 1950s and 1960s have rerecorded their better-known material for a succession of labels. Almost invariably these rerecordings are inferior to the originals. With labels leasing masters to other labels, and big labels gobbling up little labels, it's sometimes difficult to tell just by looking at a release whether or not you have the original recordings. A knowledgeable independent dealer can help you—folks at the chain stores in the mall seldom have a clue. (Look in the yellow pages under "compact discs"—the "record store" heading has been deleted.) I must make mention of one trustworthy reissue label: Rhino. There are other good ones out there, but nobody does it better than Rhino.

Don't overlook the possibilities of your neighborhood mom-and-pop outfit. Many independent record stores buy and sell used CDs and/or cassettes, and you may find some real bargains. Many of these stores also deal in used vinyl LPs. Hey, just because they're old doesn't necessarily mean they're expensive to buy. For those listeners who still have turntables, these LPs can be a joy to own. Some of the cover graphics can never be fully appreciated in smaller formats, and there's still a lot of out-of-print LPs out there that have never been reissued in other formats.

A word of caution: This rock and roll is highly addictive. When you find you can't pay the rent or stock the fridge because you spent your last dollar to obtain a rare alternate-mix B-side released only in Japan, don't say I didn't warn you!

A note about the compiler of this discography: Jivin' Johnny Etheredge is a record collector who has hosted his "Son of Saturday Gold" rock and roll oldies radio show since 1971. His "Jivin' John's Country Classics" has aired since 1974. Both programs are currently airing each week on KRVM-FM in Eugene, Oregon, and KSYD-FM in Reedsport, Oregon.

## CHAPTER 2

**Robert Johnson:** *King of the Delta Blues Singers,* Columbia Legacy
**Leadbelly:** *Leadbelly,* Columbia
**Muddy Waters:** *Best of,* Chess
**B. B. King:** *Best of Volume One,* Flair/Virgin (1950s recordings); *Best of,* MCA (1960s/1970s recordings)
**Howlin' Wolf:** *His Greatest Sides Volume One,* Chess (cassette only); or *Moanin' in the Moonlight/Howlin' Wolf,* Chess (CD only)
**The Soul Stirrers with Sam Cooke:** *Jesus Gave Me Water,* Specialty (CD only)
**The Dixie Hummingbirds:** *Best of,* MCA Special Products
**The Swan Silvertones:** *Pray for Me/Let's Go to Church Together,* VeeJay
**Louis Jordan:** *Best of,* MCA
**Lionel Hampton:** *Flying Home 1942–1945,* MCA
**Jimmie Rodgers:** *My Old Pal,* ASV (cassette only); or *Train Whistle Blues,* ASV (CD only)
**The Carter Family:** *Anchored In Love,* Rounder
**Bob Wills:** *Anthology,* Rhino
**Hank Williams:** *24 Greatest Hits,* Polydor
**Billy Ward and the Dominoes:** *60 Minute Man/Best of,* Rhino (CD only); or *21 Original Golden Hits,* Deluxe (cassette only)
**Big Joe Turner:** *Greatest Hits,* Rhino
**Ruth Brown:** *Miss Rhythm/Greatest Hits and More,* Rhino (CD only)
**Various artists:** *Atlantic History of Rhythm'n'Blues 1947–1974,* Atlantic. (This is a seven-CD boxed set. The first three discs cover many of the artists mentioned in this chapter. The remaining discs feature music discussed in Chapter 12.)
**Elvis Presley:** *The Complete Sun Sessions,* RCA
**Carl Perkins:** *Original Sun Greatest Hits,* Rhino
**Johnny Cash:** *The Sun Years,* Rhino

## CHAPTER 3

**Fats Domino:** *My Blue Heaven,* EMI
**Bill Haley:** *From the Original Master Tapes,* MCA (CD only); or *Greatest Hits,* MCA
**Chuck Berry:** *The Great Twenty-Eight,* Chess
**Little Richard:** *The Essential,* Specialty

## CHAPTER 4

**Elvis Presley:** *Elvis Presley,* RCA (his first album); *Elvis,* RCA (his second album); *The Top Ten Hits,* RCA (all of them, from the 1950s to the 1970s)
**Jerry Lee Lewis:** *Eighteen Original Sun Greatest Hits,* Rhino
**Buddy Holly:** *From the Original Master Tapes,* MCA (CD only); or *Twenty Golden Greats,* MCA (cassette only)
**The Everly Brothers:** *Cadence Classics,* Rhino (CD only); or *Best of: Golden Archives,* Rhino (cassette only)
**Bo Diddley:** *Bo Diddley/Go Bo Diddley,* Chess (CD only); or *His Greatest Sides,* Chess (cassette only)
**Gene Vincent:** *Capitol Collector's Series,* Capitol/EMI

Eddie Cochran: *Greatest Hits,* Curb

Ricky Nelson: *Ricky Nelson, Volume One,* EMI; *Ricky Nelson, Volume Two,* EMI

## CHAPTER 5

The Platters: *Anthology,* Rhino (cassette only and the superior collection); or *Only Their Best for You,* Pair

The Coasters: *Very Best of,* Rhino

Frankie Lymon and the Teenagers: *Best of,* Rhino

The Drifters: *Let the Boogie Woogie Roll/Greatest Hits 1953–1958,* Atlantic; *Very Best of,* Rhino (covers 1959–1964)

The Orioles: *Sing Their Greatest Hits,* Collectables

Various artists: *Best of Doo Wop Ballads,* Rhino; *Best of Doo Wop Uptempo,* Rhino. (Many vocal groups of the 1950s were "one-hit wonders." These two releases are indispensable.)

## CHAPTER 6

Note: There's nothing in print by Frankie Avalon, Fabian, or Bobby Rydell, perhaps evidence that there is justice in the world!

Connie Francis: *Very Best of,* Polydor

Dion: *The Wanderer,* Laurie (CD only); or *Greatest Hits,* Columbia (cassette only)

Bobby Darin: *Story,* Atlantic

Brenda Lee: *Story,* MCA

Various artists: *Best of the Girl Groups,* Rhino (cassette only and highly recommended)

The Shirelles: *Anthology,* Rhino

The Crystals: *Best of,* Abko

The Ronettes: *Best of,* Abko

Darlene Love: *Best of,* Abko

(Note: Instead of the three single CDs immediately above, you might prefer *Back to Mono,* a four-CD boxed set on Abko that includes Phil Spector productions by the above three artists, plus Ike and Tina Turner, the Righteous Brothers, and many more.)

The Kingston Trio: *Capitol Collector's Series,* Capitol/EMI

Peter, Paul, and Mary: *Best of,* Warner Brothers (cassette only)

Harry Belafonte: *Pure Gold,* RCA

Jan and Dean: *All Time Greatest Hits,* Curb

The Beach Boys: *Absolute Best of, Volume One,* Capitol/EMI; *Absolute Best of, Volume Two,* Capitol/EMI. (These anthologies, and there are dozens of others, intelligently and concisely repackage their best, in chronological order.)

The Ventures: *Walk, Don't Run,* EMI

Duane Eddy: *Twang Thang,* Rhino

## CHAPTER 7

The Beatles: *1962–1966 (The Red Album),* Capitol/EMI; *1967–1970 (The Blue Album),* Capitol/EMI

The anthologies listed above are a good place to start, but the group's entire output is really indispensable. Beatles albums before *Sgt. Pepper's Lonely Hearts Club Band* differed in their British and American versions. Only the British versions are available on both CD and cassette. There are cassette-only issues of some of the early American albums. I recommend the British versions. This gives you the music in its original context and gives you a more complete collection with less duplication of tracks. The American versions of both *A Hard Day's Night* and *Help!* are marred by the inclusion of non-Beatle instrumental music from the film soundtracks. The British versions of these albums omit this instrumental material in favor of additional tracks by the Beatles. The British and American versions of *Yellow Submarine* were identical, and they both suffered from the inclusion of instrumental movie music.

All of the following releases are on Capitol/EMI:

*Please Please Me*
*With the Beatles*
*A Hard Day's Night*
*Beatles for Sale*
*Help!*
*Rubber Soul*
*Revolver*
*Sgt. Pepper's Lonely Hearts Club Band*
*Magical Mystery Tour*
*The Beatles (The White Album)*
*Yellow Submarine*
*Abbey Road*
*Let It Be*
*Past Masters, Volume One*
*Past Masters, Volume Two*
(These last two releases collect non-LP singles.)

**John Lennon:** *Collection,* Capitol/EMI (CD only: and the superior collection); or *Imagine (Soundtrack),* Capitol/EMI

**Paul McCartney:** *All the Best,* Capitol/EMI

**George Harrison:** *Best of,* Parlophone/EMI

**Ringo Starr:** *Blast from Your Past,* Capitol/EMI (CD only)

## CHAPTER 8

**The Rolling Stones:** *Hot Rocks 1964–1971,* Abko

(The two-CD set listed above is the essential one. A less essential two-CD set that covers the same period is *More Hot Rocks,* Abko. All of the Rolling Stones albums have something to recommend them, but those listed below are among the best. All are on Abko.)

*The Rolling Stones/England's Newest Hitmakers*
*Aftermath*
*Beggars Banquet*
*Let It Bleed*
*Get Yer Ya-Yas Out*
*Sticky Fingers*
*Exile on Main Street*

## CHAPTER 9

**The Who:** *Greatest Hits,* MCA
  (After the one above, try these originals, all on MCA):
  *Tommy*
  *Who's Next*
  *Quadrophenia*
  *Who Are You*

## CHAPTER 10

**Woody Guthrie:** *Dust Bowl Ballads,* Rounder
**The Weavers:** *Greatest Hits,* Vanguard
**Joan Baez:** *Hits, Greatest and Others,* Vanguard; *Best of Joan C. Baez,* A&M
**Pete Seeger:** *Greatest Hits,* Columbia
**Bob Dylan** (all releases listed are on Columbia): *Greatest Hits; Greatest Hits, Volume Two*
(The two releases above do a good job of distilling his 1960s output. *Greatest Hits, Volume*
  *Three* gives you the best of his 1970s and 1980s work. *Biograph,* on Columbia, is a
  three-CD boxed set that covers from the early 1960s into the 1980s. The originals listed
  below are all worthwhile.)
  *Bob Dylan*
  *The Freewheelin'*
  *The Times They Are a-Changin'*
  *Another Side of*
  *Highway 61 Revisited*
  *Bringing It All Back Home*
  *Blonde on Blonde*
  *John Wesley Harding*
  *Nashville Skyline*
  *Self-Portrait*
  *New Morning*
  *Before the Flood*
  *Blood on the Tracks*
  *Desire*
  *Slow Train Coming*

## CHAPTER 11

**The Byrds:** *Twenty Essential Tracks from the Boxed Set,* Columbia
**Buffalo Springfield:** *Retrospective/Best of,* Atco
**Poco:** *Very Best of,* Epic
**Crosby, Stills, and Nash (and Young):** *So Far,* Atlantic (a "best of" set); *Crosby, Stills and*
  *Nash,* Atlantic; *CSN,* Atlantic; *Deja Vu,* Atlantic; *Four Way Street,* Atlantic
**The Flying Burrito Brothers:** *Farther Along/Best of,* A&M (CD only)
**The Eagles:** *Very Best of,* Elektra

**The Mamas and the Papas:** *16 Greatest Hits,* MCA (cassette only); or *16 of Their Greatest Hits,* MCA (CD only)

**The Lovin' Spoonful:** *Anthology,* Rhino

**The Band:** *Best of,* Capitol/EMI; *Music From Big Pink,* Capitol/EMI; *Rock of Ages,* Capitol/EMI

## CHAPTER 12

**Ray Charles:** *Best of: The Atlantic Years,* Rhino (covers the 1950s); *Anthology,* Rhino (CD only); or *Greatest Hits, Volume One,* Rhino (cassette only) and *Greatest Hits, Volume Two,* Rhino (cassette only). The last three releases cover the ABC years, 1959 through the 1960s.

**James Brown:** *Twenty All Time Greatest Hits,* Polydor

**Sam Cooke:** *The Man and His Music,* RCA

**Booker T. and the M.G.s:** *Very Best of,* Rhino

**Otis Redding:** *Very Best of,* Rhino

**Wilson Pickett:** *Very Best of,* Rhino

**Sam and Dave:** *Best of,* Atlantic

**Solomon Burke:** *Home In Your Heart/Best of,* Rhino

**Aretha Franklin:** *30 Greatest Hits,* Rhino

**Joe Tex:** *I Believe I'm Gonna Make It/Best of,* Rhino

## CHAPTER 13

**Smokey Robinson and the Miracles:** *Anthology,* Motown

**The Temptations:** *Anthology,* Motown

**Mary Wells:** *Greatest Hits,* Motown

**Martha and the Vandellas:** *Live Wire! The Singles 1962–1972,* Motown

**The Supremes:** *Anthology,* Motown

**The Four Tops:** *Anthology,* Motown

**Marvin Gaye:** *Anthology,* Motown

**Stevie Wonder:** *Greatest Hits, Volume One,* Motown; *Greatest Hits, Volume Two,* Motown; *Original Musicquarium: Greatest Hits,* Motown

**Gladys Knight and the Pips:** *Anthology,* Motown

**The Jackson 5:** *Anthology,* Motown

(Much of the Motown material listed above, and some by other Motown artists, is distilled into the four-CD boxed set *Hitsville, USA: The Motown Singles Collection, Volume One,* Motown.)

## CHAPTER 14

**The Jefferson Airplane:** *2400 Fulton Street,* RCA (a "best of" collection)

**Janis Joplin:** *Greatest Hits,* Columbia; *Cheap Thrills* (Big Brother and the Holding Company), Columbia

**Creedence Clearwater Revival:** *Chronicle/The 20 Greatest Hits,* Fantasy

**The Grateful Dead:** *Skeletons From the Closet/Best of,* Warner Brothers; *American Beauty,* Warner Brothers; *Europe '72,* Warner Brothers; *Live Dead,* Warner Brothers

**Santana:** *Greatest Hits,* Columbia

Country Joe and the Fish: *Collected, 1965–1970,* Vanguard
Quicksilver Messenger Service: *Sons of Mercury (1968–1975),* Rhino
The Steve Miller Band: *Best of 1968–1973,* Capitol/EMI
Moby Grape: *Vintage/Very Best of,* Columbia Legacy
The Youngbloods: *Best of,* RCA
Dan Hicks and his Hot Licks: *Last Train to Hicksville,* MCA (CD only)

## CHAPTER 15

Eric Clapton: *Crossroads,* Polydor. (This is a four-CD boxed set, but it's the one you want. It covers Clapton's career with the Yardbirds and Cream, his solo efforts, and other stops along the way.)
Jimi Hendrix: *The Ultimate Experience,* MCA (a "best of" collection); *Are You Experienced,* MCA; *Axis: Bold As Love,* MCA; *Electric Ladyland,* MCA; *Band of Gypsys,* Capitol/EMI

## CHAPTER 16

Led Zeppelin: *Led Zeppelin,* Atlantic; *Led Zeppelin 2,* Atlantic; *Led Zeppelin 3,* Atlantic; *Led Zeppelin 4,* Atlantic; *Houses of the Holy,* Atlantic; *Physical Graffiti,* Swan Song
MC5: *Kick Out the Jams,* Elektra (CD only)
Vanilla Fudge: *Psychedelic Sundae: Best of,* Rhino
Iron Butterfly: *In-A-Gadda-Da-Vida,* Rhino
Black Sabbath: *We Sold Our Souls for Rock'n'Roll,* Warner Brothers (a "best of" collection)
Deep Purple: *When We Rock We Rock and When We Roll We Roll,* Warner Brothers (a "best of" collection)
Alice Cooper: *Greatest Hits,* Warner Brothers
Aerosmith: *Greatest Hits,* Columbia; *Big Ones,* Geffen
Boston: *Boston,* Epic
Heart: *Greatest Hits/Live,* Epic
Journey: *Greatest Hits,* Columbia
Rush: *Chronicles,* Mercury
Kiss: *Double Platinum,* Casablanca/Mercury
Bad Company: *10 from 6/Best of,* Atlantic
AC/DC: *Who Made Who,* Atlantic (a "best of" collection)
Pink Floyd: *Works,* Capitol/EMI (a "best of" collection); *The Dark Side of the Moon,* Capitol/EMI
Yes: *Very Best of,* Atlantic
King Crimson: *In the Court of the Crimson King,* Editions E.G.
Genesis: *Abacab,* Atlantic
Moody Blues: *This Is,* Threshold (a "best of" collection)
Jethro Tull: *Twenty Years of,* Chrysalis
David Bowie: *Changesbowie,* Rykodisc (a "best of" collection)
Elton John: *Greatest Hits,* MCA; *Greatest Hits, Volume II,* MCA; *Greatest Hits 1976–1986,* MCA
Fleetwood Mac: *Greatest Hits,* Warner Brothers
Chicago: *Chicago Transit Authority,* Columbia
Linda Ronstadt: *Greatest Hits,* Elektra; *Greatest Hits, Volume Two,* Elektra

## CHAPTER 17

**The Velvet Underground:** *Best of,* Polydor
**The Doors:** *Best of,* Elektra
**The Stooges:** *Fun House,* Elektra (CD only)
**The Ramones:** *Ramones Mania/Best of,* Sire
**The Sex Pistols:** *Never Mind the Bollocks, Here's the Sex Pistols,* Warner Brothers
**The Clash:** *The Story of, Volume One,* Epic
**Elvis Costello:** *The Very Best of,* Rykodisc
**The Pretenders:** *The Singles,* Sire
**The Talking Heads:** *Popular Favorites 1976–1992,* Sire
**The B-52s:** *The B-52s,* Warner Brothers; *Wild Planet,* Warner Brothers
**Devo:** *Greatest Hits,* Warner Brothers
**Blondie:** *Best of,* Chrysalis
**The Dead Kennedys:** *Fresh Fruit for Rotting Vegetables,* Alternative Tentacles
**XTC:** *Waxworks,* Geffen
**Bruce Springsteen:** *Born to Run; The River; Nebraska; Born in the U.S.A* (all on Columbia)
**Prince:** *The Hits 1,* Paisley Park; *The Hits 2,* Paisley Park
**The Police:** *Every Breath You Take/The Singles,* A&M

## CHAPTER 18

**Various Artist Anthologies:**
   *Alternative NRG,* Hollywood (Proceeds benefit Greenpeace.)
   *Born to Choose,* Rykodisc (Proceeds benefit abortion-rights groups.)
   *Sweet Relief,* Chaos (Proceeds benefit Victoria Williams.)
   *In Defense of Animals Benefit Compilation,* Restless (Proceeds benefit animal-rights groups.)
   *Peace Together,* Island (Proceeds benefit youth of Northern Ireland.)
   *Sun City: Artists United Against Apartheid,* Razor and Tie (CD only)
**Michael Jackson:** *Off the Wall; Thriller; Bad; Dangerous* (all on Epic)
**Madonna:** *The Immaculate Collection,* Sire (a "best of" collection)
**U2:** *October; The Unforgettable Fire; Rattle and Hum; The Joshua Tree; Achtung Baby* (all on Island)
**Van Halen:** *Van Halen; Van Halen II; 1984* (all on Warner Brothers)
**Mötley Crüe:** *Decade of Decadence 1981–1991,* Elektra
**Def Leppard:** *On Through the Night; Pyromania; Hysteria* (all on Mercury)
**Metallica:** *Kill 'Em All; Ride the Lightning; Master of Puppets; And Justice for All; Metallica* (all on Elektra)
**Guns 'n' Roses:** *Appetite for Destruction; Lies; Use Your Illusion I; Use Your Illusion II* (all on Geffen)
**Grandmaster Flash:** *Message From Beat Street: The Best of,* Rhino
**Run-D.M.C.:** *Together Forever: Greatest Hits,* Profile
**Kurtis Blow:** *Best of,* Mercury
**L. L. Cool J:** *Radio; Bigger and Deffer; Walking with a Panther* (all on Def Jam)
**Beastie Boys:** *Licensed to Ill,* Def Jam; *Paul's Boutique,* Capitol/EMI
**Ice-T:** *Rhyme Pays; Power; O.G. (Original Gangster)* (all on Sire)

**Queen Latifah:** *All Hail the Queen,* Tommy Boy (CD only); *Nature of a Sista',* Tommy Boy

**Public Enemy:** *Yo! Bum Rush the Show; It Takes a Nation of Millions to Hold Us Back; Fear of a Black Planet* (all on Def Jam)

**N.W.A.:** *Straight Outta Compton,* Ruthless. (The unedited version is CD only. An edited version is available on both CD and cassette.)

**2 Live Crew:** *Greatest Hits,* Luke. (The unedited version is CD only. An edited version is available on both CD and cassette.)

## APPENDIX A

**The Kinks:** *Greatest Hits,* Rhino (covers the 1960s); *Come Dancing With the Kinks/Best of 1977–1986,* Arista

**The Animals:** *Best of,* Abko

**Sly and the Family Stone:** *Anthology,* Epic

**Traffic:** *Traffic,* Island

**Van Morrison:** *Best of,* Polydor

**Various Artists:** *Woodstock: Three Days of Peace and Music,* Atlantic (a four-CD set)

**Donna Summer:** *Anthology,* Casablanca/Mercury

**The Bee Gees:** *Greatest,* Polydor

**The Village People:** *Greatest Hits,* Rhino

**Various artists:** *Saturday Night Fever (Soundtrack),* Polydor

**Bob Marley:** *Legend/Best of,* Tuffgong

**Various Artists:** *The Harder They Come (Soundtrack)* (Jimmy Cliff and others), Mango

**The Allman Brothers:** *A Decade of Hits 1969–1979,* Polydor

**Frank Zappa:** *Freak Out!* (The Mothers of Invention), Rykodisc

**Jackie Wilson:** *Very Best of,* Rhino

**Steely Dan:** *Greatest Hits,* MCA (cassette only); or *A Decade of,* MCA (CD only)

**Simon and Garfunkel:** *Greatest Hits,* Columbia

**Paul Simon:** *Graceland,* Warner Brothers; *1964/1993,* Warner Brothers (a three-CD boxed set that covers the best of both Simon and Garfunkel and Paul Simon as a solo artist)

**Roy Orbison:** *For the Lonely: A Roy Orbison Anthology 1956–1965,* Rhino

# Selected Bibliography

GENERAL

Chapple, Steve, and Reebee Garofalo. *Rock and Roll Is Here to Pay: The History and Politics of the Music Industry.* Chicago: Nelson-Hall, 1977.

Charlton, Katherine. *Rock Music Styles: A History.* 2nd Edition. Madison, Wisc.: W.C.B. Brown and Benchmark, 1994.

Dannon, Fredric. *Hit Men.* New York: Random House, 1990.

Davis, Clive, with James Willwerth. *Clive: Inside the Record Business.* New York: Ballantine Books, 1974.

DeCurtis, Anthony, and James Henke, with Holly George-Warren, eds. *The Rolling Stone Illustrated Encyclopedia of Rock and Roll.* New York: Random House, 1992.

Denisoff, Serve, and Richard Peterson. *The Sounds of Social Change.* New York: Rand McNally and Co., 1972.

Frame, Peter. *Rock Family Trees.* New York: Quick Fox, 1979.

———. *Rock Family Trees, vol.* 2. New York: Omnibus Press, 1983.

Frith, Simon. *Sound Effects: Youth, Leisure, and the Politics of Rock 'n' Roll.* New York: Pantheon Books, 1982.

Frith, Simon, ed. *Facing the Music.* New York: Pantheon Books, 1988.

Frith, Simon, and Andrew Goodwin, eds. *On Record.* New York: Pantheon,1990.

Gambaccini, Paul. *Critics' Choice: The Top 100 Rock 'n' Roll Albums of All Time.* New York: Harmony Books, 1987.

Gillett, Charlie. *Making Tracks: Atlantic Records and the Growth of a Multi-Billion-Dollar Industry.* New York: E. P. Dutton and Co., 1974.

Gitlin, Todd. *The Sixties: Years of Rage, Days of Rage.* New York: Bantam Books, 1987.

*Guitar Player* Magazine. *Rock Guitarists.* New York: Guitar Player Books, 1975.

———. *Rock Guitarists, vol.* 2. New York: Guitar Player Books, 1978.

Hammond, John, with Irving Townsend. *John Hammond on Record: An Autobiography.* New York: Penguin Books, 1981.

Hart, Mickey, with Jay Stevens. *Drumming at the Edge of Magic.* New York: Harper, 1990.

Hibbard, Don J., with Carol Kaleialoha. *The Role of Rock.* Englewood Cliffs, N.J.: Prentice-Hall, Inc., 1983.

Kooper, Al, with Ben Edmonds. *Backstage Pass: Rock 'n' Roll Life in the Sixties.* New York: Stein and Day, 1977.

Lull, James, ed. *Popular Music and Communication.* Newbury Park, Calif.: Sage, 1992.

Marsh, Dave, and Kevin Stein. *The New Book of Rock Lists.* New York: Simon and Schuster, 1994.

Ochs, Michael. *Rock Archives: A Photographic Journey Through the First Two Decades of Rock and Roll.* Garden City, N.Y.: Doubleday and Co., Inc., 1984.

Peellaert, Guy, and Nik Cohn. *Rock Dreams.* New York: Popular Library, 1973.

Pichaske, David. *A Generation in Motion: Popular Music and Culture in the Sixties.* New York: Schirmer Books, 1979.

The Editors of *Rolling Stone* Magazine. *The Rolling Stone Interviews: Talking with the Legends of Rock and Roll, 1967–1980.* New York: St. Martin's Press/Rolling Stone Press, 1981.

———. *The Rolling Stone Interviews: The 1980s.* New York: St. Martin's Press/Rolling Stone Press, 1989.

Schaffner, Nicholas. *The British Invasion: From the First Wave to the New Wave.* New York: McGraw-Hill, 1982.

Stokes, Geoffrey. *Star-Making Machinery: Inside the Business of Rock and Roll.* New York: Vintage Books, 1977.

Ward, Ed, Geoffrey Stokes, and Ken Tucker. *Rock of Ages: The Rolling Stone History of Rock and Roll.* New York: Rolling Stone Press/Summit Books, 1986.

Whitburn, Joel. *The Billboard Book of Top 40 Hits.* New York: Billboard Books, 1992.

———. *The Billboard Book of Top 40 Albums.* New York: Billboard Books, 1991.

## CHAPTER 2

Gillett, Charlie. *The Sound of the City: The Rise of Rock and Roll.* New York: Outerbridge and Dienstfrey, 1970.

Jones, LeRoi. *Blues People.* New York: William Morrow, 1963.

Keil, Charles. *Urban Blues.* Chicago: University of Chicago Press, 1966.

Malone, Bill C. *Country Music, U.S.A.: A Fifty-Year History.* Austin: University of Texas Press, 1975.

Morrow, Cousin Brucie, and Laura Baudo. *Cousin Brucie: My Life in Rock and Roll Radio.* New York: Beech Tree Books, 1987.

Oliver, Paul. *The Story of the Blues.* Radnor, Penn.: Chilton, 1982.

Shaw, Arnold. *The Rockin' '50s: The Decade That Transformed the Pop Music Scene.* New York: Hawthorne Books, 1974.

———. *Honkers and Shouters: The Golden Years of Rhythm & Blues.* New York: Collier Books, 1978.

## CHAPTER 3

Berry, Chuck. *The Autobiography.* New York: Harmony Books, 1987.

Friedlander, Paul. "A Characteristics Profile of the Eight Classic Rock Era Artists, 1954–1959." Unpublished dissertation, University of Oregon, 1987.

Gillett, Charlie. *The Sound of the City.* New York: Dell Publishing, 1972.

Grossman, Loyd. *A Social History of Rock Music.* New York: David McKay Company, 1976.

Guralnick, Peter. *Feel Like Going Home: Portraits in Blues and Rock 'n' Roll.* New York: Outerbridge and Dienstfrey, 1971.

Hopkins, Jerry. *The Rock Story.* New York: Signet Books, 1970.

Swenson, John. *Bill Haley: The Daddy of Rock and Roll.* New York: Stein and Day, 1983.

White, Charles. *The Life and Times of Little Richard.* New York: Pocket Books, 1984.

## CHAPTER 4

Goldman, Albert. *Elvis.* New York: Avon Books, 1981.

Guralnick, Peter. *Lost Highway: Journeys and Arrivals of American Musicians.* Boston: David R. Godine, 1979.

Goldrosen, John. *The Buddy Holly Story.* New York: Quick Fox, 1975.

Hagarty, Britt. *The Day the World Turned Blue: A Biography of Gene Vincent.* Vancouver: Talonbooks, 1983.

Hopkins, Jerry. *Elvis: A Biography.* New York: Warner Paperback Library, 1972.

———. *Elvis: The Final Years.* New York: Berkeley Books, 1983.

Lewis, Myra, with Murray Silver. *Great Balls of Fire: The Uncensored Story of Jerry Lee Lewis.* New York: Quill, 1982.

O'Grady, Terence J. *The Beatles.* Boston: Twayne Publishers, 1983.

Pollack, Bruce. *In Their Own Words.* New York: Collier Books, 1975.

Wertheimer, Alfred. *Elvis '56.* New York: Collier Books, 1979.

West, Red, Sonny West, and Dave Hebler (as told to Steve Dunleavy). *Elvis: What Happened?* New York: Ballantine Books, 1977.


## CHAPTER 6

Betrock, Alan. *Girl Groups: The Story of a Sound.* New York: Delilah Books, 1982.

Gaines, Steven. *Heroes and Villains: The True Story of the Beach Boys.* New York: New American Library, 1986.


## CHAPTER 7

Carr, Roy, and Tony Tyler. *The Beatles: An Illustrated Record.* New York: Harmony Books, 1981.

Coleman, Ray. *Lennon.* New York: McGraw-Hill, 1984.

Davies, Hunter. *The Beatles.* New York: McGraw-Hill, 1986.

Dilello, Richard. *The Longest Cocktail Party.* New York: Playboy Paperbacks, 1972.

Golson, Barry G., ed. *The Playboy Interviews with John Lennon and Yoko Ono.* New York: Playboy Press, 1981.

Harry, Bill. *The Ultimate Beatles Encyclopedia.* New York: Hyperion, 1992.

Harry, Bill, ed. *Mersey Beat and the Beginnings of the Beatles.* New York: Omnibus Press, 1977.

Lennon, Cynthia. *A Twist of Lennon.* New York: Avon Books, 1980.

Lewisohn, Mark. *The Beatles: Recording Sessions.* New York: Harmony Books, 1988.

McCabe, Peter, and Robert D. Schonfeld. *Apple to the Core: The Unmaking of the Beatles.* New York: Pocket Books, 1974.

Martin, George, with Jeremy Hornsby. *All You Need Is Ears.* New York: St. Martin's Press, 1979.

Norman, Philip. *Shout! The Beatles in Their Generation.* New York: Simon and Schuster, 1981.

Schaffner, Nicholas. *The Beatles Forever.* New York: McGraw-Hill, 1978.


## CHAPTER 8

Booth, Stanley. *The True Adventures of the Rolling Stones.* New York: Vintage Books, 1985.

Flippo, Chet. *On the Road with the Rolling Stones.* Garden City, New York: Dolphin Books, 1985.

Norman, Philip. *Symphony for the Devil: The Rolling Stones Story.* New York: Linden Press/Simon and Schuster, 1984.

Sanchez, Tony. *Up and Down with the Rolling Stones.* New York: New American Library, 1979.

## CHAPTER 9

Barnes, Richard. *The Who: Maximum R & B*. New York: St. Martin's Press, 1982.
Marsh, Dave. *Before I Get Old: The Story of the Who*. New York: St. Martin's Press, 1983.

## CHAPTER 10

Dylan, Bob.*Writings and Drawings*. New York: Alfred A. Knopf, Inc., 1973.
Eliot, Marc. *Death of a Rebel*. New York: Anchor Press, 1979.
Gray, Michael. *Song and Dance Man: The Art of Bob Dylan*. London: Abacus/Sphere Books, 1973.
Rinzler, Alan. *Bob Dylan: The Illustrated Record*. New York: Harmony Books, 1978.
Scaduto, Anthony. *Bob Dylan*. New York: Signet Books, 1973.
Seeger, Pete. *The Incompleat Folksinger*. New York: Simon and Schuster, 1972.
Shelton, Robert. *No Direction Home: The Life and Music of Bob Dylan*. New York: Ballantine Books, 1986.
Thompson, Toby. *Positively Main Street (An Unorthodox View of Bob Dylan)*. New York: Warner Paperback Library, 1972.

## CHAPTER 11

Woliver, Robbie. *Bringing It All Back Home*. New York: Pantheon Books, 1986.

## CHAPTER 12

Charles, Ray, and David Ritz. *Brother Ray: Ray Charles' Own Story*. New York: Warner Books, 1979.
Guralnik, Peter. *Sweet Soul Music: Rhythm and Blues and the Southern Dream of Freedom*. New York: Harper and Row, 1986.
Haralambos, Michael. *Soul Music: The Birth of a Sound in Black America*. New York: DaCapo Press, Inc., 1974.
Hirshey, Gerri. *Nowhere to Run: The Story of Soul Music*. New York: Penguin Books, 1985.

## CHAPTER 13

George, Nelson. *Where Did Our Love Go?* New York: St. Martin's Press, 1985.

## CHAPTER 14

Friedman, Myra. *Buried Alive: The Biography of Janis Joplin*. New York: Bantam Books, 1974.
Gans, David, and Peter Simon. *Playing in the Band*. New York: St. Martin's Press, 1985.
Gleason, Ralph J. *The Jefferson Airplane and the San Francisco Sound*. New York: Ballantine Books, 1969.
Jackson, Blair. *Grateful Dead: The Music Never Stopped*. New York: Delilah Books, 1983.
Perry, Charles. *The Haight-Ashbury: A History*. New York: Vintage Books, 1985.
Sculatti, Gene, and David Seay. *San Francisco Nights: The Psychedelic Music Trip, 1965–1968*. New York: St. Martin's Press, 1985.

## CHAPTER 15

Coleman, Ray. *Clapton!* New York: Warner Books, 1985.

Henderson, David. *'Scuse Me While I Kiss the Sky: The Life of Jimi Hendrix.* New York: Bantam Books, 1981.

Hopkins, Jerry. *Hit and Run: The Jimi Hendrix Story.* New York/Toronto: Perigee Books, 1983.

Mitchell, Mitch, with John Platt. *Jimi Hendrix: Inside the Experience.* New York: Harmony Books, 1990.

Pidgeon, John. *Eric Clapton.* Suffolk: Panther, 1976.

## CHAPTER 16

Davis, Stephen. *Hammer of the Gods: The Led Zeppelin Saga.* New York: Ballantine Books, 1986.

## CHAPTER 17

Burchill, Julie, and Tony Parsons. *The Boy Looked at Johnny: The Obituary of Rock and Roll.* Boston: Faber and Faber, 1987.

Hebdige, Dick. *Subculture: The Meaning of Style.* London: Methuen and Company, 1979.

Laing, Dave. *One Chord Wonders.* Philadelphia: Open University Press, 1985.

## CHAPTER 18

Garofalo, Reebee, ed. *Rockin' the Boat: Mass Music and Mass Movements.* Boston: South End Press, 1992.

Marsh, Dave. *Born to Run: The Bruce Springsteen Story.* Garden City, N.Y.: Dolphin Books, 1979.

———. *Glory Days.* New York: Pantheon Books, 1987.

Rose, Tricia. *Black Noise: Rap Music and Black Culture in Contemporary America.* Hanover, N.H.: Wesleyan University Press, 1994.

Schwichtenberg, Cathy, ed. *The Madonna Connection: Representational Politics, Subcultural Identities, and Cultural Theory.* Boulder, Colo.: Westview Press, 1993.

Walser, Robert. *Running with the Devil: Power, Gender, and Madness in Heavy Metal Music.* Hanover, N.H.: Wesleyan University Press, 1993.

## APPENDIX B

Rosenman, Joel, John Roberts, and Robert Pilpel. *Young Men with Unlimited Capital.* New York: Harcourt, Brace, Jovanovich, 1974.

Spitz, Robert Stephen. *Barefoot in Babylon: The Creation of the Woodstock Music Festival, 1969.* New York: Viking Press, 1979.

Davis, Stephen, and Peter Simon. *Reggae International.* New York: R&B, 1982.

White, Timothy. *Catch a Fire: The Life of Bob Marley.* New York: Holt, Rinehart, and Winston, 1983.

# About the Book and Author

The social force of rock and roll music leaps off the page as Paul Friedlander provides impressive insights based on hits from "Johnny B. Goode" to "Walk on the Wild Side" and beyond. In this musical journey, he offers the melodious strains and hard-edged riffs of Elvis Presley, the Beatles, the Who, Dylan, Clapton, Doo-Wop, Motown, the San Francisco Beat, New Wave, rap, and much more. The book is written in a refreshing, captivating style that pulls the reader in, offering no less than a complete social and cultural history of rock and roll for students and general audiences alike.

Friedlander writes, "This book chronicles the first thirty years of rock/pop music history. Picture the various musical styles as locations on a giant unfolding road map. As you open the map, you travel from place to place, stopping at each chapter to sample the artistry. Take in the tales, pictures, sounds, and feelings of each location; remember the people you met there. Don't forget to dress your imagination appropriately for this trip, because each genre is affected by the societal topography and climate that surround it." Enjoy your trip. We promise it will be a good one!

Paul Friedlander is assistant dean at the Conservatory of Music, University of the Pacific, and teaches popular music history. He is American chapter chair of the International Association for the Study of Popular Music. As a musician, he has sung with Pete Seeger's Children's Chorus at Carnegie Hall, played bluegrass banjo at southern music festivals, hit some notes with New York homeboys the Chapters, played folk music in Moscow's Gorki Park, and rock and rolled all across the U.S.A.

# Index